THE

VIRTUAL REALITY

CASEBOOK

THE

VIRTUAL REALITY

CASEBOOK

EDITORS

CARL EUGENE LOEFFLER
TIM ANDERSON

VAN NOSTRAND REINHOLD
An International Thomson Publishing Company

New York • London • Bonn • Boston • Detroit • Madrid • Melbourne • Mexico City
Paris • Singapore • Tokyo • Toronto • Albany NY • Belmont CA • Cincinnati OH

Copyright © 1994 by Van Nostrand Reinhold

Library of Congress Catalog Card Number 94-1823

ISBN 0-442-01776-6

ITP Van Nostrand Reinhold is an International Thomson Publishing Company.
ITP logo is a trademark under license.

Printed in the United States of America

Van Nostrand Reinhold
115 Fifth Avenue
New York, NY 10003

International Thomson Publishing
Berkshire House
168-173 High Holborn
London WC1V7AA
England

Thomas Nelson Australia
102 Dodds Street
South Melbourne, Victoria 3205
Australia

Nelson Canada
1120 Birchmount Road
Scarborough, Ontario
M1K 5G4, Canada

International Thomson Publishing GmbH
Königswinterer Strasse 418
53227 Bonn
Germany

International Thomson Publishing Asia
221 Henderson Road
#05 10 Henderson Building
Singapore 0315

International Thomson Publishing Japan
Hirakawacho Kyowa Building, 3F
2-2-1 Hirakawa-cho, Chiyoda-ku
Tokyo 102
Japan

ARCFF 16 15 14 13 12 11 10 9 8 7 6 5 4 5 3 2 1

Library of Congress Publication Data
The Virtual Reality Casebook/ (edited by) Carl Eugene Loeffler, Tim Anderson
    p. cm.
    Includes index.
    ISBN 0-442-01776-6
    1. Human-computer interaction. 2. Virtual reality. I. Loeffler, Carl E., 1946– .
II. Anderson, Tim.
QA76.9.H85V58   1994
006--dc20   94-1823
                                                                                   CIP

Designed by Theo Coates Design

TRADEMARKS

COPYRIGHTS

Battletech	
Boom2	Fakespace
C++	Borland
CyberGlove	Virtex Technologies
Data-Vision	Fakespace
DataGlove	VPL
DMX512	
Ethernet	
EyePhones	VPL
FingerBall	Center for Industrial Research (Oslo)
GeoBall	CIS
Indigo	Silicon Graphics
ISIS	ISIS Corporation
Macintosh	Apple
Mandala	
MidasPlus	
PerfectSound	
PicturePhoneTalk	
Polhemus	
PowerGlove	Nintendo
RS/6000	IBM
SkyWriter	Silicon Graphics
Spaceball	
SPARCstation	Sun

TRADEMARKS

Turbo C	Borland
VGX	Silicon Graphics
Virtuality	W Industries
Windows	Microsoft
WorldToolKit	Sense8

CONTENTS

PART 3—REAL–LIFE VR APPLICATIONS

PART 4—NEWS FROM ABROAD

PART 5—VR THEORY

APPENDIX A

APPENDIX B

ANNOTATED BIBLIOGRAPHY

INDEX

PREFACE

Akikazu Takeuchi

Virtual reality used to be a fantasy envisioned only in laboratories. Now, computer technologies have brought it to life. VR will soon be an endless day-dream, truly an alternative reality.

The world we live in is no longer the only world that exists. What we consider the real world is merely a starting point: "World 0." With virtual technologies, a limitless series of "real worlds" can be created that do not exist in isolation but can be combined with one another, and with World 0, to create applications that stir our dreams and have concrete practical value.

People are talking about the entertainment value of these new technologies, but perhaps the most urgent task of VR is the design of society—the design of space(s), both private and common, and the design of social structures. What VR designers should do is create places for social interaction.

The contributors to this book are constructing new worlds in which everyone can work and play. Like World 0, these new worlds have their own realities that give their inhabitants alternative lives—unbounded by physical constraints and ruled only by the imagination.

Akikazu Takeuchi is senior researcher of Sony Computer Science Laboratory, Inc., in Tokyo. Internet: <takeuchi@csl.sony.co.jp>.

INTRODUCTION

What Is Virtual Reality?

Carl Eugene Loeffler and Tim Anderson

> Case was twenty-four. At twenty-two, he'd been a cowboy, a rustler, one of the best in the Sprawl. He'd been trained by the best. He'd operated on an almost permanent adrenaline high, a byproduct of youth and proficiency, jacked into a custom cyberspace deck that projected his disembodied consciousness into the consensual hallucination that was the matrix.
>
> William Gibson, 1984[1]

WHAT IS VIRTUAL REALITY?

The idea of virtual reality has captured the popular imagination. But what exactly *is* virtual reality? What does it promise that we don't experience in real life? Like many buzzwords, *virtual reality* has come to be used very loosely. Advertising campaigns apply the term to everything from computer games to pornographic sound recordings on CD. A tabloid article on virtual reality is headlined "Have Sex with Elvis." The slick (but conventional) computer animation of love scenes in the Hollywood movie *Lawnmower Man* leads to journalistic speculation on whether hackers have invented the ultimate safe sex.

It is perhaps appropriate that these media realities are labeled *virtual*, since virtual reality, as a buzzword, has little to do with the development of virtual reality in the real world. That few people have any direct experience with virtual reality only makes it easier to use the term as a vague label for all kinds of futuristic computer applications.

But there are other problems in pinning down the meaning of the term. Whatever virtual reality is, it is still emerging from a set of rapidly evolving technologies; even serious practitioners disagree about the best definition. One purpose of this anthology is to show the variety of virtual realities being built in laboratories and studios around the world. This introduction will provide an overview, and by the last chapter, you will see what virtual realities can be, and what they are already.

A DEFINITION

As a working definition, we may say that virtual reality is a three-dimensional, computer-generated, simulated environment that is rendered in real time according to the behavior of the user. Let us examine the elements of this sentence in turn.

Virtual reality is three-dimensional. In computer interfaces, VR provides a qualitative leap beyond the two-dimensional graphical user interfaces popularized by the Macintosh and Windows, just as those represent a qualitative leap beyond the one-dimensional command-line prompt of DOS, Unix, and other early systems.

Virtual reality is computer-generated. Even before we had computers, we had simulated environments that responded to the user; for example, flight simulators and arcade games. But the gains in interactivity, speed, and accuracy that computers offer has made them central to such simulations today.

Virtual reality is a simulated environment. The simulation may represent a real environment or it may be purely imaginary. It may follow familiar laws of physics or not; it may be filled with realistic detail or be highly abstracted. But the complexity and multi-dimensionality of the interface creates in the user a sense of his or her own presence in the simulated environment. While a graphical user interface is like a window on a computer application, virtual reality interfaces are like portals that allow the user to step into the application.

Virtual reality is rendered in real time according to the behavior of the user. A virtual environment does not consist of a series of predetermined points of view, like a film or video does. It is not a static creation, like a computer drawing. The user can move around in the virtual world, and the simulation is created according to the user's movement. To operate in real time means that the displayed environment responds to the user's actions with only a slight delay. Within a simulation one can move forward or backward, left or right, and up or down simultaneously.

IMMERSION AND INTERACTIVITY

One important aspect of virtual environments is immersion, or the degree to which the user's senses are limited to the simulation and screened from the real world. In computerized environments, the degree of immersion can vary significantly. Although virtual reality is too young a field to speak of a "classic" model, the "goggles and gloves" version that is often featured in the popular press represents a typical highly immersive environment. The "goggles" actually cover the eyes and ears, and are called a head-mounted display (HMD) by VR practitioners. The HMD offers both visual and audio display, and cuts off, or at least heavily screens, sights and sounds from outside the virtual world. Navigation is by hand gestures and body position; there is no computer mouse or keyboard, no real-world hardware to intrude on the virtual world.

A similar, but less intensive, experience may be obtained through a flight simulator, or even through a pod-type computer-arcade game in which the user and the screen display are well shielded from reality by the simulated cockpit of a jumbo jet or the interior of a space ship.

The least immersion is offered by desktop virtual reality systems. These are exemplified by computer games, but are also used for scientific visualization, database display, and other purposes. Here a user can have an emotional sense of immersion by being absorbed in the game or the data, but at any moment can disengage and look around.

Another aspect is VR interactivity, which may include navigating within the virtual world, turning features on and off, and interacting with other users. Many installations also allow the user to interact with agents, which are computer-simulated characters that inhabit the virtual world.

Virtual realities, then, vary widely in crucial aspects. There is a great deal of difference between immersive and nonimmersive, interactive and noninteractive experiences. This is perhaps best illustrated by the difference between looking at a swimming pool and taking a swim. Put on an HMD and dive in!

WHERE DID VR COME FROM?

In his book *Virtual Reality*, writer Howard Rheingold suggests that virtual reality traces back to religious rituals conducted in caves in France and Australia that immersed participants in three-dimensional, multisensory, simulated environments. Though such a comparison may seem stretched, VR grew from the basic human desire to explore alternative realities; computer technology merely facilitates the necessary leap of imagination, much as theater and art have done for centuries.

The flight simulator, which was a strictly mechanical device before the invention of computers, is a close predecessor to virtual reality as we know it today. Flight simulators track movement and produce an appropriate audio and visual display in a convincing manner; their purpose is to train the operators of aircraft and other vehicles. For example, hundreds of military personnel were trained for Operation Desert Storm in war games using simulators.

Virtual reality became possible in recent years when major advances were made in several independent areas of computing. These include rapid growth in computing power, new graphics techniques, and innovative input and output devices. Computer systems are now able to integrate multiple input devices as varied as three-dimensional mice, joy sticks, bicycles, and wands. Output devices now include 3D audio, or sound, whose direction is localized in three dimensions; force feedback, or mechanical hands and arms that create resistance when the user "touches" a virtual object, and more.

The success of graphical user interfaces opened the way for more direct and intuitive interfaces, and insights gained from applying visualization to different scientific fields encouraged experimentation with three-dimensional, multisensory information displays. Finally, although HMDs were designed thirty years ago, they have been refined a great deal during the past decade.

These developments allowed systems to combine great computational power with input tracking and real-time graphics and sound output. With this, one could produce a virtual world, become immersed in it, and navigate through it. An industry was born.

COMPUTER SYSTEMS FOR VIRTUAL REALITY

Three-dimensional databases are well known by specialists in computer visualization for automobile design, architecture, medical imaging, and so forth; VR brings these one step further to render a real-time, three-dimensional database with an immersion-technology interface. A virtual reality installation is a complex assembly of systems-integration that combines a host of devices and software. Because of this, the systems often fail; virtual reality is complex and volatile.

Essential to the immersion experience is the real-time rendering capability of the system. When a user turns his or her head from left to right, the application alters the audio and visual displays to match the movement. Users can ride, walk, or fly within an application, and these movements are also matched. Imagine the computational and rendering complexity involved when a system is required to match the movement of a user moving forward while looking left or right, up or down. To match these movements, the system needs to track the position of the user, and call up and render the necessary display in real time. The speed and quality of the audio and video are determined in large part by what kind of computer and supporting peripheral devices are used. For example, a personal computer provides lower resolution and slower response time than a workstation.

The quality of the visual simulation is largely determined by the frame rate (in frames per second, or fps), resolution, and visual complexity of the application. Commercial 35 mm sound films are shown at 24 fps, which is widely accepted as rapid enough for a convincing illusion. The graphics in virtual worlds are generally based on wire-frame models much like the wire frames that sculptors use. These are then rendered in solid or shaded forms in plain colors or texture maps, which are graphics that wrap or project over objects to add considerable visual detail without additional modeling.

Input devices for tracking the user's position and direction of travel are necessary for determining the movement of the displays. There are a number of devices, or travel sensors, for this. For visual and aural displays, the head position can be tracked using sound, optics, or electromagnetic fields. The direction of travel can be determined using gloves or even body suits equipped with electromagnetic and other types of sensing devices. The travel sensors also allow the user to navigate within the application while automatically telling the system what is going on. Other navigation devices include flight yokes and even machine vision, in which a video camera allows the system to observe the user's hand or body motions.

STILL A FEW GLITCHES

Effective rendering and accurate tracking are essential, though problems do occur. For example, rendering speed can be slowed by loading a personal computer with a complex graphic world intended for a workstation. This results in a low frame rate, if not a complete freeze.

When coupled with latency, the experience of a slow frame rate is less than satisfactory. *Latency* is the amount of time it takes the system to respond to the user's head movement or direction of travel. All movement is represented by the rendering, so if the frame rate is slow, the system must spend a lot of time playing catch-up. One unpleasant result is simulation sickness.

Obviously, virtual reality cannot happen without a good deal of software, including an underlying virtual-world–building program, coupled with the computer's operating system, position tracking, graphics, and sound. Thus, a virtual reality installation is a technical challenge involving complex systems integration.

One factor driving the development of virtual reality applications at this point is the availability of virtual world-building programs that can run on inexpensive personal computers. Commercial packages can now be bought off the shelf, and there are several other programs available from universities and special interest groups.

Now that virtual reality technology has been released from the enormously expensive domain of the flight simulator, and has entered the realm of the personal computer, people can experiment with many different kinds of applications.

DISTRIBUTED VIRTUAL REALITY

We foresee that computing environments in the next decade will be very widely distributed, ubiquitous, open-ended, and ever changing. All the computers in the world will be mutually connected. New services will be added from time to time, while old services will be replaced. New computers will be connected, and the network topology and capacity will be changing almost continually. Users will demand the same interface to the environment regardless of login sites. Users will move with computers and will move even while using them. Users will also demand much better user interfaces, so that they will be able to communicate with computers as if they are communicating with humans.　　←

Mario Tokoro, 1991[2]

One of the most exciting aspects of virtual reality is that it can be networked to join multiple user-immersion environments over long distances. The promise of virtual reality has captured our imagination; networks will render it accessible. There can be little doubt that networked immersion environments, cyberspace, artificial or virtual reality—whatever you want to call it—will evolve into one of the greatest ventures ever to come forward. Virtual reality will draw from and affect the entire spectrum of culture, science, and commerce, including education, entertainment, and industry. It will be multinational, and will introduce new hybrids of experience for which descriptors presently do not exist.

Three essential areas of recent cultural and technical development are:

1. The formation of a cyberculture around individuals who prefer to inhabit the domain of distributed digital media—electronic bulletin boards, databases, and multi-user simulated environments. These people more or less live in such domains, spending the majority of their time there. In virtual worlds they can alter their identities, their manner of social interaction, and their relationships within society. They become virtual beings in a virtual place. When people live in such a domain, a society becomes established, and a morality may emerge. What kind of morality will this be? Will it be governed? By whom and for what? This line of questioning becomes even more involved when one considers distributed virtual reality as a three-dimensional environment that may contain private spaces or residences that hold personal objects and possessions.

2. The emulation of the physical world may have doors, closets, and windows that look out onto multidimensional vistas. Toolkits allow for the transformation of the virtual world, which is comprised of a never-ending field of pure data. Some experiences in the virtual world will be familiar, like going shopping or going to a concert. Others will be unusual, like going to an ancient place or another planet.

3. The data field is everywhere, and people are moving through it using futuristic computer devices. Interfaces will become intuitive. Guides, or agents, will co-inhabit the domains, acquiring knowledge, becoming familiar, and growing old with us.

Though this seems like science fiction, extensive research is already being conducted in networked or distributed virtual reality. It currently constitutes a very small industry, but one with great potential for growth. At the STUDIO for Creative Inquiry at Carnegie Mellon University in Pittsburgh, we are investigating networked virtual reality and relevant applications.[3] Let's survey some examples of networked virtual reality, applying the term broadly.

Literature

The novelist William Gibson is often cited as the one who sparked the imagination of legions who are waiting for their moment to "jack into the Sendai Deck."[4] Their efforts have spawned myriad Gibson-like multi-user dimension (MUD) and multi-user simulation environment (MUSE) systems that catapult the user into a spiraling online matrix of experiential role-playing and other amusements. Here users employ text to describe the world, themselves, and their interaction with other users.

For example, MUD systems have been influential in Carnegie Mellon's development of the Oz Project, conceived by Joseph Bates of the School of Computer Science (see his essay in this collection). Predominantly a text-based narrative environment, the project explores the creation of the personality of artificial characters, which ultimately will be expressed as three-dimensional animations. Bates argues that though most virtual worlds express the concerns of replicating the physical nature and the functions of objects, other directions are equally important and must be informed by the cinematic conventions of character, plot, and story. If the entertainment of the future will be networked virtual reality, an essential study is mimesis of cinematic or narrative interaction.

THE MILITARY

The origins of virtual reality are largely to be found in the military. One current focus is SIMNET, a nonimmersive virtual environment project involving armored tank simulation with remote nodes, linked in real time. When SIMNET was used to train personnel for Operation Desert Storm it evoked strong physical and emotional reactions among the trainees. SIMNET was partly developed at the University of Central Florida, along with a number of other networked projects. The Department of Computer Science at the Naval Postgraduate School has recently launched NPSNET, with the goal to establish a government-owned, workstation-based network of visual simulators that employ SIMNET databases.

VIRTUAL COMMUNITIES

One can also point toward growing numbers of online virtual communities that introduce social, if not cinematic, interactions in a virtual place.

The Whole Earth 'Lectronic Link (WELL) is an exemplary online service that offers an expanded electronic bulletin board service (BBS). One example of an interdisciplinary virtual crossroads on the WELL is the Art Com Electronic Network (ACEN), which was founded in 1986 by Fred Truck and Carl Loeffler.[5] A real feeling of community and familiar social interaction exists among the user base. Sometimes, entire stories are written by the users, who assume the role of distinct characters that unfold a plot. ACEN focuses on the interface of contemporary art and communication technologies—and offers a discussion board, electronic art galleries, and even an electronic shopping mall for art-related books, software, and videos.

The overall shape and flavor of online services is staggering in variety. In Japan the Coara network, based in Oita Prefecture, has been operating for several years. The Oita local government is highly supportive and encourages the growth of the network. And in Korea the Association for Computer Communication Amateur Network functions as a service group for emerging grassroots networking efforts in Southeast Asia. There are countless other examples.[6]

ENTERTAINMENT

It is not by chance that Fujitsu, Ltd. of Japan has supported the work of both the Oz Project, which investigates interactive drama, and Habitat, which is a virtual world originated by Randall Farmer and Chip Morningstar at LucasFilms (see Farmer's essay in this collection). These projects and others with similar concerns indicate the advancing edge of dramatic entertainment accessed through networked immersion environments.

Farmer has demonstrated that the argument for connectivity and virtual reality is not about bandwidth; Habitat employs simple low-speed 300 baud modems. For display, it uses a simple monitor; it is not an immersion environment. The core requirements for networked virtual environments are a processor with an operating program; display and navigation devices; distribution, using computer networks, television or telephone; and thoughtful world design, employing cinematic conventions.

The addition of an HMD and other immersion devices is a relatively simple matter, and does not add considerably to the complexity of the operating program. The difficulty is economic—few of the users of Habitat, a consumer-based network, could afford an HMD for their personal computer. However, in the coming years, possessing a consumer-grade HMD will become an option.

In addition to drama there is music. The Grateful Dead's Jerry Garcia is reportly discussing interactive concerts where the audience could participate in creating the performance. Move over MTV, here comes MVR (Music Virtual Reality).

EDUCATION

The field of education offers an opportunity for applications to investigate the otherwise inaccessible, and to present challenges for the representation of and interaction with information. Scientific visualization is one area noted for advances in imaging applications. For example, Warren Robinett at the University of North Carolina has introduced a project that allows users to "fly" through protein molecules scaled to gigantic proportions. Robinett, who began at Atari and worked at NASA before UNC, has produced a number of advanced immersion applications.[7]

Another project is ExploreNet, developed by Charles Hughes and Michael Moshell at the University of Central Florida. It is a simulation network that assists in teaching core disciplines in elementary schools. Inspired by Habitat, Hughes and Moshell have produced two prototypes and have simulated Caruba, a wild world with caves, jungles, deserts, waterfalls, and mountains. ExploreNet addresses immersion experience as a psychological phenomenon, where a head mounted display is less important than compelling, dramatic interaction (see the piece by Hughes and Moshell in this collection).

The cognitive and behavioral sciences suggest that the capacity for learning is greatly enhanced when sight, sound, and touch augment the presentation of text or numerical data. Sound is especially important, as it naturally directs our eyes. From this perspective the flight simulator and the computer game may be considered advanced educational tools. Virtual reality—and eventually virtual reality networked over long distance—will be employed to conduct a multitude of education and training projects, ranging from grade-school classes to corporate seminar applications and beyond. Long-distance education will benefit tremendously, and students will have the opportunity to visualize and even touch the otherwise inaccessible.

THE WORKPLACE

Yet another direction is represented by the Team Work Station by Hiroshi Ishii of NTT, Japan. This project, which is in search of the paperless office, consists of linked multimedia work stations.[8] There are also a number of other networked workstation applications under development.

Telepresence can also be considered a networked extension of virtual reality, especially with regard to operators manipulating robots located in remote factories or perhaps in outer space. Force feedback is an essential aspect of telepresence.

TELECONFERENCING AND DESIGN

When distributed virtual reality is used as an interface for teleconferencing and design, the range of possible applications is broad, but education and industry are obvious examples.

Education can benefit with regard to long-distance learning, and industry can gain from a higher level of video teleconferencing, which will provide a more intimate relationship between the participants and the subject they are discussing.

In a teleconferencing session employing distributed virtual reality, multiple participants can share a dynamic relationship with their subject. For example, imagine a team of automobile designers discussing options via video teleconferencing. To look at the subject, they might program a prerecorded videotape, highlighting the desired aspects. Participants might even use a VR teleconference as a building site.

The salient aspects of a design studio employing distributed virtual reality are:

- The virtual environment supports interaction among networked remote production teams, for the purpose of industrial design and teleconferencing.

- The application establishes a relationship between an actual workstation and a virtual workstation, and operators can switch back and forth using a windowing method.

- Tele-existence is made evident through synchronous voice communication, and the capability of each member to "see" the other members in the virtual environmen.

- Stations consist of display, stylus, keyboard, and mouse; additional input devices include head trackers, data gloves, and machine vision for voice- and gesture-recognition; and output devices include head mounted displays.

- Design teams use proprietary software to produce wire-frame geometric models, painting, and mapping.

The advantages of distributed design stations are numerous, but an essential point is economy. Teams can be located in remote sites and benefit from a collective design experience.

CONNECTIVITY

The basis for distributed virtual reality is telecommunications. Two or more sites are joined by an operating system that can employ a number of telecommunication delivery services, including direct-dial lines, the Internet, high-bandwidth networks, cable television, and wireless.

The distributed virtual reality project at CMU is at the forefront of the investigation of connected immersion environments. Presently, a single point-to-point link, employing low bandwidth (9,600 baud) modems is available, as well as a client-server mode using the Internet. Recent demonstrations between CMU, Munich, and Tokyo proved successful, and the update-delay between each pair of cities was a barely perceptible hundred milliseconds or less. Servers and broadband telecommunications are being planned.

Select functions for point-to-point connectivity include:

- Providing all functions of the virtual world-building software in a distributed manner; the world and its attributes are distributed to each node, and one node is specified to be the controller.

- Providing constant views and updates of each user's object manipulations: users can move objects, including themselves; and updates to position and change occur with imperceptible update cycles.

- Writing and saving files to record the manipulations to objects; users can change worlds and carry an object with them into another world.

A new distributed client-server code allows multiple users to share an immersion environment by interfacing with a node. The following are key points of investigation:

- A client-server model, where multiple users can simultaneously share immersion environments, must be formed.

- The servers or nodes located across the world must be automatically updateable via the Internet.

- The nodes must offer sites for access and distribution of virtual reality software

- The nodes must support multiple platforms.

The next phase of the project will support broadband connectivity. To facilitate this phase, a consortium has recently been developed with associates in Japan, Scandinavia, and the United States. Members will conduct technology transfers and testbed projects. Actual applications are scheduled for development. Members of the consortium will collaborate to produce basic elements of connectivity for distributed simulations from client-server systems over the Internet to broadband ATM (asynchronous transmission mode), cross-platform graphical user interfaces, and executables of VR applications.

ABOUT THIS BOOK

As you can see, virtual reality is developing rapidly and in many directions. The contributors to this anthology analyze the issues and report on projects in several areas of industry and culture.

Noting the relative lack of commercial applications at this point, some observers have described virtual reality as a "zero billion dollar industry." Others have called it a technology in search of an application, which is a more relevant description. Although not yet widely adopted commercially, a wide variety of experimental virtual worlds are being created, and some general questions about how best to design them are coming to the fore.

Not surprisingly, some of the most innovative VR designs are coming from creative artists, who are helping to provide an answer to the question, "Now that we have this technology, what are we going to do with it?" We are beginning to see the first true works of art produced in the medium of virtual reality. Part 1, "Virtual Reality and the Arts," examines some of these installations from the point of view of the artists, who discuss not only the technical aspects of their cutting-edge works, but the philosophical aspects as well.

Part 2, "Ongoing VR Projects," addresses longer term projects relating to interactivity and telecommunications. Many of these projects, including Habitat and CMU's Virtual Polis, focus heavily on distributed virtual reality as the final frontier.

As mentioned earlier, education and corporate training represent broad opportunities for the use of virtual environments. Equally important is the work being done in virtual worlds for the handicapped. Such areas are covered in Part 3, "Real-Life VR Applications."

Part 4 examines the "News from Abroad" by surveying the advances in virtual reality technologies in Europe and Japan.

More far-reaching than design questions, and less often asked, are questions about the ethical, political and cultural implications of creating worlds which are "merely" virtual, and yet interact with the human body so much more intimately than computers have before. Part 5, "VR Theory," addresses these questions.

Finally, the bibliography and appendix provide guides to the literature and to suppliers.

The contributing authors were selected because of their outstanding competence in the field. And when considered as a whole, their efforts create a broad survey about virtual reality in industry and culture, telling us where it came from, what it is, and where it is going.

CONCLUSION

The server model of virtual reality points toward the Matrix to which Gibson so often refers in *Neuromancer*. In addition to various worlds, the server will contain rooms in which users can construct other virtual objects, including entire other worlds. Imagine a networked immersion environment, capable of supporting multiple users, each of whom can to change the existing virtual world or construct a new one: the bulletin board model applied to networked virtual reality. This could make for a continuously changing reality, which may produce anarchy, though the promise of constructing virtual worlds within an immersion environment is open-ended. This approach could be extended to any number of educational, entertainment, and industrial purposes. Distributed virtual reality has a rich history and the promise of an even greater future.

Note

Carl Eugene Loeffler is a pioneer in telecommunications and art, and is project director of Telecommunications and Virtual Reality at the STUDIO for Creative Inquiry, Carnegie Mellon University, and a visiting senior scientist at Norwegian Telecom Research and the University of Oslo.
Internet: <cel@well.sf.ca.us>.

Tim Anderson is Fine Arts Services Coordinator at the University Libraries and a Fellow of The STUDIO for Creative Inquiry at Carnegie Mellon University, Pittsburg, PA 15213. Internet: <ta1Ø@andrew.cmu.edu>

REFERENCES

1. William Gibson, *Neuromancer*, New York: Ace, 1984, 5.

2. Mario Tokoro, *Toward Computing Systems for the 2000's*, Tokyo: Sony Computer Science Laboratory, Inc., 1991, Technical Report SCSL-TR-91-005, 17-23.

3. For their support and interest we gratefully acknowledge the STUDIO for Creative Inquiry, Carnegie Mellon University; Ascension Technology Corporation of Bennington, Vermont; Sense8 Corporation of Sausalito, California; and Virtual Research, Inc., of San Jose, California.

4. The Sendai Deck is an electronic interface device often mentioned in Gibson's *Neuromancer*, one would "jack," or plug, into it to connect to cyberspace.

5. See Carl Eugene Loeffler, "The Art Com Electronic Network," *Leonardo*, 1988 21(3): 320-1.

6. A global perspective on the massive growth of computer networks is provided by John Quarterman in *The Matrix: Computer Networks and Conferencing Systems Worldwide*, Bedford, Mass.: Digital Press, 1990.

7. See Warren Robinett, "Electronic Expansion of Human Perception," *Whole Earth Review*, Fall 1991.

8. See Ishii and Miyake, "Toward an Open Shared Workspace: Computer and Video Fusion Approach of TeamWorkStation," *Communications of the ACM*, December 1991; 34(12): 37-50.

PART ONE

VIRTUAL REALITY

AND THE ARTS

ANGELS: A VIRTUAL MOVIE

Nicole Stenger

When this book is published, the *Angels* project will be completed in its high-res version, and will be ready to invite adults and children, art epicures, techno-freaks or simple discoverers of the world, real or virtual, to a virtual reality paradise.

In 1989, after years of artistic research into personal origin and historical identity, my desire to go back to universal values fortunately met with the emergence of a technology that was suddenly opening a window into an ontological time and reality.

I am primarily a writer of poetry and stories. Better still, I am a language *bricoleur*, or do-it-yourselfer. Any collection of objects will do for material: words bundled up together, words with a voice, artifacts combined, revealed with light, computer models in motion. The computer is a good typewriter—VR technology is the perceptual entrance to the direct manipulation of three-dimensional objects, words, sounds, and events. The ultimate for the language bricoleur!

In January 1990, I had my first VR experience at one of the first public demonstrations of the new technology, at Autodesk in Sausalito; I then attended a presentation of VR at the Human Interface Technology (HIT) Laboratory in Seattle. It was obvious to me that virtual reality was meant to convey pleasurable experiences—that it was a reward, a reassurance, a balm for some of the wounds of life. Why not start from the beginning, from a sense of well-being—from paradise?

I am a romantic, born in the misty climate of Ile de France, near Paris. I believe that love is important. Heart pains are soothed by the contemplation of nature. Exaltation of the soul travels through the gates of passion. Angels have the substance of inhabitants of paradise, as Milton describes it. They have the grace, joy, and playfulness you would expect from guides to the virtual world, and the knowledge of love. Entering virtual reality through the digitization of myself felt like experiencing my own angelic identity. Angels would thus welcome new travelers with words that would reflect on this new experience, and initiate them to the many facets of love.

When you enter *Angels*, you discover a first environment in space, a kind of "pie in the sky" immersed in music (see figures 1-1 to 1-3). Except you can grasp this apparition with your virtual hand. The doorway to *Angels* is the gateway to paradise. Fruits are dangling there in the form of three pulsating hearts—angels' hearts. You enter the revolving vestibule and, like a kid, touch one of the hearts. But you are not expelled from this paradise—on the contrary, you are invited to a new level: an island where an angel is waiting to greet you. Each encounter with an angel is a variation on the theme of love. It is a short love story that becomes your story, now that you are included in the virtual movie—now that you are the movie. The result of a dialogue between the angel's voice and your virtual body language provokes instant transformations in the environments that bring about a happy, sad, or whimsical end to each story. Back to the gateway, you choose another heart, or you go back to your first love.

I view virtual reality as a literary medium with rhythmical qualities. Thus the challenge of *Angels* was to organize a composition from what had yet no form, to draw a map from a void. I sought to play with the elasticity of time, to bounce the straying traveler back into the action, to organize three senses (though real touch is still missing at this point) into a meaningful language—to provide an experience that feels complete, no matter how long you decide to stay with it. *Angels* is a simple clockwork with few elements, but it already demonstrates that virtual reality movies are energetic organisms waiting to be optimized by the enthusiasm, humor, and inventiveness of the participants.

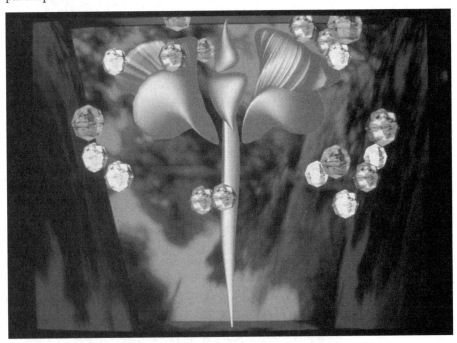

Figure 1-1. *Angels*, The Gateway • Credit: Nicole Stenger, 1990

Figure 1-2. *Angels*, Bliss. • Credit: Nicole Stenger, 1990.

Figure 1-3. *Angels,* Fusion. • Credit: Nicole Stenger, 1990.

Beyond *Angels*, three areas of artistic research seem to me to lie ahead: "adaptive computing," human interfaces, and work in collaboration with younger generations. As the complexity of virtual reality increases, new ways of computing will be needed. "Adaptive computing" might be a way to manage this complexity by developing evolutionary processes that combine familiar cards with unexpected ones in what always feels like the same game. The refinement and diversification of interfaces, by increasingly involving the body, will provide tools for a new sensorial poetry. Work in collaboration with younger people, who understand virtual reality technology better than anyone, will expand the culture of VR to its true dimensions.

For we are just building the ships for the imaginary travels of our children, providing them with food, water, a compass, and a map of the virtual world that is probably as inaccurate as a map from the fifteenth century. But this will be plenty for them to discover the virtual world!

Nicole Stenger is a poet, writer, artist, and designer. She can be reached at 146 Belvedere St., San Francisco, CA 94117.

Note

Angels was funded by Prix Villa Medicis and Eurekam. The project would not have been possible without hardware from Silicon Graphics, DEC, VPL Research, Crystal River Engineering; software from Wavefront, VPL Research; and the use of laboratories at MIT and the University of Washington at Seattle.

VERY NERVOUS SYSTEM

David Rokeby

In the series of installations that fall under the general title *Very Nervous System*, I use video cameras, image processors, computers, synthesizers, and a sound system to create a space in which the movements of one's body create sound and/or music. It has been presented primarily as an installation in galleries, but has also been installed in public outdoor spaces, and has been used in a number of performances. It has also found a number of interesting applications in the area of rehabilitation for the disabled, including facial-gesture tracking and physio- and music therapy.

The primary input device is a standard video camera. Images from it are analyzed by a hand-built video processor that determines the dynamics of physical gestures that take place within the frame. The initial level of analysis is the comparison of consecutive video frames. The result of this comparison is a representation of what has moved within the frame in the last thirtieth of a second. This information is further processed to give a sense of "gesture history," which may be described as the history of changes in the intensity (a combination of velocity and size of the moving object, a sort of momentum, perhaps) of movement over the period of a physical gesture; for example, the waving of an arm. From this gesture history, the video processor derives more qualitative information, to balance the purely quantitative character of the initial analysis. Therefore, the gathered information ranges from the amount of perceived movement at any instant, to time-based notions of consistency, unpredictability, and rhythm.

This gestural information is further processed by a Macintosh computer. The Macintosh runs a language that I call IntAct, which allows me to define the interactive behaviors of attached input and output devices. For example, physical movement might be translated into music through a set of instrument "behaviors." Each behavior is really a set of relationships between movement information and musical parameters. A wide variety of possible relationships can be imagined and defined. Many behaviors can coexist simultaneously, creating the equivalent of a band or orchestra. Behaviors can be created and shaped while an interaction is in progress (such as during a live performance), adding yet another layer of interaction.

Although this system is quite different from others currently gathered under the banner of virtual reality, it does present an experience that has several of the defining qualities of the VR experience. In *Very Nervous System*, the interactor feels truly immersed in the acoustic reality created by the system. Sound surrounds the body, providing a sensation of buoyancy and giving the interactor a sense of the physical presence of the "empty" space. The experience is somewhat like swimming. I am tempted to suggest that *Very Nervous System* is more closely allied to force-feedback systems than to three-dimensional visual worlds. The focus is on a kind of tactility, rather than on visual experience.

I created the work for many reasons, but perhaps the most pervasive reason was a simple impulse toward contrariness. The computer as a medium is strongly biased, so my impulse while using the computer was to work solidly against these biases. Because the computer is purely logical, the language of interaction should strive to be intuitive. Because the computer removes you from your body, it should strongly engage the body. Because the computer's activity takes place on the tiny playing fields of integrated circuits, the encounter with the computer should take place in human-scaled physical space. Because the computer is objective and disinterested, the experience should be intimate.

The active ingredient of the work is its interface. The interface is unusual because it is invisible and very diffuse, occupying a large volume of space, whereas most interfaces are focused and definite. Though diffuse, the interface is vital and strongly textured through time and space. The interface becomes a zone of experience, of multidimensional encounter. The language of encounter is initially unclear, but evolves as one explores and experiences.

The installation is a complex but quick feedback loop. The feedback is not simply negative or positive, inhibitory or reinforcing; the loop is subject to constant transformation as the elements, human and computer, change in response to each other. The two interact until the notion of control is lost and the relationship becomes encounter and involvement.

The diffuse, parallel nature of the interaction and the intensity of the interactive feedback loop can produce a state that is almost shamanistic. The self expands (and loses itself) to fill the installation environment, and by implication the world. After fifteen minutes in the installation people often feel an afterimage of the experience, feeling directly involved in the random actions of the street.

The installation could be described as a sort of instrument that you play with your body, but that implies a level of control in which I am not particularly interested. I am interested in creating a complex and resonant relationship between the interactor and the system.

In addition to the movement-to-music translation, *Very Nervous System* has also been used for gesturally interactive video disc installations and for interactive processing of incoming MIDI (musical instrument digital interface) data for interactive music performance.

David Rokeby is a specialist in sound-intensive spatial environments. He can be reached at 349a Spadina Avenue, Toronto, Ontario, Canada M5T 2G3; telephone: (416) 596-1428; fax: (416) 408-0080.

LEONARDO'S FLYING MACHINE AND ARCHAEOPTERYX

Fred Truck

The Model

For Leonardo da Vinci, swimming under water was the original flight simulator. In *Codex Atlanticus*, he notes: "Write of swimming under water and you will have the flight of the bird through the air." Nowadays, we can use computer technology in the form of virtual reality to create credible flight simulations for jet fighter pilot training. What, I wondered, could I do with virtual reality techniques to construct an artist's flight simulator based on one of Leonardo's flying machines?

I based my computer model of Leonardo's ornithopter on one of his early designs, from the 1490s. Rather than try to model in detail all the ropes and pulleys that provide Leonardo's machine with avionics, I eliminated them, emphasizing instead its spare, geometric lines, and of course, the batlike wings he drew so often.

Leonardo's Flying Machine and Virtual Reality

The three-dimensional computer model of Leonardo's ornithopter exists in two forms. The first form is in several animations with solid-modeled wings, which flap realistically, allowing the model to go through basic flight patterns. In the second form, the ornithopter has only the wing spars without the fleshed-out bat wings; this model has been successfully loaded in the Sense8 Virtual Reality Development System. Defying gravity, it floats, motionless, in a landscape containing nine telephone poles. As such, this work is a virtual sculpture that can exist only in the mind, and in interior computer space. The purpose of my virtual sculpture is to explore in a conscious state the common human experience of flying dreams, as reflected in the currently less common experience of flying through a virtual world. The array of nine telephone poles represents the obstructions to completely free flight often found in dreams of flying. The virtual sculpture is called *The Flying Dream*, and its exploration by technical assistants John Harrison and Colin Griffiths is the subject of a video of the same name.

Several directions are planned for the future. These include, but are not limited to: 1) testing texture-mapped wings and animation in the virtual environment; 2) comparison of third-person virtual reality, in which the user sees himself or herself, and immersive virtual reality, in which the user experiences the virtual environment directly; and 3) construction of a hardware interface for the Leonardo computer model, which will give the user the physical experience of piloting the flying machine. The name of this interface is Archaeopteryx (see figures 3-1 to 3-2 and color insert # 12).

Figure 3-1. The solid-winged animation model was the project's starting point.
• Credit: Fred Truck, 1992

Figure 3-2. The Flying Dream, the model without wings, is a study for future projects.
• Credit: Fred Truck, 1992.

The Design

Two tubular rings, placed at right angles to each other, represent the horizontal and vertical axes of Archaeopteryx. The single, mobile equatorial ring suspends a shortened fuselage based on Leonardo's flying machine design. The equatorial ring responds to the pilot's requests for directional change. The polar ring is fixed in position. It contains a complex head-tracking system, which updates the 3D world shown in the EyePhones as the pilot's head moves. The fuselage parts are:

- The sled, named after the Flexible Flyer sled, which it resembles. It consists of the headset, the torsion bar, and the pedals. The pilot of Archaeopteryx rides the sled, placing his heart very near the center of gravity. The straps of the sled are thick and padded, and extremely strong.

- The headset, which consists of VPL EyePhones for visual, stereoscopic, color display; a head tracker that cues the inertial guidance system; and a voice-input system. An inertial guidance system begins at a fixed position, then measures every move the pilot's head makes during the flight. Over time, there is some drift, but for Archaeopteryx, the inertial guidance system will provide an excellent way to update the virtual world.

- The torsion bar, which is a unique hand-tracking device that resembles a section of broom handle, but its surface is relatively soft and pliable. It is the kind of thing people like to squeeze. Inside the torsion bar are devices that read the amount of pressure the pilot's hands put on it, and the angle of force. To assist in clarifying the direction of the force, the torsion bar may move slightly in its allowed directions. The torsion bar is concerned only with hand tracking while flying, and does not preclude the integration of other forms of hand tracking, such as a DataGlove.

- The pedals, which are typical bicycle pedals that move the wings up and down when rotated. The faster Archaeopteryx is pedaled, the faster the wings beat.

Flight Simulation and Leonardo's Avionics

Microcomputer flight simulators usually present a sedentary pilot with a control panel including a number of instruments for monitoring the airplane, and flight controls for climbing, turning, engine speed, and so on, that are operated from a computer keyboard. Flight simulators that are more advanced, such as those the military uses, place the pilot in a more realistic environment that may manipulate him or her physically to create the physical sensation of the airplane bouncing off the runway during a landing, or other effects.

Leonardo's flying machine differs from conventional aircraft in several major ways. First, since the pilot's muscles provide energy for flight, the pilot cannot be sedentary. Additionally, the flight controls of Leonardo's machines are based on bats or birds, which do not use the principles of fixed-wing aircraft. The wing flaps up and down, rather than being equipped with flaps. Second, Leonardo's designs have no instrument panel. Flying is done "by the seat of the pants." Finally, in Leonardo's design, the foremost object is the pilot's head, rather than a windshield, cockpit canopy, or engine and nose.

This raises a good question. How much of the 3D model needs to reside in the computer memory? If the pilot is immersed in the virtual world, he or she will see little, if any, of the model. If the virtual world is of the third-person variety, in which the pilot watches the performance of the craft, the model needs to be available at all times, in the correct attitude and position. Fundamental issues of representation are at stake.

The answer to this question may be determined by practice, working in both third-person and immersive virtual realities. I recently made a 3D simulation of Archaeopteryx, and some animations, to see how the hardware interface might actually work—a simulation of the flight simulator. It became clear to me that it would be valuable to use a simulation of Archaeopteryx in third-person virtual reality to allow the user to learn how to control Leonardo's unusual flying machine by watching it respond to various commands, before tackling the immersive, first-person flight, at which point the flying machine becomes the virtual extension of the pilot's body and he or she must intuit the position of the wings.

Flying Archaeopteryx should be a physically exhilarating experience, like aerobics, gymnastics, or dance. Archaeopteryx is capable of aerobatic maneuvers, including outside loops, hammerheads, and inverted and knife-edge passes. It is a machine for the adventurous, for those who want to swim through the air, for those who want to explore their flying dreams wide awake.

Fred Truck is an artist working with computer technology, and is president of the artists' data resource, Electric Bank, 4225 University, Des Moines, IA 50311; telephone: (515) 255-3552; Internet: <fjt@well.sf.ca.us>.

ABOUT FIVE IDYLLS

The Narcissist

Robert McFadden

bout Five Idylls (The Narcissist) is a virtual reality environment integrating binocular three-dimensional video and binaural three-dimensional audio. The environment is experienced by means of a headset incorporating two small liquid-crystal video screens (one for each eye), audio headphones, a three-dimensional position detector, and a mouse. Produced in 1991, this was the first virtual reality project at the Banff Centre for the Arts in Banff, Alberta, Canada.

ENVIRONMENT

Visually, the environment consists of an immense white cube containing a small four-sided enclosure. Black on the outside, this enclosure has cropped photographic images of my body (legs, groin, arms, and torso) on its interior surfaces (see figure 4-1). Centered in this enclosure is a minuscule cube, proportionally equal to the first, with white top and bottom and reproductions of covers from "Doctor Strange" comic books on its rectangular sides (see figure 4-2). The sizes of the cubes and the enclosure differ radically from one another: the enclosure is barely visible from the surfaces of the white cube, as is the "comic-book" cube from the edges of the enclosure. The cube and enclosure are viewed in three dimensions. The photographic and comic-book images are two-dimensional.

Sound in *About Five Idylls (The Narcissist)* originates from two sources: a microphone mounted in the user's headset and a sample of my whispering a text from Euripides' *Alcestis*. The microphone integrates the real-time sound of the user's breathing and voice into the environment. The sampled text is controlled by a series of sequencing functions that radically alter and edit it in relation to the location and movement of the user's viewpoint (the virtual position of the user within the environment). Variations of this sampled text are experienced within the environment as triggered events (see below) and as continually present fields. The black exterior of the enclosure, for example, "emits" a "growl" (produced by layering the audio sample at an extremely low pitch). The location and volume of the growl within the three-dimensional audio mix is determined by the position of the viewpoint relative to the exterior of the enclosure. If the enclosure is to the upper right behind the user's viewpoint, this is the direction from which its sound is heard. Similarly, the spaces between the tops and bottoms of the two cubes are defined by a dense layering of whispering. This ambient sound, fairly loud at the top and bottom surfaces of the white cube, diminishes to inaudibility near the top and bottom surfaces of the "comic-book" cube.

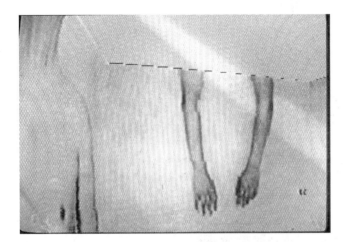

Figure 4-1.
The enclosure with body photographs.
• Credit: Robert McFadden, 1991.

Figure 4-2.   The Comic-book cube. • Credit: Robert McFadden, 1991.

NAVIGATION

Navigation of the user's viewpoint is accomplished with a hand-held mouse in combination with the three-dimensional position director built into the headset. Two buttons mounted in the mouse move the user's viewpoint forward and backward; movement is always toward or away from the viewpoint directly in front of the user. A third button, the "clutch," freezes the viewpoint. When the buttons on the mouse are not in use, the viewpoint slowly rotates in one direction, chosen at random. In other words, the viewpoint is only still when the clutch is engaged.

EVENTS

The user's viewpoint may move anywhere within the white cube and outside of the comic-book cube. Any attempt to move the viewpoint through the surfaces of the cubes and enclosure will trigger specific visual and audio events that create unique spatial relationships.

VISUAL

When the user attempts to penetrate the white cube, the viewpoint relocates to the surface of the comic-book cube; its position on the surface relative to where it "impacted" with the white cube (the dimensions of the two cubes being relative). Similarly, an attempt to enter the comic-book cube will shift the viewpoint to related coordinates on the surface of the white cube. Experiencing this event suggests a closed spatial loop between the environment's center and periphery: a circular space containing and contained by itself.

When the user tries to enter a photographic image, the viewpoint cuts to a relative position on the surface of the image located on the opposite side of the enclosure. The user experiences this event as a jump cut; a loop sequence in which the viewpoint repeatedly approaches the same photographic image.

When the viewpoint comes into contact with the black exterior of the enclosure, his or her ability to control the viewpoint's movement forward and backward is disabled. Simultaneously, a "bounce" function is activated that sends the viewpoint off through the environment on random trajectories and at random velocities. The viewer experiences this as a unique montage of images, sounds, and texts. The bounce function is stopped by using the clutch.

AUDIO

One or a combination of variations of the sampled text is triggered when the viewpoint shifts from the surface of one cube to the other. One of the text sentences may be heard in its entirety or in fragments ranging from phrases to individual syllables. The text or fragment may be heard all at once or in response to an action by the user. For instance, the full text may be "scanned" when the user's head is turned right and left, or by moving the viewpoint across areas of the environment onto which portions of the text have been mapped. Texts and fragments may be heard in three dimensions across the audio mix. They may also repeat until they are overridden by another audio event. The pitch at which my whispering voice is reproduced is random.

When the bounce function is engaged, the triggering of audio events continues to work as described above, but in relation to the visual montage. The viewer experiences this event as an audio montage in real-time synchronization with the images.

Any of the audio events described above may periodically occur in response to viewpoint movement anywhere in the environment. This presents the user with novel and unexpected combinations of images and texts at any time.

Robert McFadden is a visual artist who incorporates a variety of media and technologies, including computers, video, audio, performance, and installation. He can be reached at 8185 rue Berri, Montréal, Québec, Canada H2P 2G1; telephone (514) 279-3784.

VIRTUAL MUSICAL INSTRUMENT PROJECT

Goeff Thomas

I am currently involved with a project for a local science education center whose main purpose is to provide a demonstration of virtual reality to the general public, and to give people an idea of what VR is and what it can accomplish. The exhibit tries to give viewers a sense that musical instruments are present in the room with them, when there are none physically there.

This system differs from those usually associated with virtual reality. The main item in most VR systems is a computer-driven display that presents a stereoscopic view of a computer-created virtual world to the user. The head-mounted computer displays restrict the user's view of the real world as much as possible to enhance the feeling of being somewhere else. Typically, the user wears a glove on one or both hands that allows the computer to determine the hand's orientation and the position of the user's fingers, which can then manipulate virtual objects and change the environment.

Due to the high cost, poor image quality, and high computational demands of such a unit, we decided not to use one in the exhibit, but rather to produce virtual objects in the real world. In other words, instead of placing the user in an artificial world created by the computer, we decided to place computer-generated virtual objects in the real world.

This approach allows a head-mounted display to be added later, whereas in traditional VR it is a required component of the system. It also makes the system as a whole simpler, since only a low-end personal computer is needed, and the final cost is lower.

The exhibit will consist of an IBM-compatible PC (based on the 386 or 486 chip) or a Macintosh LC computer, a MIDI interface, a modified Nintendo PowerGlove, a synthesizer, speakers, and an audio amplifier. The virtual objects created are musical instruments such as a piano, trumpet, and drums. The users' interaction with the system basically involves waving their hands about, producing sounds when they "strike" one of these virtual instruments. To enhance the sensation of these instruments being present in the real world, we hope to add touch and/or force feedback at a later date.

We will use the system to test design factors, such as the lifetime of a PowerGlove (probably less than the few years planned for the exhibit). We also hope to learn whether visitors understand that the exhibit makes a sound when they put their hand in a certain place, and whether they feel that they actually pressed some keys on a virtual piano (how realistic is the exhibit?). More generally, is this is a good way to display virtual reality technology? Do visitors leave knowing what virtual reality is?

Goeff Thomas is currently involved in research at the University of Canterbury in New Zealand. He can be reached at the Computer Science Department, University of Canterbury, Christchurch, New Zealand; Internet: <geoffrey@cosc.canterbury.ac.nz>.

THE NEXUS PROJECT

Tim Gruchy

NEW FORMS, NEW AUDIENCES

The fundamental notion underpinning the work is that not only must new art forms grow and develop, but they must exist within new contexts. Theater, music, and cinema are all historical forms, but attending these events no longer has the cultural import it once did.

The Nexus project is the culmination of the endeavors of participants spanning the past fourteen years. It is a constantly evolving event that combines three main elements into a night's entertainment, situated somewhere between the experiences of theater, concert, and party. The elements of theatrical performances, a techno-band, and audience interaction are combined with an integrated system of interactive computer graphics, digital audio lighting, and lasers.

Nexus has been staged in entirety twice to date; once in Brisbane, Australia, to an audience of six hundred, and once in Sydney to six thousand people.

Personnel includes myself as producer, technical director, performer, artist, designer and technician; Mic Gruchy as artistic director, performer, writer, and artist; Iain Reed as lighting designer and production manager; Cathy Campbell as writer and actress; Al Ferguson as production and graphic designer; Geoffrey Rose in laser design and production; Tracy Bourke as choreographer and dancer; Noel Burgess as musician and performer; Ben Suthers as programmer and technician; and Robert Campanell as producer and artist.

On stage we provide a strong visual component by way of live mixed video and computer graphics. The techno band that accompanies the performance is Vison Four Five, which is composed of Noel Burgess and me and a floating array of collaborators. The music is diverse, though centered on the techno-dance area. It ranges in dynamics from a gentle melodic ambience to a hard, driving beat. We use the Mandala system to trigger sound and vision through movement and dance. The audio rig is entirely real-time MIDI and fully interfaced to the Mandala system; it uses no audio backing tapes.

The people involved manifest their separate endeavors in various ways and within various market places. We are trying to achieve the development of new forms that rely on the emergent technologies of digital integration and interactivity. Combined with traditional performance skills and an eye to what is happening in popular culture throughout the world, the Nexus project hopes to synthesize these elements into a holistic event that speaks of the here and now, and is a portent of things to come (see figures 6-1 to 6-3).

The complete Nexus is not always possible or appropriate. It is not a fixed or finished thing but a focus for future activity.

Figure 6-1. Nexus project. • Credit: Tim Gruchy, 1992.

Figure 6-2. Nexus project. • Credit: Tim Gruchy, 1992.

Figure 6-3.   Nexus project. • Credit: Tim Gruchy, 1992.

THE TECHNOLOGY

Points of connection between the traditional media of theater, video, and computer graphics are made possible by Mandala-sensed space interactivity. The technology allows the performer to control the performance environment during the performance. Technical media traditionally controlled by external technical operators such as lighting and sound now appear in a digital performance environment.

The technical system uses Mandala as the front end to an integrated system. On the visual side, multiple Amiga personal computers, video cameras, and tape sources are combined to create a live, mixable source that is multi-switchable into a projector array. The Amigas are fitted with real-time image-manipulation hardware and software.

Three screens are the minimal configuration. The system can be configured to drive a larger projector array. Another possibility is the use of a video-wall controller to distribute the signals to the various screens. During one event we used an array of nine screens driven from a wall. This system was then interlinked into a large digital-audio setup that uses state-of-the-art synthesizer, digital mixing, and processing capabilities. The main design criteria for the system are integration and live interactive control.

The Mandala system controls the intelligent lighting. The lasers are not yet linked to the Mandala controller, although the design should allow this in the future. We have explored the use of large-scale robotics to integrate chain-motor controllers for moving sets and lighting trusses.

By moving in space, the performer can integrate video, computer graphic scenes, and digital sound and lighting cues to reinforce the dramatic content. The technology liberates the actor/performer and overcomes the need for a strict linear structure of thematic content. The actor navigates the audience through a complex landscape of ideas and images.

PERFORMANCE OUTLINES: Running Bath and VR Cell

The two dramatic performances, *Running Bath* and *VR Cell*, are expressions of the *Nexus* concept. *Running Bath* is a complex physical performance designed and performed by actor Cathy Campbell, director Mic Gruchy, and technical producer Tim Gruchy. Presented in workshop at the Queensland University of Technology, and performed for the Institute of Modern Art in Brisbane in late 1992, the piece creates a visual environment of madness and self-analysis. The female character navigates us through quiet reflection, fear, doubt, and the nightmare of loss of reason. Campbell combines highly evocative physical theater with a digital collage of visual images and dialogue. She relates to characters from memory and madness in an interactive journey through a woman's psyche.

VR Cell uses interactive technology to allow Australian actor and director Mic Gruchy to deliver a harrowing monologue while navigating through his own video environment. Triggering vision, sound, and lighting, he confesses to future crimes. Testing morality in the modern technological terrain, the piece chronicles the story of digital genetic information, the collapse of traditional society, and the artificial immortality attained by the surviving technocratic enclaves. In a stark environment of video news footage and 3D molecular animations, the political prisoner tells fables of technological and moral bankruptcy. Presented at the Queensland University of Technology, and performed for the Institute of Modern Art in Brisbane in late 1992, the piece is a fusion of theater, artificial reality, film, and video.

LASER DANCE

Geoffrey Rose and Tracy Bourke have explored a range of technologies including lasers, fiber optics, neon, and fluorescence, not to mention a host of machines. Bourke has included astonishing laser graphics throughout the night's proceedings, and has choreographed a series of specific laser dances—some solo, some for ensemble—that rely on a particular technical setup and some remarkable costumes. These have developed into spectacular segments that are woven into the event. Rose's laser work is characterized by a strong commitment to dealing with three-dimensional illusion.

AUDIENCE ENVIRONMENT

After the various performance components to the evening are complete, the stage area is turned over to the audience to provide an interactive playing field in which they may to dance and party. Using body movements, they are able to control the computer graphics, video, lighting, and, to a lesser extent, some audio events. This triggers a broad range of events within the total environment that, when combined with careful programming, alters the dynamics that depend upon whether one person or twenty or a hundred people are in the installation. The physical design to the stage area should accommodate this requirement while maintaining its other functions. This has been achieved using a low stage when there is a relatively small audience, or a large stage with steps and a temporary barrier. Another option easily achieved would be to make the dance floor the audience zone; this has also been done successfully but stage options seem to work better. We will continue to investigate the interactive playing field.

Tim Gruchy is an artist, producer, and educator. He can be reached at 387 Riley Street, Surry Hills 2010, Australia; telephone: 61-018-161-841; Internet: <timeg@peg.apc.org>.

TAPEHEAD

Robert Campanell

Tapehead is a two-minute short-story video about a guy who orders cable TV service with 250 channels and the problems that arise from having access to so much information. The object of the video was to integrate human actors with virtual actors. I used the Mandala system to create *Tapehead*. The featured virtual actor, TalkingVHS, is a VHS tape with moving lips.

The basic concept behind the video is character development for virtual actors, whose characters have to hold equal ground with the human characters. This is difficult because virtual actors have technological constraints (such as RAM and CPU). I believe that you have to bring the human actors down to the same level as the virtual actors and make the human actors work with the same technological constraints.

In order to make the human actor work with the same constraints, he uses the Mandala to trigger the sound samples to say his lines. He doesn't open his mouth.

But naturally imposed technical constraints are not limited to the virtual actors. The human actor has the physical constraints of the studio set. His ability to move about in the virtual space is very small. Therefore, the virtual actors' movements are also limited.

One must recognize the constraints on both the human and virtual actors, and make both work within the same constraints. If this is not accomplished, either the virtual actor or the human actor will have a subordinate role in the performance. The consequences may be an uneven play, underdeveloped characters, and audience/participant frustration.

I use a fixed script for both actors. The timing is controlled by the human actor. In the Mandala, the human actors use the virtual actors to trigger the sound samples. I used an Amiga system called PerfectSound to digitize the lines of dialogue. The human actor's voice sounds normal, but for the virtual actor's voice I sped up the playback and mixed the samples for a higher pitch with some reverb.

A stationary computer-graphic remote control triggers the human actor's voice, saying his or her lines and changing the scenes.

Human actors and virtual actors can coexist peacefully in the same virtual world, as long as the human actor is scripted in the starring role. It's going to take years of understudy training before any virtual actor will be able to steal the show.

Robert Campanell produces the television series Cyberia for U Network, a national network of college TV stations based at Brown University. He can be reached at Explicit, 2020 Pennsylvania Avenue NW, Suite 430, Washington, DC 20006; telephone: (202) 667-4721; fax: (202) 429-2852; Internet: <robcamp@well.sf.ca.us>.

THE VIRTUAL MUSEUM

Jeffrey Shaw

The *Virtual Museum* is a three-dimensional computer-generated museum incorporating a display of rooms and exhibits. The equipment consists of a rotating circular platform that holds a large video projection monitor, a computer, and a chair on which the viewer can sit. From this chair the viewer interactively controls his or her movement through The *Virtual Museum* (see color insert 9) .

Figure 8-1. A viewer rides through *The Legible City* at SIGGRAPH 1989 in Boston.
• Credit: J. Shaw (with Dirk Groenveld), 1989.

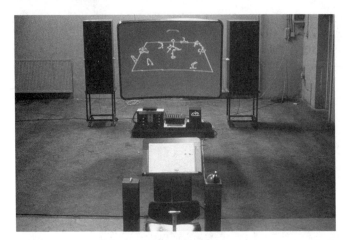

Figure 8-2. *Viewpoint* uses projection screen and viewing console to virtually project a series of images into the exhibition space. • Credit: J. Shaw (with T. Botschuijer), 1975.

Figure 8-3.   In *Revolution*, the viewer rotates a monitor in two directions; one shows a grindstone, the other shows revolutionary events 1765-1989. • Credit: J. Shaw, 1990.

Figure 8-4.   In *Going to the Heart of the Centre of the Garden of Delights*, the viewer changes the sequence of images. • Credit: J. Shaw, 1986.

Figure 8-5. In *Inventer La Terre*, a "periscope" allows the viewer to choose a path in a circular panorama of video imagery.
• Credit: J. Shaw, 1986.

Figure 8-6. In *Alice's Room* at Kanagawa Science Center, the viewer moves about in a representation of the actual room he or she is in.
• Credit: J. Shaw, 1989.

When the viewer moves the chair forward or backward, he or she moves in the same direction in the museum space represented on the screen. Turning the chair causes a rotation of this virtual image space, and also a synchronous physical rotation of the platform. Thus the viewer moves (and is moved) simultaneously in both the virtual and real environments.

The *Virtual Museum* consists of five rooms, all of which reproduce the architecture of the real room in which the installation is located, thus making a conjunction of the real and virtual spaces.

The first room shows a representation of the installation itself with its platform, computer, video monitor, and chair. Moving through The Virtual

Museum gives the viewer the effect of taking leave of the chair and transporting his or her disembodied viewpoint freely through the exhibition spaces.

The other four rooms are entered consecutively by passing through their immaterial walls. Using alphabetic and textual forms, each room has its own specific virtual contents. The arrangements in the first three rooms correspond to existing genres—painting, sculpture, and cinema. The fourth room is a wholly computer-generated environment that contains three moving signs with the symbols A, 2, and Z, which are primary tricolor light sources giving the room its physical identity.

We see around us a world that is becoming increasingly museumlike. This tendency toward premature conservation may be relieved by a virtual museum architecture that is as provisional as the culture that it embodies. *The Virtual Museum* delineates certain modalities of an interactive and virtual space. It locates the virtual space in a contiguous relationship with the real space, and establishes a discourse in the fine zone that exists between the real and the virtual.

Jeffrey Shaw is an artist who has been making interactive electronic installations since the mid-1960s. He is director of the Institute for Image Media, Zentrum für Kunst und Medientechnologie, Kaiserstrasse 64, Postfach 6919, 76049 Karlsruhe 1, Germany.

Note

Application software: Gideon May; platform engineering: Huib Nelissen; computer system: Silicon Graphics 4D/31OVGX. The Virtual Museum has been shown at "Das Beleibte Bild," Art Frankfurt, 1991; "Machines à Communiquer," La Villete, Cité des Sciences et de l'Industrie, Paris, 1991; "The Robots," Nagashima Spaland, Nagoya, Japan, 1992; and "Ars Electronica," Linz, Austria, 1992.

THE NETWORKED VIRTUAL ART MUSEUM AND OTHER PROJECTS

Carl Eugene Loeffler

The Networked Virtual Art Museum, designed and constructed by the STUDIO for Creative Inquiry, Carnegie Mellon University, joins telecommunications and virtual reality through the design and development of multiple-user immersion environments, networked over long distance.

The essential areas investigated through the project include: world-building software, visual art and architecture, telecommunications, computer programming, human interface design, artificial intelligence, communication protocol, and cost analysis.

AREAS INVESTIGATED

VISUAL ART AND ARCHITECTURE

The fusion of disciplines is the basis for collaborative authorship of virtual worlds. The construction of the virtual museum involves the participation of visual artists, architects, computer-aided design teams, computer programmers, musicians, recording specialists, and others.

WORLD-BUILDING

The project serves as a testing site for world-building software and associated hardware.[1] The programming teams have added considerably to the functions of the software tested. Public releases are in planning.

TELECOMMUNICATIONS

Critical to the project is the development and implementation of networking approaches, including modem-to-modem, server, and high-bandwidth connectivity. Telecommunications specialists collaborate with the design team to resolve problems of connectivity in immersion environments.

ARTIFICIAL INTELLIGENCE

The application of artificial intelligence, in the form of agents, or guides, and smart objects, is an essential area of development. The Networked Virtual Art Museum project involves researchers in the areas of interface design, smart objects, and artificial intelligence.

GROUPWARE AND COMMUNICATION PROTOCOL

The project documents multi-user interaction and groupware performance, establishes protocols within networked immersion environments, and suggests telecommunications standards. The contribution of communication specialists addresses aspects of documentation and standardization.

COST ANALYSIS

Future study will address the practical nature of networked immersion environments, investigate the effectiveness of information access for the end user, and profile the end-user experience. The project involves the participation of cost-analysis specialists, who will formulate a practical cost basis for networked immersion environments.

The project team has designed and constructed a multinational art museum in immersion-based virtual reality. The construction of the museum involves a developing grid of participants located in remote geographical locations. The nodes are networked using modem-to-modem telephone lines and the Internet, and will eventually use high-bandwidth telecommunications.

Each participating node will have the option to interact with the virtual environment and contribute to its shape and content. Participants are invited to create additions or galleries, install works, or commission researchers and artists to originate new works for the museum. Tool rooms will be available, so that participants can construct additional objects and functions for existing worlds, or build completely new worlds. Guest curators will have the opportunity to organize special exhibitions, explore advanced concepts, and investigate critical theory pertaining to virtual reality and cultural expression.

The museum also functions as a stand-alone installation, and is easily transportable for presentation in cultural, educational, or industrial venues.

The design of the museum centers on a main lobby, from which one can access adjoining wings or galleries (see color insert # 14). Several exhibitions are completed, while others are under construction. The first exhibition to be completed, called *Fun House*, is based on the traditional fun house found in amusement parks. The museum also contains the *Archaeopteryx*, conceived by Fred Truck and based on the Ornithopter, a flying machine designed by Leonardo da Vinci.[2] The team is also collaborating with Lynn Holden, a specialist in Egyptian culture, to complete *Virtual Ancient Egypt*, an educational application based on classic temples mapped to scale (this installation is also a part of Virtual Polis, as noted elsewhere in this volume). These exhibitions are all being constructed at CMU; however, we anticipate additions from participating nodes in Australia, Canada, Japan, and Scandinavia.

Now that the framework of the museum project has been described, perhaps it would be useful to discuss the essential points of one application.

THE FUN HOUSE

Webster's Dictionary describes a fun house as "a building in an amusement park that contains various devices designed to startle or amuse."

For the first installation in the Networked Virtual Art Museum, a fun house was designed (see figures 9-1 to 9-2). While making metaphorical reference to the fun houses found in traditional amusement parks, the application is an investigation of interaction and perception employing networked, immersion-based virtual reality. It was this world that was used during the first long-range demonstration conducted between Carnegie Mellon University and Expedition '92 in Munich in September 1992. A more recent demonstration, featuring a different virtual world, was conducted between CMU and Tokyo, sponsored by the International Conference on Artificial Reality and Tele-existence, July 1993, Japan.

The fun-house metaphor is particularly applicable as a container for virtual experience. Upon entering a fun house, one is acutely aware of being cast into a different world. The senses are amused and assaulted by a number of devices—trick mirrors, fantasy characters, manipulation of gravity, spatial disorientation, mazes, and sound, for example. In the virtual fun house, various traditional devices are adapted and some new ones are offered.

Figure 9-1. A UFO waits outside the museum. • Credit: Jeremy Epstein, **STUDIO for Creative Inquiry, Carnegie Mellon University, 1992.**

Key attributes to be found in the *Fun House* include:

- Objectification of the self within an immersion environment. Users can select their image from a library including Frankenstein, Dracula, and a doctor, among others; the Cookie Man has proved to be a favorite. When entering the *Fun House*, users can see their image reflected in real time in a mirror. They can also see the images of other users. Users can extend their hands and wave at one another—a basic and highly communicative form of human expression.

- Interaction with a client (or agent) that has artificial intelligence. When you enter the *Fun House*, a client greets you and speaks. It has a polite behavior and is programmed to face you, follow at a certain distance, and stay out of your way. After a while, the client stops following and says goodbye. Smart objects are also incorporated; touching them invokes events within the program.

- Interaction with multiple users in real time. Networked telecommunications allow for the simultaneous support of multiple users within the *Fun House*. For the demonstration between CMU and Munich, the users selected the Dracula and Cookie Man personas from the library. Each user could see the other, had an independent point of view, and could move objects.

- Links to moving objects. The *Fun House* features a merry-go-round; users can grab hold and catch a ride while music plays.

- Objects attach themselves to users. The *Fun House* features a flying saucer ride; users are transported up into the space craft, and can pilot its flight. The event calls the "beaming up" of the user and a whirring sound associated with flying saucers (see color insert #3).

- Attributes of physical laws. The *Fun House* features a ball game, where users pick up a ball and throw it at targets. The ball falls, bounces, and loses velocity. Thus gravity, velocity, and friction are articulated. The motion of the ball is sound-intensive.

Figure 9-2. The ball used for the investigation of physics.
• Credit: Jeremy Epstein, STUDIO for Creative Inquiry, Carnegie Mellon University, 1992.

NEW DIRECTIONS

Following the *Fun House*, the STUDIO created a number of applications for Ford Motor Company, including a virtual showroom (see figures 9-3 and 9-4) and a virtual test track (see figure 9-5). The participants can actually walk around the car; open doors, hood, and trunk; and even test-drive it. In detailed applications, users can examine specific—even minute—parts in detail.

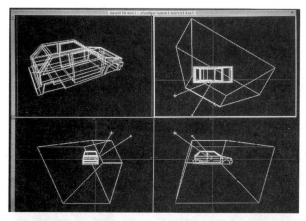

Figure 9-3. The wire-frame model of a car in the Virtual Show Room by Carl Eugene Loeffler.
• Credit: Jeremy Epstein, STUDIO for Creative Inquiry, Carnegie Mellon University, 1993.

Figure 9-4. The solid model of the car.
• Credit: Jeremy Epstein, STUDIO for Creative Inquiry, Carnegie Mellon University, 1993.

Figure 9-5. In scale, the Virtual Test Track is two miles long.
• Credit: Jeremy Epstein, STUDIO for Creative Inquiry, Carnegie Mellon University, 1993.

While working on the applications, the project team became increasingly interested in approaching the immersion environment as a site where things can be constructed or created. For Ford, virtual reality was to be used as a virtual design studio, but what are other approaches?

Currently under design are three network-capable applications for a public institution or educational setting: the Music Room, Construction Room, and Painting Room. These are friendly and intuitive environments that require only a short learning curve. Instructions are in Spanish and English, and the environment is co-inhabited by small agents, or "beasons" (named after CMU programmer Curtis Beason) that are programmed with a low-level artificial intelligence. They are guides to the various interactive objects, and they demonstrate how the environment functions by literal illustration. In the Music Room the beasons run around and make contact with the instruments, thus playing music. This shows users which instruments produce what sounds and how to use them. There are a number of other intuitive controls for navigating around in the room.

The Music Room contains three basic instruments. The largest is a large six-note keyboard attached to a wall. This instrument plays a pentatonic scale in three voices—orchestra, choir, and percussion. It is performed by touching the keys, or by simply waving one's hand in close proximity; this requires the use of a glove input device. The other instruments are a drum and shakers.

The Construction Room is designed for young children. It contains building blocks that can be assembled to construct objects—sort of a virtual Lego set. There is a nearly infinite supply of blocks, and if a user creates an object large enough, such as a house, he or she can enter it. The beasons co-inhabit this site as well, bounce merrily on the blocks, and illustrate how to stack them.

The Painting Studio is quite literal—a site for making paintings or graffiti. The user can select from a number of brush effects, and choose colors.

As of this writing, negotiations are underway to present these three applications in a public science museum setting, and to network the facility with other facilities, so that people in different locations can simultaneously interact. They are also designed for use by school districts and other institutions.

Carl Eugene Loeffler is a pioneer in telecommunications and art, and is project director of Telecommunications and Virtual Reality at Carnegie Mellon University and a visiting senior scientist at Norwegian Telecom Research and the University of Oslo; Internet: <cel@well.sf.ca.us>.

REFERENCES

1. For further information, see the WorldToolKit Manual, Sausalito, Calif: Sense8 Corporation. WorldToolKit is a computer program for the creation of virtual reality applications.

2. See Truck's contribution to this collection, "Leonardo's Flying Machine and Archaeopteryx," and, for a fuller account, his *Archaeopteryx*, Des Moines, Ia.: Fred Truck, 1992.

INHERENT RIGHTS: VISION RIGHTS

Lawrence Paul Yuxweluptun

I am an artist of two cultural circumstances. Since I happen to be a native, I paint the color of life. I see all this land in a native way. I was born to see it this way.

I find my life painting history from a native point of view. I was born in the time of the nuclear weapon, which was invented even before I was born. I am documenting neo-times. I approach my work and have always approached it taking my social and ideological responsibility as an artist first, as they relate to this time in history.

I cannot celebrate or feel any national allegiance to the Canadian flag while such racist legislation as the Indian Act remains in force: the system under which native people are governed is the despotism of white self-interest. Because of this, a lot of my pieces are historical. You cannot hide real history or even the censorship of native history, a colonial syndrome. You can hide Department of Indian Affairs documents from the time of Confederation, but you cannot hide my paintings. They are there for all people to see.

I paint on a reservation, to feel this perspective on life—the racist segregation of Canadian history, the so-called "Indian problem." I will paint you, O Canada. For all your atrocities, face my paint, for they are part of my life. Try to read the symbols for what they are.

I am concerned with the colonial mentality that is directly responsible for the killing of wolves, buffalo, whales, grizzly bears, and migratory birds, to the point that some species are now extinct. That mentality is behind the depletion of fish stocks on the West and East costs, acid rain, nuclear waste, land fills, smog, the greenhouse effect, the emission of methane gas, mining tailings, endangered animals, pollution of freshwater reservoirs, toxic wastes of all kinds, oil spills, uranium mining, and nuclear testing. The next step toward decolonization of First Nations must be recognition by the provincial governments of our sovereign indigenous government. As sovereign caretakers of the land, our forebears were always the protectors of the biosphere.

My work is very different from traditional art work. How do you paint a land-claim? You can't carve a totem pole that has a beer bottle on it. I find myself coming back to the land. Is it necessary to totally butcher all of this land? The grizzly bear has never signed away his land, why on earth should I, or a fish, or a bird? To slowly kill my ancestral land? All the money in the bank cannot buy or magically bring back a dead biosystem. I paint this for what it is—a very toxic landbase. This is what my ancestral motherland is becoming. Painting is a form of political activism, a way to exercise my inherent right, my right to authority, my freedom. This is a real freedom for me. I am proud these days. I have self-dignity in my art when I paint this world. I see environmental "shmuk," so I paint "shmuk"-art in all its toxicological bliss. I can speak out in my paintings even without the recognition of self-government. I dance around in a longhouse. I dance around fires in turn, like my forebears have done since time immemorial. I am a preservationist, continuing my heritage.

Inherent Rights, Vision Rights is a virtual reality project I have been involved with for some time now (see Figure 10-1). I approach it from the aspect of the fear others have of native people, and from their lack of understanding of our spirit world. In the piece, the longhouse is a given space in time to show a religious concept, to physically bring people into contact with a native-worshiping aspect of life, with praying Indians; to bring others close to my heart so they can understand my belief system. You learn what it is like to be in a possessed state, to feel rhythmic sounds in a longhouse, to feel sounds go through yourself, to feel a spirit inside you. I have a been a Blackface dancer eighteen years now, a masked dancer, a *Sxuwyxwey* dancer since I was fourteen. I have been able to draw from these native experiences, combining them with Western world experiences and technology to make my work. Employing technology that in the past has been used against native people, I created *Inherent Rights, Vision Rights* to show people what is happening to me spiritually. Always, I create art to communicate with others, to let other cultures see things for themselves. To show my world, the *Indian* world, to show that we do have a spirit, a place to go to, so people will understand who I am as a West Coast native person.

Although this particular virtual reality is very primitive at this point—it

Figure 10-1. Still from *Inherent Rights: Vision Rights*, 1991-1992. • Credit: Lawrence Paul Yuxweluptun, 1991.

has limited visual resolution—the capabilities of the technology will change in years to come. At the moment, the piece consists of a white man's mask, the "helmet," as it is called by the computer program. A screen goes over your eyes covering part of your face, an electronic mask with an electronic-motion hand. You start to experience a new art form. As you look into the mask, the screen shows you a piece of art work, computer-stimulated into color. Sound can be brought in at the same time. I think this first mask will end up in museums just like other masks! Very primitive, with numbers on them, and the date they were made.

I'm also a British Columbian artist painting from a B. C. position. This is different from some other native points of view. But the destruction of the ozone layer is still my problem. The ozone layer is a rare form of oxygen found nine to thirty miles above this planet's surface.[1] The chlorofluorocarbons (CFCs) used in spray cans, refrigerators, and air conditioners have gradually released chlorine atoms that have destroyed the ozone above the Antarctic and the North Pole. Ten percent of the ozone will vanish by the decade's end. In response to this threat the industrial nations have agreed to phase out CFCs and other ozone-depleting chemicals by the year 2000. It will take a hundred-year ban to bring ozone levels back to pre-1985 levels.

I don't have any rights in this country, so I paint the ozone as a problem.

Other environmental hazards are destroying and disrupting the ecosystems of First Nations' lands. They include groundwater evaporation because of big cities, and clear-cut logging, in both Canada and the United States. The province of British Columbia alone is sixty years behind in silviculture; it is cutting trees faster than it is replacing them. There is a need for a moratorium on the number of logging-truck licenses granted to the forestry industry. There is a need for an overall environmental audit to track companies' ecological performance on an annual basis and to inform the public, as well as for information-sharing on green environmental policies and programs at the governmental and community levels.

At the same time, the world's population is growing and will double in the next thirty-eight years. It is imperative to apply First World environmental standards to Third World factories, but global treaties to extend economic and technical assistance to developing nations are needed to help them help themselves to develop ecologically safe practices. We need these treaties to integrate environmental criteria into economic practices, and to provide management and technical and financial resources to tackle global problems. The economic efficiency of green policies must be improved, because the toxicological time bomb has already gone off, threatening all life forms with health hazards and, ultimately, with toxic death.

Good luck, O Civilization, for every hundred years I will ask you to drink the water with me, my Brother and Sister, and I will wait for you to take the first drink.

Yuxweluptun (white man's alias **Lawrence Paul**) is a painter and also works with advanced technologies, in particular, virtual reality.

BIBLIOGRAPHY

Linsley, Robert. "Painting and the Social History of British Columbia." In *The Vancouver Anthology*, Stan Douglas, ed. Vancouver: Talonbooks; 1991.

Townsend-Gault, Charlotte. "Having Voices and Using Them: First Nations Artists and 'Native Art.'" *Arts Magazine*, February 1991, 65(6): 65-70.

Note

This essay was reprinted with permission from *Land, Spirit, Power: First Nations at the National Gallery of Canada*, Diana Nemiroff, ed., Ottawa: National Gallery of Canada, 1992.

REFERENCE

1. Figures quoted in this essay are from Ed Magnuson, et al., "Poisoning of America," *Time* (October 14, 1985): 64-80 and Melanie Menagh, "Reportcard on the Planet," *Omni* (July 1992): 30-40.

THE WORKROOM

Ken Pimentel

A bright ray stabs out from the tip of the wand you hold as you press a button on it. A slight movement of your hand causes the beam to slice through various walls, roofs, and floors, which briefly light up and sound a musical note as the ray intersects each in turn. As you turn your head, you notice a series of walls, doorways, and columns lined up on one edge of the large green rectangular field you are hovering above.

You decide to build your virtual house by first constructing the front door wall. Pointing your wand at an object that looks like a wall with a door cut in the center of it, you press the wand button once again. The laserlike ray intersects the wall, causing a simple wire-frame box composed of thin blue lines to surround the wall, signifying its selection. With your other hand, you control a joystick that moves both your viewpoint and the selected wall. Pulling back on the joystick moves you backward, while the wall slides along the ground to keep pace with you. You move backward, not sure you've positioned the wall correctly. You ask your partner for an opinion. Turning your head, you can see her bright red wand wavering nearby. The sound of her reply appears to come from the same location as the bobbing red wand. As she moves closer, her voice grows louder.

Based on her suggestions, you make a few quick adjustments with the joystick to position the wall perfectly. Next, you alter the wall's appearance by pressing a button on the base of the joystick. Each time it is pressed, a different image is mapped onto the wall's surface. A staggered pattern of bricks, wood paneling, a granite surface, and even a zebra-skin design are potential choices. You decide on the faux zebra-skin for an avant-garde look. Meanwhile, your partner has dragged a sloped roof over and raised it into position. She selects the granitelike surface for the roof, then rotates it midair to a different orientation.

Wondering what the structure looks like from inside, you point your wand at the "get small" sign hanging in the background. Pressing the wand button causes the ray to momentarily stab out and intersect the sign before disappearing. You're suddenly dropped down to eye level with the building.

Moving forward, you approach your construction. As you get closer, you notice that the structure now seems like a correctly scaled building—whereas before it seemed more like a toy-sized collection of building blocks. As you wander the structure, you can look out windows and walk through doorways, making small adjustments to the position of an object. Finally, you point your wand at the "get large" sign and grow back to your original size. After you and your partner add a few more walls and roofs, your new virtual home is completed and the simulation is over.

This virtual home-building application, labeled The Workroom and exhibited at the Computer Museum in Boston in April 1992, represents one of the more complex shared virtual environments yet constructed. Technologies like MIDI sound, voice communications, 3D sound, head-mounted displays, six-degrees-of-freedom wands, joysticks, and an Ethernet communication link were tied together with Sense8's virtual reality development tool, WorldToolKit, as part of a single simulation (see color insert # 10). The purpose of this Intel-funded project was to demonstrate the potential of virtual technologies in collaborative design.

DESIGN GOALS

At this time, the only other public demonstrations of shared virtual worlds have been limited to either shoot-'em-up games or simple walkthrough applications. The Workroom was intended to demonstrate the capability that virtual environments provide for relatively complex design tasks. The goal was to build an environment in which two people could work jointly to construct a virtual building using a small set of preconstructed design elements. We were interested to learn how people might interact and collaborate in the design process. We also wanted to see how various VR technologies might help or hinder this process.

We based the virtual world on a children's toy—building blocks—to simplify the users' learning the new design tool. Users were given fifteen minutes or less to sit down, plug in, and jointly attempt to build a structure. There was not time to learn a complex set of tools. Elements of the virtual world had to be obvious and work in a natural manner. We also wanted to create the effect of constructing a virtual structure with toy building blocks and then shrinking the person down to the size of the building blocks so that they could explore the structure they had created when they were "larger."

SYSTEM CONFIGURATION

Each participant had two Intel-based PCs and two graphics boards (one for each eye) generating the stereo images seen in their HMDs. An ultrasonic head-tracking device monitored the direction and orientation of their heads while an electromagnetic sensor tracked the position and orientation of their wand as they waved it about. If someone spoke, the signal was picked up by a small microphone mounted on the HMD, and fed into the other person's 3D sound processor. This signal was then convolved (spatially placed in the virtual world), along with other MIDI-generated sounds, and fed into stereo headphones built into the head-mounted display. A standard PC local area network (LAN) board was used to provide an Ethernet link between the two sets of PCs.

CONCLUSION

Most of the participants were able to achieve some level of building construction in the time allowed. Relatively few people actively collaborated, or even tried to talk to each other, while performing their tasks. This could be because of the pressure of having a limited amount of time to use the system, or because many participants were working with strangers; pairs of people who knew each other were more likely to communicate and interact. When a few people were given an unlimited amount of time to use the system, they were more likely to explore the possibilities of collaboration and experiment with different aspects of the simulation.

We also learned that the technology required to mimic the naturalness of human interaction grows more complex with the degree of naturalness that is sought. Virtual reality represents a potentially natural method of computer interaction, but this is obtained at the expense of using a complicated array of technologies. The promise of virtual environments remains an elusive goal as we fumble and play with our shiny new toy. What can we make it do next?

Note

Intel provided funding for this project, and the Computer Museum in Boston provided staffing and a public site for the demonstration. The networking code and much of The Workroom demonstration were created at the Institute for Simulation and Training in Orlando, Florida, based on Sense8's design specifications. Also thanks to Polhemus and Crystal River Engineering for the loan of equipment.

Ken Pimentel is the product manager for WorldToolKit at Sense8. Prior to joining Sense8, he worked at Intel's Advanced Human Interfaces Group. He can be reached at Sense8 Corporation, 4000 Bridgeway, Suite 101, Sausalito, CA 94965; telephone: (415) 331-6318; Internet: <kp@well.sf.ca.us>.

ONGOING

PART TWO

VR PROJECTS

DESIGNING VIRTUAL ENVIRONMENTS

Mark Bolas

This paper investigates the relationship between the design process and virtual environment systems. This relationship is explored in three sections: design with virtual environments, design for virtual environments, and design of virtual environments. Each category is discussed with examples drawn from my experience.

According to the American Heritage Dictionary, design means "to conceive, invent, contrive." It is useful to look at the relationship between the design process and virtual environment (VE) systems from three points of view:

- Design with virtual environments refers to the use of virtual reality to help solve a problem or invent something new.

- Design for virtual environments refers to the task of improving the hardware and software of VE systems themselves.

- Design of virtual environments is the creation of completely synthetic environments, or virtual worlds.

DESIGN WITH VIRTUAL ENVIRONMENTS

Virtual environment systems can be used to enhance the creative ability of designers, engineers, and scientists. Quick prototypes can be made out of thin air; complicated combinations of parts can be arranged and rearranged without tools; mathematical analysis can be visually presented while the design process is occurring. In all cases, virtual reality is being used to enhance the speed and quality of the human creative process.

This is perhaps the most powerful and exciting current use of virtual systems—VR transforms the computer into a tool that amplifies human intelligence. This power is already being harnessed for a number of down-to-earth problems, as shown in the examples below.

MOLECULAR MODELING

SRI International is using the Fakespace Data-Vision system with software from the University of California at San Francisco to visualize and work with molecular models and data. Users gain an intuitive feeling for their data by moving around and manipulating molecular models. Thus, virtual reality extends the three-dimensional design process into realms that are impossible for humans to perceive and are difficult to comprehend—such as the visualization and understanding of receptor sites in complicated protein structures.

SCIENTIFIC VISUALIZATION

It has been notoriously difficult to give computers the innate human ability to match and recognize patterns in complicated situations. By presenting data to scientists through VR systems, the scientist's pattern-recognition ability can be used in data sets that are impossible to visualize because they are completely synthetic or of a nonhuman size.

For example, astronomical data provided by the Harvard-Smithsonian Center for Astrophysics is being visualized on a Fakespace Boom2 head-coupled viewer and a Silicon Graphics VGX computer at the National Center for Super Computing Applications in Urbana, Illinois. The Boom2 is a new addition to an ongoing, ten-year-old data-analysis project. Of the work, researcher Margaret Geller has said: "Even though I'm used to looking at this data, the thing that really strikes me is how clearly you can see the structures [in virtual reality]. I think this is going to have an influence on the statistical tools that we use."[1]

COMPUTER-AIDED DESIGN

Product designers and architects are finding that enhancing computer-aided design (CAD) systems with aspects of virtual reality makes them easier to use and more accurate; they allow the user to visualize and manipulate models directly in three dimensions.

Alias Research has incorporated a Boom2 viewer with sophisticated software to create a general-purpose design and visualization system. The company believes it will be useful in many fields, including automobile design, architecture, and aerospace engineering. An exciting aspect of the system is the seamless interface it maintains between its existing mouse-based software and its VE modes. Users simply turn from their workstation and look into a Boom2 viewer when head-coupled interactive-viewpoint control is desired.

JUST ANOTHER MEDIUM

When using virtual reality to aid in the design process, it is important to compare its strengths and weaknesses with those of other visualization systems. For example, blueprints and scale models often represent design data in ways that convey important information that can be lost in VR systems. Likewise, the palette and ease-of-use of VR systems cannot always match those of a pen and pad in the hands of a skilled design artist.

VR systems should complement, not replace, these other media. It is important to note that virtual reality is just another medium. It does not provide a perfect representation of a design and never will. It should be used as one of many design-visualization tools—in this way, a spectrum of viewpoints and insights will be achieved.

DESIGN FOR VIRTUAL ENVIRONMENTS

There is a need for better-designed and more effective virtual environment systems. VE systems are new tools and need refinement before they achieve the ease of use and fluid feeling of more established design tools. Toward this end, the work at Fakespace has centered on building friendly and effective VR tools by creating better human-interaction metaphors for VR software, and by building higher-quality visual displays and interaction devices.

METAPHORS FOR MANIPULATION

Just as the desktop metaphor allows users to interact easily with a computer's file structure, useful interaction metaphors are needed for virtual environment systems. Because Fakespace provides a VE software toolkit, the invention and analysis of such metaphors are important parts of our software design process. One example of this process is presented here: the creation and evolution of the "flying arrow" metaphor.

A key element of a virtual environment is the ability to move in three dimensions, often by letting the user "fly" through the air, gaining a bird's-eye view. This freedom of movement presents the VE designer with a difficult task: how to allow the user to control such motion effectively. For example, users with head-mounted displays and flex-sensing gloves can:

- Point and fly toward an object with speed proportional to hand position;

- Grab at empty air, and pull along in the direction of the grab;

- Swing their arms by the sides of their bodies and translate through the VE as if walking forward;

- Hold their arms straight out and fly through the virtual environment like a bird.

I tried each of these ideas in conjunction with the VIEW lab at NASA Ames Research Center and Stanford University in 1988. Our goal was to develop better metaphors for movement through virtual environments. While each of the above ideas had good and bad points, a detailed look at the "point to fly" metaphor illustrates the issues that must be addressed when designing a VE metaphor.

To test the point-to-fly metaphor, users were placed inside a virtual test track and instructed to fly around the track as quickly as possible. By observing the users and using lap times as a measure of performance, we identified two problems.

First, when going around corners, users became confused because the point-to-fly gesture was counter-intuitive to the familiar experience of driving a car. Automobiles rotate the user's frame of reference as a turn is being made, while the point-to-fly metaphor does not. Users would point around a corner, but forget to turn their body in a corresponding manner.

The second problem was that some users would lean into turns as if on a motorcycle, while continuing to point straight ahead, thinking this would cause them to turn. The farther off course they became, the farther they would lean while continuing to point straight ahead. While this works on a motorcycle, no rotation takes place with the point-to-fly gesture.

These observations led us to develop the follow-the-leader metaphor. Basically, this is the same as the point-to-fly metaphor except that a virtual airplane is placed in front of the user. This airplane indicates where the user is flying; thus, as the plane moves around a corner, it visually leads the user to turn around the corner to follow the lead of the plane. The dynamics of the airplane also take the user's leaning into consideration. As the user leans left, the plane banks left and turns further than it would with no lean.

This metaphor proved to be successful, because users' performance increased and they required no instruction on how to fly through a space. The airplane served as a familiar reference. If a plane banks left, it goes left. Although metaphors need not duplicate familiar experiences exactly, the follow-the-leader metaphor works because it is based on an experience (flying an airplane) that is easily understood.

DISPLAY AND INTERACTION DEVICES

To gain wide acceptance, virtual reality hardware needs to be comfortable, easy to use, and accessible. Most VR displays ignore these requirements. The typical head-mounted display is heavy and based on low-resolution technology. Users complain that they cannot see the images clearly, and that they are encumbered by the weight and claustrophobia.

Alternative display designs are currently being pursued. The University of Illinois has created a multisided video projection room called the Cave. While inside the Cave, one user sees stereoscopic images coupled to his or her head position and movement. Other participants in the Cave see the same images, but do not have head-coupled perspective control. The Cave appears to be comfortable to use and well suited for collaborative design work.

The Boom2 is a head-coupled display that uses a counterbalancing mechanism to achieve a weightless and comfortable interface.[2] It is based on a pair of custom displays that achieve resolution that is higher than that of high-definition TV (1,280 x 1,024 pixels per eye). It uses optical encoding technology to provide head tracking that is noise free, with very little tracking delay.

Because the Boom2 is not head-mounted, it is easy to use, making it a tool that designers (and others) are eager to incorporate into their work. It is similar to a telephone handset in that the user can enter an environment without needing to suit-up, and can easily share it without adjusting settings. The Boom2 is also designed for public viewing areas since it takes little floor space, can accommodate a large volume of users, and is very robust.

The Cave, HMDs, and the Boom2 are all forms of virtual environment displays. It is important to realize that VR hardware will take many different forms as it becomes comfortable and effective for a variety of uses.

DESIGN OF VIRTUAL ENVIRONMENTS

The design of virtual environments is perhaps the most exciting and challenging VR design task. One reason it is so difficult is that the designer must abandon the physical environment of everyday perception and the characteristics of other media to embrace the nature of virtual environments.

To fully gain a feeling for the nature of a virtual environment system, it is useful to approach it as a new medium for artistic expression. From this viewpoint, many virtual environment demonstrations seem trite. For instance, a three-dimensional representation of an office, complete with filing cabinets, sidesteps the true nature of virtual reality by using only existing concepts and images.

While working with VR pioneer Scott Fisher at the NASA Ames VIEW laboratory and studying at the Stanford University Design Program, I experimented with the VIEW system in order to explore the nature of this medium called virtual reality. I created and experienced many different worlds for hours at a time. It was only through such extended immersion that I was able to come close to feeling this new medium.

To conduct a more abstract investigation of the medium, I undertook the task of interpreting various works of art in a virtual reality system. One environment that was created, *Flatlands* (see figures 12-1 and 12-2), is an interpretation of a work by Piet Mondrian called *Composition with Line*. Mondrian's piece consists of a series of black horizontal and vertical lines of differing lengths against a white background.

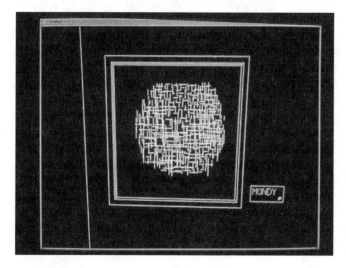

Figure 12-1.
Flatlands is based on Mondrian's *Composition with Line*.
• Credit: Mark Bolas.

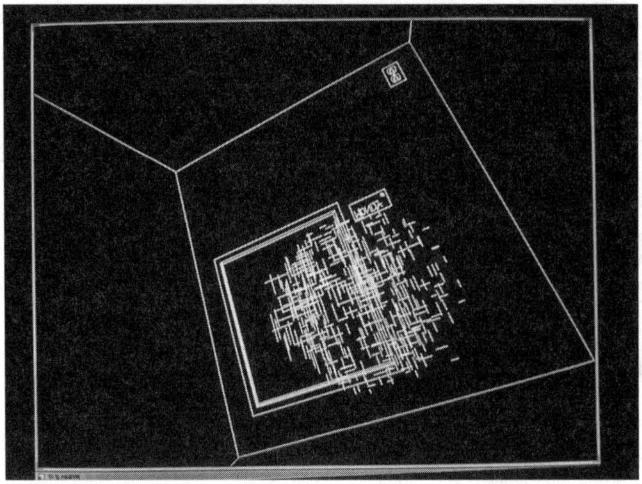

Figure 12-2.
Flatlands can be appreciated only in a three-dimensional environment.
• Credit: Mark Bolas.

While Mondrian's work was inherently two-dimensional, *Flatlands* creates an environment that can be appreciated only in a three-dimensional environment. *Flatlands* consists of the same set of elemental lines found in the Mondrian painting. When standing inside the virtual art gallery, the Mondrian appears to be hanging on a wall in a frame. As the user flies into the painting, the perspective shift causes the painting to disintegrate into a collection of abstract lines that form a huge three-dimensional sculpture. The painting becomes a forest of lines to fly through and experience—the lines continuously defining space and challenging the user to visually interpret the patterns formed by perspective shifts. The experience highlights two essential characteristics of the virtual environment medium: the ability to disregard physical laws and concentrate solely on form, and the recognition of and respect for the user's continuous ability and desire to choose new points of view.

Flatlands is one example of an attempt to design a virtual environment that fulfills the nature of virtual reality as a medium. Mondrian reminded us of this mandate when he said, "Painting occupies a plane surface. The plane surface is integral with the physical and psychological being of the painting. Hence the plane surface must be allowed to declare itself, must not be falsified by imitations of volume. Painting must be as flat as the surface it is painted on."[3] The painter should never try to imitate the three-dimensional world on a two-dimensional canvas. It seems ironic, then, that when the empowering tools of virtual environment systems are available, we limit ourselves to trying to emulate our lowly three-dimensional world.

VR AS AN ENTERTAINMENT MEDIUM

We must develop software that creates dense and rich virtual environments based on a small number of parameters. A world of this type was demonstrated by interactive artist Creon Levit at SIGGRAPH '91. Levit's work,

Tapeworld, placed each participant in a room filled with unique stringlike and tapelike formations that were based on randomly generated values. This world demonstrated the power of algorithmic generated environments.

While industry is rushing to develop VR game systems, the real task will be to fill these systems with interesting and entertaining environments. This task is challenging because the medium is more demanding than existing video games. While a conventional game requires the designer to create a two-dimensional video environment, the nature of virtual reality requires a rich, interactive environment.

Mark Bolas is president of Fakespace, Inc., 935 Hamilton Ave., Menlo Park, CA; telephone: (415) 688-1940; fax: (415) 688-1949.

Note

My work has been supported by the Stanford University Design Program, NASA Ames Research Center VIEW Lab, and the NASA Ames Research Center NAS program. MidasPlus visualization software courtesy of Tom Ferrin, University of California, San Francisco.

Parts of this essay were adapted from a presentation at ICAT '92: *The Second International Conference on Artificial Reality and Tele-Existence*, July 1-3, 1992, at Tokyo, Japan.

REFERENCES

1. Margaret Geller, *Supercomputing* Review, January 1992.

2. I. E. McDowall et al., "Implementation and Integration of a Counterbalanced CRT-based Stereoscopic Display for Interactive Viewpoint Control in Virtual Environment Applications," *Stereoscopic Displays and Applications: Proceedings of the SPIE*. Conference held February 12, 1990. Santa Clara, Calif.: SPIE, 1990, vol. 1256: 136-46.

3. Piet Mondrian, quoted in *Artists on Art*, Robert Goldwater and Marco Treveg, eds., New York: Pantheon, 1972.

THE REND386 PROJECT: HISTORY AND CURRENT STATUS

Dave Stampe and Bernie Roehl

In the summer and fall of 1991, virtual reality was becoming a hot topic. The discussions on the Usenet newsgroup sci.virtual-worlds centered on low-end systems, the so-called "home-brew VR" or "garage VR" approaches. It is in this context that work on the REND386 project began.

At the time, we were both based at the University of Waterloo, so it was easy for us to meet and work together on the project. From the outset, the basic goal of REND386 was clear: to create a simple VR programming environment for widely available 386- and 486-based IBM-compatible systems. No special hardware would be required; a minimal configuration would be a 386SX personal computer and any standard VGA graphics card.

We began with a PC interface system for the Nintendo PowerGlove, then worked on the 3D renderer that would become REND386. At the beginning, we planned only to develop a fast, polygon-based rendering system; however, it quickly became clear that support for a limited number of peripheral devices was needed, as well as support for animation, jointed figures, databases, and head trackers. The result would eventually become a complete VR system.

Since only two people were working on the project, it developed rapidly. We would get together and brainstorm about what we wanted to do; we would first select the algorithms, then Bernie would program them in C and Dave would optimize the result in C and assembly language for speed.

SPEED AND RENDERING

Speed, we decided, is what it's all about. For VR applications, especially those involving head-mounted displays and real-time interaction, a frame rate of at least ten frames per second is essential. Whenever we were faced with a tradeoff between functionality and speed, speed won out; the result is that REND386 is an extremely fast rendering system. The rendering was optimized for full-screen updates, as these are needed for walkthroughs and head-mounted displays.

56

The feasibility of the project hung on beating the VGA-access bottleneck inherent in the PC's design. This was tested by Dave's fast polygon blitter, a specialized piece of software that draws color polygons on the screen. Using the undocumented mode Y of the VGA card (available on all VGAs through direct-register programming), it can write four pixels to the screen in the time it would normally take to do one. The polygon blitter's speed of 22,000 polygons per second (50,000 for local-bus VGA cards) is a key element in the performance of REND386.

Next, we designed the core of the renderer: the "graphics pipeline" that would take the data describing the objects in the scene and transform it into a sequence of calls to the polygon blitter. A series of mathematical transformations determines where on the screen each point of a polygon should go, and clips the polygons to fit the screen. The renderer is optimized to ignore objects that are behind the viewer, or outside the field of view, tripling its speed. As a further optimization, each shared vertex (where the corners of several polygons meet) in a figure is transformed only once, again tripling rendering speed.

The renderer also supports multiple representations of an object—if an object will look smaller than a preset size on the screen, a less detailed representation is used. This can make the rendering process faster, and is a key component of most 3D video games. Switching between representations can also be used for simple animations.

The renderer uses a programming tool called the "painter's algorithm" to determine which objects are visible by drawing more distant objects first. However, visibility errors can occur; for instance, objects are sometimes visible through solid walls. To circumvent such problems, we used splitting planes, which divide the virtual world into small areas along parallel planes, making proper depth-sorting very fast. In addition, the subdivision of the world makes collision-detection between objects, and removal of invisible objects, simpler.

The renderer was written in floating-point C, then major portions were converted to fixed-point calculations and assembler. Although floating-point is faster than fixed-point on 486 PCs, using fixed-point math keeps hardware requirements needed to run REND386 low. An extensive matrix calculation library uses 32-bit integer math, and includes its own trigonometric routines, inverse matrix support, and square root functions, which are as fast as their floating-point counterparts.

A VR TOOLKIT

The current release of REND386 can support many popular VR devices, and allows programmers to add their own. Display devices that can be driven by REND386 include most monitors and HMDs. Support for stereoscopic 3D displays has also been formalized in REND386; by specifying a few key parameters, such as the viewer's distance from the screen, the proper left- and right-eye views are created automatically. Several display methods are supported, including HMDs, side-by-side images on the screen viewed with lenses or a mirror, and time-multiplexed devices such as the Sega LCD shutter glasses. With time-multiplexing, left- and right-eye views are displayed alternately on the monitor, with the glasses blanking the eye that should not see the image.

Many interface devices are supported by REND386, including the Nintendo PowerGlove, a 3D pointing device originally created for use with a home video-game system. In "Reach Out and Touch Your Data" (*BYTE*, July 1990), writer Howard Eglowstein had shown how to interface the glove to the computer's printer port, and work by several people in various countries (including Dave, who contributed some good deglitching code) made it usable in a high-resolution mode. The combination of the Sega glasses and the Nintendo glove allowed users not only to see objects in three dimensions, but to actually reach out and grab them. The mouse and joystick can be used for moving about in the world or selecting objects for manipulation.

REND386 was designed as an open VR toolkit, and programmers are encouraged to write their own applications using the extensive library of 3D object manipulation and interface support routines. An example of object-manipulation support is "segmented" figures, in which one object can be attached to another by a "joint"; the most common use would be for things like human figures, where, for example, moving an upper-arm segment would cause the lower-arm segment to move along with it. The position of any part of the figure can be specified in terms of joint angles, making animation and manipulation easier to implement. This also simplifies making complex machinery models with rotating wheels or parts. Segmented-figure support requires the use of matrix calculations, so an extensive matrix calculation library was added to REND386. This library uses 32-bit integer math, and includes its own trigonometric routines. It has proved invaluable for the support of HMDs and the PowerGlove manipulation system as well.

In the fall of 1993, Waite Group Press published *Virtual Reality Creations*, by Dave Stampe, Bernie Roehl, and John Eagan. This book documents how to create worlds with REND386, and includes a disk of animated worlds and instructions for device interfacing. Bundled with the book, Release 5.0 of REND386 added a better menu system, an animation language, and support for more devices, including stereoscopic viewers. Some of the worlds included on the disk used the animation language for fairground rides and portals from world to world.

NEW PROJECTS

REND386 was an experimental VR development system: it just grew from a fast 3D renderer to a full-fledged VR system, resulting in complex code that was hard for programmers to work with. By the fall of 1993, it was clear that a complete reworking of the software was needed. We decided to pursue independent development paths, and the result was two new packages, VR-386 and AVRIL.

In January 1994, Dave launched VR-386, a complete rewrite of REND386 designed to make future extensions easier and to improve programmer access. More of the modules—such as fixed-point math, the renderer, and PC device support—can be used on their own, and the addition of a simple API (application program interface) makes creation of applications simpler. The rewritten code will make future features, such as texture mapping, easier to add. The goal was to retain all the VR tools, such as HMD support and stereoscopic rendering, while maximizing the performance of the system.

In May 1994, Bernie released AVRIL, a rendering library designed for simplicity of use and portability (without the VR interface toolkit). By eliminating the use of assembly language in the code, interplatform portability is possible: AVRIL has been ported to the Macintosh and the Power PC (in native mode).

Whatever their future, REND386, VR-386 and AVRIL have met their goal. They have brought VR to the widest possible audience of enthusiasts, and at the lowest possible cost: free. In doing so, they have brought the hacker ethic to the new frontier and helped to launch many new careers and products.

Note

A demonstration version of REND386 is bundled with *Virtual Reality Creations* (Corte Madera, Calif.: Waite Group Press, 1993). Source code is available by FTP from <sunee.uwaterloo.ca> in the directory pub/rend386.

The programming toolkit and source code for VR-386 are available by FTP from <psych.utoronto.ca> in the directory pub/vr-386.

The libraries for AVRIL are available by FTP from <sunee. uwaterloo.ca> in the directory pub/avril.

Bernie Roehl is a systems programmer and computer system administrator at the University of Waterloo, who teaches Unix system administration and networking at Conestoga College. He can be reached at the Department of Electrical and Computer Engineering, University of Waterloo, Waterloo, Ontario, N2L 3G1, Canada; telephone: 1-519-885-1211 x 2607; Internet: <broehl@sunee.UWaterloo.ca>.

Dave Stampe is working on a graduate degree in cognitive psychology, researching eye-tracking interfaces. His background includes telerobotics, stereoscopic television, computer graphics, and virtual reality. Internet: <dstampe@psych.toronto.edu>.

VIRTUAL POLIS: A NETWORKED VIRTUAL REALITY APPLICATION

Carl Eugene Loeffler

So Hiro's not actually here at all. He's in a computer-generated universe that his computer is drawing onto his goggles and pumping into his earphones. In the lingo, this imaginary place is known as the Metaverse. Hiro spends a lot of time in the Metaverse.

Neal Stephenson, *Snow Crash*[1]

VIRTUAL CITIES

The Virtual Polis is a virtual reality application of a three-dimensional, computer-generated city, inhabited by a multitude of participants joined by means of telecommunications. Tele-existence is an essential aspect: imagine a virtual city complete with people, private homes, museums, parks, stores, and entertainment centers. The city is both real and false at the same time. In the words of Umberto Eco, it is "not a city like the others, which communicate in order to function, but rather a city that functions in order to communicate."[2] This city functions because of programming options; here the original and copy exist as natural extensions of each other, forming a perfect simulacrum.

But for what purpose? For one thing, there are now societies in which the market is reaching the limit on consumer goods that can be manufactured, bought, and used in the physical world. In his book, *Virtual Worlds*, author Benjamin Woolley explains the case of Japan, for example: "By the mid 1980s, its exports had so saturated world markets that Japan began to look for further room for expansion at home. The problem was that the domestic market was saturated, too; everyone owned at least one of everything—what they did not own, such as a second car or reasonably sized house, they could not own, because there was simply not enough space."[3] Video artist Nam June Paik says simply, "There is nothing more to buy." This makes it necessary, he continues, to "invent new software [to] stimulate [the] economy."[4] What this points toward is the virtual domain: virtual beings, manufacturing virtual things, for virtual people. However, there are other reasons for the virtual city as well.

As much as a social experiment, the virtual city is also a far-reaching graphical user interface (GUI) for cultural expression, electronic home shopping, and entertainment, with implications for society as a whole. What sounds like science fiction is no longer so. One could largely exist in the city, conducting day-to-day activities from work to play. As the poet and artist Nicole Stenger envisions it, "We would celebrate in cyberspace, rocking and humming in televirtuality, inhabitants of a country that is nowhere, above the busy networks of money laundering. Over the rainbow."[5]

Writer Howard Rheingold, however, questions such rosy assumptions: "Nobody knows whether this will turn out to be the best or the worst thing the human race has done to itself, because the outcome will depend in large part on how we react to it and what we choose to do with it."[6]

The Virtual Polis is a project of the STUDIO for Creative Inquiry at Carnegie Mellon University:

- it is a distributed, three-dimensional inhabitable environment;

- it can support a potentially unlimited number of participants;

- it has private spaces and personal and public property;

- participants use tools to alter the environment while inhabiting it; and

- it includes an interface for home shopping, entertainment, and work.

This inhabited city allows for investigation of tele-existence in a distributed virtual construct. The city provides a meeting site and offers many opportunities. However, it also poses questions about how to develop moral and legal codes for virtual worlds.

There are other virtual city projects being conceptualized, and in his book *Mirror Worlds*, writer David Gelernter provides a compelling description: "The software model of your city, once it's set up, will be available (like a public park) to however many people are interested, hundreds or thousands or millions at the same time. It will show each visitor exactly what he wants to see—it will sustain a million different views, a million different focuses on the same city simultaneously. Each visitor will zoom in and pan around the room through the model as he chooses, at whatever pace and level of detail he likes. On departing, he will leave a bevy of software alter-egos behind, to keep tabs on whatever interests him."[7] Gelernter presents a sketch of what a virtual city and world may be, and many hope he will be able to produce his design. A limitless number of virtual cities can exist in the data stream, including cities that are personalized by each user. This will formulate a society and culture based in software.

Habitat, a commercial online service that features two-dimensional applications and currently has ten thousand subscribers, is a precursor to Virtual Polis. Habitat was developed by Randy Farmer and Chip Morningstar, and later licensed to Fujitsu in Japan (see Farmer's essay in this volume). Under the direction of Kazuo Fukuda, Fujitsu later released its own version, though Habitat will soon expand back to where it originated, the United States.

As Morningstar and Farmer describe it, Habitat is "a far cry from many laboratory research efforts based on sophisticated interface hardware and tens of thousands of dollars per user of dedicated computing power." It is "built on top of an ordinary commercial online service and uses an inexpensive—some would say toy—home computer to support user interaction. In spite of these somewhat plebeian underpinnings, Habitat is ambitious in scope. The system we developed can support a population of thousands of users in a single shared cyberspace. Habitat presents its users with a real time animated view into an on-line simulated world in which users can communicate play games, go on adventures, fall in love, get married, get divorced, start businesses, found religions, wage wars, protest against them, and experiment with self government."[8]

Habitat was one of the first cyberspace environments available on a commercial basis, and is a rich resource for the Virtual Polis. However, three things place Virtual Polis in a class of its own as an emerging prototype: the distributed three-dimensional environment that comprises it; the articulated, three-dimensional representations of the participants; and its projected interface for art, education, home-based entertainment, and work.

VIRTUAL POLIS

The prototype of the Virtual Polis premiered at VR Vienna-'93, a virtual reality conference conducted in Austria in December 1993. For the premiere, participants located in Pittsburgh, Tokyo, and Vienna donned head-mounted displays and explored the city together.

The Virtual Polis is presented as a contemporary, Western city. Some of the buildings are new, bright, and shiny; others are so tattered they appear to have plaster falling off the walls. It is a city of contrasts. Participants can "hang out" in private spaces, go to the park, or shop for virtual objects to bring "home." Journeys to distant times and places—ancient Egypt, for example—are options at the travel store (see color insert # 15). Future versions will include entertainment centers at which participants can experience the latest media events. The city is populated, so participants may find themselves in a crowded elevator, and virtual friends may be invited over for a party. There are agents, presented as people or animals, who can lend elements of surprise. The possibilities for club-hopping are evident.

Future applications of the virtual city may be thematic in nature, adding new meaning to terms like "Latin Quarter" and other cultural distinctions.

The virtual city will not be all play and consumption, however. In an essay entitled "Corporate Virtual Workspace," Steve Pruitt and Tom Barrett describe a typical worker's day: "By donning his customized computer clothing and logging in to the fiber optic network via his home reality engine, he has attached his Personal Virtual Workspace (PVW) to his employer's CVW (i.e., Corporate Virtual Workspace). His PVW, analogous to the physical cubicle he inhabited back in the old days, provides a personal working environment rich in tools he has developed and collected over the years. These tools greatly extend his productivity, communication skills, and access to knowledge."[9] Workspaces can exist as both public and private virtual spaces. For example, the user may traverse the virtual city to reach the public site, in the form of office buildings, design studios, or production facilities. In the production facility, virtual copy machines make virtual copies of yet-to-be-named and described virtual goods. The personal workspaces are located in one's virtual apartment or home. In either case, the model of the personal virtual workspace put forward by Pruitt and Barrett is compelling, especially when you consider the city as an interface. It has become increasingly evident that the Virtual Polis or an equivalent will eventually serve as such an interface.

ACCESS

The city is a distributed virtual reality application, which means that the application employs a distribution network for end users. Currently, a client-server scheme is employed, in which end users tele-connect with a host computer that servers as a traffic manager and maintains a system of locks on objects and a database of changes that may have occurred while a user was disconnected. When the user reconnects, the server updates his or her data, maintaining continuity. Eventually, a network of multiple servers will emerge, and perhaps advanced distribution models will be installed.

Connecting to the server can be done with a standard modem, over direct-dial lines or the Internet. Multiple platforms will be supported; that is, a participant is not required to use the same computer at each log-on, though performance will be determined by the user's own machine. Presently the city is a research project, although it is intended for introduction to the general public.

PRIVATE SPACES

While a city is the meeting place of a population, it is as much about interior places as public places. The ultimate private space is home. The premiere version of Virtual Polis features high-rise apartment buildings that contain individual apartments with varied room configurations, interior lights, furniture, customized interior design, and windows that offer a view of the city (see figure 14-1). Here a number of activities can be conducted on an individual or group basis. One can, for instance:

- enter through a door (pass key required),

- invite fellow inhabitants inside,

- sit on and rearrange furnishings,

- look out windows, and

- store objects.

Figure 14-1. The Virtual apartment is a private space. • Credit: Nicole Jackson, STUDIO for Creative Inquiry, Carnegie Mellon University, 1993.

In future applications, it is conceivable that virtual home-entertainment centers will be able to access a variety of distributed games and infotainment services. The initial version of the Virtual City features a combination entertainment center and workstation; it is one interface with two purposes, and is located in the wall between two rooms. In the living room, one can access the entertainment center, while the work room contains a center for future applications dedicated to computer-supported cooperative work, or virtucommuting, as described below.

The private spaces in Virtual Polis are prototypes that suggest distributed graphical environments for entertainment, education, and the electronic cottage industry, that are interfaced with programming services or a head office, for example. Thus the private space could be used to listen to music or "radio," watch video or multimedia, play games, learn new things, or do office work.

In their book *Virtual Reality and Its Implications*, Barrie Sherman and Phil Judkins make a distinction between telecommuting, where one works at home via computer, telephone, and modem, and virtucommuting, which is a home-based virtual-reality teleconferencing system. "Virtucommuting will have several advantages." they write. "Up to a certain point, it will allow employees to pace their work while fitting it around their lifestyle. There will be fewer commuter journeys, expenses will be lower, time will be saved and in many cases job satisfaction will be increased. From an employer's point of view it will cut overhead costs (office blocks can be sold) and increase efficiency. It will reduce the distractions when office relationships go sour, defuse the interminable round of office politics, and diminish the thorny problem of sexual harassment."[10] Though the telecommuting office has not yet proved successful, many industries have benefited from telecommunications. It seems reasonable that entertainment and education will be the cutting edge for distributed virtual reality, followed by work-oriented applications. Although not all work can be conducted at home, telecommuting is acceptable for a variety of professions. And if it becomes an available option, it will have a huge impact on the businesses and services that depend on the daily migration of workers. It is hoped that new services will offset deficiencies.

Another aspect of the private space in Virtual Polis is that it can contain personal property, which can take different forms, from furniture to communication centers. As in the real world, such items are often expensive. Virtual apartments present the option of custom decor; the premiere version featured paintings on the walls and distinctive carpeting, among other items. Because the application stresses tele-existence, some kind of clothing, or way of presenting an appearance, is a real necessity. Probably, as in Habitat, the participants will stockpile elements of apparel. This implies private property, assuming that such items possess either a personal or financial value. The apartments, then, are also for storage and perhaps protection of property. This raises questions of ownership, security, morality, and law. The system designers of Habitat rendered theft largely impossible through system programming, but enforcing honesty in this way does not fully address the issue.

The city and its components, including the apartments, are not just abstract, mathematical constructs, but places that have the aura of a frontier. John Perry Barlow, co-founder of the Electronic Frontier Foundation, summed it up in the Winter 1991 issue of *Mondo 2000*: "Cyberspace...is presently inhabited almost exclusively by mountain men, desperadoes and vigilantes, kind of a rough bunch. And, as long as that's the case, it's gonna be the Law of the Wild in there....So we feel that the way to minimize anxiety, and to make certain that the freedoms we have in the so-called real world stay intact in the virtual world, is to make it inhabitable by ordinary settlers. You know, move the homesteader in."[11] Barlow was describing cyberspace in broad terms, including applications like the city. His "homesteader" is an apt description; in Habitat, wild behavior and gun play resulted in a virtual sheriff arriving on the scene to keep the anarchy more or less healthy. In addition to theft and horseplay, there are other possible problems to confront, largely involving viruses and their effects. "Viruses can be made to affect a virtual world," explain Sherman and Judkins. "They may not only act on the shapes and contours of users, but also the user's behavior in relation to the world, indeed the behavior of other objects in it. The first virtual 'deaths' will come when viruses destroy virtual images of people in precisely the same way as they destroy other digital representations, for example conventional computer data and text."[12] This is why private space is important. It is a safety zone; users can go in there and close the door behind them. A number of sociologists and cognitive scientists have expressed interest in the study of the city as a social phenomenon, and steps are being taken in this direction. One researcher, Ola Ødegård, has commented that "using distributed communication technology, people can interact without being in the same place....As people start to use different media they must develop conventions, etiquette and norms for behavior or apply a priori social knowledge on how to interact with each other....To apply insight into the social processes has to be a fundamental part of designing functioning networked applications."[13] Indeed, it will be an understatement to refer to the observations of the first pioneering inhabitants as essential research.

PARKS

The city features a park that contains walkways, grass, trees, equipment for climbing, a fountain, and a merry-go-round. The fountain and merry-go-round are animated, and they are presented realistically (see color insert # 13). In future versions, games like soccer can be played in the park. From a user-interface standpoint, the parks serve as passageways, or portals, to other sectors of the city, such as the apartment buildings and stores.

Users can visit the park, see others seated on the benches or playing games, relax, and listen to the wind in the leaves and birds in the trees. But why a virtual park when we have real parks to visit? For one thing, not everyone has easy access to parks; consider the disabled, for example. Also, some cultures have a different relationship to technology than we do in the West. The Japanese, for example, look upon technology as an extension of nature. It is common in Japan to find open areas located in a shopping complex several stories beneath the ground, where banks of video monitors present a nature scene or waterfall; this is a park. Thus Virtual Polis, too, has a park, available for different uses and interpretations.

STORES

The city serves as a graphical user interface for electronic home shopping. Customers enter a three-dimensional virtual catalog of merchandise offering varied goods and services:

- clothing and other apparel,

- furniture and home decoration,

- digital media, and

- leisure and travel.

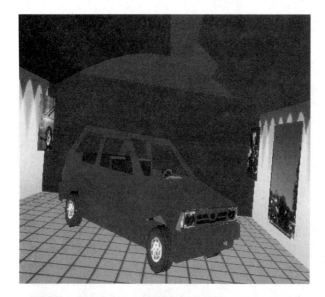

Figure 14-2. The full-scale virtual auto may be test-driven in future versions.
• Credit: Jeremy Epstein, STUDIO for Creative Inquiry, Carnegie Mellon University, 1993.

Figure 14-3. Virtual clothing helps to change the virtual appearance of users.
• Credit: Nicole Jackson, STUDIO for Creative Inquiry, Carnegie Mellon University, 1993.

Figure 14-4. The travel store will offer many virtual vacations.
• Credit: Nicole Jackson, STUDIO for Creative Inquiry, Carnegie Mellon University, 1993.

In the current version of the city, three stores are available: an automobile showroom, a clothing store, and a travel store. In the showroom, one can interact with a full-scale auto: open doors, play the radio, and change parts such as the grille and body color (see figure 14-2). The hood opens to reveal an engine. Ultimately, the car could be test-driven. Imagine entering the car, sitting behind the wheel, and touching the ignition. Suddenly you're driving on a mountain highway. The showroom and driving applications were initially developed for the Ford Motor Company, and linking them together as an option in the city would not be problematic.

In the clothing store, users can try on clothes and see their image reflected in mirrors (see figure 14-3). The ramifications here are broad. In one sense, the store can function as an outlet, offering the latest for electronic home shoppers. And, because tele-existence is an essential aspect of this project, one's tele-appearance is important. In previous examples of networked virtual reality produced by the STUDIO for Creative Inquiry, participants could choose their appearance from an on-screen menu that correlated to images of people and animals, for example. This concept is now extended to include virtual clothes and costumes available from the store. Perhaps the most intriguing option is the one that allows inhabitants to stockpile clothes in their apartments. As mentioned earlier, this raises issues of property, morality, and law.

The travel store is different from those in the real world in that it offers instantaneous experiences (see figure 14-4). In the current version, one can enter the travel store, and step into ancient Egypt through a portal. A number of other "vacations" are being planned. The travel industry hopes to benefit from virtual reality by allowing prospective vacationers to "visit" their holiday spots in advance. Also, as with the park, there is a segment of the population that may require or prefer the simulated vacation.

The city is a prototype for electronic home shopping, but how will billing and financial transactions be conducted? One model is for the city to relate to an external economy. In this case, inhabitants are billed for purchases or activities conducted in the city by an outside agency. The infamous 900 numbers that offer a dizzying variety of services from tele-sex to astrology to virtual reality reports are examples of this model. In a conceptual sense, it would be interesting to blur the distinctions between life in and out of the city. If you purchase a sweater at the virtual Gap shop, it can be used in the city, but it can also show up the next day at your doorstep; the notion of electronic home shopping will take on a new dimension. Another model is Habitat's internal economy. Participants are awarded a certain number of tokens when they join, and earn additional tokens for logging on and playing games. Perhaps the most interesting possibility is that Habitat users could earn tokens from business activities. The city has yet to achieve commercialization, so there is much to be resolved in this area.

ENTERTAINMENT CENTERS

Diverse entertainment centers are being planned for future versions of Virtual Polis. The idea is to provide a "place" for what can be considered "live" entertainment with a public audience. Such centers can assume various forms, including:

- arcades,

- clubs and discos, and

- concert and multimedia halls.

The arcades will present the latest in location-based entertainment, and will operate on a pay-per-play basis—although, as in the case of the stores, the actual economics are yet to be realized.

The idea of going to a concert hall in the city to experience the latest event performed by a favorite media star is compelling. A number of projects currently point toward this direction, such as "voomies," a kind of interactive theater proposed by Jaron Lanier. No doubt the present movement in the United States toward interactive television will ultimately embrace the virtual arcade and concert hall.

But what do people want? R. U. Sirius, editor of *Mondo 2000* , suggests "channels for consensual VR, cybererotica, personal soap operas, alternative news, and the conspiracy du jour."[14]

Who will actually come forward with solid examples of programming? Once the music industry decides it can use this marketing device, it could be a matter of roll over MTV, here comes MVR (Music Virtual Reality). But what is an example of MVR? Not simply a choice of camera angles or time sequences will do. And not all the issues are technical—many are concerned with semantics. If these are not addressed, meaning will be lost to all but a limited number of *illuminati*. But the music industry does have a track record of innovation and willingness to invest, so MVR has a good chance to surface, and with it, truly interactive media may well be born.

MUSEUMS

The first virtual world constructed at the STUDIO for Creative Inquiry was an art museum, which is incorporated in Virtual Polis (see my essay in this collection, "The Networked Virtual Art Museum and Other Projects"). The design of the museum centers on a main lobby, from which one can access adjoining wings or galleries. Several exhibitions for the museum are completed and were shown in the Machine Culture section of SIGGRAPH '93, while others are under construction. The first exhibition to be completed, *Fun House*, is based on the traditional fun house found in amusement parks. The museum contains the *Archaeopteryx*, conceived by Fred Truck and based on the Ornithopter designed by Leonardo da Vinci. Imagine flying a machine designed by one of the world's greatest inventors (see essay, page 10). The team also collaborated with Lynn Holden, a specialist in Egyptian culture, to complete Virtual Ancient Egypt, which is used in the travel store in Virtual Polis. An educational application based on classic temples mapped to scale, the piece was presented at the Guggenheim Museum in New York, and is scheduled to tour (see color insert # 15 and # 16).

Virtual theme parks could flourish as well. Recently, many parks employing virtual reality have been proposed—including Star Trek, zoos, and aquariums—but none have appeared. However, what theme park executives call virtual reality is quite unlike our definition of the term. For instance, the theme parks should abandon the notion that the public must travel to their site to participate, and begin to concentrate on distributed modalities. But at least they're on to something, as the success of VR arcades Battletech and W Industries show.

TELE-EXISTENCE

Tele-existence is the concept of "existing" within a tele-environment. Tele-existence raises many sociological and psychological questions. For instance, will it alter our perception? Morton Søby, a sociologist of virtual communities, writes that "the debate on virtual reality should quickly change its focus from hardware and software to the individual's perception and cognitive experience. In relation to our consciousness we can say that virtual reality simulates the reality processes direct into the brain. Through virtual reality the outer world begins to think inside us. Virtual reality generates real experience in an electronically mediated world for the self."[15]

Tele-existence, which gives users realistic sensations within a distributed graphical environment, is core of the virtual city. The initial features of tele-existence are based on the user's virtual self—his or her virtual body and its ability to perceive and act. Key features of the virtual body are that it:

- allows the user to see other inhabitants,

- allows the user to maintain a consistent individual point of view,

- allows independent motion, and

- provides the ability to move virtual objects.

Altogether, tele-existence is not that different from life itself, except that the experience resides in the virtual domain. In his 1964 book *Understanding Media: Extensions of Man*, Marshall McLuhan writes, "During the mechanical age we had extended our bodies in space. Today, after more than a century of electric technology, we have extended our central nervous system itself in a global embrace, abolishing both space and time as far as our planet is concerned."[16] Some wonder whether tele-existence is a metaphor, while Søby reminds us it is "real experience."

Tele-existence in the virtual city is social; other inhabitants "live" there, too, have their own apartments, enjoy the park, and carry on as in any city.

They communicate in various ways, and are attentive to their virtual bodies (see figure 14-5). Authors Steve Aukstakalnis and David Blatner have noted that "one of the first things people do in exploring a virtual reality is to orient to their own virtual body. And because this virtual body usually consists of only a hand, people become fascinated with this virtual hand....After people get used to their virtual body and are comfortably moving around the virtual space, they generally settle into a pattern of movement."[17]

Key functions of a virtual body now include:

- moving arms and hands—waving, for example;
- walking and other forms of mobility,
- changing facial expression; and
- changing costume and other aspects of self-representation.

The option to combine voice is posited in a number of ways. Keyboard- or text-generated exchanges could appear as text on the screen, resembling the balloons of text found in comics, or text could be translated to audible speech, using the kind of output devices employed in text communications for the visually impaired. The goal is the inclusion of real-time voice. Synthesizers can easily alter the voice, to produce convincing or amusing transformations.

The bodies of the inhabitants are formed by an assembly of separate objects—the head, torso, upper and lower arms, and legs are independent objects strung together. The head motion—movement from left to right, and up and down—is governed by a tracking device in the HMD, while the motion of the arms is a function of variable input devices, including data gloves, joysticks, multidimensional mice, and more. In this schema, the body is a vehicle; the motion of the legs is timed with the movement of the body, which is also determined by input devices.

Figure 14-5. The virtual body takes some getting used to.
• Credit: Nicole Jackson, STUDIO for Creative Inquiry, Carnegie Mellon University, 1993.

All the functions listed earlier, except for facial expression, are currently supported. Facial expressions are extremely important to communication, and in future versions of the Virtual Polis, facial modality and real-time voice communication will be options.

AGENTS

The city is also designed to be populated with computer-generated clients, or agents, that have artificial intelligence and sometimes closely resemble the participants in geometric and graphical respects.

The types of agents include adults of both genders and varied morphology, children, animals, and objects.

Distinctions between agents and participants can become blurred, especially when agents are programmed with social behaviors such as flocking, which directs them to mingle with participants. Flocking is a common behavior among many animals, including certain birds and fish, and is not so different from some human social behaviors. Walking around the city with a flock of agents can result in complex interactions such as sharing a park bench with an agent or inviting an agent to a party.

Animal agents are possible; a favorite in the present city is a striped yellow alley cat that has a loud, distinctive *meow*. The animal agent was first introduced in the Virtual Ancient Egypt application, mentioned earlier, and inhabitants enjoyed playing a game of hide-and-seek with the temple cat. The cat had an advantage, for it was programmed to run away when seen, which it did, over and over, in various locations in the temple; no one could catch it, but the thrill of trying was worth the chase (see color insert # 16).

Subsequent applications will feature yet another class of agents, that seemingly could pass the Turing test, described by author J. David Bolter: "Turing envisioned a game in which a human player is seated in a teletype console, by which he can communicate with a teletype in another room. Controlling this second console would be either another human or a digital computer. The player could ask any questions he wished through his console in order to determine whether he was in contact with a man or machine....Men can solve problems one way, machines another."[18] The concept in Virtual Polis would be to support natural language dialogue between an inhabitant and an agent. Thus, agents possibly could become subject experts, conversationalists, museum tour guides, or clerks in the stores, for example.

Aki Takeuchi, of Sony Computer Science in Toyko, is researching artificial intelligence. In a recent demonstration, Takeuchi not only employed facial gestures, but a natural language scheme that allowed an agent to answer questions and engage in dialogue, in this case about SONY's product line. Advances of this nature can enable the agents that co-inhabit Virtual Polis to share their expertise in a given subject, exchange conversation, and accumulate memories.

The basis for the "common ground" between users and agents, according to author Marcos Novack, isthat "cyberspace involves a reversal of the current mode of interaction with computerized information. At present such information is external to us. The idea of cyberspace subverts that relation; we are now within information. In order to [get there] we ourselves must be reduced to bits, represented in the system, and in the process become information anew."[19]

This sort of interaction further blurs the distinction between agent and participant. As writer Brenda Laurel says, "The notion of common ground not only provides a superior representation of the conversational process but also supports the idea that an interface is not simply the means whereby a person and a computer represent themselves to one another; rather it is a shared context for action in which both are agents."[20] In the Polis, the inhabitants and agents are, in the end, one and same. They are, after all, bits, enjoying the benefits of functionality in a shared informational space. Invite an agent home for a party.

SOUND

As noted earlier, the city is a three-dimensional, sound-intensive environment. Localized sound is implemented from a cinematic perspective, and sources include:

- ambient, environmental sounds,

- specific sounds assigned to objects, both moving and stationary, and

- music tracks.

Sound is an essential aspect of the city as a virtual reality application. A number of key attributes have been investigated, but the most important is sound localization. This establishes an audio map of the environment, which adds considerably to the immersion experience. The impression of three-dimensionality depends on stereo audio imaging and differences in interaural intensity; that is, localizing the sound in the left or right ear. Other areas of investigation may include reflected sounds, which make the auditory environment responsive to the inhabitants. Finally, because the city is a mediated experience, sound is essential to the suspension of disbelief. It is basic to our nature to associate sounds with objects and events, and the application of sound in the city reinforces this expectation.

CONCLUSION

It is easy to find a healthy dose of enthusiasm in this essay, and why not? Virtual Polis as a distributed graphical environment is a far-reaching virtual reality application. The premier of the city at the VR Vienna-'93 conference was met with a high level of success. The telecommunications program effectively linked users in three locations to the same virtual site; the graphic quality and the programmed functionality of the city were far more than the

STUDIO team had hoped for. But in order not to seem like screaming "yahoos," we must keep things in perspective. Artist David Rokeby provides a necessary caution: "There is a kind of colonialism implicit in western approaches to the unexplored territories of virtual realities. We seem to assume that virtual space is our for the taking and that we can colonize this space, imbuing it with our own notions....I believe that we will spend more and more time living in virtual spaces, in virtual relationships, even perhaps in virtual time. It would seem that, if general trends continue, we will be spending this time living within our models. We are already capable of ignoring perceptions that run counter to our conceptions. We will have to take care to avoid massive collective self-delusion with these self constructed models." [21]

So in the end, the issue is not the technology of virtual reality, but rather the people using it. The city is populated; it contains "real" people having "real" experiences—and the people there have a social responsibility. Many believe that technology—virtual reality included—must remain only an augmentation to our capacities as human beings; that our ethics must remain intact. While some consider this an optimistic view, it is preferable to the techno-destruction of humanity—though at the same time it demands our responsibility to render ourselves "intact."

Rokeby also refers to "the privileged ones who design, program, and have access to the technology that will define the models and rules, much as the Europeans coming to North America defined the rules and models of the `New World' society."[22] There is an element of truth to his statement, but again, there are other viewpoints. The designers and users of applications like the city have the opportunity to establish a different model. For example, the designers of Habitat quickly learned that they were not "in control"; in fact, the more users they involved, the less control they had. The designers altered their style of operation, increasingly allowing the participants to direct the evolving design. Likewise, Virtual Polis will not be centralized and dominated by plans. Rather, freely available toolkits will encourage the inhabitants to build upon it, expand and change its shape and purpose, much the way electronic bulletin boards function today. We must expect and demand the same from distributed virtual reality, and this is part of our responsibility, for such worlds exist only because we have willed them to exist.

Still, there is the problem of inequality. While the visualization capabilities achievable through virtual reality can address multiculturalism, this says nothing of the simple case of individuals and entire countries that struggle to exist day to day, where lack of access to a network is less a problem than obtaining pure water, for example. Without access to the network, the inequalities will no doubt continue to increase, though of course this problem extends far beyond virtual reality alone. As Barrie Sherman and Phil Judkins note, "This is because late twentieth-century technological advances have actually reinforced global inequalities. The industrialized countries are leaving the nonindustrialized further behind with each successive wave of developments."[23] Again, we are reminded of our responsibility.

What if the network were accessible to everyone? Would this result in a common global society in which cultural differences would no longer exist? Noted sociologist Anthony Smith negates the prospect of this "constructed" commonality, because there is no common heritage of socio-history that would allow such a construction to occur.

Advocates for cultural diversity through the growth of telecommunications, however, believe otherwise. Researcher Patricia Search has studied this question at length, and believes that "in the future, the potential for reaffirming and preserving cultural diversity will increase as global networks provide users with a wider range of interactive applications and expand the use of audio-visual data.....The user interface must reflect the psychological, historical, and social forces that form the foundation of cultural diversity....However, before we can evaluate design criteria for such interfaces, we must understand the differences between the psychodynamics of oral culture (where the seeds of cultural diversity were sewn) and of multimedia computing."[24]

Perhaps this is where the "art" of the interface design becomes essential, since the merging of cognitive and perceptual information is largely the domain of art. It is at this point that artists meet their responsibility toward advancing technology.

The traditions advanced by the city are well grounded in artistic expression, and include painting, sculpture, and conceptualism—namely, information and performance art. Remember, the entire application is comprised of bits of data, which are everywhere, and have no beginning, no middle, and no end. What does this have to do with art? Consider what the critic Clement Greenberg wrote in 1961 on the demise of the pictorial tradition: "The very notion of uniformity is antiaesthetic. Yet many 'all-over' pictures seem to succeed precisely by virtue of their uniformity, their sheer monotony. The dissolution of the pictorial into sheer texture, into apparently sheer sensation, into an accumulation of repetitions, seems to speak for and answer something profound in contemporary sensibility....The `all-over' may answer the feeling that all hierarchical distinctions have been, literally, exhausted and invalidated; that no area or order of experience is intrinsically superior, on any final scale of values, to any other area or order of experience."[25]

In the immersion experience of the virtual city, an inhabitant's view is governed by the twin rectangles of meshed pixels that comprise the visual display. The repetition of the bits underscoring the city, augmented by color, establishes the semantic basis for the visual perception of users. As their gaze moves, the twin rectangles perfectly reproduce, and "frame" before their eyes, the never-ending bits. This is their "window on the world." However, in this "picture," there is no vanishing point, no illusion of linear perspective, and no decorative frame, except for the techno-glitz of the head-mounted display. This is "all-overness" to the extreme, and at last, the easel painting, which Greenberg called "the movable picture hung on a wall," has been displaced. Fulfilling the best of all possible conceptual dreams, the city is a self-reflexive tautology of pure information, where everything is at once the subject and the object.

Carl Eugene Loeffler is a pioneer in telecommunications and art, and is project director of Telecommunications and Virtual Reality at Carnegie Mellon University and a visiting senior scientist at Norwegian Telecom Research and the University of Oslo; Internet: <cel@well.sf.ca.us>.

REFERENCES

1. New York: Bantam Books, 1976: 25.

2. Eco, *Travels in Hyper-reality*, London: Picdor, 1992: 41.

3. Woolley, *Virtual Worlds: A Journey in Hype and Hyperreality*, Cambridge: Blackwell, 1992: 206.

4. Paik, *Venice-4-1993*, Bill Clinton Stole My Idea (exhibition catalog), Venice, Italy: Venice Bienale, 1993: 131

5. Stenger, "Mind Is a Leaking Rainbow," in *Cyberspace: First Steps*, Michael Benedikt, ed., Cambridge: MIT Press, 1991: 54.

6. Rheingold, *Tools for Thought*, New York: Simon & Schuster, 1985.

7. Gelernter, *Mirror Worlds*, New York: Oxford University Press, 1992: 5.

8. Chip Morningstar and F. Randall Farmer, "The Lessons of Lucasfilm's Habitat" in *Cyberspace: First Steps*, edited by Michael Benedikt, Cambridge: MIT Press, 1991: 273.

9. Steve Pruitt and Tom Barrett, "Corporate Virtual Workspace" in *Cyberspace: First Steps*, Michael Benedikt, ed., (Cambridge: MIT Press, 1991): 384-5.

10. Barrie Sherman and Phil Judkins, *Virtual Reality and Its Implications*, London: Coronet Books, 1993: 199.

11. Quoted in David Gans and R. U. Sirius, "Civilizing the Electronic Frontier," *Mondo 2000*, No. 3, Winter 1991: 49.

12. Sherman and Judkins, op. cit.: 190.

13. Ola Ødegård, "Telecommunications and Social Interaction: Social Constructions in Virtual Space," *Telektronikk*, 89(4), 1993: 76, 81.

14. Quoted in Wes Thomas, "Postlinear Media," *Mondo 2000*, No. 10, 1993: 21.

15. Morten Søby, "Living and Working in Virtual Spaces," research paper, University of Oslo, 1993: 12.

16. Marshall McLuhan, *Understanding Media: The Extensions of Man*, London: Routledge, 1964: 5.

17. Steve Aukstakalnis and David Blatner, *Silicon Mirage: The Art and Science of Virtual Reality*, Berkeley, Calif.: Peachpit Press, 1992: 271.

18. J. David Bolter, *Turing's Man: Western Culture in the Computer Age*, Chapel Hill, N. C.: University of North Carolina Press, 1984:191-193.

19. Marcos Novack, "Liquid Architectures in Cyberspace," *Cyberspace: First Steps*, Michael Benedikt, ed., Cambridge Mass.: Cambridge University Press, 1991: 223.

20. Brenda Laurel, *Computers as Theatre*, Menlo Park, Calif.: Addison Wesley, 1991: 4.

21. David Rokeby, "Evolution and the Bioapparatus", *Virtual Seminar on the Bioapparatus*, proceedings of a seminar held October 28 and 29, 1991 at Banff, Alberta, Canada. Banff: Banff Centre for the Arts, 1991: 18.

22. Sherman and Judkins, op. cit.: 191.

23. Anthony Smith, cited in Patricia Search, "The Rhythm and Structure of Multicultural Communication," *Media Information Australia*, August 1993.

24. Patricia Search, "The Rhythm and Structure of Multicultural Communication," op. cit.: 62.

25. Clement Greenberg, "The Crisis of the Easel Picture," in his *Art and Culture: Critical Essays*, Boston: Beacon Press, 1961: 157.

To Live in Virtual Polis

Ola Ødegård

A networked virtual city environment changes the implications of being a user. For Virtual Polis (see figure 15-1), the terms *resident, citizen, or inhabitant* would be more suitable than user, as they imply a social and virtual space for potential interaction with other inhabitants. The developers of Virtual Polis have attempted to abstain from setting standards for social behavior and to enable the inhabitants to express their individuality. For example, Japanese users must be allowed to greet by pressing their palms together, just as the American and European users must be granted the freedom to express their special customs. There are also degrees of responsibility connected to the role of inhabitants; for instance, for the welfare of other inhabitants, or for the environment in general. The computer-generated agents can also be considered "inhabitants" of the polis, although of a different category. Their artificial intelligence includes elementary social attributes, but their behavior is limited.

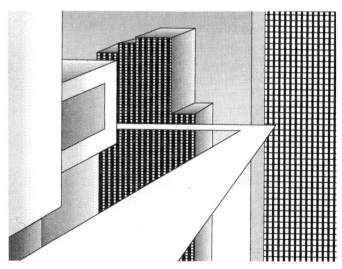

Figure 15-1.
Virtual Polis.
• Credit: Fortuna Group, Norwegian Telecom Research, 1994.

It remains to be seen whether the basic principles of human communication can be fulfilled in Virtual Polis. This chapter will discuss some important issues that developers take into consideration when creating social environments, as well as what life may be like in such a virtual environment.

PHYSICAL LAWS AND VIRTUAL REALITY

To develop appealing and user-friendly virtual reality applications requires particular analytic and interdisciplinary skills. The developers must interpret and recreate the factual world, beginning with its physical laws such as gravity, centrifugal force, ricochet, and so forth. They must then define the attributes of objects that are to move, including for example, the rules for how a car runs, how a UFO flies, or how a human being walks. At the same time, however, it is not necessarily desirable to transfer all the possibilities and limitations of the factual world into the virtual world. Virtual realities have unique possibilities that ought to be used precisely because of their liberating, intensifying effects. During the development of virtual reality applications it is important to create a balance between what is known from the factual world and the freedom that can be obtained in virtual reality. There are esthetic and pedagogical challenges in mastering this balance. An important pedagogical principle is the interdisciplinary orientation of the development group. Another central issue is the user perspective, meaning that users in networks are to enjoy a user friendly environment.

NORMATIVE LAWS IN VIRTUAL WORLDS

Prior to the programming and design of virtual worlds, many choices regarding cultural and social values must be considered. At this point it is especially important to review the ethical and normative choices the virtual reality application represents. The creators of virtual worlds are themselves part of a culture, a nation, a political and social system that constitutes the bases for their specific cultural and social interpretations. This may determine the virtual development process. Developers must be self-reflective and interdisciplinary if their work is to succeed. This is important in assigning programmed interactivity for users, but also in art, architecture and layout.

To be interdisciplinary means to use insight from fields like cognitive science, ethnology, sociology, and media studies, in addition to technical fields like computer programming and telecommunications. This may be crucial for the future distribution and use of this technology. Virtual worlds must choreograph all interactivity, yet must allow room for the personal fulfillment of users by allowing them to choose social roles, personal attributes, and names, for example.

VIRTUAL POLIS

There are two kinds of inhabitants in this virtual city: real users, and computer-generated agents with a low-level artificial intelligence. At first sight, the agents cannot be distinguished from the virtual humans; all bodies can move arms and legs. The agents have social behavior such as the ability to flock, imitating modern human beings in cities. (Today, an estimated 80 percent of the earth's population lives in urban areas.) To make things more complex, the agents also flock around the users! They are programmed to selectively follow the users wherever they move, which would become interesting if the agents were to try to follow the users into their apartments, for instance. It is a challenge for new users to tell the agents apart from other users.

In this virtual city the users can move around freely, just as in the real world. Actually, in many ways they have even more freedom, since Virtual Polis has no cars, no apparent crime, and no disease (though simulations can be implemented if desired).

If distributed applications will be accessible in networks, they will no doubt be attractive for hackers. Further, if hackers manage to place viruses in virtual worlds, we can only imagine what these viruses might look like and what characteristics they may have.

PHYSICAL AND SOCIAL EXPERIENCES IN VIRTUAL REALITY

In networked virtual environments the social space can be a physical experience. The immersive environment of the head-mounted display sometimes creates a physical sense of simulation sickness because of time delay in the video representation of the physical movements. More important, VR immersion can be perceived by users as so close to realistic that it can be classified as a physical experience. The user can, for instance, drive a virtual car and experience physical sensations; move the steering wheel and the car turns, accelerate and the car runs faster through the environment.

Media research and pedagogical research employ the notions of primary and secondary experiences. Primary experiences are personally experienced, factual life situations—anything from using tools, driving a car, or visiting a museum, to emotional or sexual experiences. Secondary experiences are also personal experiences, though they are experienced in the third person through media (usually television) in a passive way. Because the perception of "being there," "doing things," or "meeting with" in distributed virtual environments can be so realistic, the distinction between primary and secondary experiences is diminished. This phenomenon underlines the potential of virtual reality as a tool for socialization.

Socially, telecommunication is based on some fundamental principles of human communication. For instance, to have meaningful social interaction it is necessary for the participants to share a few social and cultural symbols and values; in networked interaction, too, the participants use shared symbols. Together, users create social space while using the media.

Through the telecom network the virtual world will be accessible for users independent of location. Virtual worlds will be meeting places where the users can see representations of each other.

In Virtual Polis the park, lobby, elevator, and stores are arenas for interaction, the content of which is determined by the users themselves. Interaction will take place between various users, and between users and agents. In subsequent versions the inhabitants will have rather advanced bodies with moving body parts; they can greet each other, dance, touch each other, and so on. This is a new arena for network interaction, and it can be liberating for future users. Normal behavior will be regulated by conditions such as social control and conventions for behavior, depending on the social context or situation in which the user is engaged. Comparative research has shown that different communication media provide different settings for social interaction, which in turn regulates and stimulates social interaction.

If one compares virtual reality with computer-mediated communication (CMC) and distributed multimedia applications, the difference in the possibilities for interaction becomes obvious: CMC shows rather limited capabilities for communicating social control and social information among users, as the social world materializes only through words and symbols conveyed through keyboard and monitor. Virtual worlds based on CMC offer possibilities of interaction that can be liberating and polyfaced exactly because the visual aspect is largely absent. Multimedia applications, on the other hand, allow users to communicate using video images, through which social information and social control have a stronger impact; this is the type of computer-based communication that comes closest to regular face-to-face communication. Distributed virtual reality applications offer possibilities for personal freedom similar to those of CMC, while its computer-generated visualization and representation give increased freedom when compared to multimedia applications. Social control is limited, which favors interaction. The differences among these three types of media are expressed from a comparative standpoint in figure 15-2.

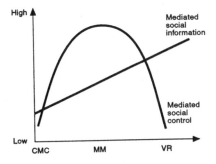

Figure 15-2. Interaction and social control in computer media.
• Credit: Fortuna Group, Norwegian Telecom Research, 1994.

VIRTUAL POLIS: A SOCIAL EXPERIMENT?

Virtual Polis is a social experiment with implications for the development of future distributed virtual reality applications. In theory there is no limit to the number of simultaneous users of such networked applications. The possibilities for individual expression will be improved in the next generations of Virtual Polis. Users will be able to furnish their apartments with objects bought in the virtual stores, and the application will memorize the changes and special characteristics. This brings up the question of security: Who will have access to the apartment—the owner only?

Further down the road, inhabitants themselves may be able to build in Virtual Polis by means of online programming and access to a library of existing objects and functions.

There should be cafés and other places where people can meet. The next challenge for distributed virtual reality applications is two-way audio communication, through which inhabitants in Virtual Polis can talk to one another when they are in the same virtual area or within some specified distance from each other. This will add yet another dimension to virtual worlds.

VIRTUAL POLIS NEEDS NO VIRTUAL POLICE?

Virtual Polis also adds new perspectives to the discussion of suspension of time, space, personality, and identity. The social aspects of the virtual reality technology will be on various levels. Leaving one's physical body, choosing another identity, meeting others in a computer generated world, and simply opening one's eyes to new perspectives by moving freely in a computer-generated universe are liberating elements of the technology. Virtual reality could enable us to edit animation, just as we edit videos and text files, and then play it interactively. As a distributed communication medium, this technology has the potential to revolutionize the human-to-human interface.

Ola Ødegård is a sociologist at Norwegian Telecom Research investigating virtual reality and telecommunication networks; Internet: <ola.odegard@tf.tele.no>.

REFERENCES

Ola Ødegård, "Telecommunications and Social Interaction: Social Construction of Virtual Space," *Telektronikk* (Kjeller, Norway), special edition on "Cyberspace" edited by W. H. Lie, April 1993, 89(4): 76-82.

———, "Hvordan skapes elektronisk kultur? Endrede vilkr med datakommunikasjon," paper presented at Pedagogosk Online Seminar (POS) No. TF F 22/92, Televerkets Forskningsinstitutt, 1992.

———, ed., *Virtuell virkelighet og det sosiale liv*, Technical Report TF R 32/93, Kjeller, Norway: Norwegian Telecom Research, 1993.

Morten Søby, "Virtuell virkelighet: en reiserapport fra cyberspace," Kulturens digitale felt. *Essays om informasjonsteknologiens betydning*, T. Rasmussen and M. Søby, eds., Oslo, Norway: Aventura, 1993.

VIRTUAL POLIS: MEDIA PROGRAMMING IS NO LONGER LINEAR

Richard Lynn

A true virtual reality interface for networks explodes our current ideas of programming for television. First of all, networks no longer mean just television networks; moreover, programming is no longer simply linear. Indeed, programming now becomes truly creative in every way.

New worlds can be created that can be explored both in the traditional linear way and in newer ways. A linear story can take place within the context of another world. The types of buildings and agents created, and the services available, are all programming. Worlds, as well as specific shows within those worlds, can now be created. The interweaving of linear and nonlinear will produce many marketing opportunities.

CHOICES

The means of distribution currently available for virtual reality are the various platforms now in use, such as CD-ROM, 3DO, and CDI, as well as game platforms like Sega. In addition, there are emerging networks, including the Internet—on which VR has already been networked among multiple users in various international sites, newly emerging telephone company networks, and satellite, to name a few. And there is no reason that broadcast networks cannot join in. The Public Broadcasting System (PBS), the educational network, would be a likely candidate because virtual reality and interactive multimedia are ideal platforms for learning.

Of the various programming elements possible, the most obvious are home shopping and travel. Virtual home shopping, which allows a person to "enter" a store and have a look around without leaving home, is interactive and protective at the same time. One does not have to brave the elements, and can interact with others or cut off the interaction by exiting VR.

If users merely want to try another experience or level of interest, they can go directly to that experience. If home shopping bores the interactive party, he or she may want to go see a concert. Again, it will be a simple gesture, as opposed to standing in line for tickets, waiting in line again to see the show, and the other tribulations that go along with actually attending such an event. Interacting with other crowd members is possible, but not required. You can see your fellow audience members or choose not to.

It is the choice of interaction with one's counterparts, coupled with limitless possibilities to experience and explore, that will make networked virtual reality desirable. It is also the immediacy of those choices.

Another programming possibility is the creation of the virtual world itself. Each building, each city block, each pasture, each vehicle allows the possibility to create something. Whether this will be done by network owners or by individuals accessing the networks remains to be seen. It is possible for individuals to enter the network and create, and allowing them to do so could enhance the experience for everyone. Users could simply decorate their own apartments, or accomplish much more complex tasks, such as creating a new city or even a new invention.

Travel in virtual worlds also offers new opportunities. This is true on two levels, the simplest being economics. While some may not be able to visit Africa or Russia, or even Florida, VR allows them the opportunity to see some of the sights that they might not be able to visit physically.

On a more complex level, with the help of experts, VR can bring worlds that are no longer available, such as ancient Egypt or Mexico, to the inquisitive eye of anyone who wishes to explore. An authority on ancient peoples of North America can create a prehistoric Native American village, which can be explored and lived in. Here travel merges with education.

Education is another facet, perhaps the most important aspect of networked virtual reality. Virtual reality, via networking, is an obvious way to allow interactivity and exploration, which are the most enticing ways for individuals to learn. Virtual environments allow students to ask questions of an authority in their field; Einstein can teach physics, and Descartes, math. Students can question them and they can give examples to illustrate their answers.

Virtual reality offers many ways to provide entertainment programming. It can deliver two-dimensional entertainment, such as video, audio, or films, that can be experienced in a virtual environment with others. Movies and television-type shows can also be created completely within virtual reality, and can be either linear or interactive.

A VR movie might be three-dimensional, making users feel part of the experience. For example, viewers can follow the detective in a murder movie. Or the experience can be truly interactive, allowing users to explore the virtual environment created and join the plot going on within the environment, or even take part in the plot.

BANDWITH AND COPYRIGHT

All of this is exciting, but the possibilities lie in the hands of the folks with the bandwidth. Will they create one VR environment? Or will they portion it into several? Will they allow only one group to provide home shopping and a separate one to provide travel, and so on? Or will the VR interface be used as an environment within which various types of programming interact and intersect?

Questions are also raised about copyrights and ethics. What will be the criteria for who is allowed to create or program? Who gets access to the media? If everyone is allowed to enter and create, will users need to pay for access to the parts others have created? In this new world, any experience that now exists in the real world can be recreated and sold, as can experiences that are not currently available.

What should be allowed in the new world will be difficult to determine. If existing programming entities are given this new domain, there will probably be traditional forms of censorship. If, on the other hand, it may be used by anyone with access to the network, other forms of censorship are likely to be determined. If not, legal complications will ensue rapidly.

While networked virtual reality may be just a new avenue for traditional media programmers, it may also be the first step in a new world in which everyone is a programmer.

Richard Lynn is a producer of video and television programs, and director of New Media for QED Enterprises. Internet: <rlynn2@aol.com>.

SOCIAL DIMENSIONS OF HABITAT'S CITIZENRY

F. Randall Farmer

I was the oracle, or system administrator, for the cyberspace known as Habitat, by Lucasfilm, during its shakedown period from June 1986 to May 1988. Here are a few observations about the unique social dimensions of online communities. Most of these ideas were composed while I reigned over a small Habitat town named Populopolis, which had a population of 500 online citizens. The oracles of the currently operating Habitats—Club Caribe in the United States and Fujitsu Habitat in Japan—have contributed much to later refinement of these thoughts.[1]

WHAT IS HABITAT?

Habitat is a multiparticipant online virtual environment, or cyberspace (see figures 17-1 to 17-4 and color insert # 2). Each participant, or player, uses a home computer and is interactive, communicating by modem and telephone over a commercial data network to a centralized, mainframe host system. The client software provides the user interface, generating a real-time animated display of what is going on and translating input from the player into mes-

Figure 17-1. In Fujitsu Habitat, objects are created by vendo-machines (shown here) and recycled by pawn machines.
• Credit: Fujitsu.

Figure 17-2. The Red-Shirt Troupe, an all-volunteer entertainment company in Fujitsu Habitat.
• Credit: Fujitsu.

Figure 17-3. In Habitat, the primary means of locomotion is walking and teleporting. A Fujitsu Habitat port is shown here.
• Credit: Fujitsu.

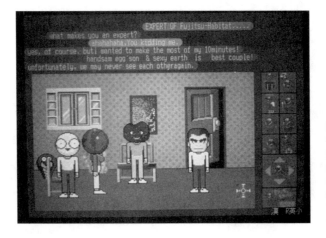

Figure 17-4. An international gathering. In Fujitsu Habitat every avatar is born with a turf, or private home for storage of personal belongings.
• Credit: Fujitsu.

sages to the host. The host maintains the system's world model, enforcing the rules and keeping each player's client informed about the constantly changing state of the universe. The various players connect to the host simultaneously and appear to be inhabiting the same imaginary world. Thus the host enables the players to interact not only with the world but with one another.

The world is built entirely with objects.[2] There are more than two-hundred object classes; the most notable are avatars, ghosts, and regions. Players may be represented either by an animated graphic figure called an avatar or by a static ghost icon. Avatars can move around, manipulate objects, talk to one another, send messages to one another by means of ESP (extrasensory perception) and mail, and make graphic gestures. Ghosts are observer-only objects, and do not interact with the environment except to transform into avatars. Regions hold the players and other objects for one screen of the world.

THE SOCIAL COMMITMENT DIMENSION

The entire point of any thriving community is *people*. Habitat is an interactive environment in which people define the parameters of their experience. Thus it is important to understand how people behave in cyberspaces. In Habitat I observed five distinct patterns of usage and social commitment:

- The passives

- The actives

- The motivators

- The caretakers

- The geek gods.

THE PASSIVES

The passive group must be led by the hand to participate. They want effortless entertainment, as though they were flipping around cable television with a remote control. They flit from place to place, staying in any single spot for only a moment.

Easily 75 percent of the players fall into this category, but they account for only perhaps 20 percent of the connect time. They tend to "cross over" into Habitat only to read their mail, collect their daily tokens, and read the weekly newspaper (and if given the chance to do any of these activities offline, they'll take it). They show up for special events intermittently and only when the mood strikes. Even when they *do* spend more than two minutes in at a time, they tend to hang around as ghosts and eavesdrop on others' conversations, rather than participating in the activities themselves. Many special events and activities have to target these "on for just a few minutes" people, and encourage their active participation.

THE ACTIVES

The active group is the next largest, and makes up the bulk of the paying customer hours. The active players typically participate in two to five hours of activities a week each. They tend to put Habitat first in their online agenda. Immediately upon entering they contact the other players online to find out the hot activity of the day. They *always* have a copy of the latest paper, and gripe if it comes out late.

The actives' biggest problem is overspending. They really like Habitat, and lose track of the time they spend in it. This sometimes leads to actives canceling their accounts when a huge bill arrives in the mail, a loss for all involved. The watchword for these people should be thrift.

During Fujitsu Habitat's first year of operations the system was available only from 1 p.m. to 11 p.m. local time. The actives in Japan developed the habit of logging in every evening at 9:00, give or take a minute. This way they maximized their social activity, since they knew everyone else was doing the same thing, but minimized their connection costs, since the system shut down at 11:00. Fujitsu Habitat usually reached peak load by 9:15. More than half these players would still be online at closing, when the host was yanked out from under them. Even now, after two years of 24-hour host operations, this peak persists.

THE MOTIVATORS

The real heroes of Habitat are the motivators. They understand that Habitat is what the players make of it. They throw parties, start institutions, open businesses, run for office, start moral debates, become outlaws, and win contests. Motivators are worth their weight in gold. One motivator for every fifty passives and actives is a wonderful ratio. Online community builders should nurture these people.

In Club Caribe, there is an official title bestowed on several of those whom the operators have recognized as motivators: The guardian angels. Each receives a male or female angel head, the honor of having the initials GA attached to his or her user name, plus access to a private clubhouse that only GAs can enter. In return, they dedicate themselves to furthering the enjoyment of all participants. When motivators are ready to make their online community "a paying job," they can become caretakers.

THE CARETAKERS

Caretakers may already be employees of the host organization, but the best caretakers are experienced motivators. They help the new players, mediate interpersonal conflicts, record bugs, suggest improvements, run their own contests, officiate at functions, and keep things running smoothly. There are far fewer caretakers than motivators.

Again, Club Caribe has an official title for these people: Club Caribe

Guides, or CCGs. In Club Caribe they wear distinctive heads and often receive free online time for their participation. They are on strict online schedules and can be fired. Caretakers wield significant political power in cyberspaces because the other players quickly figure out who actually "runs" the system. They often develop followers and fans, or enemies and detractors. In this way, caretakers often introduce real-world politics and egos into cyberspace, which can dramatically affect the community.

THE GEEK GODS

The original Habitat operator was known as the oracle. Having the operator's job *is* like being a god of ancient Greek mythology. The oracle grants wishes and introduces new objects and rules into the world. With one stroke of the keyboard, the operator can change the physics of the universe, create or eliminate bank accounts, entire city blocks, even the family business. This power carries a heavy burden of responsibility, since any externally imposed change to the cyberspace world can have subtle (and not-so-subtle) side effects. Think about this: would you be mad at God if one day suddenly electricity didn't work anymore? Something like this happened in Habitat. We had magic wand objects, and an oracle-in-training made dozens of them available, for a stiff price: five days' income. This was a problem because the *wands never failed*, and never ran out of charges. I had always intended to set the magic charges, so one night during host maintenance, I quietly gave each wand a random number of remaining charges. The next day, when the wands started to discharge fully, the players became furious! Some of them threatened to leave Habitat forever. Simple bug "fixes" are sometimes interpreted as the removal of a much loved "feature." Often, you cannot tell in advance what will happen. Players should be an integral part of cyberspace rule and object changes.[3]

Geek gods need to be knowledgeable about fantasy role-playing, telecommunications networks, political science, and economics, among other things. They must understand the need for consistency in a fictional world and the methods used to achieve it. They need to understand something about the real world, since that is where the players come from. They need to know the players themselves, since they are the ones who will make or break the system. Most important, they must know when *not* to wield their power.

VARIATIONS ON THE THEME

The developers of Fujitsu Habitat decided to have their geek gods operate behind the scenes rather than interact directly with the players. *All* online support personnel operate at the Caretaker level of commitment and power. This separation of powers is more politically stable and allows the programmers the luxury of remaining a comfortable distance from the daily social problems.

THE PATH OF ASCENSION

The path of ascension for users in Habitat is passive to active to motivator to caretaker to geek god

Encourage everyone to move one role to the right, and the result will be a living, self-sustaining, thriving community where new members always feel encouraged to become vital citizens.

THE DIMENSION OF BEING AND NOTHINGNESS

To consider fully the social dimensions of a cyberspace citizen, we need to consider how virtual being compares with a person's existence in the real world.

Table 17-1 shows two dimensions: level of participation and connectivity. The four quadrants are labeled with the commonly known names of these states on various online systems.

Quadrant I on most systems represents the avatar, user account, or handle. This is the most familiar state of being for a person in a cyberspace. You are logged in, doing things in the universe, even if only sending mail or copying files. You are interacting with the system, and others in the system can interact with you.

Quadrant IV is the next most familiar state: logged out. Most cyberspaces understand this state as inactive, dead, in the Void, or sleeping. Simply put, nothing happens to or for you while you are not present.

These two quadrants map nicely onto the human experience as awake (conscious) and asleep (unconscious). Most cyberspace implementors handle

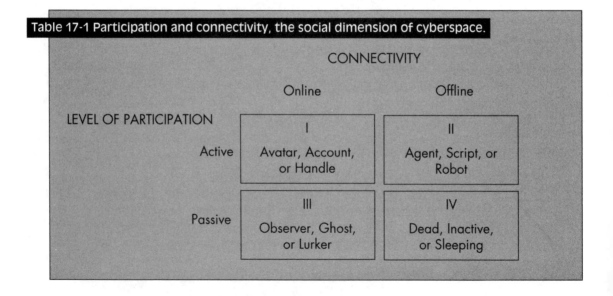

Table 17-1 Participation and connectivity, the social dimension of cyberspace.

	CONNECTIVITY	
	Online	Offline
LEVEL OF PARTICIPATION		
Active	I Avatar, Account, or Handle	II Agent, Script, or Robot
Passive	III Observer, Ghost, or Lurker	IV Dead, Inactive, or Sleeping

these cases adequately; however, cyberspace systems designers often over-look the other two quadrants.

Quadrant II describes robots and agents. These are entities that act on your behalf when you are away. The MUDs (multi-user dimensions) and MOOs (MUD-object-oriented) are text-only cyperspaces that are leading the experimentation in this area of cyberspace consciousness.[4] Of course, this raises some questions about responsibility for actions. What happens when a robot, acting in your name, does some cyberspace property damage? Or steals? Or worse yet, "harms" someone?

Quadrant III describes by far the most overlooked state of a cyberspace inhabitant's make-up, the ghost, or lurker state of existence. In this state you are an observer only, hiding just out of sight, and would prefer that others not bother you or even know that you are watching. In Habitat you could enter the ghost state instantaneously: your body would disappear from the screen, to be replaced by a single small icon in the corner of the screen repre-senting you and any other people who were also watching as ghosts. These people can usually be found hanging around in any large, public-access cyber-space.

ONLINE PERSONAE AND REAL-WORLD PERSONALITY

Cyberspaces, because they are anonymous, allow people to present them-selves in any manner they desire. Shy people can experiment with being bold, men can present themselves as women, and so on. How often are these alter-nate personalities accepted or rejected? How often are people just being themselves in these online worlds? Why do people masquerade? These ques-tions require further study, but I have collected some interesting data.

In December 1990, I met face-to-face with a group of fifty Fujitsu Habitat citizens about their avatars. During one part of the discussion I asked, Do you think of your avatar as a separate being, or is it a representa-tion of you? Half said they thought of their avatar as a separate being. The others said it was their "self."

I then asked, Do you act like your usual self when you are in Habitat, or in ways different from real life? Again the results were fifty-fifty.

This was no surprise to me, as I thought I had simply rephrased and inverted the first question. Then I realized that several who had selected "self" for the first question had not selected it for the second question! The actual distribution is presented in Table 17-2.

A minority (26 percent) prefer to project themselves fully into the online universe. Clearly, cyberspace citizens feel empowered by the technology to experiment with social interactions. They feel safe enough to try on a differ-ent skin. Given that the current players are mostly affluent, male, and com-puter-savvy, will these statistics remain meaningful when people with other interests arrive?

OTHER SOCIAL DIMENSIONS

Other social dimensions of cyberspace citizenry that should be considered include sense of place,[5] point of view,[6] government, economics, politics, religion, crime, punishment, inclusion, ostracism, and spontaneous social organization.[7] These are the issues that Habitat's citizenry cares about.

It seems that people are people, even in cyberspace. But these online communities, with the individualism and anonymity they provide, produce a unique culture, combining fictional constructs and personalities with real people and their real-world expectations.

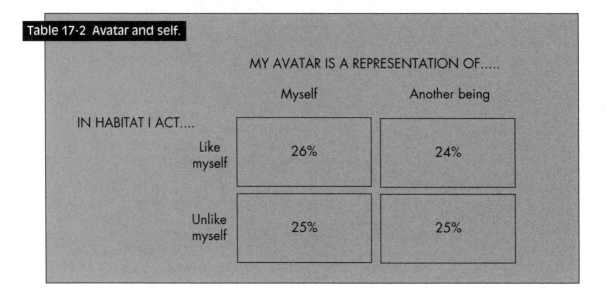

Table 17-2 Avatar and self.

	MY AVATAR IS A REPRESENTATION OF.....	
IN HABITAT I ACT....	Myself	Another being
Like myself	26%	24%
Unlike myself	25%	25%

F. Randall Farmer is a partner in Electric Communities, a cyberspace consulting group. Internet: <electric@netcom. com>.

REFERENCES

1. I am indebted to oracles Layza, Tsuo, and Z'd from Fujitsu Habitat, along with GGCs JZer0, Becky, GaryM, and GA Thistle from Club Caribe for their participation in these communities.

2. A detailed review of Habitat design goals, successes, and failures appears in Chip Morningstar and F. Randall Farmer, "The Lessons of Lucasfilm's Habitat," in *Cyberspace: First Steps*, Michael Benedikt, ed., Cambridge, Mass.: MIT Press, 1991.

3. For more about operational subtleties, see "The Lessons of Lucasfilm's Habitat."

4. Dozens of MUDs and MOOs are available worldwide via the Internet. I suggest LambdaMOO, run as a research project in secure programming languages by Pavel Curtis at Xerox PARC. Telnet to <lambda.parc.zerox.com>, port 8888.

5. Joshua Meyrowitz, *No Sense of Place: The Impact of Electronic Media on Social Behavior*, Oxford, Eng.: Oxford University Press, 1986. Recommended reading.

6. Detailed in F. Randall Farmer and Chip Morningstar, "Cyberspace Colonies," presented at the Second International Conference on Cyberspace.

7. Stories about these are in "The Lessons of Lucasfilm's Habitat."

THE NATURE OF CHARACTERS IN INTERACTIVE WORLDS AND THE OZ PROJECT

Joseph Bates

Traditional storytelling media—the novel, cinema, and television—draw much of their emotional power from characters and story. Interactive media will have their greatest impact only when they too exhibit these characteristics. However, rich interactive characters and stories are unfamiliar concepts. The Oz Project at Carnegie Mellon University is trying to bring together writers, artists, and artificial intelligence researchers to produce fundamental technology that can support this new form of art and entertainment. Our work emphasizes the construction of interactive characters for simulated worlds.[1]

THE DEMANDS OF INTERACTIVITY

Virtual reality is the most recent type of interactive world. Earlier examples include the video games that were invented in the 1960s and the text adventures that were the most popular home software in the early 1980s. However, virtual reality has touched the hearts of many people in ways that earlier simulations did not.

A result of this great popularity is widespread speculation on the future of virtual worlds. A frequent notion is that we will soon develop "interactive cinema," which will allow people to enter into immersive environments that have as much emotional impact as, say, *Citizen Kane* or *Terminator 2*. After all, we can already build simulated physical spaces and objects, so we must be about half way toward including simulated characters and an exciting story.

This speculative notion, while attractive, is flawed. Consider the simulated characters. Writing about and filming characters is not fundamentally more difficult than writing about and filming scenery. So for noninteractive media, you are indeed halfway there when you can manage scenery. By contrast, developing richly interactive characters means constructing intelligent, emotional, behaving creatures. These creatures must seem to live in the simulated world and must respond believably to the variety of human behavior in users. This kind of creature is a primary goal of basic research in artificial intelligence; it is not merely a next obvious step for designers of virtual reality systems.[2]

Similarly, the interactive story is not an obvious extension of the traditional linear story. In order to feel the reality of a simulated world, users must be free to behave in any way that might fit within the theme of that world. For instance, a flight simulator need not support stopping for lunch at a McDonald's, but it must permit the freedom to use the airplane controls in any reasonable way. However, a story by nature imposes structure on the user, because whatever the user chooses to do must inevitably lead to the climax of some storylike experience. Thus, an interactive story system must provide a computational solution to the apparent clash between free will and destiny. This is unlike the requirements of story in traditional media, and is more than a minor extension to existing virtual reality technology.

If one views a VR system as producing surface-level phenomena via the hardware interface and associated software, then the organization and content of software behind the interface constitute a "deep structure" for the virtual world. This is the arrangement of code and data that produces the central meanings of the interactive experience. For the reasons suggested, those involved in the Oz Project believe that for VR to join the novel, cinema, and television as a broadly successful artistic medium, the technology must provide a sufficiently rich deep structure. In particular, it must provide computational theories for interactive characters and stories.

The Oz Project at Carnegie Mellon is our attempt to work toward these goals. The project includes artists, writers, and artificial-intelligence and computing researchers. We believe that such collaboration is necessary to capture the artistic knowledge, sensibilities, and capabilities needed to provide a deep structure for dramatic worlds.

Current Oz research falls into three areas:

- the construction of broadly capable, though perhaps shallow, autonomous agents that integrate elements of perception, cognition, emotion, action, and language;

- the construction of a computational theory of interactive drama, to gently shape the user's overall experience; and

- the development of computational methods for varying the presentation style of the experience, thus providing the interactive analog of film technique and writing style.

Our work is described in detail in a number of reports.[3] The rest of this essay summarizes our research on the construction of agents.

INTERACTIVE CHARACTERS

One of the keys to an effective virtual world is that the user be able to suspend disbelief, or imagine that the world portrayed is real, without being jarred out of that belief by the world's behavior. In existing works of interactive fiction and other simulated worlds, the unnatural behavior of simulated agents is perhaps the primary impediment to fully suspending disbelief.

Traditional research on agents in artificial intelligence demands that constructed creatures be highly competent. Our central requirement, that users be able to suspend disbelief, requires not that agents be especially active and smart, but only that they not be clearly stupid or unreal. An agent that keeps quiet may appear wise, whereas one that oversteps its abilities will probably destroy the suspension of disbelief. Thus, in Oz we try to take advantage of what we call the "Eliza effect," which allows people to see subtlety, understanding, and emotion in an agent as long as the agent does not actively destroy the illusion.[4]

In order to foster this illusion of reality, we believe our agents must have broad capabilities. To this end, we have developed a model for mind, called Tok, that exhibits some signs of internal goals, reactivity, emotion, natural language ability, and knowledge of agents (self and other) as well as of the simulated world.

Rather than describing Tok in detail, we will convey the flavor of our work by presenting a particular agent built in Tok. That agent is a simulated house cat named Lyotard. Our goal in developing Lyotard was to build a creature that could believably pass for a cat in an Oz micro-world.

Table 18-1 lists the emotions and behaviors from our original informal design document for Lyotard. The emotions are those naturally available in the current version of Tok, though in the end we did not use all of them. The behaviors were developed over several hours of brainstorming by several cat owners in our group. The behavioral features are used to modify the details of Lyotard's behaviors, according to Lyotard's mood.

THE BEHAVIOR OF LYOTARD

Whether an agent's behavior produces a suspension of disbelief can be determined only empirically. The agent must be embedded in a world, and a variety of users must report their subjective experiences with the agent.

Table 18-2 shows a small excerpt of a session with Lyotard that provides a sense of Lyotard's behavior and of his internal mental causes for the behavior. In this session a human user interacted with Lyotard in a simulated six-room house. Because we are interested in the actions of the agents, the table presents the actions of both the agent and the user from an omniscient perspective. The normal output from the Oz system to the human user, such as English descriptions of what the human perceives, prompts for the human's action, and so forth, have been omitted.

Table 18-1. Original Lyotard design

EMOTIONS	BEHAVIORS		FEATURES
hope	wanting to be petted or *brushed*	purring	curiosity
fear	cleaning self	arching back	contentment
happiness	wanting to go out/in	hissing	aggression
sadness	eating	swatting	ability to ignore
pride	wanting to eat	biting	friendliness
shame	getting object (using human or tool)	escaping/running away	*pride*
reproach	searching for something	*pouncing on creatures*	energy
gratitude	*carrying mouse*	chasing ball/*creatures*	
remorse	playing with ball	rubbing against things	
gratitude	playing with mouse	licking	
anger	*crazy hour*	watching/starting at	
love	hiding	sitting on a sunny ledge	
hate	pushing things around	having fun	

Italicized items were not included in the final implementation.

Just prior to the beginning of this excerpt, Lyotard had successfully finished exploring part of the house. This success made Lyotard mildly happy. The happy emotion led to the contentment feature being set, which gave rise to Lyotard's behavior to find a comfortable place to sit. In doing this, Lyotard remembers places that he believes to be comfortable and chooses one of them, a particular chair in the spare room. He then goes there, jumps on the chair, sits down, and starts cleaning himself.

At this point, the human user, whom Lyotard dislikes, walks into the room. Since Tok models "like" and "dislike" to be relatively long-lasting attitudes toward external entities, the initial mild dislike of the user gives rise to an emotion of some hatred toward the user. Further, Tok notices that one of Lyotard's goals—not being hurt—is threatened by the disliked user's prox-

Table 18-2. Section of an interaction with Lyotard

Lyotard:	(*GO-TO "the bedroom").	Lyotard:	(*GO-TO "the kitchen").
	(*GO-TO "the sunroom").		(*Meow).
	(*GO-TO "the spare room").	Player:	(*GO-TO "the sunroom").
	(*JUMP-ON "the chair").	Lyotard:	(*Meow).
	(*SIT-DOWN).	Player:	(*GO-TO "the diningroom").
	(*LICK "Lyotard").	Lyotard:	(*WAIT).
	(*LICK "Lyotard").	Player:	(*TAKE "the glass jar").
Player:	(*GO-TO "the spare room").	Lyotard:	(*GO-TO "the diningroom").
Lyotard:	(*JUMP-OFF "the chair").	Player:	(*GO-TO "the kitchen").
	(*RUN-TO "the sunroom").	Lyotard:	(*JUMP-ON "the table").
Player:	(*GO-TO "the sunroom").	Lyotard:	(*JUMP-OFF "the table").
Lyotard:	(*LOOKAROUND NERVOUSLY).		(*GO-TO "the kitchen").
Player:	(*PET "Lyotard").		(*Meow).
Lyotard:	(*BITE "Player").	Player:	(*POUR "the glass jar" IN "the kitty bowl").
	(*RUN-TO "the diningroom").		
Player:	(*GO-TO "the spare room").	Lyotard:	(*EAT "the sardine").
Lyotard:	(*LOOKAROUND NERVOUSLY).		(*EAT "the sardine").
	(*GO-TO "the sunroom").		(*EAT "the sardine").
	(*POUNCE-ON "the superball").		(*EAT "the sardine").
	(*LOOKAT "the superball").		(*EAT "the sardine").
	(*NUDGE "the superball").	Player:	(*PET "Lyotard").
	(*POUNCE-ON "the superball").	Lyotard:	(*CLOSE-EYES LAZILY).
	(*POUNCE-ON "the superball").	Player:	(*TAKE "Lyotard").
Lyotard:	(*GO-TO "the diningroom").	Lyotard:	(*CLOSE-EYES LAZILY).

imity. This prospect of a goal failure generates fear in Lyotard. The fear and hate combine to generate a strong aggressive feature that diminishes the previous contentment. The fear emotion and the proximity of its cause give rise to an avoid-harm goal, while the aggressive feature gives rise to a goal to threaten the user. In this case the avoid-harm goal wins out, creating a subsidiary escape/run-away behavior that leads Lyotard to jump off the chair and run out of the room.

When the user follows Lyotard into the sunroom and tries to pet him, Lyotard sees the action and notices that the actor trying to touch him is one toward whom he feels mild hate. This generates another goal: respond-negatively-to-contact. Lyotard responds to this rather than to his escape/run-away goal or any of his other goals because we declared it as having a high priority when we created Lyotard. Further refinement of this goal through a series of choices leads to Lyotard biting the player.

As the player leaves Lyotard alone, the emotions engendered by the player start to decay, and Lyotard again pursues his amusement goal. This time he is no longer content, which is one of several changes to his emotional state, so a slightly different set of amusement choices is available. He chooses to play with one of his toys, and so goes to find his superball.

As the simulation has progressed, Lyotard has been getting hungry. After he plays with the superball for a bit, Lyotard's hunger crosses a threshold so that his mind notices it as a feeling of hunger. This triggers a feeding goal that causes him to go to his bowl, but it is empty so he complains by meowing. After a while, he gives up on this technique for getting food, and tries another; he goes looking for food himself. He remembers places where he has seen food that was reachable, and goes to one of them, passing by the user in the process. At this point he again feels fear and aggression, but he ignores these feelings because dealing with the hunger is more important to him. As he reaches the place where he expected to find the food, he notices that it is gone (taken by the user when Lyotard couldn't see him), so Lyotard again considers other techniques to get food. He could try to find a human and suggest he be fed, but instead he chooses to try his bowl again. This time the human feeds him, and Lyotard eats. As he eats he feels happy because his emotionally important goal of eating is succeeding, and he also feels gratitude toward the user, because he believes the user helped to satisfy this goal. This gratitude in turn gradually neutralizes Lyotard's attitude toward the user.

Now when the user pets Lyotard, Lyotard responds favorably to the action by closing his eyes lazily. Lyotard wants to be petted because he no longer dislikes or fears the user. Thus, being petted causes a goal success, which causes happiness, and because the goal success was attributed to the user, increases gratitude toward the user. The result is that Lyotard now strongly likes the player.

The trace shown in Table 18-2 was produced by the interactive fiction version of the Oz software, which is written in Common Lisp. Of the 50,000 lines of code that comprise Oz, the Tok architecture uses roughly 7,500 lines. Lyotard is an additional 2,000 lines of code. Running on a Hewlett Packard

720 workstation (55 million instructions per second), Lyotard takes roughly two seconds for processing between acts.

CONCLUSION

The virtual reality community has generally focused on VR as a human-interface technique, giving some attention to modeling physical space and objects as well. While these topics are important, we see exclusive focus on them as something like studying celluloid instead of cinema, paper instead of literature, or cathode ray tubes instead of television. To reach our dream of interactive cinema, we must also look at the underlying content of the worlds we want to model. This means studying interactive characters, story, and presentation style, and that in turn means studying artificial intelligence.

Joseph Bates is Senior Research Computer Scientist at the School of Computer Science and a Fellow of the STUDIO for Creative Inquiry in the College of Fine Arts at Carnegie Mellon University, Pittsburgh, PA 15213. Internet: <joseph.bates@cs.cmu.edu>.

REFERENCES

1. We gratefully acknowledge the support of Fujitsu Laboratories, Ltd. for our research.

2. Joseph Bates, "The Role of Emotion in Believable Agents," *Communications of the ACM*, special issue on agents, July 1994.

3. Joseph Bates, "Virtual Reality, Art, and Entertainment," *Presence*, December 1992, 1(1): 133-138; A. Bryan Loyall and Joseph Bates, "Real-Time Control of Animated Broad Agents," *Proceedings of the 15th Annual Conference of the Cognitive Science Society*, Hillsdale, N.J., L. Erlbaum, 1993, conference held in Boulder, Colo., June 1993; Joseph Bates, A. Bryan Loyall, and W. Scott Reilly, "Integrating Reactivity, Goals, and Emotion in a Broad Agent," in *Proceedings of the Fourteenth Annual Conference of the Cognitive Science Society*, Bloomington, Ind., July 1992; Mark Kantrowitz and Joseph Bates, "Integrated Natural Language Generation Systems," in *Aspects of Automated Natural Language Generation*, R. Dale, E. Hovy, D. Rosner and O. Stock, eds., LNAI Volume 587, Berlin: Springer-Verlag, 1992; Margaret Kelso, Peter Weyhrauch, and Joseph Bates, "Dramatic Presence," *Presence*, Winter 1993, 2(1):1-15.

4. Joseph Weizenbaum, "Eliza" *Communications of the ACM*, 9 (1966): 36-45.

REAL LIFE

PART THREE

VR APPLICATIONS

THE PROMISE OF VIRTUAL REALITY FOR LEARNING

David C. Traub

Like every evolutionary concept, the promise of virtual reality in education will be grossly abused. Simulations of this, comparisons with that, virtual visits here and there...anchored by the promise that all will *soon* be possible.

But the real question remains: once affordable, will virtual reality be an effective tool for learning?

Immersive games exist that demand that users manipulate floating icons into meaningful sequences—no doubt a feisty tonic for motor skills. And minimally interactive polygon characters presented as user representations have been the stuff of virtual environments for several years—great fun unless you are expecting *Terminator 2* or *Lawnmower Man.*

That the technology is evolving exponentially and will find myriad brilliant uses in education and learning is not in question. What is in question is when? How? More important, how best can the potential of VR be tapped? How might the evolution of virtual environments be optimized to exploit the unique attributes of the immersive interface in the service of learning?

WHAT IS VIRTUAL REALITY?

Virtual reality (cyberspace, telepresence, artificial reality, immersion computing) is not a technology. Nor is it a fad that will fade when the next hype-train arrives. Rather, it is the natural extension of the classic two-dimensional computer, telephone, or television interface into the third dimension—an electronic means by which various display technologies allow a user to access and interact with electronic information in the first person as if sharing its physical domain.

According to this definition, VR embraces the use of interface clothing such as head-mounted displays and Datagloves equipped with position and orientation sensors. It also includes immersive experiences such as Disney's Captain EO and Virtual Worlds Entertainment's BattleTech Center, in which a user is seated in a cab that serves as the fulcrum for a projected experience. The term *virtual reality* will evolve toward ubiquity as it comes to describe any interactive three-dimensional projection scenario that eliminates the distance between user and machine—such as the display of speed-limit information on LCD driving glasses, or the act of quieting your coffeemaker with the wave of a hand.

Eventually such interfaces will be everywhere. Virtual reality will be part of everything we do, including learning.

WHAT ARE LEARNING AND INSTRUCTION?

There are several concepts and learning models to ponder when determining how best to apply virtual reality to education. As context, let us first consider the concept of learning itself. What is learning? According to educational theorist Robert Gagne, it is "the process by which human behaviors are changed within certain identifiable situations."[1] This definition suggests that behavioral change is realized by interaction with specifically defined environments—a deliberate arrangement of external events to support internal learning processes. Key here is the importance of design in instruction. One must make decisions in order to teach.

Next we ask, When does one learn? With nearly every unique sensory input. When is one educated? When an instructor's intent is successfully realized within the universe of a student's knowledge base, through appropriate use of human- and/or machine-based technologies. This is a key point, given that the designers of any virtual environment are inevitably teaching their users, whether or not that is their intention. Those interested in education and learning must come to appreciate the educational power of nonconventional delivery systems such as entertainment television and virtual reality.

How does one learn? Though it is a gross simplification, consider my three-step model, which indicates where technology might or might not be appropriate:

1. Data acquisition. Whether by lecture, book, or high-tech delivery system, the first step to learning is the acquisition of patterns, symbols, modeled behaviors, processes, and so forth. This is where interactive technology shines, principally because the stimulus-response mechanism it embraces replicates the positive human process of reinforcement.

2. Collaborative learning. Popular educational theory suggests that the optimal path to learning features social interaction whereupon two or more speakers join to agree on the meaning of symbols and reinforce each other's understanding through empathy. Here technology plays a lesser role than a teacher, except in the case of collaborative computing scenarios, in which users collaborate over a computer or an expert system facilitates collaboration.

3. Reflection. Once acquired data have been internalized, the personal process of reflecting upon and applying that data to real-life circum-

stances speeds the integration of the information that is truly useful into longterm behavior. In the short term, reflection is not likely to involve technology; in the long term, technology may evolve to simulate realities that allow users to interact with an environment as if it were real.

The significance of this model is fourfold. First, it presents simple distinctions among various phases of learning, each of which requires different strategies and technologies of instruction. Second, these distinctions begin to point to areas where technology might be more appropriate (data acquisition) or less appropriate (collaborative learning). Third, this model emphasizes the importance of direct human interaction—an educational necessity for which there will never be a complete substitute. Finally, it emphasizes another key, if neglected, part of learning design: the value of time for reflection.

In developing this model, my first assumption was the importance of design. My second assumption was that learning takes place throughout all phases of life (work and play). My third was the notion that learning takes place in stages, more or less amenable to high-tech support. Finally, I assumed that there are different kinds of learning, each more or less amenable to technological interventions.

According to Gagne, we experience five types of learning, each best suited for a unique set of instructional scenarios. Technology might or might not fit in with each type of learning:

1. Verbal information: the facts and knowledge of the world that one accumulates to facilitate other activities. Here technology is probably most logical because of its ability to facilitate contiguity, repetition, and reinforcement—time-tested learning principles employed to facilitate memorization. Rote-oriented interactive technology would be most valuable here because it could free teachers to focus on the most valuable and complex of instructional skills (reinforcement, cheerleading, esteembuilding) and the teaching of more challenging skill sets such as cognitive strategies and intellectual skills.

2. Intellectual skills: symbolic processes such as language and quantification. These skills are best learned with a combination of mentoring (collaborative processes) and practice; a variety of tools can be applied to these individualized phases of learning, including pen and paper, calculator, and computer-based instruction.

3. Cognitive strategies: the higher-order means by which one exerts control over one's learning processes. Problem-solving and self-imposed behavior modification are the most challenging skills to teach, and are optimized by interpersonal instruction. Software to facilitate problem-solving and other high-order activities is evolving, but is best applied with the supervision of a discerning mentor.

4. Attitudes: internal states of being that evolve over time and influence action. These in turn are influenced by the environment. At present, television is probably the most pervasive delivery system for influencing attitude.

5. Motor skills: skeletal/muscular activities. Presently an experiential rather than technological issue, though simulations featuring accurate body tracking might teach intricate motor skills.

These taxonomies emphasize that learning can be broken into classes and phases, each more or less amenable to complementary technology. So which is which? I have already stated that interpersonal collaboration is a vital, minimally technological step to learning. I have also suggested that certain classes of learning—such as the development of cognitive strategies and the acquisition of motor skills—are best realized through experiential and interpersonal learning.

Finally, I have suggested that other classes of learning—such as verbal and intellectual skills—could be facilitated by interactive technologies. There are six distinct methods of learning that are effectively facilitated by technology.

These six methods are posited by educators Stephen M. Alessi and Stanley R. Trollop in their book *Computer-Based Interaction*. They include:

1. Tutorial instruction: dialogue with the student;

2. Drills: a sequence of questions or problems presented repeatedly;

3. Simulations: the multidimensional representation of physical phenomenon;

4. Instructional games: instructional representations optimized for their motivation quality;

5. Tests: drills designed to test learning; and

6. Problem-solving environments: complex simulations embedded with user-derived outcomes.[2]

In other words, certain learning mechanisms are interactive, or "stimulus-response," and machines are good at facilitating these. But what about virtual reality? In those categories of learning where technological support is valuable, what are the qualities of interactive virtual environments that suggest they might be more or less effective than other technologies? And where might virtual reality's other experiential assets suggest a new role previously inappropriate for technological solutions?

WHY VIRTUAL REALITY AND LEARNING: What the Experts Say

I recently did some telephone interviews with industry experts. Their comments show that there are many reasons to contemplate the role of virtual reality in learning. For example, Anne McCormick of Media 3 and the Neuva School, an innovative pre-kindergarten through eighth grade school for gifted students, suggests that the multimodal kinesthetic and sensory feedback that virtual reality enables is critical to the learning experience, particularly with children not yet acclimated to the passive receipt of information. Kicha Ganapathy, manager of AT&T Bell Lab's Machine Perception Research Department, sees virtual reality's interactivity and ability to be personalized as its principal values.

Wes Regian, senior scientist for the Intelligent Training Branch at the U. S. Air Force's Armstrong Laboratory, sees several reasons why virtual reality is particularly appropriate to education. First, he claims that the human information processing system is primarily visual—and virtual reality, of course, has a strong visual component. Second, Regian believes that the ability to "situate cognition" within real-world contexts optimizes the chances for the transfer of learned knowledge to the real world. Finally, he sees virtual reality as a way to optimize motivation, a key factor to learning.

Randy Walser, an independent consultant formerly with Autodesk, suggests that "the deep way by which a user interacts with Cyberspace enables a significantly greater emphasis on experiential forms of learning which go well beyond today's tremendous focus on factual knowledge and facts." Another former member of Autodesk's team sees the assets of virtual reality in a similar vein. Meredith Bricken, who is a partner in Oz...Ellipsis, suggests that because learning is not just a mental process, but rather an activity of the entire physiology, the ability to use virtual reality to teach within an actual or simulated physical context optimizes the brain's ability to make new neurobiological connections by replicating the phenomena of real-life interaction.

THE KEY: Suspension of Disbelief

The future of virtual reality in learning may be seen in educational philosopher Jean Piaget's observation that the ultimate path to learning is life itself. This is the power and promise of virtual reality. The technology is developing the ability to achieve such a comprehensive suspension of disbelief that it will challenge users to learn as they would in real life.

So what is the suspension of disbelief? If a filmmaker is successful in building a good plot, strong characters, and a compelling *mise-en-scène*, he or she is able to cause the audience to suspend disbelief, temporarily losing a conscious sense of the distinction between themselves and their environment. They come to consider the filmed entertainment they are viewing as real, and to identify with its characters.

As virtual reality evolves in its ability to provide stimulus-response mechanisms, real-time correspondence of perspective cues, realistic immersion, and compelling narrative and characters, it too will enable users to suspend disbelief. However, a virtual suspension of disbelief may have a deeper imprint on the subconscious for several reasons. First, in the case of increasingly high-resolution projection scenarios such as direct retinal projection, the sense of immersion will become more immediate and powerful than it is in a darkened theater. Second, the virtual experience embraces interaction, enabling the user to relate directly to the projected world, making that world—and the response that it projects—that much more real.

To put it more directly, virtual reality portends a learning environment in which an educator's intended communication can be built into an experience the user perceives—and learns from—as real.

One can argue that the comparison between the psychological impact of cinema and virtual reality is flawed due to differences between the subconscious states of moviegoers and computer users.[3] However, virtual reality is swiftly evolving as an integration of the best of the educational qualities of computing (stimulus-response and simulation), communications (collaboration), and cinema and television (suspension of disbelief). Because of this, interactive immersion will facilitate new educational capacities—and will have a significant impact on the future of learning.

EXAMPLES

What are some of these capacities? Below are brief examples of current projects focused on integrating virtual reality into the educational mix.

MEDICAL

There is extensive activity in the use of virtual environments for training in the medical field. One of the hotbeds of development for medical VR is Dartmouth College, where Joseph Henderson, director of the Interactive Media Lab at the Dartmouth-Hitchcock Medical School, and Joseph Rosen, head of the school's surgical simulation unit and president of Medical Media Systems, are focusing on three areas: information access, experiential learning, and collaborative application. Henderson is concentrating on evolving the "social gestalt" of virtual environments whereby simulations evoke a strong sense of reality, history, and importance. Rosen is using VPL's technology to develop both the interface and dynamic modeling of geometrically represented virtual environments. Their work focuses on providing a practicum, or practice-based tutorial, to teach caregivers how to deal with the swampy problems of everyday medical decision-making by simulating clinical situations. Over the long term, Henderson and Rosen's vision is to provide access to these environments over high-bandwidth networks so that people who are geographically separated can work together to learn and provide service.

MILITARY

The military has been the fountainhead of virtual environments, especially in their application to flight training. As the interface technologies associated with immersion become more complex, virtual reality scenarios are being applied to a broader set of learning goals. For example, Wes Regian is using HMD configurations at the Air Force's Armstrong Lab in Brooks, Texas, to facilitate the acquisition of long sequences of actions and psychomotor skills in small spaces, the development of large-scale spatial skills via maze research (useful, for example, in teaching astronauts how to get around a space station they have never visited), and procedural expertise with large, complex consoles. His thesis is that virtual environments can be used to optimize the adaptation of required motor skills and other knowledge within a simulated environment. He anticipates that the type of training he is developing will be used in other industries involving psychomotor skills, such as air traffic control and nuclear power plant management.

THE CLASSROOM

One of the most interesting applications that is likely to make it to the classroom in the next year or so is another of Regian's projects funded by the Air Force: a bus for a teacher and thirty students that features workstations with head-mounted displays and earphones. This bus would be district-owned, and would travel from school to school offering a variety of simulation-oriented educational applications that would ordinarily be beyond the reach of the classroom. This project, to be developed by a major aircraft company, not only exemplifies the military's efforts to develop nondefense business, but also reflects its evolving role in education. It is a logical first step in exploiting a tool that will remain financially impossible for most schools for quite some time.

Another experiment with virtual reality in the classroom has been conducted over the past year at the University of Washington's Human Interface Technology (HIT) Lab. It introduces virtual reality to ten- to fifteen-year-old technology-camp students to determine whether they would be motivated to work with virtual reality when given access to the technology in an open-ended context. The children were fascinated by the experience of creating and entering virtual worlds. Students learned a series of new technological and mathematical skills and concepts, researchers gained insight into human factors issues, and both groups agreed that virtual reality was an optimal medium for constructionist learning.

A third center for educational research in virtual reality and classroom education is the San Francisco Bay area. Autodesk, a company known for its computer-aided design (CAD) software, has paired with cognitive psychologist Mark Merickel to experiment with local school children on the value of virtual reality as a research tool. The experiments focused on how people visualize geometric information; children were introduced to cyberspace environments featuring unique geometric shapes and representations that they were asked to describe. Merickel not only gained key insights into spatial perception, but both he and Autodesk observed how naturally the children took to the virtual worlds. Both intend to continue riding the wave of educational virtual reality.

Perhaps the first company to experiment with virtual reality and the classroom was VPL, also in the Bay Area. The company conducted classroom experiments at the Nueva School, introducing virtual world-building to students as young as six. The principal finding was that children of all ages readily adapted to the paradigm of virtual environments and expression—an insight that was confirmed at a conference on virtual reality at Stanford Research Institute during which, according to the Nueva School's Ann McCormick, it was the children who were best able to describe to the audience the experience of virtual reality.

HIGHER EDUCATION

A number of universities are experimenting with virtual reality, principally in the area of scientific visualization. Perhaps the most prolific is the University of North Carolina at Chapel Hill, which has been a leader in computer, interface, and hypertext innovation for the past decade. One of the more interesting projects, funded by a major news corporation, explores virtual reality as a means of transmitting social information such as news and entertainment. Communications researcher Frank Biocca and his associates are trying to determine whether a virtual interface to the news or other forms of public information will cause users to change their habits: Will they spend more time with the news? Will they take a more active, even editorial stance to their news, pursuing hypertext links between current news and historical context? Will this extension of sensory channels cause consumers to stop buying newspapers?

DISTANCE LEARNING AND CORPORATE TRAINING

Universities are the not the only ones interested in higher education, particularly as it applies to distance leaning. ATT's Kicha Ganapathy sees concurrent education—featuring collaborative learning partners in geographically distant locations—as a major area of opportunity for telecommunications. John Thomas, executive director of artificial intelligence research at NYNEX Technology, sees networked virtual reality as a boon for distance education, and is developing the notion of "augmented reality." According to this scenario, a worker is "augmented" by special glasses that are able to project technological schematics and instructions as she or he conducts a project outside the office.

"Empathy training" is another concept introduced by Thomas and his associate Rory Stuart of NYNEX's intelligent interface group. It allows a user to experience another person's perspective from a distance by means of virtual technologies. One application for empathy training allows an on-site worker to call upon the expertise of a retired worker merely by donning an interface device. Myriad other networked virtual reality applications could facilitate educational applications that support decision-making, medicine, architecture, planning—even motor skills such as ballet, music, and hurdling. Stuart, however, warns about "literalization," in which consistent users of virtual technologies might begin to perceive virtual representations as reality—a real concern, as limited virtual reality devices are beginning to hit the mainstream consumer market.

THE HOME

A number of developers, both large and small, are already trying to determine just how cheaply they can produce and package head-mounted VR simulators for the home, without undermining the high-end market they might already be serving. Accordingly, they are pondering the software titles that will be needed to drive sales. And of course, many of these early titles will be educational, for two reasons: to inspire parents at the point of purchase, and because the low capacity of these early machines will likely enable little more than interesting navigational explorations and mildly interactive simulations. Kicha Ganapathy says, "You will see educational software for the home and school that specializes in modeling worlds like the planetary system such that a child might be able to travel to the moon, then look back and observe the earth."

WHEN WILL VR REACH EDUCATION?

Wes Regian suggests that it will take from eight to ten years for a nonmilitary, SIMNET-like networked virtual resource to be made available for education. Most believe that it will take even longer—perhaps ten to fifteen years—before the real obstacle to adaptation is overcome: ignorance and fear on the part of senior administrators, who consider financial problems the principal reason that appropriate multimedia technologies have not found their way into the schools.

The problem, in other words, is that VR software is still being produced largely by engineers. Most of the systems are too difficult for those who have content to share—artists, teachers, musicians, publishers—to manufacture VR software easily.

Both Ann McCormick and Meredith Bricken suggest that one solution would be the evolution of appropriately user-friendly and powerful authoring systems—versus canned titles—that would be designed to enable experts in education and other fields to produce significantly rich environments.

Michael Benedikt is the Meadows Foundation Centennial Professor of Architecture at the University of Texas at Austin, editor of *Cyberspace: First Steps,* and an artist/researcher who is exploring what it takes to build a cogent virtual world. He believes it may be as long as twenty-five years before there is easy access to complex 3D virtual databases, and notes that there is no good substitute for an exhilarating give-and-take presentation with a fine teacher.

Others suggested specific areas in which technological innovation should continue at full speed (displays, CPUs, and so forth), and believed that additional empirical evidence would help VR's potential for adaptation. Most felt extremely confident in the future of virtual environments, but with regard for learning and education, believed that issues of government economics, societal values, and administrative malaise would impair a healthy rate of progress beyond specialized adoption by visionaries. All said they would continue with their own unique contributions.

Nancy Young is media director for the Edison Project, which brings private enterprise to the classroom. Young says that Edison's answer to the issue of educational malaise is to build a new kind of world-class school from the ground up. She says the project is currently evolving the educational structure of its first two hundred schools by taking a fresh look at all collaborative, interactive, and immersive simulation technologies. The intent is to draw from them the best creative technological assets available, then to mix these with a forward-thinking faculty and administration that appreciates the commercial value of excellence, fiscal responsibility, and esprit de corps.

CONCLUSION

Virtual reality continues to experience many technological, presentational, and cultural limitations. These problems portend many years of meaningless digital worlds we can explore but never believe—a swirl of digital bliss that will do little more than entice idealistic entrepreneurs to the edge.

But as virtual technology evolves in its ability to comprehensively engage a user in an immersive reality embedded with valuable lessons, it *will* help to build a new means of learning by which both humans and technology are optimized according to the nature of the lesson and the type of learning to be realized. As an ultimate learning technology, virtual reality will also serve to help redefine the role of educators. The teacher will be less administrator and test-giver, and more thinking mentor and reinforcer of self-esteem.

In doing this, virtual reality may also serve to remind us what it means to be human.

David C. Traub is an independent new-media producer and journalist. He can be reached at 343 Soquel Ave., #240, Santa Cruz, CA 95062.

Note

This essay is based on a paper entitled "Virtual Reality and the Future of Edutainment" presented at ICAT '92 *The Second International Conference on Artificial Reality and Tele-Existence*, Tokyo, July 8, 1992.

REFERENCES

1. Robert Gagne, Leslie Briggs, and Walter Wager, *The Principles of Instructional Design,* Holt, Rinehart and Winston, Inc., 1988, 6.

2. Stephen M. Alessi and Stanley R. Trollop, *Computer-Based Instruction: Methods and Development* , Prentice-Hall, Inc., 1985, 50.

3. Phenomenologists may argue with this comparison, especially considering the gross psychological difference between the experience realized by the passive cinema-goer and the active arbiter of a virtual experience. However, both the cinema and virtual reality strive to solicit the full subconscious attention of the user, and when successful, realize a significant opportunity for impressing the subconscious.

EXPLORENET

Charles E. Hughes and J. Michael Moshell

ExploreNet is a networked simulator designed to support the presentation of virtual worlds that aid in the teaching of core disciplines (mathematics, and social and natural sciences) for grades 6 through 12. Inspired by the Habitat project,[1] ExploreNet uses role playing to encourage cooperative problem-solving. Students share experiences and work in teams to reach their goals, even though they may be geographically and culturally separated, or physically isolated, perhaps by illness or disability. (see figure 20-1)

A student enters the graphically simulated worlds of ExploreNet via a personal computer, and can participate in an ongoing simulation, start a new "world," or become a nonparticipating observer within an existing world.

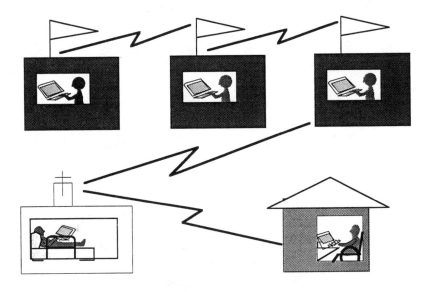

Figure 20-1. Remote access to ExploreNet.

Each student sees animated human forms (called actors) representing his or her own presence and the presence of other students. Each student controls his or her own actor in explorations that require cooperation, the employment of mathematical skills, and the development of thoughtful experiments.

A typical world might include a scene in which students need to explore an unlit cave. The scenario is designed so that in order to enter the cave, our adventurers must realize that lanterns found in an earlier scene can provide the needed light. This leads them to estimate the volume of kerosene required to fuel the lanterns. The scenario includes unpleasant consequences of overfilling and underfilling, plus the need for at least two participants to bring along lanterns.

The goal of the ExploreNet project is to produce a simulation-based system that:

- Emphasizes cooperative problem-solving,

- Provides innovative access to learning,

- Fits into existing school settings,

- Captivates the attention of students, and

- Is scalable to newer technologies.

To achieve these goals the ExploreNet system provides a framework in which worlds can be designed and run. Some worlds may include mathematical tools that do automatic unit-management and even perform symbolic evaluation of sets of equations. Others may come with a simple calculator.

As of this writing, we have produced two prototypes and applied the first of these to the simulation of a complete world—Caruba Island—designed for middle and high school students.

CARUBA ISLAND: A Typical Scenario

The initial world we have created for ExploreNet is called Escape from Caruba Island. This adventure is first presented to our students when they see a map of a picturesque island over which a bird lazily flies. The students read the following introduction.

It's Spring Break. After hours of begging, your parents finally agree to let you join your friends on a vacation. Not just any vacation...a vacation to Caruba Island!

Caruba Island is a remote isle. Long ago, Caruba was the home to many native Carubans. However, upon the discovery of modern transportation, technology and MTV, the Carubans abandoned their native land for the gold-paved streets of the United States. Now, Caruba Island is totally deserted. That is, until you arrive.

Whirlpools, caves, jungles, deserts, waterfalls, and mountains await your arrival. Your escape to the Island should take only a few minutes. However, your Escape from Caruba Island will take much longer.

When a student finishes reading this introductory text, he or she starts the simulated adventure. The adventure involves many scenes in which the student must carry out analytical tasks, recognize potentially useful objects, and, above all, work cooperatively with team members (see figure 20-2).

In the Caruba Island scenario, success can occur only when at least one other student enters the simulated world from a networked computer. Cooperation is usually initiated by message sending, but may also involve coordinated actions on the parts of the figures controlled by students (see figure 20-3).

BRINGING VIRTUAL REALITY TO EXPLORENET

In its present form, ExploreNet provides a limited form of presence in its simulated worlds—each participant has a corresponding animated actor, and each user's view of the simulation is that of an observer from on-high. The simulated world can seem remote and the animated actor's needs may not feel like our own real needs.

True VR requires a system with a deep sense of immersion (presence), realistic behavior (autonomy), and rapid responses to a range of natural inputs such as gestures (interaction).[2] But is this really necessary to an educational application like ExploreNet? Can we achieve desirable effects in a desktop VR system—without the cost and effort required to provide visual presence?

Immersion is a psychological phenomenon. Chess players, for instance, are immersed in the rich, discrete world of decision trees and zones of control. Not all virtual worlds require total sensory immersion to achieve psychic commitment. The current design of ExploreNet is based on the belief that the properties of autonomy and interaction are more essential to success in education than are 3-D stereo immersion graphics.

Indeed, the primary educational concern with presence will probably be that it provides an axis of literalness in learning space. When the lesson designer chooses to invoke the deepest nonrational, passionate part of a student's psyche (that is, to "hook 'em" on the story line), then full immersion may be appropriate. When the intent is for the students to pause, reflect, and step out of the story, freezing a screen view may achieve the necessary distancing, the chance to reflect.

STATUS OF EXPLORENET PROJECT

The first two prototypes of ExploreNet, both written in C++, have been used in several experimental settings that provide us with feedback that we are using to improve the user interface and functionality. The version now under

Figure 20-2. A meeting of adventurers on Escape to Caruba Island.

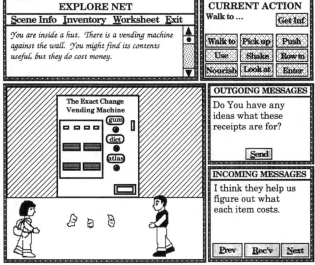

Figure 20-3. Applying analytical problem-solving

development is written in Digitalk's Smalltalk-V/Win 32 to take advantage of that system's ability to support an evolving set of behaviors and interactions among objects within the simulated worlds.

Scenarios for ExploreNet are now being developed by a multidisciplinary team of animators, educators, philosophers, psychologists, and script writers. One such scenario provides the opportunity for middle-school students to mentor younger children acting out African-American heritage stories written by Zora Neale Hurston.[3] In a second scenario, children explore at-risk situations that emphasize personal responsibility and adaptive problem-solving. These scenarios will be used in several schools in the Fall of 1994.

Anyone interested in learning more about ExploreNet or perhaps in participating in experiments or designing new scenarios should contact either of the authors.

Charles E. Hughes is professor of computer science at the University of Central Florida. His current research interests include networked graphical simulations, and virtual environments. He can be reached at University of Central Florida, Orlando, FL 32816; telephone: (407) 823-2762; Internet: <ceh@cs.ucf.edu>.

J. Michael Moshell is an associate professor at Computer Science Department, and chief scientist at Visual Systems Lab, Institute for Simulation and Training, University of Central Florida. He is presently working on educational applications of virtual environment technology, and can be contacted at University of Central Florida, Orlando, FL 32816; Internet: <moshell@cs.ucf.edu>.

REFERENCES

1. See Randall Farmer's essay in this collection, and also Chip Morningstar and F. Randall Farmer, "The Lessons of Lucasfilm's Habitat," *Cyberspace: First Steps*, Michael Benedikt, ed., Cambridge: MIT Press 1991.

2. David Zeltzer, "Autonomy, Interaction, and Presence," *Presence* 1(1), December 1992: 127-132 .

3. Zora Neale Hurston. *Their Eyes Were Watching God.* Philadelphia: J. B. Lippincott, 1937. Reprinted by Harper & Row, New York, 1990.

SIGN-LANGUAGE RECOGNITION USING VIRTUAL REALITY GLOVES

Peter Vamplew

The development of instrumented gloves capable of measuring the movements of a user's hands has been one of the major steps in allowing natural interaction with a computer-generated environment. The measurements made by the gloves can be used to directly model the movements of the hand—thus creating a virtual hand within the virtual world—or to interpret the user's movements as gestures. A simple example of the gesture-recognition approach is the common convention of pointing with the hand to move around the virtual world. While this gesture consists of only a hand shape, it is possible to develop systems that will be able to recognize more complex gestures based on other features such as hand motion and orientation. This leads to the possibility of creating a computer system capable of recognizing the component gestures of the sign languages used by many deaf people.

MANUAL LANGUAGES

The deaf community communicates effectively through manual languages such as American Sign Language (ASL) and Australian Sign Language (Auslan). However, the vast majority of hearing individuals are ignorant of these languages. This lack of knowledge causes problems for signers who cannot speak and wish to interact with the hearing community. Simple gestures such as pointing at objects or message writing can be used in some situations; in other circumstances such methods are inappropriate (for example, communicating at a distance) or cumbersome (conversing at a party). Technological "solutions" that alleviate some problems still often fail to provide natural means of communication. As described earlier, the instrumented gloves developed for virtual reality allow the creation of gesture-recognition systems, and thus may offer a technological bridge between manual and vocal languages.

MANUAL LANGUAGES AND INSTRUMENTED GLOVES

Some pioneering research along these lines has already taken place. The GloveTalker system, developed by researcher Sidney Fels of the University of Toronto, is capable of converting hand gestures into spoken words from a carefully selected small vocabulary.[1] The gestures used are only loosely based on ASL signs and require a certain amount of training on the part of the user. More closely based on ASL, and therefore more natural, is the Talking Glove developed by Jim Kramer of Stanford University.[2] This system currently is capable of converting letters created using the ASL manual alphabet into spoken words. Kramer's research aims to extend the system to the more complex gestures involved in Pidgin Signed English (a more Englishlike variant of ASL often used when native signers converse with nonnative signers).

SLARTI

These systems have demonstrated that translating hand gestures into speech is indeed possible. The aim of the Slarti (Sign Language Recognition) system under development at the University of Tasmania is to extend these principles to Auslan, the primary language of the Australian deaf community. The project uses the CyberGlove, which contains artificial neural networks (ANNs) that perform the recognition task based on glove data.[3] ANNs have been selected for the recognition process because of their ability to perform the type of "fuzzy" pattern-matching required by such a task. This should enable Slarti to handle the quirks of signing, such as the variation among signers, the modifications made to an individual sign depending on the signs made before and after it, and the natural lack of repeatability of the basic act of signing.

Slarti is not intended to provide a complete Auslan-to-English translation system. While such a system would be the ideal communications device, it is simply beyond the limits of existing knowledge of language translation. Auslan is not, as many hearing people imagine, merely a manual representation of English allowing direct word-for-word translation. It is a distinct, though closely related, language with its own conventions of grammar and semantics. Auslan language conventions, because they are specifically tailored for efficient communication in a manual medium, often vary greatly from those of a spoken language such as English. Therefore, the Slarti system will concentrate on the sign recognition task, rather than on providing complete translation facilities.

This does not mean that Slarti will be merely a prototype with no practical application. Even if translation is provided only at the word level, Auslan and English still have enough similarities for such a translation to augment communication, conveying more information than the signing alone would to someone with limited knowledge of Auslan. In addition, Slarti may serve as a training aid for hearing people learning Auslan. Correct pronunciation is a major difficulty in learning a new spoken language without feedback from an experienced speaker. Similarly, with sign language it can be hard to know whether the signs are being formed correctly. Slarti can provide such feedback by telling the trainee whether or not it can recognize the sign being performed (and by extension, possibly even explain how to correct mistakes).

GESTURE RECOGNITION AND VIRTUAL WORLD BUILDING

The techniques developed within Slarti can also be applied to developing gesture-recognition interfaces more complex than those in existing VR systems. It may be beneficial to incorporate elements of existing sign languages into such gestural systems. For example, the gestures used to depict and reference objects in Auslan would appear to provide a basis for creating an interface for the rapid creation of new objects in a world-building utility.

Peter Vamplew is a lecturer with the Artificial Neural Networks Research Group of the Department of Computer Science, University of Tasmania, GPO Box 252C, Hobart, Tasmania 7001, Australia; telephone: 61-002-202-932; fax: 61-002-202-913; Internet: <vamplew@cs.utas.edu.au>.

REFERENCES

1. S. Fels and G. Hinton, "Building Adaptive Interfaces with Neural Networks: The Glove Talk Pilot Study," *Proceedings of the IFIP TC 13 Third International Conference on Human-Computer Interaction*, D. Daiper et al., eds. Amsterdam: North-Holland, 683-688; S. Fels, *Building Adaptive Interfaces with Neural Networks: The Glove Talk Pilot Study*, Toronto: Department of Computer Science, University of Toronto, February 1990, Technical Report CRG-TR-90-1.

2. J. Kramer and L. Leifer, "The Talking Glove: An Expressive and Receptive 'Verbal' Communication Aid for the Deaf, Deaf-Blind, and Nonvocal," *Proceedings of the Third Annual Conference on Computer Technology/Special Education/Rehabilitation*, Harry J. Murphy, ed., conference held at California State University, Northridge, October 15-17, 1987; J. Kramer and L. Leifer, "The Talking Glove: A Speaking Aid for Nonvocal Deaf and Deaf-Blind Individuals" RESNA 12th Annual Conference, New Orleans, La., 1989.

3. For a simple introduction to ANNs see W. Allman, *Apprentices of Wonder: Inside the Neural Network Revolution*, New York: Bantam, 1990; for a more rigorous treatment see J. Hertz, A. Krogh, and R. G. Palmer, *Introduction to the Theory of Neural Computation*, Reading, Mass.: Addison-Wesley, 1991.

A LOW-COST VIRTUAL REALITY SYSTEM FOR ACCESSING BARRIER-FREE DESIGN

John Trimble and Ted Morris

Traditionally, the built environment has been designed with an average user in mind. This idea did not include the range of abilities of persons with physical disabilities or with impairments related to the aging process. The idea of "barrier-free design" evolved in the 1970s and 1980s, largely through the work of individual architects like Ronald Mace, director of the Center of Accessible Housing in Raleigh, N.C. As the name implies, barrier-free design refers to designs that do not impose barriers on their users, regardless of their abilities. Although the idea of barrier-free, or accessible, design is more than two decades old, it was not until the recent passage of legislation that it gained wide recognition.

Public awareness and public laws now mandate equal opportunity for individuals with disabilities in employment, public accommodations, transportation, state and local government services, and telecommunications. As of July 26, 1992, businesses with more than twenty-five employees must be accessible to and usable by disabled and older persons. On July 26, 1994, this extended to businesses with more than fifteen employees. All forms of public transportation will also be affected in the coming years. This has created a significant incentive for businesses, government, and schools to create accessible environments—which is not always easy.

People's physical and cognitive functions vary along a continuum. Accordingly, individual differences in functional abilities present a design problem. While some designs may be evaluated by a consensus of clients (for example, public bathroom designs), others are best evaluated on an individual basis (such as work stations or offices). Additionally, designs often must be assessed with small- or full-scale models that may lead to a costly iterative development process.

The tools available to help designers solve these problems are limited. Most AEC/CAD software is for visualizing designs, not necessarily for testing their ergonomics. Software for architectural walkthroughs is only incrementally better. Programs for ergonomic analysis lack the architectural features needed to evaluate prospective designs.

WHEEL-CHAIR ACCESSIBLE VIRTUAL ENVIRONMENTS

Our system, the WAVE-4-1 (Wheelchair Accessible Virtual Environment for one user), gives people who use wheelchairs a way to test proposed designs before they are built. This is achieved by immersing the user in a three-dimensional representation of the designs (see figure 22-1 and color insert # 11). The user views the 3D representation with a stereoscopic wide-field-of-view HMD that contains two miniature color monitors displaying slightly shifted images of the scene. The images on each monitor are controlled by individual computers according to the person's position and line of sight. A sensor affixed to the HMD tracks the position and orientation of the person's head, providing data to the computer to determine the line of sight.

The user moves through the virtual environment using a wheelchair that is mounted on an instrumented roller platform. Transducers in the platform provide data that allow computation of the user's direction and distance of

Figure 22-1. The view of a stove as seen from the point of view of the person in a wheelchair, who is reaching for a pot. • Credit: Hines VA Hospital/ Prairie Virtual Systems Corp.

travel. Thus, when a user turns his or her head and rolls forward, his or her view of the virtual world changes the way it would in the real world, creating a feeling of being immersed within the visual scene. Entire buildings can be evaluated by creating "portals" into different CAD designs. The system also provides a means of displaying scaled 3D CAD representations of the person and the chair using anthropometric and wheelchair dimensions. This gives designers a way to quantify environmental or architectural barriers.

A collision-detection algorithm is used to determine when the person or chair is bumping into surfaces. Navigation can be completely unconstrained by the surroundings by deactivating collision detection. This makes navigation easier and gives people the freedom to go through windows and view environments from the outside.

The WAVE-4-1 also allows people to interact with things in the virtual environment using a glove whose sensors provide data on finger-flexing and the position and orientation of the hand in space. These data are used to control the position, orientation, and configuration of a "virtual hand" with which the user can manipulate virtual objects. Thus, if an object is out of reach, for instance, the user can readjust its position so that it becomes accessible.

Users may also use hand gestures to remove barriers. Environmental objects like walls, cabinets, and toilets can be moved or resized simply by grasping and manipulating them. Door handles may be relocated. When the environment has been modified to suit the user's needs, the design can be saved so that the designer can incorporate the modifications in the CAD model.

The WAVE-4-1 is currently one of the most cost-effective way to evaluate the accessibility of designs. Development cost for the entire system was under $30,000, as the project uses two high-speed IBM-compatible 80486 PCs and several sensing devices to control navigation, line of sight, and object manipulation.

The WAVE-4-1 brings users into the decision-making process. It also allows architects and designers to see their designs through their clients' eyes, which lets them appreciate and understand ergonomic and other functional barriers in designs. A second system, WAVE-4-2, which allows architects or designers to share the space with their clients, is under development. This should further increase the effectiveness of the WAVE as a medium for communicating the effectiveness of designs.

John Trimble, founder and president of Prairie Virtual Systems Corporation, has more than twenty years experience in research and development. Prairie Virtual Systems, 2201 West Campbell Park Drive, Chicago, IL 60612; telephone: (312) 243-8744; fax: (312) 829-4069; Internet: <j.trimble@well.sf.ca.us>.

Ted Morris is associate director for engineering visualization at the Center for Advanced Manufacturing Design and Control at the Institute of Technology, University of Minnesota, Minneapolis. He can be reached at (612) 625-3520.

NEWS

PART

FROM

FOUR

ABROAD

LOOKING AT CYBERSPACE FROM JAPAN

Katsura Hattori

October 6, 1990, marked the opening of Cyberthon—the Woodstock of the 1990s, heralding the advent of Cyberculture—at Colossal Pictures Studio in suburban San Francisco. This conference ran nonstop for twenty-four hours, enveloped in the enthusiasm of cybernauts about to launch into the twenty-first century.

This large studio, designed for special effects, was partitioned in several sections: two halls for discussion, an exhibition area, and a virtual kitchen in the center of the studio. Presentations were made in both halls simultaneously while visitors moved continuously from one area to another. The exhibition area between the halls was partitioned like a labyrinth, and various kinds of devices were jammed in to the point of overcrowding. The exhibition made me feel like Alice in Wonderland, slipping into another dimension.

Debate was opened by the chairperson, Howard Rheingold, wearing a hat set with twinkling LEDs; he was followed by Warren Robinett of the University of North Carolina, Tom Furness of the University of Washington, and, wearing his usual dreadlocks, Jaron Lanier of VPL Research, Inc., a company that at the time was the Apple Computer of virtual reality. Their speeches were enthusiastically received. Around midnight, Michael McGreevy, disguised as a clown, got his audience to put brown paper bags over their heads and sing "The Song of a Miserable Clown." When Timothy Leary shouted, "Everything is virtual!" the excitement of the conference climaxed.

After the long night, the participants dispersed into a real Sunday, still looking feverish from the heated discussions and demonstrations of the previous day. Following the conference, I began to meet many American cybernauts, some of whom have contributed to this book.

It wasn't until 1991 that the fever reached Japan in earnest. However, in the previous year, the exhibition for new computer human interfaces in Tokyo presented demonstrations using a head-mounted display, data gloves, and a data suit developed by VPL Research.

JAPAN'S CYBERNAUTS

As in the futuristic cityscape in the movie *Blade Runner* and Chiba City in William Gibson's *Neuromancer*, a smell of Japan hangs in the air of cyberculture. Although Gibson has said he was not conscious of imitating Japanese, he invented Japanese-sounding words in his pioneering cyberpunk writings; at Cyberthon, there were graphics that reminded me of the Japanese cartoon "Gundam," with strange Japanese-like characters in a calligraphic form. I wonder why there is a glimpse of the Far East in these premonitions of the yet unseen world of cyberspace.

Although no Japanese products were exhibited at Cyberthon, Japanese cybernauts have been opening up their worlds steadily. Susumu Tachi, for example, created for the Ministry of International Trade and Industry a remote-control robot that operates under extreme conditions of temperature and stress. Tachi had previously been developing prosthetic devices for physically challenged people, and did research in rehabilitation engineering at MIT. Tachi gave the name "tele-existence" to the sensation of perceiving another place by sending a robot as your clone, connecting the robot's senses and those of its operators by telecommunication.

Tachi, whom I met at a presentation of the Robotic Society of Japan, showed me a video of a humanoid robot that was developed at his lab. The user manipulates the robot by remote control, while wearing an HMD whose video display is produced by camera eyes on the robot. The robot imitates the operator's action in detail. To me, the robot almost seemed human; the distant world that it saw and heard seemed awfully familiar through my eyes and ears.

Researchers have suggested we develop more advanced humanoid robots that can travel through space and upload their experience into humans. Some, such as Hans Moravec of Carnegie Mellon University, suggest that we could even download our psyches from our real bodies into robots, thus ridding ourselves of flesh to achieve immortality. Robotic research will continue to break the human limits on space and time, and will ultimately challenge our ideas of what it means to be human.

I visited Hiroo Iwata's laboratory at Tsukuba University. Iwata had written a paper on virtual reality for *Nikkei CG* magazine and has been studying this field extensively. Iwata showed me a force-feedback device in which the user wears a mechanical hand and arm. When he or she grabs an object in a virtual display, motors in the machine activate to simulate the hardness of the object.

Simulating an object's hardness was also achieved by Makoto Sato of Tokyo Institute of Technology with a device called SPIDAR, which shapes objects with wires. I experimented with a virtual potter's wheel that can manipulate a pot drawn on a computer system. This system was originally made for one-hand use, but was later developed for both hands. This research on virtual force is receiving quite a lot of attention.

In another laboratory, Iwata had an HMD that employed displays from Sony's liquid crystal TV and was used in a virtual walkthrough demonstration. Most large VR systems are image based with no whole-body movement involved. However, his system changes the landscape as you walk, and can add resistance until you even experience moderate fatigue. On top of that, Iwata built a force-feedback system for the legs by attaching wires to a leg harness. The wires pull on the legs when the user climbs a virtual stairway. This system has been extended and developed into a larger system, combined with a force-feedback system for the arms, as part of project to test the comfort of houses using virtual layouts.

Takemochi Ishii recently changed the focus of his studies from medical science to engineering, and is researching the intersection of these two fields. He is attempting to decipher the communication between mothers and babies by doing image-analysis of babies' facial expressions on tape. Ishii attends the government's inquiry commission frequently, and has greatly influenced the direction of Japanese technology.

Michitaka Hirose of Tokyo University researched virtual reality under L. W. Stark at the University of California at Berkeley. His papers showed more imagination than any others I had read, and he is the most promising of the young VR researchers in Japan. He is interested in the relationship between imagination and engineering; when he visited Disney's Epcot Center in Orlando in 1982, he returned overwhelmed by the fantastic image technology. His sensitivity to images and science fiction has been a driving force behind his virtual reality research.

Hirose's laboratory houses a homemade HMD and a unique force-feedback device that traces three-dimensional movement in detail. It was like a VR toy box, where one tries to avoid virtual danger zones; it seemed perfect as a new kind of a theme park program. Hirose's collaborative research with Tokyo Electricity on representing software programs and complicated processing in virtual reality is the first attempt to use virtual reality for visualization of industrial processes.

At Advanced Telecommunication Research Communication Systems Research Labs in Kansai Cultural Technology and Art City, research is being conducted by researcher Fumio Kishino on pseudo-presence communication systems, combining virtual reality with telecommunication for virtual meetings or joint work. Also, at the NTT Human Interface research lab, research is being conducted on controlling, through VR, a digital-circuit-linked robot in a distant place.

In 1991, the Japan Industry & Technology Promotion Association—a body of the Ministry of International Trade and Industry—founded the Virtual Reality and Tele-existence Research Society with members from various fields including computing, construction, machinery, and trade. In July 1991, the society held its first international conference, the International Conference on Artificial Reality and Tele-Existence, ICAT '91. The success of this initial conference led to the even larger ICAT '92 and ICAT '93.

Virtual reality is also being researched at Fujitsu, NEC, and other companies as a computer interface model, and unique results, such as imaginary creatures and a ski simulator, have been announced. Also, arcade game companies like Sega and Namco are incorporating virtual reality into entertainment, so that we can experience the sensation of motion at various game arcades in Japan. Matsushita Electronics' showroom contains the world's first practical sales application of virtual reality in its Kitchen Experience system, which allows potential customers to create and step into the virtual kitchen of their dreams. At Toyota and Fujita's showrooms, motion-sensation theaters have been installed. A few hundred Japanese theme parks use these devices.

VR'S FUTURE

As you can see, in Japan virtual reality has gone beyond fad: it is working its way into popular culture. It has drawn attention from many fields, and at the same time, has influenced those fields. I can hear the rumble of the tectonic forces that VR is bringing to bear on the world.

Technical questions have always taken precedence in the world of VR. The wonders and deep meaning that virtual reality will bring to humankind have not yet been deciphered. For that, a greater variety of people must participate and tackle the ultimate question, Reality.

I have great expectations for the future of VR. But internal strife at certain research organizations gives me a feeling of the difficulties that will occur as VR transforms from a fad into a full-fledged industry.

System and device developments occur almost daily—advances in computer speed and refinement and invention of peripherals are just matter of time. But as we try to connect VR with the human psyche and the outside world, it will become progressively more difficult to fill in the last few centimeters between VR simulations and human sensory organs. Also, developing a software to replicate our mental processes will be a major point in future.

The general audience brings to VR high expectations. They are often disappointed, partly because of a mismatch between the imprecision of VR devices and human senses. Also, we do not know the fundamental mechanisms of how humans grasp reality or how the mind works. The three-dimensional combat games that have been used to demonstrate VR are good enough to surprise a general audience, but they are not meant for sustained use.

In the future, we must put more energy into developing applications. And when virtual reality gains popularity, humanity will face a new reality with new possibilities and unexpected problems. As a mirror that reflects the human psyche faithfully, virtual reality will unleash desires and needs.

Note

This essay was adapted from the preface to *Virtual Realities: Anthology of Industry and Cultlure*, edited by Carl Eugene Loeffler, Tokyo: Gitjusu Hyoron Sha, 1993.

Katsura Hattori is a journalist specializing in new computer technology, and the author of the first book on cyberspace to be published in Japan. Internet: <hattori@pub.asahinp.co.ip>.

AN OVERVIEW OF VIRTUAL REALITY RESEARCH IN THE NORDIC COUNTRIES

Kai-Mikael Jää-Aro

While work in simulators and three-dimensional modeling software for conventional applications has a strong position in Scandinavian industry, research in and applications of virtual reality technology have remained confined to scattered work within the academic community. The recent upsurge of popular interest in virtual reality may lead to more projects and increased cooperation among projects.

DENMARK

The Department of Computer Science at Aarhus University is considering a project to build a virtual reality system using the agent-based programming paradigm developed by Yoav Shoham of Stanford University.

Also, VR is coming to the public in Denmark. W Industries has an agent in Copenhagen—Key Sales—that rents Virtuality arcade games to Scandinavian amusement establishments.

FINLAND

Tapio Takala, a professor at the Helsinki University of Technology, has worked at George Washington University with the problem of rendering sound. In an animation, sound can be generated (and thus automatically synchronized) according to physical models of the objects that cause the sound. The propagation of sound in three-dimensional space can then be computed using information about objects that surround the listener and the sound source.[1] Takala intends to continue this work at HUT and possibly extend it to other areas of virtual reality research.

NORWAY

The Center for Industrial Research/Stiftelsen for Industriteknisk forskning (SI/SINTEF) has several VR-related projects. In cooperation with

Kronprinsesse Märthas Institutt (KMI), a leading hand-surgery clinic, SI/SINTEF has designed FingerBall, a suite of video games that use a VPL DataGlove connected to a personal computer. The video games require the use and constant movement of the fingers, and thus speed recovery after hand surgery. FingerBall has been in daily use for months at a time for the rehabilitation and training of patients at KMI since January 1990.[2]

SI/SINTEF has initiated a large cooperative effort in the Nordic countries among disability-research organizations such as the Nordic Development Center for Handicap Aids (NUH), the Invalid Foundation in Finland, the Center for Rehabilitation Technology (CERTEC) in Sweden, KMI and Sunnaas Hospital in Norway, and the Danish Technology Center for the Handicapped (DATCH). Its goal is to spin off from DataGlove-based technology to aid the handicapped. Projects planned include sign-language interpretation and generation, cognitive training with VR interfaces, and home robot operation, to name just a few.

A very different project has been prompted by the needs of the Norwegian offshore oil industry. Starting in 1988, workers at the Department for Automatization at SI/SINTEF have built enhanced human-machine interfaces for remotely operated vehicles (ROVs)—submarines, in this case (see figures 24-1 and 24-2). Input to the ROV is through speech and body position, in addition to the usual keyboard and mouse interface. Feedback from the ROV is on a large video wall, where live video from the submarine is enhanced by overlays of images generated from CAD data about the structures worked upon. The video image is synchronized with the posture of the operator for increased feel of presence, and stabilized against movement through the use of pattern-recognition software.

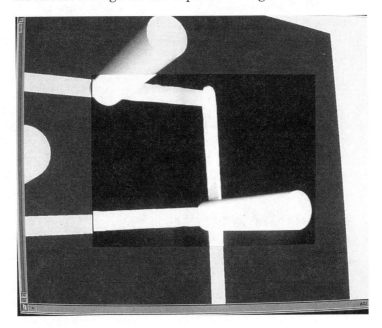

Figure 24-1. SI/SINTEF ROV-MIMIC (Multisensory integrated Man-machine interaction and Control) mock-up template with live video image in the center.
•Credit: SINTEF, 1992.

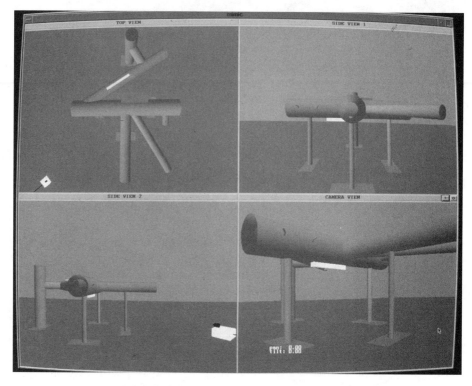

Figure 24-2. Overviews of the SI/SINTEF screen used in sea test. • Credit: SiINTEF, 1992.

SI/SINTEF has also been researching acoustic interfaces, mainly focusing on active earplugs generating sounds in counter-phase, with noise to enhance hearing in noisy environments. The research on sound-generation may impact audio spatialization.

BERGEN

Inspired by the experiments at the University of North Carolina, a small group of researchers in Bergen, Mexico, and the U.K., led and financed by Raul Lopez Almaraz, M.D., of Guadalajara, have recently initiated a project whose goal is to superimpose real-time computer-aided tomography (CAT) imagery of a patient onto semitransparent glasses worn by a surgeon, permitting a combined view of internal and external organs.

LOOKING AT USE

Morten Søby, a research fellow at the Institute of Educational Research at the University of Oslo, has started a three-year project called "Living and Learning in Electropolis: To Connect or Not to Connect Is the Question." Søby intends to study the cultural impact of advanced computer technologies, from electronic mail to virtual reality.

Børre Ludvigsen, an architect and associate professor at the Department of Computer Science at Østfold Distriktshøgskole in Halden, has studied the architecture of cyberspace and has taught courses and published articles on the subject.[3]

Kim Baumann Larsen, a former student of Ludvigsen who is now at Arkitekthøgskolen in Oslo, has plans for virtual reality extensions of constructions in extreme environments—for instance, polar research stations and underwater habitats—and intends to pursue these ideas at Sasakawa International Center for Space Architecture in Houston. He also operates the virtual reality conference on the Zirkonium bboard.

SWEDEN

Swedish virtual-worlds research is concentrated in two academic groups, one at Linköping University and one split between the Swedish Institute of Computer Science and the Royal Institute of Technology in Stockholm.

LINKÖPING

Robert Forchheimer, associate professor at the Department of Electrical Engineering at Linköping University, and his colleagues have worked on image compression since the 1970s, and since 1988 have applied their results to video teleconferencing over narrow-bandwidth communication lines.[4]

Telephone conferences lose valuable nuances of gesture and facial expressions, and even, of course, the ability merely to see who is present. On the other hand, using video systems usually requires the participants at a certain site to crowd together in front of a camera and employ special high-bandwidth communication lines for the connection.

The method developed by the Linköping group for video conferencing involves the encoding of the faces and bodies of the participants as three-dimensional geometric models. During the connection phase of a conference, the local computer unit of each participant in a conference transfers the model of that participant to the local computers of every other participant. During the conference the faces and bodies of the participants are tracked by video cameras, and image-analysis software decides what parts have moved. The changes are mapped to the geometric models, and only the changed parameters are sent to a central computer that forwards the updates to the other participants. The participants thus see computer-reconstructed polygon images of the faces of their partners.[5] The central telepresence unit, in addition to working as an exchange, also contains the description of the virtual conference setting.[6]

While the largest emphasis so far has been on the modeling of human faces,[7] in 1989 the group built a head-mounted display using camcorder viewfinders, stereo headphones and a Polhemus position sensor. They also have developed models for audio spatialization.[8]

The work in Linköping inspired the formation in 1991 of the Working Group for Virtual Reality in Teleconferencing within the program for Digital

Signal Processing Methods for Telecommunications, a research area within COST, a European research program. The COST working group intends to have biannual workshops, of which the first was held in Linköping in October 1991.[9] The Linköping project has an ongoing exchange of ideas and workers with the MultiG telepresence project in Stockholm.

STOCKHOLM

In 1990, the MultiG research program was started as an effort to lay down the infrastructure for a multigigabyte data and telecommunications network in Sweden and research basic issues related to this at all levels—from the actual optical fibers and protocols for data transmission hardware to operating systems for distributed computing and software systems enabled by high-bandwidth communication. Several Swedish academic institutions and high-technology enterprises participate in MultiG, including the Royal Institute of Technology (KTH), the Swedish Institute of Computer Science (SICS), Ericsson Telecom, Swedish Telecom, and their joint subsidiary Ellemtel Utvecklings AB.

One of the subprojects of MultiG is the TelePresence project, which began as an attempt to experiment with 3D graphics for computer supported cooperative work. Since then it has taken on a life of its own as virtual reality research, with an investigative group of about ten people led by Lennart E. Fahlén and Olof Hagsand at SICS.[10]

The main part of the group is situated at the Distributed Systems Laboratory (DSLab) at SICS, but a few workers are affiliated with the Interaction and Presentation Laboratory (IPLab) of the Department of Numerical Analysis and Computing Science (NADA) at KTH. Cooperation with several research locations in Europe, notably the Universities of Nottingham and Lancaster in the UK, has been undertaken within COMIC (Computer-Based Mechanisms of Interaction in Cooperative Work), a Basic Research Action within the ESPRIT research program of the European Community.

While independent, the MultiG subprojects work in concert. The Telepresence project has a constant exchange of goals and ideas with the Collaborative Desktop, a project aimed at more conventional two-dimensional computer-supported collaborative work (CSCW) applications and PicturePhoneTalk, an IP-based video conferencing system for workstations with local cameras. The intention is to integrate all these into a seamless 2D-within-3D environment (see color insert # 6 to # 8).

The VR system developed is called Distributed Interactive Virtual Environments, or DIVE (see figures 24-3 to 24-6). Central to DIVE is the replicated object database, which is programmed in the ISIS environment from Cornell University (though SID, or SICS Distribution, another MultiG subproject, is intended to supersede ISIS). Every process in the system thus has a copy of all objects; updates are kept consistent through the virtual synchronicity of ISIS communication. The processes can run on any machines registered as ISIS nodes; thus, computation can be split between the visualization and interaction nodes running on graphics servers and the computational nodes running on servers. Any number of processes may control the objects in a given world.[11]

Figure 24-3. DIVE, aerial view of the entrance world. The boxes contain gateways to other worlds.
• Credit: MultiG, 1992.

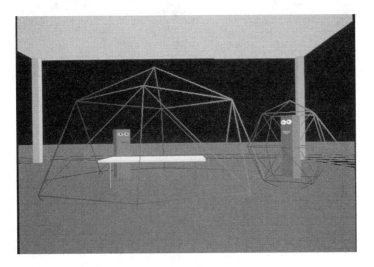

Figure 24-4. Inanimate objects may also extend an aura. Here, a new member joins a conference by entering the aura of the conference table.
• Credit: MultiG, 1992.

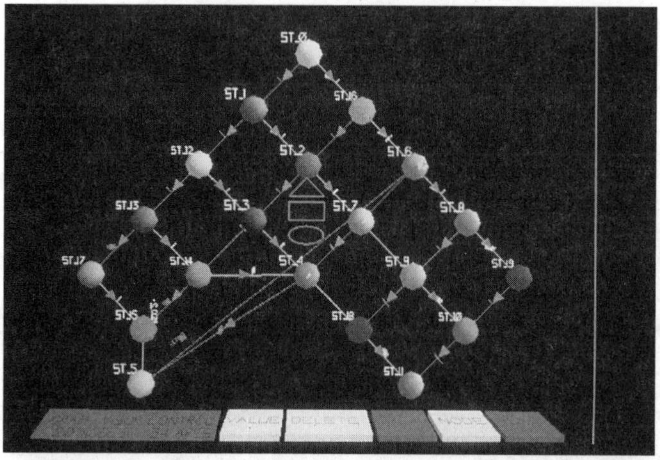

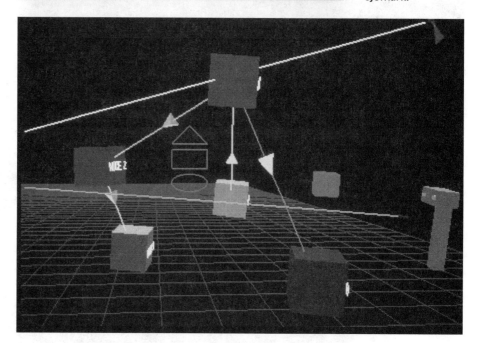

Figure 24-5. Ur2, a fantasy landscape using the DIVE system, was designed by students from the National School of Arts, Craft and Design in Stockholm.
• Credit: CarlJohan Rydell and Johan Sjömark.

Figure 24-6. Another application for the DIVE system, was designed by students from the National School of Arts, Craft and Design in Stockholm. • Credit: Lena Paulsson.

The renderers can display real-time video as well as polygon graphics. By mounting the cameras on a robot arm controlled from within the virtual environment, the participants can look around a remote real-world room. The system is explicitly meant for cooperation, and one of the main lines of investigation concerns focus, projection, and awareness in conference systems and other cooperative settings.[12] There is also a conferencing system that can support simultaneous conferences, each in its own virtual space.

The home robot control system for the mobility impaired, a subproject of the Nordic DataGlove project, is being implemented at SICS in cooperation with Handikappinstitutet (see Figure 24-7).

Other prototype applications include graphics and text processors for group access, a 3D graph editor, and a visualization system for local area networks (see figures 24-8 to 24-10).

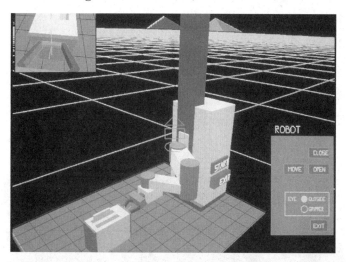

Figure 24-7. Joint project between SICS and the Swedish Handicap Institute. Small robot in the home is remotely controlled via a VR-based interface to perform everyday tasks, such as making toast.
• Credit: Magnus Andersson, SICS.

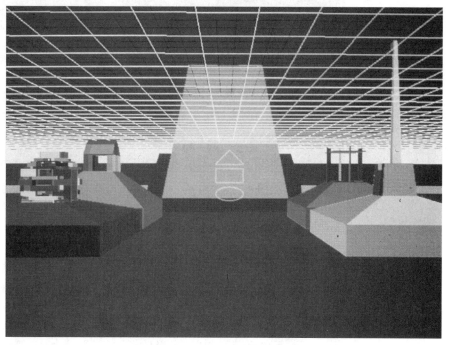

Figure 24-8. A three-dimensional graph editor, created by Rolf Staflin at SICS. The command console is at the bottom. •Credit: Rolf Staflin.

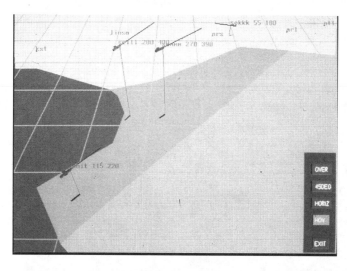

Figure 24-9. Several people can concurrently edit the graph with the rays emanating from their magic wands, a 3-D interaction tool.
• Credit: Rolf Staflin.

Figure 24-10. Net, a LAN monitoring application, designed by Kai-Mikael Jää-Aro.
• Credit: Kai-Mikael Jää-Aro, Royal Institute of Technology.

The system has to date been through-the-window (nonimmersive), with graphics displayed on ordinary graphics workstations such as Sun SPARCstations, IBM RS/6000s, and Silicon Graphics Indigos. However, one of the recent successes of the project has been the development of a lightweight, high-resolution color display based on Tektronix liquid crystal shutters (rapidly switching color filters) and small (centimeter-sized) black-and-white monitors. It is hoped that this will result in a revolutionary new head-mounted display design.[13] Reports of the work have been published in the proceedings of the semiannual MultiG workshops.[14]

LUND

The Department of Industrial Management and Working Environment at the Lund University Institute of Science and Technology is cooperating with the Center Rehabilitation Engineering (CERTEC) at Lund University and the Institute for Handicap, Work, Computers and Rehabilitation (HADAR) on using a DataGlove for user interfaces. One project, initiated by Charlotte Magnusson at CERTEC, is concerned with text input using the Swedish sign alphabet.

Other work is concerned with improving the user interface for creating three-dimensional models of working environments for planning and study purposes, a project funded by the Working Environment Fund and the Swedish Board for Industrial and Technical Development.[15]

GOTHENBURG

Johan Andersson, while a student at the Chalmers University of Technology, did his M.S. thesis work at the Human Interface Technology Laboratory of the Washington Technology Center in Seattle, Washington.[16] Using the VEOS software of HIT Lab, he implemented a prototype remote-inclusive interface for LPmud, a multi-user dimension (mud) system created by Lars Pensjö at the same institution.

The system developed by Andersson is called MIVE, for Multiply Interfaced Virtual Environment. It uses a central world server (based on LPmud, in this case) that keeps the world model consistent and handles requests by clients to access and modify objects in the world database. The players communicate with the world server via a MIVE client called the ProtoDeck. Depending on what equipment is available to the player, interaction can be either through a text interface or through the full array of immersive VR gear.

BIBLIOGRAPHY

Andersson, Jerker and Lasse Hellquist. "Telepresence, Some Aspects of the Interface." *Telepresence: A New Concept for Teleconferencing: Proceedings of the First COST #229 WG.5 Workshop*; Robert Forchheimer, ed. Conference held October 1991. Linköping, 1991.

Andersson, Johan. "Prototype Remote Inclusive Interface." *Telepresence: A New Concept for Teleconferencing: Proceedings of the First COST #229 WG.5 Workshop*; Robert Forchheimer, ed. Conference held October 1991. Linköping, 1991.

Andersson, Johan. "MIVE: Multi-interfaced Virtual Environments [Virtuella Omgivningar: Simuler ing och Gränssnittsmöjligheter]." Master's thesis, Chalmers University of Technology, 1992.

Bajura, Michael, Henry Fuchs, and Ryutarou Ohbuchi. *Merging Virtual Reality with the Real World: Seeing Ultrasound Imagery within the Patient*. Chapel Hill, N.C.: Computer Science Department, University of North Carolina, Chapel Hill, 1992. Technical Report TR92-005.

Bogdanski, Jan. "Color Helmet Mounted Display." *Proceedings from the 4th MultiG Workshop*; Björn Pehrson, ed. Conference held May 1992 at Stockholm. Stockholm, 1992: 89-96.

Brooks, Martin. "The DataGlove as a Man-Machine Interface for Robotics." *Second IARP Workshop on Medical and Healthcare Robotics*, September 1989: 213-225.

Edgren, Bent. "Modellering av tillverkningssystem i dator." Summary 1434, Arbetsmiljöfonden, March 1991. (In Swedish)

Eriksson, Joakim, G. I. Johansson, and K. R. Akselsson. "Participative Environment Planning for the Physically Disabled Using Computer-Aided Design." *3rd International Conference on Computers for Handicapped Persons*, July 1992: 150-156.

Fahlén, Lennart E. "Issues in Telepresence." *Proceedings from the 2nd MultiG Workshop*; Björn Pehrson and Yngve Sundblad, eds. Conference held June 1991 at Stockholm. Stockholm, 1991: 31-41.

Fahlén, Lennart E. "The MultiG TelePresence System." *Proceedings from the 3rd MultiG Workshop;* Yngve Sundblad, ed. Conference held December 1991 at Stockholm. Stockholm, 1991: 33-57.

Fahlén, Lennart E., and Charles Brown. "Use of a 3D Aura Metaphor for Computer Based Conferencing and Teleworking." *Proceedings from the 4th MultiG Workshop*; Björn Pehrson, ed. Conference held May 1992 at Stockholm. Stockholm, 1992: 69-74.

Fahlén, Lennart E., and Olof Hagsand. "The SICS TelePresence System." *Telepresence: A New Concept for Teleconferencing: Proceedings of the*

First COST #229 WG.5 Workshop; Robert Forchheimer, ed. Conference held October 1991. Linköping, 1991.

Forchheimer, Robert, ed. *Telepresence: A New Concept for Teleconferencing: Proceedings of the First COST #229 WG.5* Workshop. Conference held October 1991. Linköping; 1991.

Forchheimer, Robert and Torbjörn Kronander. "Image Coding: from Waveforms to Animation." *IEEE Transactions on ASSP*, December 1989 37(12).

Hägglund, Per. "Användning av Datahandsken för Navigering i en Enkel 3D-miljö." Master's thesis, Royal Institute of Technology, 1989. (In Swedish).

Hagsand, Olof. "Consistency and Concurrency Control in Distributed Virtual Worlds." *Proceedings from the 2nd MultiG Workshop*; Björn Pehrson and Yngve Sundblad, eds. Conference held June 1991 at Stockholm. Stockholm, 1991: 43-56.

Jää-Aro, Kai-Mikael. "The X-ray Factory: Some Experiments with Three-dimensional, Iconic Control Displays." *Proceedings from the 3rd MultiG Workshop*; Yngve Sundblad, ed. Conference held December 1991 at Stockholm. Stockholm, 1991: 59-67.

Jää-Aro, Kai-Mikael. *Tankathon: A Process Plant Simulation*. Stockholm: IPLab-52, MultiG-6, Royal Institute of Technology, 1992. Technical Report TRITA-NA-P9207.

Johansson, Curt R., Roland Akselsson, and Jonas af Klercker. "Dynamisk Beskrivning med Datorstödd Bild." Summary 1495, Arbetsmiljöfonden, May 1992. (In Swedish.)

Kvarnström, Bengt. "Telepresence: A Proposal for Communication between Humans." *Telepresence—A New Concept for Teleconferencing: Proceedings of the First COST #229 WG.5 Workshop*; Robert Forchheimer, ed. Conference held October 1991. Linköping, 1991.

Lee, Haibo, Pertti Roivainen, and Robert Forchheimer. "Analysis/Synthesis of Human Facial Movements." *Telepresence: A New Concept for Teleconferencing: Proceedings of the First COST #229 WG.5 Workshop*; Robert Forchheimer, ed. Conference held October 1991. Linköping; 1991.

Linderhed, Anna. *Algorithms for Three-dimensional Sounds*. Linköping: Linköping University, 1991. Technical Report LiTH-ISY-EX-0954. (In Swedish).

Ludvigsen, Børre. "Content and Context in the Architecture of Cyberspace." Norwegian Informatics Conference; November 1992, Norway.

Ludvigsen, Børre. "Presence and Form in the Architecture of Cyberspace." Norwegian AI Magazine, 1992.

Øderud, Tone and Eivind Kjennerud. "Man-Machine Interactions Applied to ROV Operations."

Pehrson, Björn, ed. *Proceedings from the 1st MultiG Workshop*. Conference held November 1990 at Stockholm. Stockholm, 1990.

Pehrson, Björn, ed. *Proceedings from the 4th MultiG Workshop*. Conference held May 1992 at Stockholm. Stockholm, 1992.

Pehrson, Björn, and Yngve Sundblad, eds. *Proceedings from the 2nd MultiG Workshop*. Conference held June 1991 at Stockholm. Stockholm, 1991.

Roivainen, Pertti. "Motion Estimation in Model-Based Coding of Human Faces." Licentiate thesis LIU-TEK-LIC-1990:25, Department of Electrical Engineering, Linköping University, 1990.

Rydfalk, M. *CANDIDE*: *A Parameterized Face*. Technical Report LiTH-ISY-I-0866, Department of Electrical Engineering, Linköping University, 1987.

Skjørten, Ariel and Martin Brooks. "FingerBall: A Hand Rehabilitation Activity Based on the DataGlove."

Ståhl, Olov. "Tools for Cooperative Work in the MultiG TelePresence Environment." *Proceedings from the 4th MultiG workshop*; Björn Pehrson, ed. Conference held May 1992 at Stockholm. Stockholm, 1992: 75-88.

Sundblad, Yngve, ed. *Proceedings from the 3rd MultiG Workshop*. Conference held December 1991 at Stockholm. Stockholm, 1991.

Takala, Tapio, and James Hahn. "Sound Rendering." *Computer Graphics*. July 1992, 26(2): 211-219.

Mats Werke. "Virtual Reality: en Förstudie." Overview IVF 92809, Institutet för verkstadsteknisk forskning, 1992. (In Swedish).

REFERENCES

1. Takala and Hahn, "Sound Rendering."

2. Skjørten and Brooks, "FingerBall," and Brooks, "The DataGlove as a Man-Machine Interface for Robotics."

3. Ludvigsen, "Content and Context in the Architecture of Cyberspace," and "Presence and Form in the Architecture of Cyberspace."

4. Forchheimer and Kronander, "Image Coding."

5. Roivainen, "Motion Estimation in Model-based Coding of Human Faces."

6. Kvarnström, "Telepresence: A Proposal for Communication between Humans."

7. Lee, Roivainen, and Forchheimer, "Analysis/Synthesis of Human Facial Movements."

8. Linderhed, *Algorithms for Three-Dimensional Sounds*.

9. Forchheimer, ed., *Telepresence: Proceedings of the First COST #229 WG.5 Workshop*.

10. Fahlén, "Issues in Telepresence," and "The MultiG TelePresence System"; also Fahlén and Hagsand, "The SICS TelePresence System."

11. Hagsand, "Consistency and Concurrency Control in Distributed Virtual Worlds."

12. Fahlén and Brown, "Use of a 3D Aura Metaphor."

13. Bogdanski, "Color Helmet Mounted Display."

14. Pehrson, ed., *Proceedings from the 1st MultiG Workshop, and Proceedings from the 4th MultiG Workshop*; Pehrson and Sundblad, eds., *Proceedings from the 2nd MultiG Workshop*; and Sundblad, ed., *Proceedings from the 3rd MultiG Workshop*.

15. Edgren, "Modellering av Tillverkningssystem i Dator," and Eriksson, Johansson, and Akselsson, "Participative Environment Planning for the Physically Disabled Using Computer-Aided Design."

16. Johan Andersson, "Prototype Remote Inclusive Interface," and "MIVE: Multi-interfaced Virtual Environments."

Kai-Mikael Jää-Aro is a doctoral student at the Interaction and Presentation Laboratory, Department of Numerical Analysis and Computing Science, Royal Institute of Technology, S-100 44 Stockholm, Sweden. Internet: <kai@nada.kth.se>.

WE CONTINUE SEARCHING: VIRTUAL REALITY RESEARCH IN GERMANY

Tom Sperlich

For the superficial observer, at least, it often seems that though virtual reality is a frequent topic in international media reports, most research occurs in the United States. But how real is cyberspace in Germany? What is going on there? What projects exist, beyond the one or two demonstration projects? There is much activity in German cyberspace: At present there are at least ten institutes and companies at which researchers explore virtual worlds.

THE "EYEFLY" AT ART + COM

Let us begin our alphabetical survey with Art + Com, the Center for Computer-supported Design and Presentation, located in Berlin. The objective of the nonprofit private research institute is to provide professional working conditions for architects, designers, film experts, graphic designers, and musicians.

In Art + Com's *Cyber City Flights*, users can take a virtual walk through Berlin. You can stroll through the city two dimensionally—as you move a sensor along the streets of an aerial photo of the district, models of the streets are projected on a screen. Or you can immerse yourself in the simulation using a DataGlove and an EyePhone HMD. The quality of the graphics, rendered on Silicon Graphics workstations, is high. Art + Com has linked a high-quality renderer into VPL's system, which enhances the models with realistic lighting, improving depth perception. Multimedia events within the virtual worlds, like the input of video clips from a laserdisc, are triggered when a virtual object is touched. The images—for instance, historical film sequences—are mapped on or around a polygon as real-time texture. *Cyber City Flights* is a project sponsored by Detecon, a consulting company of the German telephone company Telekom. Since the reunification of the divided country in 1989, Berlin has again become the capital of Germany, and large parts of the city are being developed. This provides a good opportunity for an advanced simulation technique like virtual reality to prove its aptitude for city planning and architecture.

The researchers at Art + Com have two central concerns: the development of immaterial interfaces between man and machine, and the search for a specific media language for virtual reality computing. "We don't want to copy reality," says German artist Joachim Sauter, "that is in any case only feasible in a very limited way, because reality has eighty million polygons per second. But the new technical media demand a new media language if they are to be maintained as specific, independent artistic media. In the field of virtual reality we are still where the movies were at the time of the brothers Lumière. But we continue searching...."

Art + Com also continues to search for the definitive virtual interface. DataGlove and EyePhone are employed increasingly less often, not only because of stagnating quality. Are *eye tracking* and *biofeedback* the magic words of the new media language? *Der Zerseher* (translated by Art + Com as *The Iconoclast*), a prize-winning installation by Sauter shown at the international annual art congress Ars Electronica in Linz, Austria, provides an interesting example for Art + Com's eye-tracking application EyeFly. In *Der Zerseher*, the image reacts to the view of the beholder and starts to crumble apart exactly at the point where the viewer focuses. Normally, the image leaves an impression on the viewer; here, the observer leaves an impact on the image. The reaction of the image is triggered by view-detection technology. The video camera built into the image detects where the computer has to interrupt the pixel arrangement, which is restored after thirty seconds if the viewer does not look there anymore. Subsequently, Art + Com began employing aspects of eye-tracking technology.

TELEROBOTICS FOR SPACE

The scientists of the German Aerospace Research Establishment (DLR) are in completely different new worlds . In the framework of virtual reality technologies, the scientists of the Institute for Robotics and System Dynamics in Oberpfaffenhofen near Munich work for the DLR telepresence project ROTEX (Space Robot Technology Experiment).

Telerobotics, a new technology for supporting costly operations in space, hitherto seemed to be the domain of NASA, known among practitioners as a cradle of VR technology. But the DLR, in cooperation with several other German companies and institutions, surpassed NASA in plans to send the first telerobot into space. ROTEX, under development since 1985, is scheduled for tests on board the second German Space Lab Mission this year.

In order to proceed with further exploration of space, all nations must to decrease its cost. In the future, therefore, robots and telepresence systems will undertake extensive work in space, including assembly, repair, and service tasks, carrying out experiments and production processes, as well as the management of "space junk."

The virtual world of the ROTEX interface is an interactive, stereoscopic 3D computer graphic installed on a Silicon Graphics workstation. The screen is viewed through glasses that, in combination with the stereo picture on the monitor, provide a 3D image. These shutter glasses are employed from the ground station as well as by the astronauts on board the space lab to control the experiments of the space robots with the help of a special control ball. With this six-axis hand controller ball, the gross control of the manipulator arm of ROTEX can be performed by the ground station or the space lab. The movement around the six axes is converted into rotation and translated in three-dimensional space. Today, control balls of this kind are increasingly employed in VR systems, especially in three-dimensional CAD/CAM applications—they have literally become "Spaceballs" (one of the brand names).

Online teleoperation of the robot and offline programming on the ground is done by simulation in the three-dimensional model. Gerhard Hirzinger, the head of the institute, says, "We merely program the gross robot positions and the simulated sensor patterns. At the end, the robot itself undertakes the 'fine work,' via a unique sensor feedback/feedforward system that is built into the complex DLR gripper." Hirzinger also sees a terrestrial benefit: "It is an acknowledged goal of space robotics to provide new, intelligent sensors and gripper systems for industrial applications."

ROBOT CONTROL AT THE IPA

A similar objective is shared by the Fraunhofer Institute for Production Technology and Automation (IPA), located in Stuttgart. In the spring of 1992, the IPA presented VR4RobotS (Virtual Reality for Robot Systems) at the worlds' largest computer fair, CeBIT, in Hannover, Germany. VR4RobotS is an application for the simulation, control, and programming of an industry robot. The IPA employs explicit VR technology—researchers there are working with EyePhone and DataGlove, as well as with software from VPL. If the user moves his or her hand in the glove controller, the robot receives the required path data directly, and thus the gripper is forced to corresponding actions. The Spaceball serves only to move the user's viewpoint through the virtual space.

Further basic research areas at the IPA concerning VR technologies are rapid prototyping and simultaneous engineering, which are intended to minimize costs by reducing product-introduction times. To allow broader user circles to benefit from their findings, various Fraunhofer Institutes will establish demonstration centers for virtual reality in their respective cities. The institutes (IPA jointly with the IAO and the Institute for Building Physics; the other demonstration center will be at the IGD) are going to set up a showroom where developers and users can learn about the latest technology. These locations will also conduct independent hardware and software evaluations and training seminars, and will provide consultation concerning specific development of applications.

THE IAO: Planning with Different Methods

At the Fraunhofer Institute for Industrial Engineering (IAO), research and development focus on application: room and office planning, architecture and building planning, and ergonomic product design (see figure 25-1). Here, scientists work on one of the most powerful VR computers, a Silicon Graphics SkyWriter (with four RISC-based CPUs and two graphic pipelines) running hardware and software from VPL. A staff of eleven develops ambitious applications, says the head of the VR team, engineer Oliver Riedel: "At the moment, for instance, we are optimizing a radiosity method with which one can simulate realistic lighting situations in rooms. But we are interested in all areas that are involved in VR technology. So, a psychologist at our institute is engaged with psychological/somatical problems [known as 'lock-problems'] that can occur while using VR."

Recently, the IAO has gone beyond pure research. A technology center for virtual reality is being set up that interested companies can join. In addition, work is underway on explicit applications jointly with the experienced scientists of the IAO. This recently resulted, for example, in a program to interactively simulate the design of an entire office in virtual space. With one of the members of the consortium, a German office-furniture company, the application was successfully presented in Cologne at Orgatec, one of the largest international office fairs.

Figure 25-1. Architectural model at the Fraunhofer Institute for Industrial Engineering.
• Credit: Tom Sperlich, 1992.

VIRTUAL RHYTHMS IN DARMSTADT

At the Fraunhofer Institute for Computer Graphics in Darmstadt, the scientists developed their own VR interface. With help from the nonprofit research institute Computer Graphics Center (ZGDV) and the Interactive Graphic Systems Group of the Technical University Darmstadt (THD-GRIS), they have developed the only existing German VR software. About 120 scientists are teaching and doing research in-house. They are developing a variety of applications, in areas such as visualization, multimedia interaction technologies, and integration solutions, particularly for documentation and publication applications, including prepress and reproduction techniques.

A three-dimensional toolkit named GIVEN (Gesturebased Interaction In Virtual ENvironments) has been developed at the ZGDV Media & Vision lab to simplify work in 3D environments. "The available input devices like DataGlove and Spaceball show deficits in handling and feedback, and therefore they must be improved," says Wolfgang Huebner, head of the VR project at the ZGDV.

This judgment may already be obsolete, however, because the latest development concerning 3D input devices is the introduction of a new mouse, from the DLR, one of the inventors of the six-axis control ball technology (CIS GeoBall). The scientists of the Institute for Robotics and System Dynamics showed their Space Mouse (see figure 25-2) at the SYSTEC fair in Munich in October 1992. The Space Mouse combines the conventional 2D

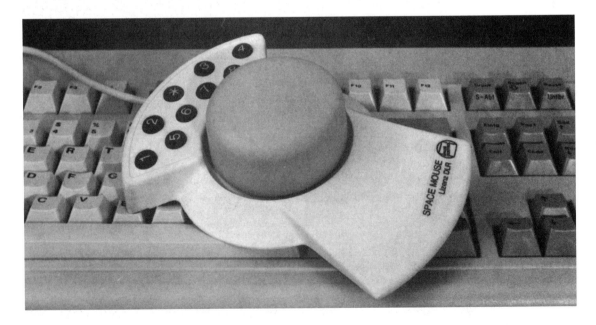

Figure 25-2. Space Mouse, Institute for Robotics and System Dynamics. • Credit: Institute for Robotics and System Dynamics, 1992.

mouse functions with comfortable 3D functions, and is different from other available 3D input devices. The instrument resembles a Geo/Space-Ball, where the hand now rests on a cap and slight finger-pressure is sufficient to grasp a 3D graphical object, or to fly through virtual space.

The IGD's Department of Simulation and Visualisation, headed by Martin Goebel, controls its VR applications with the more common Spaceballs and DataGloves. With the latter, users can already interact in astonishing ways in artificial worlds. With IGD's VR software (running on diverse Silicon Graphics workstations), researchers have constructed a virtual building in which users can go to different rooms via a graphical menu designed like an elevator. In one room you can play "cyberdrums" with your gloved hand (see figure 25-3). "The acoustic feedback, which we generate with the help of our AudioServer, we call sonification," explains Goebel. It can also be understood as the transformation of scientific data into tones. "In virtual space, one also has to serve the users' sense of hearing, to synchronize the visual impressions with the acoustic. This we call sound rendering."

The IGD has also developed a 3D puzzle with acoustical feedback functions (see figure 25-4) that is used for the development of new instruments for planning in very tight spaces. One of several other interesting applications is a virtual potter's wheel for simulation of direct surface modeling.

Figure 25-3. Virtual drums, Institute for Computer Graphics (IGD). • Credit: IGD, 1992.

Figure 25-4. 3-D puzzle, Institute for Computer Graphics (IGD). • Credit: IGD, 1992.

According to Goebel, the IGD will never research military applications; future work will instead concentrate on the social and ethical implications of VR technology.

VR FOR SHOOT-OUTS IN MAINZ

Not far from Darmstadt, in Mainz, one can find Germany's first VR entertainment system, Loewenplay, located in a busy shopping area. In many countries, people already play the system Virtuality from the British manufacturer W Industries. In Mainz, a three-minute shootout in cyberspace costs two dollars. Despite its commercial success to this point, W Industries has not provided its systems with a matching software design. While the equipment is almost overstyled externally, the virtual worlds are simple. "Quite satisfied," however, are the managers of Loewenplay, who say they haven't had any complaints yet. A problem for the managers, though, is the law prohibiting cyberenthusiasts under eighteen years of age from entering the arcade. Maybe this is one reason that the hobby cybernauts are not waiting in long lines, as is the case when the Phillip Morris promotion team sets up their mobile version of W Industries' VR system.

DISAPPOINTING GRAPHICS FOR CIGARETTE PROMOTION

Active in Germany with almost everything that can be linked to future topics, Phillip Morris has toured with cyberspace equipment since 1991 and has attracted much attention, since they have been the first in the country to show working cyberspace equipment. But most of the people trying the Virtuality system, by W Industries, have been disappointed with cyberspace. Almost every video game five years ago looked more realistic than this simple world. A Phillip Morris slogan proclaims: "Cyberspace—take your brain to nowhere," and when the tour began you really did have to deposit your brain at the entrance to believe that "the artificial reality is hardly discernible form the real one," as asserted by a press release. Although the program has been improved since its first release, the essential problem remains: these virtual worlds look cartoonlike.

However, graphics performance is a matter of the computing power of the hardware and the available budget, and the Virtuality machines are at the low end in both. The overall concept of W Industries is on target, and in the long run, the entertainment industry certainly will be one of the major players in the VR trade.

TEXTURE-MAPPING WITH THE WORLDTOOLKIT IN HAMBURG

One of the first companies in the VR trade was the California company Sense8, which employs design aids for visually appealing environments—especially for low-cost VR systems on a PC base. The company's WorldToolKit software offers texture mapping, in which digitized images of surfaces, structures, or objects are mapped around polygons in the model, allowing for more lifelike graphics. "Textures need more computing power than ordinary shaded polygons, but, reasonably employed, they can substitute for a large number of [complex] polygons. Therefore, [they] provide an enhanced realism," explains Martin Weidt, VR programmer with the Hamburg company Megabrain, which is distributing Sense8's WorldToolKit and is the first purely commercial distribution company for VR tools in Germany.

HOLO-OPTICS IN MUNICH

The objective of the company VIERTE ART in Munich is to propel the transition from two-dimensional to three-dimensional display methods and media. Since 1987, VIERTE ART has provided services for high-end computer animation; the company works under the general term "information design" in the areas of industrial design, film, user interfacing, multimedia, three-dimensional animation, system design, and consulting. Founder and CEO Olaf E.

Schirm says, "We are continually developing new ways to support our customers with their ideas and product conceptions. We work on the generation of a total illusion, but always in regard to the usefulness for the customer."

Seeking the ultimate illusion, VIERTE ART is optimizing holo-optics (stereoscopic 3D viewing of print, slide, video, and film), and offers an image with intense full-screen resolution. For instance, users can display computer animation fully 3D on any regular television with the help of the TV spacer, which employs shutter glasses and a regular VHS cassette. Says Schirm, "Now we work on software and hardware for 3D multimedia applications. Here, besides holo-optic perception, interaction is also possible." Schirm works with the specialist for information design at VIERTE ART and the industrial designer Lenz Lampertsdoerfer to develop concepts for projects that will lead to virtual realities. "At the moment, we are working on a housing vision system, which will be employed in the interior architecture area and in which holo-optics plays a significant role," explains Lampertsdoerfer.

"The main focus of research at VIERTE ART," says Schirm, "is the direction we call mixed reality, or MR. With that, the really occurring outside world of the user is enhanced with objects or presentations of information, which are being produced by VR technology. Thus it will be possible to generate some real objects without physical presence and to distribute, use, and own them."

These designers see mixed reality as an objective that can be reached in the short range, and they want to transform their ideas through projects from the industry and the entertainment trade. Lampertsdoerfer explains, "We also want to show that VR developed an internal dynamic in the laboratories that is hard to employ in industry. The decisive mistake was made, too, to favor the application over the needs of the user. VR users look clumsy and inelegant [as they try to maneuver]. One gets the feeling inside the virtual world that even the simplest things like grabbing and pointing have to be learned anew, and, fatigued, one wants to stop after ten minutes. We will supply the user of VR/MR with abilities and a user interface, which secure him or her a clear advantage compared with the previous interactions."

Furthermore, VIERTE ART founded a discussion platform, the Cybercafé. This forum serves as a medium for exchanging expert information and speculative opinions about the entire area of cyberspace. In its existing form, the Cybercafé is a mailbox with links to some networks, though it is hoped that the development of the Cybercafé might lead to a real café with VR terminals.

UNCOMMON REALITY IN KARLSRUHE

To establish a link between arts and new media technologies, like multimedia, virtual reality, computer animation, and so forth, is the base for the activities of the Center for Art and Media Technology in Karlsruhe (ZKM). At the moment ZKM is still provisionally accommodated in different places; by 1996, work will be completed on a hall that will house all the institutes of the ZKM. These include the Institute for Image Media, the Institute for Music and Acoustics, the Media Museum, the Museum of Contemporary Art, the Media Theater, and the Mediathek. Many artists will produce new works with the most modern media technologies, and present them in the new location.

Uncommon people work here, with uncommon ideas, employing uncommon aids—for instance, a flight simulator. A focus of the work of the Institute for Image Media will be in the area of simulation and interaction, says the head of the institute, the Australian interactive-computer-graphics artist Jeffrey Shaw. Shaw explains that the flight simulator "gives us new, very radical, and direct possibilities to communicate with the spectator. We send movement directly through his or her body," he says, "and thus we can tie the viewer to the installation more directly than it was possible ever before. This topic, to let the spectator interact with the art work via his movement, has engaged me for years" (see figures 8-2 to 8-6).

The *Legible City* installation is another example: the user sits on a stationary bicycle and simulates a ride through a virtual, three-dimensional urban space (see figure 8-1). The architecture of the actual cities of Manhattan, Amsterdam, and Karlsruhe is displayed as letters and words that can be read as text as the user "rides" through. The text consists of either story lines by fictional citizens or quotes from existing people of public interest, historical accounts relating to the city, or promotional text from contemporary tourist brochures. Says Shaw: "Choosing the path one takes is a choice of certain texts and their spontaneous juxtapositions. The identity of these new cities thus becomes the conjunction of the meanings these words generate, as one travels freely around in the virtual space."

For this and other artistic applications, several Silicon Graphic workstations are being used at the Institute for Image Media. Recently, special VR-software from the University of North Carolina at Chapel Hill has been installed on them. The computer science department of UNC has an almost legendary repute amongst experts. UNC scientists have been investigating virtual realities since the 1960s, and are in the forefront in the development of hardware.

The growing collaboration between this high-end American laboratory and the ZKM gives rise to the question whether Karlsruhe is going to become a Swabian Silicon Valley, or a German version of the famous Media Lab at the Massachusetts Institute of Technology. Jeffrey Shaw smiles and says, "Unfortunately, we don't have as much money available as the Americans have. We are also doing research in the artistic, not in the commercial field. We want to maintain our independence, and also I don't want to come into any situation where the industrial sponsors decide about our work. But on the other hand, it would be rather important for the development of Europe's technology if initiatives like the ZKM were better subsidized, in order to better face the strain from Japan, for instance."

Not only in Germany can one start from this assumption—for the Japanese economic power is already massively engaged in virtual reality technologies. The Japanese realize that these are key technologies for the world of tomorrow. In any case, there have already been significant developments in Germany that can stand up to any international comparison.

SELECTED BIBLIOGRAPHY

Art + Com, Berlin

Krueger, W. "Volume Rendering and Data Feature Enhancement." 1990 Workshop on Volume Visualization, conference held December 10-11, 1990 at San Diego, Calif., *Computer Graphics*. November 1990; 24(5): 21-6.

Paulousek, P. "The Project 'Centre for Multimedia Telecommunication.'" *Informatik Spektrum*; 14(5) October 1991: 291-5. (In German).

German Aerospace Research Establishment (DLR), Oberpfaffenhofen

Hirzinger, G. "Sensory Feedback in Robotics: State-of-the-art in Research and Industry. *Automatic Control—World Congress, 1987. Selected Papers from the 10th Triennial World Congress of the International Federation of Automatic Control*, R. Isermann, ed. Conference held July 27-31, 1987, at Munich. Oxford, Eng.: Pergamon, 193-206.

Hirzinger, G., J. Dietrich, and B. Brunner. "Multisensory Telerobotic Concepts." *Intelligent Motion Control. Proceedings of the IEEE International Workshop*, O. Kaynak, ed. Conference held August 20-22, 1990 at Istanbul, Turkey. New York: IEEE; 1990: SL43-53 vol. 1.

Hirzinger, G., J. Heindl, and K. Landzettel. "Predictive and Knowledge-Based Telerobotic Control Concepts." *Proceedings. 1989 IEEE International Conference on Robotics and Automation*. Conference held May 14-19, 1989 at Scottsdale, Ariz. Washington, D.C.: IEEE Computer Society Press, 1989: 1768-77 vol. 3.

Sanchez, V.D., Sr., and G. Hirzinger. "Real-time Polyhedra Localization in 3D Space." *Applications of Transputers 3. Proceedings of the Third International Conference on Applications of Transputers*, T. S. Durrani, et al., eds. Conference held August 28-30, 1991, at Glasgow, Scotland. Amsterdam, The Netherlands: IOS, 1991: 295-300.

Skofteland, G., and G. Hirzinger. "Computing Position and Orientation of Free-flying Polyhedron from 3D Data." *Proceedings. 1991 IEEE International Conference on Robotics and Automation*. Conference held April 9-11, 1991, at Sacramento, Calif. Los Alamitos, Calif.: IEEE Computer Society Press, 1991: 150-5 vol.1.

Fraunhofer-Institut für Produktionstech und Automatisierung (Institute for Manufacturing Engineering and Automation) IPA, Stuttgart

Flaig, T. "Einsatz von Transputersystemen zur Simulation und Steuerung von Industrierobotern." *IPA/IAO Forum Virtual Reality 93*; Stuttgart, Germany.

Goebel, Martin. "Virtuelle, Realität: Technologie und Anwendungen." *Multimedia und Imageprozessing*, L. Nastansky, ed. AIT Verlag, 1992.

Neugebauer, J. G. "Virtual Reality Applied to Industry." *Imagina 93*, Conference held 1993 at Monte Carlo.

Neugebauer, J. G. "Virtual Reality: The Demonstration Centre." *Virtual Reality 93*. Conference held 1993. London, 1993.

Neugebauer, J. G., and W. M. Strommer. "Virtual Reality Applied to Industrial Robot Control and Simulation." *Automation 92*. Conference held 1992 at Genoa, Italy.

Schraft, R. D., W. M. Strommer, and J. G. Neugebauer. "A Virtual Reality Testbed for Robot Applications." *International Symposium for Industrial Robots (ISIR 92)*. Conference held 1992 at Barcelona, Spain.

Strommer, W. M., and J. G. Neugebauer. "Robot Simulation with Virtual Reality." *ESA Workshop on Simulators for the European Space Programmes*. Conference held 1992 at ESTEC, Noordwijk, Netherlands.

Strommer, W. M., J. G. Neugebauer, and T. Flaig. "Transputerbased Virtual Reality Workstation." *Informatique '92. International Conference. Interface to Real and Virtual Worlds*. Conference held March 23, 1992, at Montpellier, France. Nanterre, France: EC2, 1992.

Schraft, R. D., W. M. Strommer, and J. G. Neugebauer. "Virtual Reality Applied to Industrial Robots." *Informatique '92. International Conference Interface to Real and Virtual Worlds*. Conference held March 23, 1992, at Montpellier, France. Nanterre, France: EC2, 1992: 297-307.

Fraunhofer-Institut für Arbeitswirtschaft und Organisation (Institute for Industrial Engineering) IAO, Stuttgart

Bauer, W. "VODIS: Virtual Office Design, ein Konzept für die Ganzheltllche Bürogestaltung." *Forschung und Praxis*, H. J. Warnecke and H. J. Bullinger, eds.1993, T 35: 281-297.

Bauer, W., H. J. Bullinger, and O. Riedel. "Virtual Reality as a Tool for Office Design Applications: Visions and Realities." *HCI International '93*. Conference held 1993 at Orlando, Fla.

Bauer, W., and O. Riedel. *Der Blick in eine Faszinierende Künstliche Welt*. Stuttgart: Fraunhofer Institut für Arbeitswirtschaft und Organisation IAO, 1993. Technical Report 15/93.

Bauer, W., and O. Riedel. "New Techniques for Interaction in Virtual Worlds: Development and Examples." *HCI International '93*. Conference held 1993 at Orlando, FL.

Bauer, W., and O. Riedel. "VILAGE: Virtueller Layoutgestalter." *Forschung und Praxis*, H. J. Warnecke and H. J. Bullinger, eds. 1993, T 35: 47-59.

Bauer, W., and O. Riedel. "Virtual Reality Design in Office Workplaces." ICPR '93; conference held 1993 at Lappeenranta.

Bauer, W., and O. Riedel. "Virtuelle Realität als Werkzeug für die Bürogestaltung." *Office Design*. 1992: 36-41.

Degenhart, E., J. Neugebauer, and M. Wapler. "VR4RobotS: Virtual Reality for Robot Systems." In *IPA/IAO Forum Virtual Reality '93*. Conference held 1993 at Stuttgart.

Herrmann, G., and O. Riedel. "VIRUSI: Virtual User Interface— Iconorlentierte Benutzerschnittstelle für VR-Applikationen." *Forschung und Praxis*, H. J. Warnecke and H. J. Bullinger, H. J., eds. 1993, T 35: 227-243.

Riedel, O. *Faktor 10 : Cyberspace auf dem Mac*. Stuttgart: Fraunhofer Institut für Arbeitswirtschaft und Organisation IAO, 1992. Technical Report 8/92.

Riedel, O. "Fraunhofer Institut Develops Office Design Tools." *VR News*. 1992: 8.

Riedel, O., and A. Ebeling. *Begrenzte Welten: Fraunhofer Institut (IAO) Präsentiert Virtuelle Realität auf dem Grafikrechner "SkyWriter."* Stuttgart: Fraunhofer Institut für Arbeitswirtschaft und Organisation IAO, May 1992. Technical Report.

Institut für Graphische Datenverarbeitung (Institute for Computer Graphics) IGD, Darmstadt

Astheimer, Peter. "Real-time Sonification to Enhance the Human-Computer-Interaction in Virtual Worlds." Fourth Eurographics Workshop on Visualization in Scientific Computing. Conference held April 1993 at Abingdon, England.

Astheimer, Peter. "Sonification Tools to Supplement Dataflow Visualization." Third Eurographics Workshop on Visualization in Scientific Computing. Conference held April 1992 at Vlareggio, Italy.

Astheimer, Peter. "Sonification in Scientific Visualization and Virtual Reality Applications." GI-Workshop "Visuallsierung: Rolle von Interaktivität und Echtzeit." Conference held June 1992 at St. Augustin.

Astheimer, Peter, and Wolfgang Felger. "Virtuelle Realität in der Architektur." *Bau-Informatik*, Part 2. Düsseldorf: Werner-Verlag, 1993.

Astheimer, Peter, and Martin Goebel. "Integration Akustischer Effekte und Simulationen in VR-Entwicklungsumgebungen." *Virtual Reality '93*, H. J. Bullinger and H. J. Warnecke, eds. Conference held February 1993. Springer-Verlag, 1993: 187-208.

Encarnacao, Jose L., et al. "Graphics and Visualization: The Essential Features for the Classification of Systems." IFIP International Conference on Computer Graphics. Conference held February 1993 at Bombay, India.

Felger, Wolfgang. "How Interactive Visualization Can Benefit from Multidimensional Input Devices." GI-Workshop "Visuallsierung: Rolle von Interaktivität und Echtzeit." Conference held June 1992 at St. Augustin.

Felger, Wolfgang. "Konzept und Realisierung eines Labors fuer Anwendungen der Virtuellen Realitaet angenommen fuer." *Proceedings. GI-Workshop "Sichtsysteme- Visualisierung in der Simulationstechnik."* Conference held November 1993. Springer-Verlag; 1993.

Felger, Wolfgang, Torsten Froehlich, and Martin Goebel. "Techniken sur Navigation durch Virtuelle Welten." *Virtual Reality '93*; H. J. Bullinger and H. J. Warnecke, eds. Conference held February 1993. Springer-Verlag, 1993: 209-222.

Mueller, Stefan, Matthias Unbescheiden, and Martin Goebel. "GENESIS: Eine Interaktive Forschungsumgebung zur Entwicklung Effizienter und Parallelislerter Algorithmen fuer VR-Anwendungen." *Virtual Reality '93*; H. J. Bullinger and H. J. Warnecke, eds. Conference held February 1993. Springer-Verlag, 1993: 321-341.

Center for Art and Media Technology in Karlsruhe (ZKM)

Shaw, Jeffrey. "The Legible City." *Ten.8*, 1991, 2(2): 46-48.

Shaw, Jeffrey. "Revolution/Revolutions" (interactive video sculpture). *Leonardo*, 1991, 24(4): 489.

Tom Sperlich is a developer of virtual reality applications, and a leading journalist in the field. Auf der Eierwiese 14, D-8022 Grünwald, Germany; telephone: 89-641-55-28; fax: 89-641-54-97.

VR

PART

FIVE

THEORY

REAL ARTIFICE: MYRON KRUEGER'S BEAUTIFUL INTERFACE

Interview by Jas. Morgan

Artificial reality is a term Myron Krueger coined back in 1974. Since then he has been called variously the father, grandfather, and godfather of artificial reality. Whatever the paternity, Myron Krueger is an artist/scientist who has been creating computer-generated full-body telecommunication experiences for twenty-three years. He is also the author of the books *Artificial Reality* and *Artificial Reality II*.

VIDEOPLACE is Krueger's interactive installation located, when not on tour, at the Connecticut Museum of Natural History in Storrs. Participants can perform digital painting, three-dimensional gymnastics, touch one another, and perform other interactive feats in cyberspace.

Jas. Morgan

Jas. Morgan: Tell me, Myron, how did you get like this?

Myron Krueger: Well, it was quite unexpected. There was nothing more unlikely than for me to become an artist. I fouled out of any art class I had in grammar school. When I started working with computers in the mid-sixties, I had a liberal-arts background, so I was more interested in philosophical issues than transient technical problems. In particular, I was interested in the confrontation between man and machine—in the human-machine interface. If people were going to use computers all day, every day, the design of such machines was not solely a technical problem—it was also an aesthetic one. A lousy interface would mean a lousy life. I decided that the proper goal was a beautiful interface.

When I wondered what a beautiful interface might be, I thought of artists with their brushes and musicians with their instruments. So, I taught a computer course for artists, in order to see how they might want to relate to computers. I found that computers didn't do anything artists cared about: they just sat there, read in programs, and spat out text. So, I hooked up a Moog synthesizer and a visual display, and created a system in which any program you wrote made sounds and visual patterns. While I was somewhat successful in moving artists toward technology, I was far more so in moving myself toward the arts.

While I had always thought of art and technology as antithetical, I discovered that it was not that artists didn't use technology, it was that the technology they used was obsolete. For the first time, I realized why I had never been interested in art. I imagined illiterate people who had never seen an illustration walking into a cathedral during the Renaissance. They would have been absolutely knocked out. I thought: that's what art should do—it should blow you away.

During that time, I became aware that artists were using the computer to create art, but art as it was traditionally understood. I didn't know anything about art, but I did know about computers. It seemed to me that an art form based on computers should be impossible without them.

The unique capability the computer offered was its ability to make decisions in real time—which implied an interactive art form. In fact, it was not enough to make art interactive, it was necessary to make interactivity itself the art form. When I imagined what such an art form might be like, it excited me the way I imagined that earlier art forms had moved those who created them.

When I tried to communicate my vision of an art form based on composed interactivity to artists, they weren't interested. It was simply too far from their definitions of art. Furthermore, they didn't have the technical skills needed to conceptualize, let alone implement it. The traditional fine arts were static, and this would be a temporal medium—more like music or film than painting. I realized that if I was going to see the kind of art that I wanted, I would have to do it.

At that time, most artists, most intellectuals, and all self-described humanists were antagonistic toward technology. But I loved technology and the potential of computers. (I hated the way we program. I still do—I have a padded monitor so I won't punch it out.) So I had a passion to communicate.

While I had originally wanted to use the computer to teach programming, I decided that most people didn't need to know how to program, or even how the computer worked. I wanted people to walk into a room, have a brief pleasant experience, and leave knowing that computers could be playful, creative, vested with the humanity of humane programmers. I thought in terms of an aesthetic medium that would celebrate technology and show how rich and unexpected the future would be.

That's how I got into it. It was an unexpected opportunity that touched everything—it was a cosmic concept. I reacted to VR in 1969 the way people do today.

WILL THE REAL BODY PLEASE STAND UP AND WIGGLE...

The thing I hated about computers was that you had to sit down to use them. (Actually, this has always been true of intellectual work). How could you talk about human-machine interaction when all you could do was wiggle your fingers on a hundred-year-old keyboard? Some interaction!

I wanted to wiggle the rest of me. I wanted to use my whole body to interact with computers. At that time, computers received input from users. Instead, I wanted them to perceive participants in computer-generated experiences. I thought in terms of *computer-controlled responsive environments.* That was the title of my 1974 dissertation; my term *artificial reality* was a little too far out for a dissertation title.

In 1970, I didn't know how to get the computer to perceive people, so I faked it. In a show called METAPLAY, I used my own perception and my own intelligence to control computer-graphic responses. I pointed a video camera at the computer screen and projected the image onto one end of the gallery. (What I really wanted was a completely environmental display, with floor, walls, and ceiling covered with computer-generated images.)

When people entered the gallery, they saw their images projected life-size in front of them. Then they saw computer-graphic graffiti appearing on their images: I was drawing on their images with a data tablet a mile away. When they got the idea, they would duck when they saw the cursor coming toward them. Or bat it away. When I put a graphic ball at the top of the screen, they would reach up and hit it, and I would move it across the screen. Sometimes I would put my own image on the screen to interact with them.

Now, when I put my image on the screen, I noticed that they avoided touching my image with theirs, as if we were together—they maintained a personal space around themselves.

That led me to reformulate the concept of telecommunication—as creating a new place, maintained by the information that was available to all participants simultaneously. VIDEOPLACE was the name for such a space that had no physical existence and was created with live video images and computer graphics.

In 1974, the day after my Ph.D. orals, I went to Washington to propose a worldwide artificial reality with many participants as the theme of the Bicentennial. At NSF [the National Science Foundation], they turned up their noses and said that it sounded like engineering. At NASA [the National Aeronautics and Space Administration], they said there was a satellite that I could use—if I could get it launched.

Finally, I went to the one place that I was sure would be interested—the Japanese embassy. They were delighted at the thought of being part of our Bicentennial and were sure their government would want to participate. It was obvious then that the United States was a lazy tortoise and Japan a hard-working hare.

Two years later, I received funding from the NEA [National Endowment for the Arts], and VIDEOPLACE was an official Bicentennial project. It was shown on a less-than-global scale—two interconnected installations at the Milwaukee Art Museum.

When you enter the VIDEOPLACE environment, you see your silhouette image life-size on a projection screen in front of you. The computer views you through a video camera below the screen. A graphic creature named CRITTER flies out on the screen and chases your image. If you hold out your hand, CRITTER will land on it. It's like playing with a pet. After a while, you can get it to do tricks. You can get it to dangle from your fingertip or even explode.

CRITTER is one of about fifty interactions. When the image of a remote person touches yours, the contact may make a sound, push you across the screen, or even knock you over. (There's usually a genuine belly laugh when this happens. That was a goal—to make people laugh.) You can retaliate with a karate chop, cutting off the other person's hand.

In the past, humankind could only afford a few artists who would create for the rest of us. That elitist tradition has intimidated nonartists, stifled their confidence. I give visitors an aesthetic medium for which there are no rules, and invite them to experiment.

Adults in our society allow themselves an incredibly restricted repertoire of physical behaviors. My interactions are operated by the body, so people will forget what they are doing with their bodies as they try to achieve an effect on the screen. They find themselves in postures they have not been in since they were children. Some people even assume that I am directing my work at children. My goal has always been to awaken the child in the adult.

I finesse the hard problems of seeing people in a complex world by having them stand in front of a back-lit background to provide a high-contrast image with good edges for the computers to analyze. Their video image goes through a bank of twelve specialized processors that locate the head, hands, and fingers, and detect motion. The specialized processors can be as much as a thousand times faster than off-the-shelf microprocessors. We have to have an instantaneous response.

No one else in the VR community even seems to think about real-time design. For years, software engineering people and computer scientists refused to think about speed. You wouldn't find more than two or three papers in a decade on the subject. And they'd have titles like "The Lost World of Real-Time Programming." Even now that they have conferences about it, they're not doing it. It's considered a lower form of activity. But it happens to be absolutely necessary for this work.

If the responses follow your actions instantaneously, you feel a real sense of cause and effect. The experience is real. That speed requirement is a cognitive imperative. If you have to wait for the response, you're distanced from the experience. Either you make it, or you are not doing it. Period. You don't show slides and say you're showing a movie. I don't understand how the head-mount crowd has exempted themselves from this requirement.

Our specialized processors are not the only reason our system is fast. The key is that if we can't do something in a thirtieth of a second, we don't do it. We simply live within our budget. As a result, my work is often visually spare, but very high in interactivity—like the fish at SIGGRAPH '90. We had a laser-graphic projector mounted above a sensory floor. As you stepped on the floor, a fish came careening across the floor after you. People saw that fish coming at them and they ran.

The experience was real, even if the fish obviously was not. Even a baby on hands and knees crawled after it. (When we made the fish bigger, he crawled the other way.)

The goal is to provide an experience for the participant. How it looks in magazine pictures and video tapes is not important. Fancy graphics add to the experience only if you can meet the speed requirement. The highly rendered graphic worlds that others favor only provide a background. When you go to the theater, you may applaud the stagecraft at the beginning, but you don't go to see the set. You expect some action; you expect some drama; you expect some characters. Something had better happen pretty quickly or you'll split. So I always thought in terms of minimum stagecraft, and worked on interactivity itself. I'm a minimalist. No matter how much visual clutter is on screen, it's only stuff you can affect that matters.

SLOW, AWKWARD, YET LOW-RES

JM: Why are you opposed to the head-mounted displays?

MK: In its current form, the goggle-and-glove world offers an awkward interface that the user is expected to adapt to. It's not intuitive. You point and fly, instead of walking around. It's impossibly slow. The displays have the poorest resolution since the early PCs. I would be willing to say these problems are temporary, but the technology has been working for more than twenty years. Many of the problems are not due to limitations of today's technology. Untethered, walk-around interactions with 1/30 second delay between the participant's action and the system's response have been possible all along.

Then, part of my reaction is idiosyncratic. I don't like to wear things: watches, rings, glasses, or gloves. I was aware of Ivan Sutherland's work with a head-mounted display in the late 1960s. I saw that you could load people up with sensors, but I decided to focus on the development of a completely unencumbering technology that would let you come as you are. I wanted to make the real world virtual rather than cut you off from it. But I didn't think of this decision as permanent. I thought that I would do both technologies.

Goggles have advantages that are seldom commented upon: computers have always been sold by the pound—a small display is inherently cheaper than a large one. It's the cheapest way to do a workstation monitor or HDTV (High Definition Television). It can be shipped in a tiny box. Cardboard boxes are the reason we're cutting down the rain forests.

With high-resolution goggles, you will be able to read an electronic newspaper that looks like a real one. More forests saved! Why doesn't the environmental movement embrace electronic media? Ultimately, a low-cost head-mounted display with the resolution of an OmniMax theater will be irresistible—if it's as unencumbering as VIDEOPLACE. It is my expectation that the two approaches will merge. The light-weight goggles will fit within ordinary eyeglasses. They will superimpose graphics on the real world. They won't cut you off from your colleagues—you'll be able to make eye contact with them. If you already wear corrective glasses, you'll look the same. Or, they've already got a chip with a million lasers on it. You take that million laser thing and fit it to your cornea as a contact lens, and you have a raster blast on your retina, all in parallel. The contact lens solves the problem of how you track the eyeball.

Instead of requiring you to wear instrumented clothing and special gloves, the computer will work from a three-dimensional model of your body that includes your underlying anatomy, your muscles, your gestures, the color and texture of your skin and hair, and the clothes you're wearing. Using video cameras, the computer will locate landmarks on your body—such as the corners of your eyes—to determine the current state of that model. As it calculates what your body is doing in three dimensions, it can build the appropriate view of you to be seen by each of the other participants. Thus, you can appear in another location and interact normally with the people there.

This approach is particularly important if you want to capture people's facial expressions. The video camera is the only sensible face detector I know of. You're completely unencumbered. Especially if you already wear glasses, why would you resist such a technology? You'd have to be pretty perverse.

OFF-WORLD EMPIRICISM

JM: What about education? The theme of your installation is that you can educate over a distance.

MK: In 1976, I submitted a proposal to NSF to make children scientists landing on an alien planet. They would go into VIDEOPLACE individually and explore, and then they'd come out, compare notes, and realize that their experiences were totally different. Big kids, little kids, active kids, and inert kids would each uncover different phenomena, so they would need each other to discover all the rules. They would invent the concept of a critical experiment. They'd learn the process of science. It's not about mathematics. It's not about knowing the right answers. It's about trying to find out.

My favorite approach to education is to trust play as the proper way to learn. Young animals have never been observed to sit in chairs for long periods of time, so I can't imagine why we expect children to. I like to think of artificial reality as an electronic sandbox. A child could play with a swarm of intelligent bees or a constellation of stars. Such play would be enough to sophisticate the child. Then, what we typically consider education would be easy.

JM: What would you do with HMDs today?

MK: The initial focus would be on adding the sense of smell. I have sketched out an olfactory delivery system. You would move through a graphic space and smell graphic flowers. In the beginning I'd play it straight, but then I might not be able to resist the temptation to attach a noxious odor to an attractive visual stimulus.

As you add more instrumentation, you have some interesting opportunities. With force feedback and tactile feedback, the encumbering technology provides the ultimate Skinner Box. Since it dictates to your senses and monitors your every action, it can know exactly what information is reaching your brain. Thus, it can study perception as part of physical behavior rather than as a distinct activity. These systems will let us analyze how we use our senses while we are in motion. In particular, we will be able to understand what information athletes use as they operate at high speeds.

There are also purely tactile illusions. Researchers have shown that when a particular tendon in a your arm is vibrated, you feel that your hand is extended. If this is done as you hold your nose, you feel that your arm has straightened. But, since you still feel your nose in your fingers, your brain's interpretation is that your nose grew like Pinocchio's.

In another effect, stimulation of two points on your body leads you to perceive a phantom sensation in between. In fact, it's possible to make you interpret a concrete sensation as coming from outside your body.

A psychologist might identify the features and factors that an artist can use as compositional elements. But the artist is best equipped to play with them.

Myron Krueger is president of Artificial Reality Corp., an artist, and a pioneer in the field of artificial reality. P.O. Box 786, Vernon, CT 06066; telephone: (203) 871-1375; fax: (203) 871-7738.

Jas. Morgan is art and music editor of *Mondo 2000*. He can be reached there at P.O. Box 10171, Berkeley, CA 94709-5172; telephone: (510) 845-9018; Internet: <mondo@well.sf.ca.us>.

LEAVING THE PHYSICAL WORLD

John Perry Barlow

Like very few Americans of my generation, I come from a very physical world. I've spent much of my working life running a large cattle ranch, first as a cowboy and then as a cowman, earning a living from things I could touch and smell. This career involved the continual and palpable presence of such nonabstractions as the hindquarters of a hundred cows plodding through sagebrush before me. I found myself constantly hard up against the physical world, whether digging holes in rock-packed glacial rubble or stringing barbed wire as far as the eye could see. I conducted this enterprise in the last part of America still holding out against the advancing Information Age.

PINEDALE, WYOMING: MARLBORO COUNTRY

I come from that Great Blank Slate, the American West, universally known as Marlboro Country. When I was a kid growing up in Pinedale, Wyoming, there seemed nothing artificial, or even particularly romantic, about this place. Soon, its tarted-up advertising afterimage will be all that remains of it.

The county I grew up in is about the size of the Netherlands and even today supports fewer than five thousand people. When I was a boy, I rode horseback to a one-room schoolhouse. We didn't have television. We barely had telephone service. Here, guns were part of the furniture, and my taciturn neighbors used them on one another with heartbreaking regularity. These domestic killers rarely went to jail, since they could usually remind the jury that the deceased, whom most of the jurors knew, needed killing anyway.

This is one of the last parts of America in which, despite our vaunted independence, community not only exists but remains a practical necessity. We are united by shared adversity and a common enemy—the natural, physical world. Until recently, nature always seemed to us an implacable, irrational, invincible foe that must somehow be harnessed and turned to the work of man. It is always present and trying to kill you. Absolute temperatures of –58°F and wind chills of –94°F are not uncommon. Life sometimes feels like God's practical joke.

This is a very placeful place. In my little town people often live out their lives in the houses they were born in, a geographic relationship almost unheard of in the rest of the country, where the average citizen moves seventeen times over the course of a lifetime.

It is the sort of place where there is no privacy and little need for any. People tolerate and even brag about one another's peculiarities. We descend from people who were chased here by their unwillingness to fit into anyone's program elsewhere. Thus, this became a culture disinclined to impose any programs of its own. These people don't talk much, but are determined to be able to say whatever they want whenever they feel like it.

We remain the apotheosis of everything America for a long time thought itself to be. Around here we suspect it isn't true any more. Ours is a culture of the physical world, a place which, increasingly, the rest of America no longer inhabits. It is certainly true that America no longer earns its living there.

Instead of producing beef or steel, most of us have become "knowledge workers." We spend our days in cubicles under fluorescent lights, shipping around terabytes of data in the service of obscure purposes. We assemble presentations, reports, and memos, works as ephemeral as the electronic haze from which they emerge. We might as well be shoveling smoke. Having been driven out of the factory and off the land, we "earn" handsome livings from bytes that no one can chew, architecture no one can inhabit, and software that keeps no cold winter wind from anyone's bodies.

Whether I like what it says or not, I have never been one to ignore the handwriting on the wall. I sold the Bar Cross ranch in the spring of 1987, and am thus the first historically recorded male from either side of my family not to pass his whole career in agriculture.

I managed the ranch for the new owner a little over a year. In June 1988, I walked away from the ranch my great-great-uncle founded and became a knowledge worker myself. I was determined to make this dispiriting prospect as entertaining as possible.

Not long before this, I had been asked to co-author a book about Apple Computer. As I knew nothing about computers or corporations, I figured writing the book might be a good way to start learning about both. So I moved my little family to Silicon Valley and started looking around.

A NEW KIND OF PLACE

I wasn't there long before fleeing back to Wyoming, but I discovered a number of surprises that have commanded my attention ever since.

First, I learned that computers were not just faster adding machines, toiling the grim vineyards of columnar arithmetic. Nor were they just smart typewriters. Instead, they could become, when connected, a new kind of place.

I discovered a computer network called the WELL. Inside it were minds whose bodies were scattered all over the world. As I found myself cruising its conceptual back streets, it felt like a small town whose inhabitants were invisible but were nevertheless engaged in the kind of thing I could recognize from rural experience to be human community.

Like Pinedalians, these WELL beings were an irascible bunch, likely to go off all over you without much cause. Unlike Pinedalians, they loved to talk. About everything. Which was not so surprising when one considered that talk was literally all they were made of.

They were humanity stripped of racial characteristics, pheromones, sexual identities, personal style, and even bodies. Words were the only part of themselves they could bring here. Nevertheless, this crowd of strangers chattering at one another in the electronic darkness seemed to me pregnant with possibilities.

The WELL, I later learned, is but one small backwater in a global electronic matrix called the Internet. The Internet connects some 800,000 (mostly UNIX) computers, to any of which thousands of individual minds might also be attached. Growing exponentially since the late 1960s, the rates of Internet growth now sometimes exceed 25 percent a month! The mindscape inside this network seemed vast and wild.

Yet it appeared somehow familiar too. Despite being a very different place, it shares many of Wyoming's historical characteristics. Like the Old West into whose waning days I was born, this place has much unmapped terrain, resources that are barely understood, wild sociopaths operating in the absence of social contracts yet to be drawn, and alarming ambiguities about the nature and ownership of property.

At first, I called it the Datasphere, but then I read *Neuromancer*, a 1984 science-fiction novel by William Gibson. In it he had a twenty-first century, digitally created landscape of information and mind called cyberspace.

Gradually, I realized that cyberspace had been around since Alexander Graham Bell met someone named Watson there in 1876. Cyberspace is where you are when you're on the phone.

Despite its gathering presence among us, we had not noticed it before because, unlike computer bulletin boards and larger networks, phones have no apparent spatial dimension unless one is making a conference call—which is another fairly recent development. The linear end-to-endedness of telephones hides from callers the dark "space" that surrounds the path of conversation.

Besides, cyberspace is pretty thin at present, despite being the new home of most of the world's wealth and business. When I first happened upon it, it was so thin that I could only take my mind there. But I soon found efforts to "thicken" it using a technology called virtual reality. Jaron Lanier and others, whom I came to know well and work with, are developing methods to inject the body into the heretofore spiritual realm of the immaterial. Now, I realized, would the Flesh be made Word.

TELEVISIONLAND

Another of my disorienting Silicon Valley discoveries was that even those Americans who have never seen a modem are coming to live in environments that are almost entirely virtual. Glued to one tube all day and another all evening, they are rapidly trading the old stuff of life for information, which is, in Lanier's words, nothing more than "alienated experience."

Televisionland spreads out from the screen and across the land, covering it in one continuous array of homogenized marketing iconography—McDonald's, Toys R Us, the Mall. Generica the virtual. It smoothes the texture of place, becoming a kind of decal to be affixed to any terrain without regard to local geology or climate.

In Silicon Valley, I never know whether I'm in Mountain View or Sunnyvale or Campbell. They all look the same, and they all look more or less like any other American suburb. Most Americans can be said not to come from anywhere at all.

My studies of Apple Computer also led me to a variety of realizations about the modern corporation. (And I decided not to write the book about Apple when I realized that it was more myth than mission.) The most striking of these was that all large human organizations have more in common with collective organisms than with the machines after which their management is still designed. The American captains of industry remain pleased to think of their companies as shiplike. They imagine themselves on the bridge, their hands on the wheel that connects to the rudder.

In fact, individual humans, regardless of station, are about as likely to "run" large corporations as coral polyps are likely to run reefs. I have been told that Japanese management understands this a little better.

I further found that detachment from such artifacts of physicality as space, time, and Newtonian predictability was having a profound effect on the nature of organizations, tending to favor the creation of small, fast-moving, short-lived adhocracies—digitized hunter-gatherer groups roaming the steppes of cyberspace.

And finally, in another example of the never-ending strangeness of life, I woke to find myself something like a cross between Tom Paine and Wyatt Earp in this new electronic frontier—attempting to maintain its independence from the tyranny of the Old (physical) World it was replacing, while at the same time helping to maintain a certain measure of community and order in its wilds. (The irony of having this role thrust on a renegade physicalist was not lost on me.)

THE ELECTRONIC FRONTIER FOUNDATION

After a disorienting visit from the FBI in May of 1990, I wrote a rant called "Crime and Puzzlement," which led to my establishing with Mitch Kapor (the founder of Lotus Development Company) an organization called the Electronic Frontier Foundation.

We were joined in this effort by a group that now includes Apple founder Steve Wozniak, Whole Earth-ist Stewart Brand, computer guru Esther Dyson, cryptologist and early Sun Microsystems employee John Gilmore, Internet elder David Farber, and long-time ACLU Congressional liaison Jerry Berman. We were also joined, almost immediately, by an uncountable number of ghostly citizens of the 'net.

At first we described the purpose of the Electronic Frontier Foundation as, simply, the "civilization of Cyberspace." Now, after almost four years of operation, we also think of ourselves assisting in some Great Work, creating what may be nothing less than the united mind of humanity, hardwiring the collective organism of human consciousness.

In preparation for that distant realization, EFF seeks policies of openness and easy access, as well as freedom and privacy of expression in digital media. At first we relied on such legal protections for speech as were provided by the First Amendment of the U. S. Constitution. But we soon we realized that, in Cyberspace, the First Amendment is a local ordinance of a different territory.

As a result we have shifted to a set of strategies that we hope will result in the achievement of greatest ubiquity and redundancy of digital connections in the shortest time. We have come to see that "architecture is politics," as Mitch Kapor puts it. If no individual channels are critical to the integrity of the 'net, it will be more difficult for any government to suppress it.

That this approach works was demonstrated during the 1991 coup in the Soviet Union. The hierarchical information systems of the geriatric plotters in the Kremlin were no match for the horizontal and self-organizing networks of PCs and fax machines that informed their popular opposition in the streets.

Lately we have been working on a variety of fronts to accelerate deployment (in the United States and abroad) of the Integrated Services Digital Network (ISDN) for high-speed digital data transmission. We are also fostering the growth of the Internet, acting as a kind of informal regulatory agency while the bases for electronic capitalism are defined.

EFF has also been heavily involved in matters pertaining to intellectual property and reminding society of the fundamental differences between soft and hard goods. We work on fostering virtual community, promoting network-distributed communications multimedia, and educating law-enforcement agencies and corporate security forces on the culture and actual threat posed by computer hackers.

INFORMATION SPACE

The first half of my life was about landscape, place, dirt, physicality, facts, and experience. I now find myself trying to understand a world that has moved off the territory, where such things exist, and onto the map, where they are replaced by simulation, thought, process, image, and relationship. In other words, information.

I have profound misgivings about this weird new place, but it has several advantages over the one that I am leaving behind. (Besides, as we are headed there whether we want to be or not, we might as well enjoy the ride.)

Since most of the wealth of this place derives from the most renewable resource of all—imagination—it is potentially far richer than the last New World we entered. Its basis in mental rather than physical terrain means that its frontiers will always be expanding. Thus, restless iconoclasts like me will always have some marginal region to explore. We will never find ourselves stranded at the old frontier's terminus, as I felt myself to be while growing up in Pinedale.

Its fundamental indefinability might do a lot to eliminate the national borders across which wars are fought. And the Protean capacity of its inhabitants to present themselves any way they see fit may eliminate some of the cultural immune responses that have caused those wars in the first place.

Furthermore, it offers the promise that humans can quit spending so much of the world's treasure traveling to physical proximity with other humans. Instead, they can assemble their far-more-portable minds. Then there is the potential conservation of those resources that we have traditionally devoted to impressing one another to an extent well beyond the requirements of survival. The trappings of prestige can be as easily manufactured from bytes as from leather and brass.

We may also see something like the restoration of community, both inside and outside cyberspace. Since I came this way, I have observed many examples of social congregation that could not have taken place without these media.

Finally, if you are able to pursue any work you like while leaving your body wherever it suits you, the small towns and villages of the world may be again populated with real neighbors. Perhaps we can retire that bleak human relationship that passes for neighborhood in the global suburbs.

This is not to say that the entry into cyberspace is without hazard. For example, there may be almost no way to ensure privacy there. While these electronic thickets may afford the best guerrilla jungle that ever harbored dissidents, certain kinds of technological development could render it as flat and barren of hiding places as the salt deserts of the American West.

In its present condition, it lacks many of the communications media on which people count most heavily—body language, smell, styles of dress, and culture. Reduced to pure content, opportunities for misunderstanding are rife and cyberspace burns continuously with the flaming declarations of its inhabitants.

That there is already so much digital strife worries me. Most of the current population is male, white, affluent, young, well-educated, English-speaking, and suburban. That such a homogeneous citizenry would find so much cause for dispute does not bode well for what will follow the arrival, already well underway, of people from completely different cultures. The opportunities to create innocent offense will increase dramatically

But while the ASCII howls of violation may clog hard disks all over the 'net, virtual bullets cannot kill. And the hybrid cultures we will eventually assemble there will not have, in the absence of boundaries and limited resources, the usual bones of contention to scrap over. Perhaps they will find ways to define the cultural Self without imperiling the cultural Other.

John Perry Barlow is a lyricist for the Grateful Dead and co-founder of the Electronic Frontier Foundation. Internet: <barlow@eff.org>.

Note

This paper is based on the Introduction and Mission Statement for the Hypernetworking Conference, Oita, Japan, February 29, 1992.

CYBER STRATEGIES AND THE VIRTUAL ARM PROJECT

Stelarc

HOLLOW BODY/REMOTE DESIRES

IMMORTAL IMAGES/EPHEMERAL BODIES

At present, technologies are better life-support systems for our images than for our physical bodies. The body can no longer match the expectations of its images. In the realm of MUTATING and MULTIPLYING images, the body's *impotence* is apparent. Orbiting images pacify the body ...

ANESTHETIZED AND OBSOLETE

Images irradiate and anesthetize the body. It is MESMERIZED by the ebb and flow of images. The media become the new *membrane* of human existence. SKIN BECOMES A SCREEN. Images are engaging because they electronically etch the skin—*transient tattoos* that trigger response ...

BIOTECH TERRAINS

The body now inhabits *alien environments* that conceal countless BODY PACEMAKERS—visual and acoustical cues that alert, activate, condition and control the body. Its *circadian rhythms* need to be augmented by artificial signals. Humans are now regulated in sync with swift, circulating rhythms of pulsing images. MORPHING IMAGES MAKE THE BODY OBSOLETE ...

ARTIFICIAL INTELLIGENCE/ALTERNATE EXISTENCE

Artificial life will no longer be contained in computer programs simulating biological development. *Artificial intelligence* will no longer mean expert systems operating within specific task domains. Electronic space no longer merely generates images but extends and enhances the body's operation parameters BEYOND ITS MERE PHYSIOLOGY AND THE SPACE IT

OCCUPIES. What results is a high-fidelity interaction—a meshing of the body with its machines in ever increasing complexity. The significance of a hybrid human-machine system is that it culminates in an ALTERNATE AWARENESS—one that is PAN-HISTORIC, POST-HUMAN, and even EXTRATERRESTRIAL (though the first signs of an alien intelligence may well come from this planet) ...

PSYCHO/CYBER

The PSYCHOBODY is neither robust nor reliable. Its genetic code produces a body that *malfunctions* often and *fatigues* quickly, allowing only slim survival parameters and limiting its longevity. Its carbon chemistry GENERATES OUTMODED EMOTIONS. *The psychobody is schizophrenic.* The CYBERBODY is not a subject, but an object—not an object of desire but an object for designing. It is no longer meaningful to see the body as a site for the psyche. See the body rather as a structure. Confronted by its images of obsolescence, the body is traumatized into splitting from the realm of subjectivity and considering the necessity of reexamining and redesigning its very structure. Altering the architecture of the body results in adjusting its awareness of the world. REDESIGNING THE BODY MEANS REDEFINING WHAT IT MEANS TO BE HUMAN. The Cyberbody bristles with electrodes and antennae, amplifying its capabilities and projecting its presence to remote locations and into virtual spaces. The Cyberbody becomes a post-evolutionary projectile, departing and diversifying in form and function...

THE SHEDDING OF SKIN

Our skin is no longer an adequate interface with the world. It is neither an adequate as neither *sensory* nor *survival* clothing. The solution to radically redesigning the body is not to be found in its internal structures, but on its surface. The solution were no more than skin deep. If the body were draped with a SYNTHETIC SKIN that could absorb oxygen directly through its pores and could effectively convert light and moisture into chemical nutrients, we could eliminate many of the body's *malfunctioning* organs and *redundant* systems. The body would shed its skin, drain its emotional chemistry, and EMPTY OUT ITS ORGANS ...

HOLLOW BODY/HOST SPACE

Off the earth, the body's complexity, softness, and wetness would be difficult to sustain. The strategy should be to HOLLOW, HARDEN, and DEHYDRATE the body to make it more durable, less vulnerable, and more operationally efficient. The notion of a hollow body is seductive as it would become a better host for all the technical components that could be packed into it ...

THE VIRTUAL ARM PROJECT

Amputees often experience a phantom limb. It is now possible to have the phantom sensation of an additional arm—a virtual arm—albeit visual rather than visceral.

THE VIRTUAL ARM

The Virtual Arm is a computer-generated humanlike manipulator, interactively controlled by virtual reality equipment from VPL, Inc. (see figures 28-1 to 28-2 and color # insert 4). DataGloves with flexion and position-orientation sensors use a gesture-based command language to allow real-time intuitive operation and additional extended capabilities. Functions are mapped to finger gestures, with parameters for each function allowing mobility. For example, the continuous-rotation function can apply to the fingers as well as to the wrist, and its speed can be varied. In the future, hand state and motion gestures will also be recognized. Another strategy is to depend on a small number of gestures, with different functions mapped in different ways, to allow access to new sets of functions and parameters.

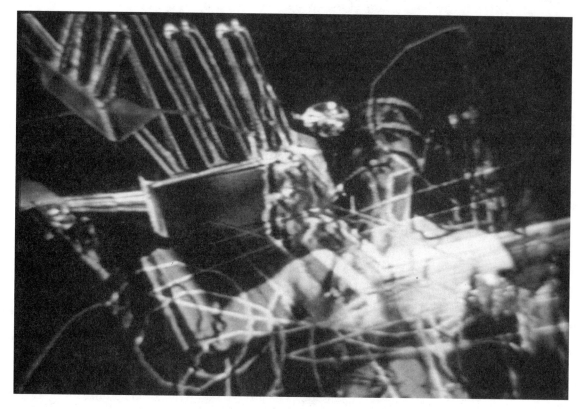

Figure 28-1. Virtual arm graft capability. • Credit: Tony Figallo

Figure 28-2. Virtual arm graft replicate. • Credit: Tony Figallo

An arm editor allows the Virtual Arm to be customized for particular performances and virtual tasks rather than limited by anatomical or engineering constraints of the real world. The Virtual Arm is able to behave ambidextrously, as a left or right hand.

Some of the Virtual Arm's extended capabilities include "stretching," or telescoping of limb and finger segments; "grafting" of extra hands on the arm; and "cloning," or calling up another arm. The record and playback function allows the sampling and looping of motion sequences. A clutch command enables the operator to freeze the arm, disengaging operation of the gloved hand. For teleoperation systems, locking allows the fixing of the limb in position for precise operations. With the hand in macro mode, complex commands can be generated with a single gesture; in fine control mode, delicate tasks can be completed by the transformation of large operator movements to small movements of the Virtual Arm.

Gesture interaction is an effective and efficient means of remotely controlling robot manipulators. Since the Virtual Arm is a generalized or universal robot with extended capabilities, it may be useful for teleoperation environments or as a sophisticated humanlike manipulator for handling objects in a virtual task environment.

HOST BODY/COUPLED GESTURES

Host Body/Coupled Gestures: Event for Virtual Arm, Robot Manipulator and Third Hand is an interactive event, or performance, that controls, counterpoints, and choreographs the motions of a virtual arm, a robot manipulator, an electronic "third hand," and the arms of the body (see figures 28-3 and 28-4 and color insert # 5). It combines real-time gesture-control of the Virtual Arm, programmed robot scanning, symbiotic electromyogram (muscle signal) activation of the third hand, and improvised body movements. Sensors on the head and limbs allow the body to alternate images received from cameras positioned above the body, on the robot manipulator, and on the left arm. The Virtual Arm is the default image.

A relationship between body posture and images is established, with body movements determining the flow of images on the large screen, displayed either singly, superimposed, or in split configurations. Amplified body and machine signals acoustically configure the virtual and robot operations. There is an interface and interplay of virtual and machine systems, of simulated and physical action, of actuation and automation. The event is about motion and surveillance. The interest is how electronic systems can extend performance parameters and how the body copes with the complexity of controlling information video and machine loops online and in real time.

Figure 28-3. Virtual Body performance by Stelarc at Obscure, Québec City, 1993.
• Credit: Stelarc, 1993.

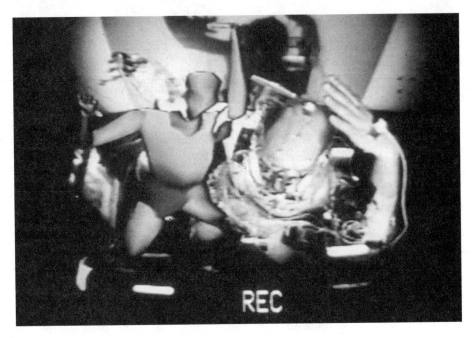

Figure 28-4. Virtual Body performance by Stelarc at Obscure, Québec City, 1993.
• Credit: Stelarc, 1993.

Stelarc is Artist in Residence and coordinator of the arts program at the Royal Melbourne Institute of Technology Advanced Computer Graphics Centre, Melbourne, Victoria 3000, Australia; Internet: <stelarc@cgl.citri. edu.au>.

Note

The Virtual Arm project was completed with the assistance of Mike Papper, Craig McNaughton, James Boyle, Dean Hansen and Robert Webb, and was supervised by Mike Gigante at the RMIT Advanced Computer Graphics Centre, CITRI in Melbourne.

Some of Stelarc's previous work leading up to his explorations of telepresence and virtuality are described in Stelarc and James D. Paffrath *Obsolete Body: Suspensions:* Stelarc, Davis, Calif.: J. P. Publications, 1984; Stelarc, "Prosthetics, Robotics and Remote Existence: Postevolutionary Strategies," *Leonardo* 24(5), 1991: 591-595; and Stelarc, "Event for Amplified Body, Laser Eyes and Third Hand," *Irrelevant Ethics: Notes on Art Practice in a Technological Context*, Simon Penny, ed., Sydney, Australia: Virtual Object, 1987.

THE BIOAPPARATUS RESIDENCY AND VIRTUAL SEMINAR

Catherine Richards and Nell Tenhaaf

INTRODUCTION

As artists who have worked in the area of new technologies for many years, we are confronted with limitations in the discourses around culture and technology. These are generally not formulated from the point of view of art practitioners, nor do theoretical premises active in the artworld interact with technological development. In the Fall of 1991 we developed a 10 week artists' residency at the Banff Centre for the Arts to look at some of these issues. *Bioapparatus* was the title of the residency and also of a two-day seminar that took place October 28 and 29, 1991. The importance of these events was their integration of many different perspectives on new technologies—cultural theory, postmodernism, feminism, postcolonialism. We wanted to engage artists from many disciplines, as well as scientists and theorists, in a discussion that would go far beyond the cliché of artists humanizing existing technologies.

Participants in the residency were: Mary Anne Amacher, Wende Bartley, Eleanor Bond, Adam Boome, Diana Burgoyne, He Gong, Doug Hall, Carl Eugene Loeffler, Robert McFadden, George Bures Miller, Robin Minard, Michael Naimark, Lawrence Paul, Catherine Richards, Warren Robinett, Kathleen Rogers, Dacid Rokeby, David Rothenberg, Daniel Scheidt, Nell Tenhaaf, Chris Titterington, David Tomas, Fred Truck, and Inez van der Spek.

We called the seminar the *Virtual Seminar* on the *Bioapparatus* since many people not in Banff for the two days participated by mail, fax and e-mail. The publication documenting the seminar can be obtained from the Banff Centre. Reprinted here is the call for submissions to the seminar, followed by our introduction to the publication. We are re-publishing this material as a historical document. At the same time, it is a successful portrait of debates that are still active.

June 1994

THE VIRTUAL SEMINAR

One of the intentions of the residency has been to expand the discourse around technology and culture. As organizers of the seminar, we wanted to encourage debate and to involve a large number of people in mapping this vast territory. To this end, we invited short submissions in response to a text outlining issues concerning the *bioapparatus*. These contributions, submitted by residents as well as interested people who could not attend the residency, formed the discussion document for what became known as the virtual seminar on the *bioapparatus*. As forums for diverse voices, the seminar and publication reflect unresolved and contentious positions in this field rather than a universal perspective.

The papers in the discussion document were grouped into ten chapters, each of which addressed a specific concern related to the *bioapparatus*. These are: natural artifice, designing the social, re-embodiment, perfect bodies, subjectivities, art machines, cyborg fictions, art in the virtual, aural/visual space, and the real interface.

GENEALOGY

The term *bioapparatus* was coined specifically by us for the residency. It combines an understanding of particular philosophies of technology with theories about the technological apparatus, the technologized body, and the new biology. To describe the origins of such an open-ended word, one that seems to resonate even without explanation, is to offer only a piece of a large and complex territory. Presented here is a synopsis of the theoretical frameworks that have shaped our conception of the bioapparatus.

The philosophical grounding of our thinking on technology is influenced by the perspectives of three thinkers working within a Canadian context. Arthur Kroker published an insightful study of the Canadian philosophers of technology Marshall McLuhan, Harold Innis and George Grant, who propose what he calls an original and comprehensive discourse on technology.[1]

McLuhan is widely known in North America as the electronic media guru of the 1960s. Kroker characterizes McLuhan as a rhetorician and a technological humanist in comparison to the existentialist Grant and Innis the realist. McLuhan's cosmos is not a futureworld of processed experience but a global information environment already in place. Among his more revolutionary propositions, several of which have become platitudes of the media age, is the idea of body extension: "All media are extensions of some human faculty – psychic or physical."[2] So the *technological sensorium* is an extension of ourselves which envelops us and in which, from McLuhan's redemptive perspective, we can all participate with creative freedom.

George Grant's lament for humanity as trapped creatures, "half-flesh/half- metal," exemplifies his Nietzschean pessimism about technological society. He envisions the emergence of the"will to technique" as "will to power," in fact the "will to will." What seems here to be an unredeemable conception of the modern world, a 1960s mindset very different from McLuhan's, offers at least a warning about the impact of the technological drive for mastery and for progress. Taken as a fixed and cul-de-sac position, it offers a starting point for deconstructive readings that break out of the limits of Grant's fundamentally conservative categories of thinking and feeling.

Innis is the political/cultural observer who saw clearly, in writings as early as the 1930s, the position of the Canadian psyche, "trapped between the cultural legacy of its European past and the expanding space of American empire."[3] For Innis, media technologies are "monopolies of space" that work against time, time as historical remembrance. His is not a nostalgic vision of the past, but a probing of possible identity and of survival.

Through this synopsized philosophical overview, the technological sensorium emerges as a reflection of shifting yet specific social and cultural value systems. The debates that developed in the mid-seventies around the workings of cinema as an ideological apparatus, particularly through the British journal *Screen*, are a second theoretical underpinning to the *bioapparatus*. Articles published around 1975 by Jean-Louis Baudry, Christian Metz and Laura Mulvey are key to this area.[4] Baudry proposes the cinematographic apparatus as constituted through the entire context, structure, and signification system of cinema. It is a closed system that creates its own desire for itself. It instills this desire, among others, in the spectator through its simulation of individual subjectivity. Metz and Mulvey add that scopophilia (pleasure in looking) and the spectator-text relationship in cinematic narrative are, in psychoanalytic terms, the very conditions of subjectivity.

Paul Virilio, on the other hand, specifically examines cinema as an apparatus of war. Many of his insights anticipated what more recent technologies have made apparent. "Space is made translucent and its military commander clairvoyant ... by technological processes of foresight and anticipation."[5] This cinematic process is no longer reserved for the high command, but has become a public visual display (in the new world order). Through these theorizations of the ideological apparatus, it is possible to conceptualize individual subjectivities as constructed through technologies. The bio of bioapparatus is primarily an issue of subjectivity, how it is constituted and how it is located in relation to the body.

The cinematic apparatus can be linked to another apparatus, the bachelor machine. Constance Penley considers Baudry's theory to be a "bachelor construct," because of its phallocentric position in the unconscious and its mechanism for reproducing itself by itself – for situating desire only within its own closed masculine terms.[6] The bachelor machine construct actually has its origins in the art domain, in Marcel Duchamp's infamous *La mariée mise à nue par ses célibataires, mêmes* of the 1920s. As a dadaist anti-art gesture and as the deconstructive device described by Penley, this artist's machine has taken on a much broader role as a literary trope referring to a (masculine) auto-erotic and nihilistic narrative logic.

In this context, a brief mention of the "influencing machine" is also in order. Joan Copjec writes about this model, proposed by Victor Tausk, a contemporary of Freud. Freud's patients describe the influencing machine as controlling them, persecuting them, and making them "see pictures: ... the machine is generally a magic lantern or cinematograph."[7] The "phallic machine reproducing only male spectators"[8] is thus deeply embedded in psychoanalytic discourse and consequently in poststructuralist thought including feminist theories.

If psychoanalytic discourse has been the central construct for examining issues of the subject, the notion of simulation has become another trope for much postmodernist theorizing. It has provided grounds for reflection on contemporary culture as well as an oblique link with developments in representational technologies (Virilio, Deleuze, Baudrillard, Lyotard, Kroker and Eco). The notion of an apparatus becomes specific - both as metaphor and diagnosis of a general condition.

Gilles Deleuze comments on the links of the apparatus of power with new technologies. He observes that "psychoanalysis ... is the forced choice ... because it gave the binary machine new material and a new extension, consistent with what we expect of an apparatus of power."[9] These observations support his encompassing reflection of "the machine as social in its primary sense ... in the structure it crosses, to the men (sic) it makes use of, the tools it selects, and the technologies it promotes":[10] that is, the apparatus can be seen as deeply embedded in the social fabric.

This conception of a fully implanted technological order is also evident in the new biology discourse of boundary transgression, whose foremost theoretician is Donna Haraway. Her conceptualization of the feminist cyborg is a triple characterization of a machine and organism hybrid, a creature of social reality and a creature of fiction.[11] Haraway describes the place for both pleasure and responsibility in the breakdown of boundaries between human, animal and machine. She merges the social with myth and fiction in perceiving both the machine and organism as "coded texts," both engaged in questions that are as radical as survival itself.

SITUATING TECHNOLOGY, CONSIDERING GENDER ISSUES

In formulating the residency, the seminar and this publication, we have approached technology in the widest possible sense. Technology often specifically refers to an instrument or a tool which might be articulated in hardware or software. Here, it is considered to be a product of cultural, social and political practices that are already firmly in place. As such, technology develops within existing frameworks that specify what counts as valid knowledge and how it can be obtained. The framework is in place long before the will or the resources are directed towards making a specific instrument: relational models are crystallized into technological objects. Therefore, technology is not neutral but embedded in social and cultural contexts.

This position on technology underlies our approach to specific technologies such as virtual reality or virtual environment technology. Virtual reality is particularly interesting for its extreme intimacy with the body. In fact, this technology is driven by reading signals from the body. As our most recent form of representational technology, it raises questions about the construction of self (or subjectivity). It also challenges traditional thinking that relies on a distinction between subject and object as it functions directly with the body's multi-sensory physiological thresholds.

The intense public attention directed toward virtual reality over the past two years has little to do with the hardware and software itself. In effect, a public mythology is being constructed about what virtual reality will be. The development of this mythology is as important as the development of the technology itself. The narratives and metaphors imply logical solutions within which research, development and representation will take place. For example, one of the phrases borrowed by the technological community from recent science fiction is "jacking into cyberspace,"[12] which is used to describe entering a virtual environment. This kind of phrase incorporates assumptions about how the simulation of communication and physical experience can be imagined and acted upon.

To address technology in a cultural context requires a range of input. The artists in this residency range from those who integrate technology as the means and/or the subject of their work to those who address issues related to the contemporary technoscape. In this way the residency was designed to generate a broa d interdisciplinary discussion, and the pertinence of various art pratices in the social field has been addressed throughout the process.

Questions concerning gender have been central to contemporary art practices of the last decade, and the *bioapparatus* is certainly a gendered territory. The body is biologically and socially gendered and, in an equally profound sense, technology can be seen as gendered. The gendered nature of technological development itself poses questions about authorship, intrinsic structure and power. The relation of technology to the body and to subjectivity and the effects of technologies on femininity and masculinity as they are constructed in different social contexts are issues that constitute a very complex subject area.

Rather than create a category in the discussion paper that focussed on gender issues, we preferred to have these questions, like questions of race, class and cultural differences integrated as much as possible into all of the discussions. For example, several of the participants addressed the ideological conditions that shape the western notion of progress through science and technology. This idea encompasses gender issues that can be raised within a reexamination of historical and contemporary constructs of nature and culture, mind and body, and machine and spirit.

What follows are the responses to the call for submissions and the discussions from the Bioapparatus Seminar.

A VIRTUAL SEMINAR ON BIOAPPARATUS

Catherine Richards
Nell Tenhaaf

BACKGROUND TO THE RESIDENCY

The Art Studio program at The Banff Center in Banff, Alberta, offers three 10-week residencies a year, bringing together a group of 20 artists, writers and theoreticians to address themes of current cultural interest.

For the Fall 1991 residency, we formulated a residency theme and suggested participants in the context of a collaboration between Art Studio and Media Arts programs of The Banff Center. The collaboration is a fortuitous one as it draws on and develops our overlapping interests as independent cultural producers in issues of new technologies, not the least of which concerns what could be meant by the term "new."

The residency is related to a longer term project at The Banff Center called *Art and Virtual Environments*, directed toward artistic use of virtual reality technology. The plan is to ultimately make virtual reality technology available to artists through the Media Arts Program of The Banff Centre. This process will begin during the *bioapparatus* residency by providing an on-site virtual reality system.

CONCEPTUAL FRAMEWORK

With Michael Century, Lorne Falk and Vern Hume (Banff Centre for the Arts directors of Program Development, Art Studio and Media Arts respectively) we constructed a residency on the *bioapparatus*. As a general framework, we agreed to look at the technological apparatus in its intimacy with the body, examining the history of this interrelationship and its sociocultural implications. Such issues have constituted the site for much of the postmodernist debate on representation and the pronounced cultural shifts of the past few decades.

The *bioapparatus* residency will explore questions of the integrity of the body and of subjectivity. The apparatus, as we construe it, is itself a perceptual model, a reflection of social and cultural value systems, of desires. It can be seen as a metaphor that not only describes but generates subjectivity, a subjectivity problematized by the objectifying effect of any technological instrument. The apparatus splits the body, the person, into subject and object, and its history thus merges with the philosophical history of dualism: body/mind, nature/culture, female/male. One question posed by feminist critiques of technology in the context of media, science and medicine is whether the historically constructed subject/object relation can be reconstituted so that its power dynamic is one of commonality and attunement rather than objectification and conquest.

Virtual reality or virtual environment technology is of particular interest in the context of the *bioapparatus*. It is a symptom as well as an instrument of a re-ordering of perception and, one can anticipate, of power relations. The current mythology surrounding the technology reconstitutes the mind/body opposition, and raises issues of "bodily materiality" (a term proposed by Rosi

Braidotti). As such, virtuality can be looked at as an expression of social discourses that are already in place. One of the intentions of the residency is to address the broader context of sociocultural shifts that are both the cause and symptom of technological changes.

Some other issues related to the *bioapparatus* are:

- the idea of machines as essentially social assemblages

- the tool as a political site for shifts in the mediascape and its definition: the military, the American "world culture" and its media, the drug cowboys, medicine

- the fictions of science and the science of fiction

- "man"/machine interaction, cyborgs, boundary degeneration

- artists' definitions of machines: futurism, bachelor machines.

PLEASE RESPOND

The apparatus has probed, extended and blurred the boundaries between viewer and viewed, knower and known. Virtual reality can be seen as one moment on this trajectory. The apparatus has now become so sophisticated that it presents itself as merging with the body – becoming the *bioapparatus* – obscuring the borders drawn by instrumentality and redefining body functions of perception, sensations, understanding.

What is the most pressing issue, for you, concerning the bioapparatus? What would you add to this description of the bioapparatus?

Please send a one-page response, typed or legibly handwritten, including original drawings or diagrams if you wish.

Catherine Richards, with Nell Tenhaaf, led the Banff seminar on the bioapparatus described in this essay. Working initially in drawing, video, and performance in Canada, Richards is interested in image-making and the simulation of the body by new technologies. 41 Delaware Avenue, Ottawa, Ontario K2P 0Z2, Canada; telephone: (613) 233-8316.

Nell Tenhaaf, with Catherine Richards, led the Banff seminar on the bioapparatus described in this essay. She is a writer and reviewer and currently teaches at the University of Ottawa. She can be reached at 4128 rue Hôtel-de-ville, Montréal, Québec H2W 2H1, Canada; telephone: (514) 844-1377 or (613) 564-6588.

Note

This paper was adapted from the proceedings of a two-day seminar held at the Banff Centre for the Arts, October 28 and 29, 1991. The seminar took place within the framework of a ten-week residency on the bioapparatus, a collaborative project of the Art Studio and Media Arts programs of the Banff Centre. Through its ongoing residency programs, the Centre offers a unique context for bringing together a multidisciplinary group to address important cultural issues. The full proceedings have been published as *Virtual Seminar on the Bioapparatus*. Banff, Alberta: Banff Centre for the Arts, 1991.

REFERENCES

1. Arthur Kroker, *Technology and the Canadian Mind: Innis/McLuhan/Grant*, Montreal: New World Perspectives, 1984, 7. Kroker has added his own perspective on technology in a series of works, the most recent being *The Possessed Individual: Technology and the French Postmodern*, Montreal: New World Perspectives, 1992.

2. Kroker, *Technology and the Canadian Mind*, 56.

3. Kroker, *Technology and the Canadian Mind*, 95.

4. Jean-Louis Baudry, "Ideological Effects of the Basic Cinematographic Apparatus," *Film Quarterly* 28:2, Winter 1974-75: 39-47; Christian Metz, "The Imaginary Signifier," *Screen* 16:2, 1975: 14-76; Laura Mulvey, "Visual Pleasure and Narrative Cinema," *Screen* 16:3, 1975: 6-18. See also *The Cinematic Apparatus*, Teresa de Lauretis and Stephen Heath, eds., New York: St. Martin's Press, 1980.

5. Paul Virilio, *War and Cinema, The Logistics of Perception*, London: Verso, 1989, 77.

6. Constance Penley, "Feminism, Film Theory and the Bachelor Machines," *m/f* 10, 1985: 39-59.

7. Joan Copjec, "The Anxiety of the Influencing Machine," *October* 23, Winter 1982, 54. See also Jeanne Randolph, "Ambiguity and the Technical Object," *Vanguard* 13:7, 1984: 24-27.

8. Copjec, "The Anxiety of the Influencing Machine," 57.

9. Gilles Deleuze and Claire Parnet, *Dialogues*, translated by Hugh Tomlinson and Barbara Habberjam, New York: Columbia University Press, 21.

10. op. cit.

11. Donna Haraway, "A Manifesto for Cyborgs: Science, Technology, and Socialist Feminism in the 1980's," *Socialist Review* 80, 1985: 65 -107.

12. William Gibson, *Neuromancer*, New York: Ace Books, 1984.

2 A typical Habitat social gathering. The strange device to the right is a sex changing machine. • Credit:: Fujitsu.

1 Woggles. • Credit: Oz/Animation Group. Carnegie Mellon University, 1992.

3 The UFO room in the *Fun House*. • Credit: Jeremy Epstein, STUDIO for Creative Inquiry, Carnegie Mellon University, 1993.

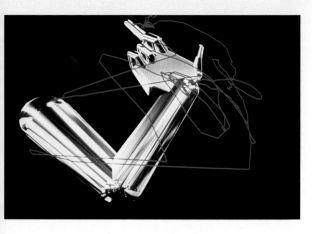

4 Virtual Arm drawing capability. RMIT, ACGC, CITRI, Melbourne 1992. • Credit: T. Figallo.

5   Actuate/Rotate: Event for virtual body held at Obscure, Québec City, 1992.
    • Credit: Video still, Stelarc.

6   DIVE, conference application. The white board allows several people to draw graphics and text, and add live or pre-recorded video.
    • Credit: Multi-G, Swedish institute of Computer Science, 1992.

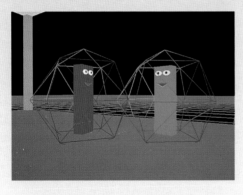

7   Users can have a conversation when their auras, or the "cages" that surround them, intersect.
    • Credit: Multi-G, Swedish institute of Computer Science, 1992.

8   Inanimate objects may also extend an aura. The conference table extends an aura that allows communication among those intersecting with it.
    • Credit: Multi-G, Swedish institute of Computer Science, 1992.

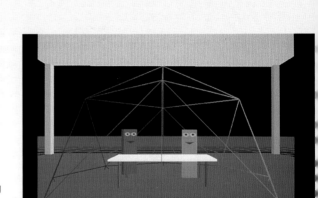

A user controlling his movement through the *Virtual Museum*. • Credit: J. Shaw, 1991

10 The Workroom at the Boston Computer Museum, 1992. • Credit: Sense 8 Corp.

11 Bird's-eye view of a stove accessible from a wheelchair, represented in violet and yellow. Inset: The wheelchair interface to this virtual kitchen.
• Credit: Hines VA Hospital/Prairie Virtual Systems Corp.

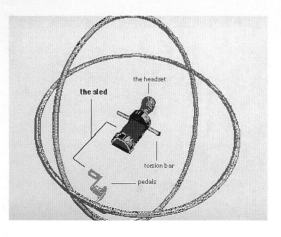

12 The design for the *Archaeopteryx* flight simulator. • Credit: Fred Truck, 1992.

13 The park in Virtual Polis contains a realistic fountain.
• Credit: Jeffrey Jacobson, STUDIO for Creative Inquiry, Carnegie Mellon University, 1994.

14 Outside view of the Virtual Art Museum.
• Credit: Jeffrey Jacobson, STUDIO for Creative Inquiry, Carnegie Mellon University, 1994.

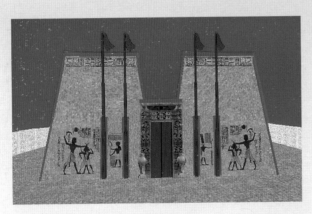

15 Virtual Ancient Egypt: Temple of Horus.
• Credit: Jeffrey Jacobson, STUDIO for Creative Inquiry, Carnegie Mellon University, 1994.

16 The cat in Virtual Ancient Egypt is an example of an agent that interacts with human users.
• Credit: Jeffrey Jacobson, STUDIO for Creative Inquiry, Carnegie Mellon University, 1994.

VIRTUAL REALITY AS THE COMPLETION OF THE ENLIGHTENMENT

Simon Penny

New technologies are often heralded by a rhetoric that locates them as futuristic, without history, or at best arising from a scientific-technical lineage that is quite separate from cultural history. This paper is an attempt to place virtual reality and its attendant rhetoric squarely within, and as a product of, the philosophical developments that began with the Enlightenment. Central to this critique is the proposition that while virtual reality is technically advanced, it (along with most computer graphics practice) is philosophically retrogressive.

The key figure here is René Descartes, whose thinking set the scientific and technological revolution in motion. In 1619, Descartes had a dream in which he was advised that he should find the unity of the sciences in purely rational terms. Here is the irony at the heart of rationalism: that it arose from a dream. Products of Descartes's career that are relevant to this discussion include his famous postulation *Cogito ergo* sum (I think, therefore I am); mind/body duality; Cartesian analytic geometry (1637); and his Treatise on *Man and the Formation of the Foetus* (1664), in which he describes animals in purely mechanistic terms.[1] These are key points in the development of the ideology of rationalism.

VIRTUAL REALITY AND CARTESIAN SPACE

Recently there has been some criticism of the computer graphic establishment for its endorsement of a (gendered?) Cartesian space. I would be the first to agree that computer graphic production, as seen in commercial cinema, video games, theme park rides, and military simulations, is dominated by a late adolescent Western male psyche and world view, but I am troubled by what appears to be an unsubstantiated conceptual leap between a critique of gendered virtual spaces and criticism of the utilization of the Cartesian grid.

One can offer any amount of criticism of the rigidifying effect of the rectilinear grid on our architecture, our city environments, even our three-dimensional modeling programs. But the Cartesian grid is built into our culture and our perception as an integral part of the rationalist determinism that we were taught in school in math and science, and that structures our thinking. To propose an alternative to Cartesian space is to propose an alternative to the philosophical and technical legacy of the Enlightenment.

Cartesian space comprises two parts: the notion of three straight infinite axes at 90 degrees to one another, and the division of those axes into discrete numerical units. Computer technology is a numerical technology. All data is converted into discrete numerical values. Space is broken into numerically defined units. Cartesian space does not privilege any part over any other.

Proto-Cartesian gridding is central to the concept of Renaissance perspective. But it is the system of perspective, the system of representing that grid from a particular (powerful and singular) viewpoint as a two-dimensional image, that contains the objectionable theoretical material, the privileging of a sole location of viewing and power.

VR AND NEO-VITALISM

A criticism leveled at computer graphics (at least until *Terminator II, Lawnmower Man, and Jurassic Park*) was that it was a cold space unable to persuasively represent the natural world. This view is equal parts New Age neo-pagan earth-motherism, Luddism, and narrow-minded critique from the world of traditional art media. It is conveniently forgotten that it took the Western tradition in painting significantly longer to develop these abilities (say, from Cimabue to Leonardo). This criticism is now a thing of the past in high-end computer graphics, although it remains a problem in VR and home computing.

Is the objection to "Cartesian space" voiced as a result of frustration with the inability of current 3D modeling and world-building kits to produce persuasive amorphous organic forms? This would fit with a somewhat simplistic set of gender-related oppositions (male/female, sharp/soft, square/round, and so on).

On a technical level, the grid (and polygonal construction within the grid) limits radically the possibility for construction of organic, amorphous forms. It privileges clean crystalline coherent independent forms; it is an articulation of the space of the Platonic Ideal, and yes, it is this world of pure form that is the premise of the scientific method and of theoretical engineering. Resolution, processor speed, bandwidth: these terms are like a mantra for computer graphics engineers. When resolution of the grid is below the threshold of vision, the problem of organic form will, ironically, disappear. Ironic, because the increase of resolution that puts the mind at rest is an expression of an increase in power of the technology that is being critiqued.

MIMESIS IN WESTERN PICTURE-MAKING

This call for the representation of the "organic" is a call for greater mimesis in computer graphics. But why this obsession with micrographic representationalism? Why should the digital allow production (simulation?) of organic form? After all, the crystalline Platonisms may be more "natural," more "native" to that space. Inevitably, terms like "natural," "simulation" and "mimesis" enter the discussion. Historically, mimesis has been a central concern of Western art.[2]

The call for a more "organic" representation in the digital realm may be regarded as a retrograde critical position. The most familiar mode of critique of electronic media is characterized by dipoles such as natural/synthetic, authentic/fake, real/artificial—critical systems that ultimately call upon the "natural" as a baseline. But this baseline has been well and truly confounded by poststructural criticism, which establishes that the natural is itself simply a cultural construct. Cultural theoretician McKenzie Wark has noted that whenever we call upon the organic, the whole, the lying in the past, the lost; we reenact in criticism the myth of the Fall, the expulsion from the garden of Eden.[3]

VR AND CHRISTIANITY

Virtual reality, like any other technology, is embedded in a cultural history that lends to the enterprise a world view. I argue that this world view is (not unexpectedly) male-gendered, patriarchal, and Christian. Jaron Lanier has announced that virtual reality is the culmination of culture. This is a somewhat conceited judgment given that he is a major developer of the technology. But my concern is with the cultural specificity of that remark. The abhorrence of the body is inherent in Christian doctrine, and Christianity has served as the basis for Western philosophy until the last century. Philosophical ideas such as the duality of René Descartes are based in Christian doctrine. Alluquere Rosanne Stone has observed that in the Greek New Testament, the word *endyo* is used in the context of narratives of Christian conversion, to mean "to put on Christ" in the sense of putting on an overcoat.[4] This condition of "stepping into" is very similar to the condition of being in virtual reality. Such suggestions strengthen the assertion that the cultural history of VR is as old as Western culture itself. William Gibson's cyberpunks proclaimed that "the body is meat," but neglected to notice just how similar their position was to that of Saint Augustine.

VR AND RENAISSANCE HUMANISM

It is a basic tenet of art history that the mode of picture-making practiced in the West is a set of representational conventions devised during the Renaissance. In the computer graphics community there is a naive acceptance that Western perspective is in some sense absolute. This comes as no surprise when various computer graphics luminaries have proclaimed that the ultimate goal of computer graphics is to achieve something indistinguishable from a color photograph. Western perspective, or for that matter any system of pictorial representation, is in no sense innate or "natural," but an often arduously learned convention.[5] The developers of virtual reality have inherited a humanistic world view (an attitude to life and a way of making pictures) that places the eye of the viewer in a position of command, a privileged viewpoint on the world. Recent art theory has examined the relationship between this Western perspective and the rise of humanism, rationalism, and empiricism.[6] Computer graphics as a field is therefore heavily invested in the possibility of the objective observer. The notion of the objective observer, outside the field of action, is precisely encapsulated in Western perspective. As Florian Rotzer has noted, "the model of the external observer...is gradually being superseded, not only in science but also in art."[7]

VR AND COLONIALISM

Technological development has always defined the location of frontiers. The Atlantic coast of Europe remained the edge of the world (to Europeans) until explorers were liberated from coast-hugging travel by accurate navigational technologies and robust ships. The American West was claimed and held only when the the steam locomotive, the telegraph, and the conoidal bullet combined into one technological complex. More recently, the space race advanced as soon as the technology was available.

With geography filled up, and the dreams of space colonization less viable every day, the drive to the frontier has collapsed in on itself. The space remaining for colonization is the space of the technology itself. No longer the tool by which the frontier is defined, the body of technology is now itself under exploration. Back in the early 1960s, one of the pioneers of computer graphics, Ivan Sutherland, declared that the goal was to "break the glass and go inside the machine."[8] More recently, Jaron Lanier says of VR that "the technology goes away, and all that's left is the cultural component." The technology "goes away" because we are inside it.

VR AND TWENTIETH-CENTURY PHILOSOPHICAL DEVELOPMENTS

No selection process is value-free, by definition. Software projects are shaped by the world views of their makers, their value systems are (often unknowingly) incorporated into the work. Computer engineering, software engineering, knowledge engineering are heirs to the tradition of Engineering, the quintessential Industrial Revolution science, concerned with production—efficient production, by means of standardization of parts and processes. A computer is a device for automating production. Production automation depends on the standardization of objects and categories.[9]

In our historical moment, ideas of "standardization" are being questioned, from social policies of multiculturalism to the instantly reprogammable robotic production line. The engineering world view is itself under examination. It seems that the value systems reified in computer technology are dangerously unsteady. One might fairly ask whether it is possible to build a postindustrial aesthetic within such a "steam-powered" technology.

One might assert that the ideas that have shaped this century are due to Marx, Freud, Einstein, and Heisenberg. What effect have their ideas had on the development of the computer? The answer must be close to none. And what of newer philosophical ideas that actively critique Cartesian rationalism: poststructuralism and feminism and other varieties of postmodern thought? We might ask ourselves, "If the computer as we know it is heir to such a philosophical system, is it possible to imagine a similar machine based in another system, or is the idea oxymoronic?"

Nell Tenhaaf states:

> The philosophy of technology...has been articulated entirely from a masculinist perspective in terms that metaphorize and marginalize the feminine. In real social discourse, this claiming of technology has been reinforced by, and has probably encouraged, a male monopoly on technical expertise, diminishing or excluding the historical contributions of women to technological developments.[10]

Tenhaaf asserts that this invisibility of the feminine calls for "a radical reconstitution of technology," but we must ask ourselves whether the architecture of the hardware and the premises of software engineering themselves are not so encumbered with old philosophical ideas that any "reconstitution" would amount only to surface decoration. Key ideas of feminism and poststructuralism include the question of gender, of re-owning the body, of the voice of the "other" and "minor literatures" of postcolonialism and subaltern theory. These discourses critique the Enlightenment values of the authority of a rational master discourse and the subjugation and rejection of the body. The standard paradigm of VR reifies a mind/body split that is essentially patriarchal and a paradigm of viewing that is phallic, colonizing, and panoptical. A case example of the culturally male perspective is the standard mode of navigation in virtual space. Simply stated, "what the eye wants, the eye gets" in this world of unhindered voyeuristic desire. It is a machine that articulates scopic desire. VR arms the eye, it gives the eye a hand of its own, propelled (apparently) by the gaze itself. The authoritative viewpoint of Renaissance pictorial space is actively empowered: action at a distance. The entire body is propelled by scopic desire.

THE GENDERED GAZE, VIRTUALITY, AND SAFE SEX

Media theorist Erkki Huhtamo has outlined a history of the "penetration shot" from early cinema, through various generations of moving image technology into the "powerful gaze" in VR.[11] He notes the preponderance of environments that allow or facilitate visual command in virtual worlds—the familiar panopticon model, in which the user oversees an expansive space, and can "zoom" to any place at high speed in order to take disciplinary action. If navigation in VR is the articulation of the phallic gaze, we might consider what a feminine alternative might be. A recent work by Agnes Hegedus neatly turns this paradigm on its head. In *Handsight*,[12] the viewer holds a position sensor with the image of an eyeball painted on it. In conventional VR, the eye can fly and grab, unhindered by the body. In *Handsight* the body helps the helpless eye about the virtual space. The virtual space is not a limitless frontier, but a closely bounded domain, whose physical boundaries prohibit the illusion of limitlessness. This inversion is experiential; one discovers it through interaction and consideration.

West Coast interactive media artist Lynn Hershman, too—in her work *Deep Contact*[13]—interrogates the gendering of electronic tools and spaces by offering the user the prospect of libidinal reward if only "he" would "break through the glass [of the monitor] and touch me." In this metaphor of penetration, there is a sideswipe at Ivan Sutherland's goal to "break the glass and go inside the machine."

British media and performance artist Paul Sermon has similarly interrogated the gendering of electronic spaces in his video telepresence performance *Telematic Dreaming*.[14] This curious work offered the visitor the pleasure of lying on a bed with a real-time interactive image of Paul, who was in another city, watching the scene on a video monitor. The image of Paul would stroke the visitor sitting or lying on the bed, and the visitor might stroke the image of Paul. Like *Deep Contact*, this work explores questions of technological telepresence via mechanisms of the erotic. A nostalgic reenactment of 1960s love-ins in the erotophobic age of AIDS, virtual sex is the ultimate prophylactic.

VR, SCIENCE FICTION AND POPULAR CULTURE

Virtual Reality is discussed here as if it exists. At the time of writing, VR in the civilian domain is a rudimentary technology, as anyone who has worn a pair of eyephones will attest. That the technology is advancing rapidly is perhaps less interesting than that virtually all commentators discuss it as if it were a fully realized technology. There is a desire in our culture for VR that one can fairly characterize as a yearning. VR has lingered prenatally in science fiction and the Star Trek Holodeck for a generation or two, but now it is being born. It will slip frictionlessly into our culture because our culture has prepared us for it. I have suggested elsewhere that every significant media-technological development since the Renaissance has been employed to create theaters of simulation. Film historian Andre Bazin noted in mid-century that "the guiding myth...inspiring the invention of cinema, is the accomplishment of that which dominated in a more or less vague fashion all the techniques of mechanical reproduction of reality in the nineteenth century, from photography to the phonograph, namely an integral realism, a recreation of the world in its own image, an image unburdened by the freedom of interpretation of the artist or the irreversibility of time."[15]

The way for VR has been prepared (most recently) by Disneyland, Hollywood, liposuction, and Nintendo. We are taught to regard our body as a an instrument, as apparel. Our culture customizes bodies like it customizes cars. The body is a representation only, an external appearance, and may be adjusted to suit the taste of the owner. The absolute malleability of the virtual body is different only in degree. VR is an easy step because the body is already a representation.

How real is virtual reality? The cultural underpinnings are already in place to lubricate the general acceptance that VR adequately represents "reality." The interchangeability of visual consumption with "experience," which we are encouraged to believe occurs via television, has certainly colored expectations of the virtual environment. Our preparation is cultural. We will accept VR as a representational scheme, no matter what its verisimilitude, in the same way that we accept a map of a city or the pieces on a chess board.

VR AND THE MIND/BODY SPLIT

I want to explore now the perceptual experience of inhabiting the virtual body with respect to Cartesian dualism. Wearing eyephones and earphones, the visual and auditory world is shut out and replaced with a representation. This leaves one part of the sensorial body in the corporeal world, the other part in the virtual world. To avoid this split-body condition, one must simulate all sensory input in a coordinated way. We might call this "total body representation." It is instructive to examine what this might imply. If in VR, I am confronted with a cast-iron chair, a typist's chair, and a lounge, I must not only be able to sit, but the sensation of texture must change. I must also be physically supported by some system. This implies a full force-feedback suit unimpeding and light enough to be unnoticeable by the wearer. This kind of apparatus is not feasible with any technology currently available or in development. Further, in order for a fully simulated representation of the body to be complete, the realm of the kinesthetic, proprioceptive sense, and sense of balance must be catered for. The internal body senses must be represented, but how can we electronically simulate the sense of a distended stomach? Sense of taste and smell are also absent. When can I eat virtual food and excrete virtual feces? Clearly no amount of external gadgetry will facilitate total body representation.[16]

The VR condition that we are discussing is therefore the limited case of a simulated interactive stereoscopic visual (and occasionally auditory) environment, in which the body is represented purely visually. The prospect of a partial but coordinated and articulated representation of the body raises the question of the repercussions, both psychological and cultural, of a double body. Virtual reality replaces the body with two partial bodies: the corporeal body and an (incomplete) electronic body image. The VR experience is therefore, on a bodily level, one of dislocation and dissociation. Can this "body without organs" cope with such fragmentation? The mind seems willing to close down sensory channels at odds with other more dominant channels. There do seem to be problems when the closed-down channels are reactivated. Simulator sickness arises from disconnected sensory modalities. "Sitting still" in a flight simulator in which the image presents the visual experience of "rolling" requires the mind to preference the visual input and ignore the kinesthetic information from the semicircular canals of the ears, to switch it off. This the mind happily does, but it takes at least twenty-four hours for the sense of balance to "reconnect." During that time people tend to fall over a lot. As a result, the Navy prohibits the piloting of a plane within twenty-four hours of being in a flight simulator.

The body representation of VR fragments the body; it produces a powerful eye mounted on a fractured body. One does not take one's body into VR, one leaves it at the door. Virtual reality reinforces the Cartesian duality, replacing the body with a body image, a creation of mind, as all objects in virtual worlds are a product of mind. As such, it is a clear continuation of the rationalist dream of disembodied mind, part of the long Western tradition of denial of the body. St. Augustine is the patron saint of cyberpunks.

Randy Walser and Eric Gullichsen of Autodesk (in one of the more striking examples of science fiction inspired VR rhetoric) have said: "In cyberspace there is no need to move about in a body like the one you possess in physical reality. As you conduct more of your life and affairs in cyberspace, your conditioned notion of a unique and immutable body will give way to a far more liberated notion of 'body' as something quite disposable and, generally, limiting. You will find that some bodies work best in some conditions while others work best in others."[17] This is a confusion, since there is no need for a body at all in virtual reality except for narcissistic or gaming purposes. All you require is an indication of the location of your VR effectors with respect to your virtual viewpoint. As the entire physical body is represented in VR by a larger and larger array of interface points, the potential diversity of one's image in VR will become more limited. The variety is possible now only because one can put almost any shape between the image of the glove and the virtual viewpoint.

As all objects in a virtual world are constructed, so is the body image itself. In "designer reality," the shape and style of the body you take into virtual reality is an open choice. You can design a body with numerous limbs—say, a giant lobster—and by attaching additional sensors to knees and elbows to control the extra limbs, you can comfortably inhabit such a body. The mind maps to this new body almost effortlessly; that is, you begin to instruct your left knee to move, fully knowing that it is in fact the third foot down on the left side. In the case of the giant lobster, Lanier reports that it takes only two to three minutes to remap arbitrarily placed sensors—on the chin or knee, for instance—as controllers for extra limbs.

These astonishing reports suggest that the mind can quickly draw a new "internal body representation" to allow control of the new body—effectively, to pull the gray matter out of one skull and drop it into another. This effect seems to be at odds with the traditional notion of the neurological homunculus inscribed on the brain. The arbitrary body suggests a way of understanding virtual body articulation as hyper-puppetry, with the homunculus functioning as a temporary map or I/O program, as opposed to "hard wired" circuitry.

The term virtual body is loosely used and should be clarified. When we discuss the perceiving body, it is in two quite different perceptual roles. We can discuss the body as *a thing that is perceived internally and understood to be the physical manifestation identified with "self."* In virtual reality this perception is purely visual and crudely fashioned. We can also discuss the body as *the thing that does the perceiving of other things outside the body.* In virtual reality this perceiving is specifically visual and auditory. Walser and Gullichsen conclude: "The ability to radically and compellingly change one's body image is bound to have a deep psychological effect, calling into question just what you consider yourself to be."[18]

There is cause for concern here if our sense of self, our sense of place in the world, remains consistent and continuous purely because external reality has a certain continuity to it. I am suggesting that we have no internal continuous self-image, that self-image is volatile, and that only a stable "reality" enforces a stable self-image by means of a continually active feedback loop. You have remained a person while reading this paper; you have not turned into a pool of red hot lava or a collection of reptiles. What, then, are the effects of longterm immersion in virtual reality, of adopting alternative bodies, and what are the effects of frequently switching in and out of a variety of bodies in a variety of worlds? Could the Walser and Gullichsen experience induce a form of schizophrenia?

There is no such thing as the virtual body in the sense that we inhabit our bodies. We live in our bodies, and our bodies both act upon the world and register the action of the world upon us. The resistance-then-collapse of frozen snow under the weight of my foot, the squeaking sound of walking in snow, the pain in my face from the cold and the gluey feeling of my upper lip as my breath condenses to ice on my mustache are all aspects of my bodily experience of winter. Such holistic body response is not available in a virtual world. In true industrial spirit, duties have been specialized, action is done by certain parts of the body, and cognition is done by others. The "meat body" becomes only a machine to press the appropriate buttons or to re-aim the viewpoint, driven by a desiring, controlling mind. The body does not feel, it does not register the virtual world. Only the eyes—privileged as the most "accurate" of the senses since the Renaissance—and sometimes the ears register the virtual world. Indeed, the virtual world is constructed primarily as a visual world—it is incorporeal!

THE CONFLATION OF REPRESENTATION WITH KINESTHETICS

Jaron Lanier argues that virtual reality sidesteps the process of translation into and out of symbolic representation; he calls this postsymbolic communication. This claim is, in my view, questionable. Lanier argues that "the way you talk to your body doesn't use symbols." Fair enough, but what he then suggests to be a logical corollary does not follow: "You can make a cup that someone else can pick up...without ever having to use a picture or the word 'cup'...you create the experiential object cup' rather than the symbolic object."[19] But it is not that simple. The cup in VR is a representation; it is a stereographic image. You cannot drink out of it.

The paradoxical nature of "body" in VR is that although the cup itself is an incorporeal image, the movements of my arm to pick up the cup, and the correlation of my proprioceptive perception of my arm moving (in coordination with the image of a hand/tool/pointer moving toward the cup) are bodily experiences. Handing someone a virtual cup resolves the mind/body duality—not because the virtual cup bypasses the symbolic, but because the willful action "passing the cup" is made. Motor action occurs as a result of will; the real arm moves the representation of the cup, the arm is moving both within virtual reality and without, the realm of representation and physiology are conflated.[20]

There is a paradigm shift in the VR experience, but it does not bypass the symbolic and replace it with an experience that is indistinguishable from corporeal experience.[21] The VR representation is an interactive stereographic representation; it is an automation of pictorial representation. The appellation *virtual reality* is unfortunate; it makes the same sort of untenable claims for the technology that the term *artificial intelligence* did. I would prefer to discuss VR as a special augmented case of representation, such that the object is simultaneously a representation and (in a limited way) a kinesthetically experiential phenomenon. VR directly interfaces with the body, bypassing textual language, but it remains a pictorial representation and is thus subject to critical analysis as such. A new critique is required: a way of thinking about the meeting point between the immediate physiological reality of the body as lived in, and the culturally specific conventions of representation.

VR AND POWER

Machine tools, including computers, are devices for exercising power over objects and sometimes people, but the role of the user in virtual reality is essentially submissive. In VR one submits to the representation and the limited freedoms it offers—a postmodern capitalist paradise! This submission is analogous to the submission of the people who are employed to actually manufacture the hardware that runs these virtual worlds. In electronic sweatshops in Taiwan, Malaysia, Mexico, and El Salvador, people (primarily women) labor to produce these goods that they will never consume. Alluquere Rosanne Stone remarked that Descartes was able to "forget the body" only because he had servants to attend to the needs of his.[22] Similarly, users of VR implicitly exploit the labor of these Third World workers. Can we interpret this swing in the technology of virtual reality from a paradigm of domination to a paradigm of submission as a *fin de siècle* malaise, a simultaneous decline in the will to control, and an acceptance of the overarching power of technology? French philosopher Gilles Deleuze has built an argument on similar terms, in which he outlines a general movement in the twentieth century from societies of overt discipline such as Foucault has described, to "ultrarapid forms of free-floating control." In the computerized workplace, real-time surveillance via the computer has been a reality for some time. Paranoia aside, your computer *is* watching you. Text workers are monitored in terms of keystrokes per minute, telephone salespeople in terms of calls per hour. If such a vision is possible in the corporeal world, the prospect of real-time surveillance is so much more simply facilitated in VR. Not only will the computer know where you are, but what kind of information you are accessing, and where your various body parts are at the time. As digital media become increasingly encapsulating, so the possibility of permanent real-time surveillance becomes real.

In terms of corporate economics, VR serves the computer industry very well. It is intuitive (which allows for an easy learning curve and thus no consumer resistance) and calls for unlimited computer power. It thus fulfills the industry's need for technological desire, the transference of libidinal desire onto fetish objects that offer the promise of ecstasy but never finally consummate, driving the consumer to the next purchase in an unending coitus interruptus.

We have no reason to delude ourselves that any new technology, as such, promises any sort of sociocultural liberation. History is against us here. We must assume that the forces of corporate consumerism will attempt to fully capitalize on the phenomenon in terms of financial profit, and that the potential for surveillance and control will be exploited by corporate and state instrumentalities. We have a responsibility to develop a critical consciousness of these possibilities, the better to prepare ourselves, our children, and our students to deal with the highly technologized lifestyle of the early decades of the twenty-first century. As they say, the future isn't what it used to be.

CONCLUSION

Technologies are products of culture. The ideas that have constructed virtual reality are not new, but have deep roots in our culture. Historically, technological development projects have been considered by their developers as noncontinuous with the world of everyday experience. Virtual reality must not be considered in this way, nor should the developers of these environments be encouraged to think in such a way. It is the fabric of everyday culture that lends, and confines, meaning to these virtual worlds. The developers and their worlds are immersed in, and informed by, the contemporary culture that is itself informed by cultural history.

I hope to have indicated that the claim that VR is a liberation from the mind/body duality is, like most rhetorics, in opposition to the experience. This is not to say that VR does not have a complex relation with the body. It is precisely this relation, a relation of instrumentalization, of specialization of parts, that shows it to be the technology at the end of the Enlightenment.

If VR can be regarded as the end point of the Enlightenment, then perhaps this completion may now allow for the "paradigm shift" that chaos theory, nonlinear dynamics, and the theory of complexity promise, not simply for computer science, but for culture in general.

Simon Penny is Associate Professor of Art and Robotics at Carnegie Mellon University, Pittsburgh. His recent activities include editing *Critical Issues in Electronic Media* (SUNY Press) and curating the Machine Culture exhibition of interactive art at SIGGRAPH '93. He makes interactive installations and mobile robotic artworks. Internet: <penny+@andrew.cmu.edu>.

Note

This is the most recent in a series of papers I have written dealing with the cultural context and philosophical implications of Virtual Reality. My previous work in this field includes "2000 Years of Virtual Reality" in *Through the Looking Glass, Artists' First Encounters with Virtual Reality* (catalog of an exhibition held at Jack Tilton Gallery, 1992), edited by Janine Cirincione and Brian D'Amato; and "Virtual Bodybuilding," *Media Information Australia*, August 1993. Aspects of this paper have their roots in these, and also in a paper presented at the Ideologies of Technology Symposium, held March 1992 at the Dia Center for the Arts in New York City, organized by Timothy Druckrey and Gretchen Bender (see *Culture on the Brink: Ideologies of Technology*, Seattle: Seattle Bay Press, 1994, in association with Dia Center for the Arts). At the outset, virtual reality boggled and challenged many in the techno-arts community, myself included. I am now of the opinion that the achievements of VR in the past have been mostly technical, rhetoric notwithstanding. The esthetically difficult work, of what to put in virtual worlds, of the ways in which they might be constrained and conformed, is yet to be done.

REFERENCES

1. Many of these ideas were "of their time." Analytic geometry, with the device of axes mutually at ninety degrees to locate points on the plane or in space, was also developed by Pierre de Fermat around the same time, but Fermat's work was not published until 1670.

2. Recall the story of a competition between two Greek painters: (Parrhasius) entered into a competition with Zeuxis. Zeuxis produced a picture of grapes so dexterously represented that birds began to fly down to eat from the painted vine. Whereupon Parrhasius designed so lifelike a picture of a curtain that Zeuxis, proud of the verdict of the birds, requested that the curtain should now be drawn back and the picture displayed. When he realized his mistake, with a modesty that did him honor, he yielded up the palm, saying that whereas he had managed to deceive only birds, Parrhasius had deceived an artist.

3. See McKenzie Wark, "Suck on This, Planet of Noise," in "Art and Cyberculture" special issue of *Media Information Australia #69*, August 1993.

4. Alluquere Rosanne Stone, quoted in *Telesthesia*, Frances Dyson and Douglas Kahn, San Francisco: Walter McBean Gallery, San Francisco Art Institute, 1991.

5. What if virtual reality had developed along pictorial principles other than Renaissance humanism? Could we feel we could inhabit it at all? In other words, how much is any so-called virtual reality dependent upon culturally acquired knowledge in order to be decipherable? Numerous experiments in visual perception performed on non-Western people attest to the cultural specificity of our particular way of pictorially representing space and distance, relative scale, and so forth. There are reports that New Guinea Highlanders were initially unable to "see" themselves, to identify their own images in Polaroid photographs.

6. Among others, Jonathan Crary discusses these issues in his excellent book *Techniques of the Observer*, Cambridge, Mass.: MIT Press, 1992.

7. Florian Rotzer, "Interaction and Play" in *Machine Culture*, Simon Penny, ed., in *Computer Graphics: Visual Proceedings*, Annual Conference Series, 1993, New York: ACM Press, 1993.

8. Ivan Sutherland, "The Ultimate Display," in *Proceedings of the IFIP Congress 65, Vol. 2.*, edited by Wayne A. Kalenich, Washington, DC: Spartan Books, 1965: 506-509. Sutherland built the first head-mounted display in 1968.

9. Manuel DeLanda, *War in the Age of Intelligent Machines*, Cambridge, Mass.: Swerve Editions, Zone Books, MIT Press, 1991.

10. Nell Tenhaaf, "Of Monitors and Men and Other Unsolved Feminist Mysteries," *Parallelogram*, 18(3).

11. Erkki Huhtamo in *Virtual Zone Symposium* (Turku, Finland, October 1992) (text in Finnish).

12. Shown at Ars Electronica, Linz, Austria, June 1992 and the Machine Culture exhibition at SIGGRAPH '93. Documented in *Computer Graphics: Visual Proceedings*, Annual Conference Series, 1993, New York: ACM Press, 1993: 130.

13. Lynn Hershman, *Deep Contact*, exhibited at Rijksmuseum Enschede, Netherlands, 1990 and elsewhere.

14. Paul Sermon, *Telematic Dreaming*, performed at Muu Media Festival, Helsinki, Finland, 1991.

15. Andre Bazin "The Myth of Total Cinema" in *What Is Cinema*, volume 1, Berkeley: University of California Press, 1967: 21.

16. For better or worse, direct neural jacks seem to loom on the horizon, and this technology will radically change the terms of this discussion.

17. Randy Walser and Eric Gulichsen, quoted by Howard Rheingold in "The Wildest Dreams of Virtual Reality," *M*, March 1992.

18. Ibid.

19. Jaron Lanier, interviewed by Tim Druckery in "Revenge of the Nerds," *Afterimage* 18(10).

20. William Bricken maintains that all the operations of symbolic logic can be performed in VR without recourse to symbolic languages, that logic is equivalent to inference in visual programming. Set theory, number theory, algebra can all be represented as objects in space that is nonsymbolic and totally math-rigorous! Binary logic can be represented as open and shut doors, knot theory as fish swimming upstream over dams. "All computation is algebraic pattern-matching and substitution (proven)" William Bricken, SIGGRAPH '91 (personal notes).

21. Cognition in VR: That virtual reality is incomplete is clear at even a cursory inspection. As a representation, virtual worlds are an abstractions. The question is not how abstract a representation will the mind/body accept as one that will stand in for reality, as "reality" is an obfuscating word in this context. The question becomes, What constitutes a continuous interactive representation? What arrangement of images and interactive cues cohere into a system with syntactic order? This question is made complex due to the confounding malleability of the mind, what William Bricken refers to as "cognitive remodeling." The mind, it seems, is quite willing to restructure itself to compensate for, or adapt to, a changing "reality." There is a peculiar cognitive feedback loop here: virtual reality, standing in for reality, begins to shape the way the mind describes its experience to itself. The current state of imagery in virtual environments is extremely simple, built as it is from several thousand polygons. Even so, William Bricken reports that as one interacts with a

virtual world, one comes to accept the polygonal representations. It becomes as valid a world as the "real." VR people refer to this as "cognitive plasticity" (William Bricken, SIGGRAPH '91, personal notes). Thomas Furness relates that if you spend a lot of time in VR, you begin to dream in polygons! (Thomas Furness, SIGGRAPH '91, personal notes). Jaron Lanier's oft-quoted definition that "reality is what is on the other side of the senses" is validated by these experiences. The VR representation is ultimately as schematic as that of a map or a chess board. These are schematic representations that are culturally learned, to which we bring meaning and from which we draw meaning. One of the techniques of virtual world design, as of other computer interface design, is to utilize familiar symbols and terminology to indicate to the user that the computer system has been modeled on a familiar "real world" system (i.e., the folders and trash can of the Macintosh interface). The learning curve is less steep because relationships are familiar. Virtual reality cannot exist outside a cultural construct.

22. Alluquere Rosanne Stone, quoted by Frances Dyson and Douglas Kahn in *Telesthesia*, catalog of an exhibition held 1991 at the Walter McBean Gallery of the San Francisco Art Institute, San Francisco, CA.

ETHICAL QUESTIONS POSED BY VIRTUAL REALITY TECHNOLOGY

Howard Rheingold

The time to discuss the ethical implications of a new technology is when the technology is young. Virtual reality is a new technology, and some of its implications are becoming clear early in its development. It will take ten or twenty years for the technology to mature enough to realize our most humane hopes and our worst nightmares about its impact.

MICROSCOPE FOR THE MIND

Virtual reality technology, when applied in medical imaging, scientific visualization, prosthetic devices, and other areas, has the potential to become a life-enhancing tool, a window onto invisible worlds, and a liberating force for good minds trapped in dysfunctional bodies. When applied to semi-autonomous weaponry, political disinfotainment, or the marketing of addictive but alienating experiences, VR technology has the potential to become a life-sapping weapon, a dangerous brainwashing device, a form of imprisonment-through-illusion. Decades of research and development lie ahead before forecasts become products. This is an ideal time for a widespread public discussion of the benefits and liabilities of VR-based applications, and in particular, the ethical implications of synthetic experience.

The use of VR as a scientific visualization tool is enough to guarantee its place in future history. The microscope made biology and modern medicine possible because it gave scientists a window onto the invisible world of the very tiny. The telescope helped create the foundation of the industrial revolution by offering a window onto the invisible world of very distant objects, thus changing our image of humanity's place in the universe. VR offers a window onto other heretofore invisible spaces, but it offers a window through which the scientist can actually climb to interact directly and bodily with scientific abstractions. In ways that we can't fully predict today, VR has the potential for becoming a microscope for the mind.

VR could be a microscope on the mind as well; well-designed virtual environments could have the power to alter consciousness, shape behavior, and influence belief systems. VR could become a powerful tool for understanding the nature of the human mind; for the same reasons, it could be a brainwashing weapon par excellence. Reacting to this possibility, the British medical journal *The Lancet* recently called for an early discussion of "Being and Believing: Ethics of Virtual Reality."

The Lancet editorial warned that the effectiveness of VR as a psychological tool for even the most altruistic purposes might lead to an ethical slippery slope:

> Although the motives behind clinical VR experimentation may be praiseworthy—e.g., it may replace the prescription of harmful psychotropics—the fact that experimentation may be well intended does not preclude early examination of ethical issues. Careful thought is required before [administering] VR-based care or clinical investigation to patients, especially those who are mentally ill. Underlying concerns include the capacity of VR to distort reality-testing in patients whose judgment is already impaired, the loss of freedom of choice of experience when in VR, and the dangers of medical paternalism. Our experience has many levels of purpose; VR provides only part of these. Continuous exposure to VR will impoverish those aspects of life that determine social development, interpersonal insight, and emotional judgment. Vulnerable patients should not be exposed to VR until the full extent of its likely impact can be reliably anticipated.[1]

When visiting the University of North Carolina at Chapel Hill, I used a force-feedback mechanical arm and head-mounted display to manipulate molecules with my hands, as if they were Tinkertoys: the shape of a potential anti-cancer molecule was represented by a three-dimensional model that floated in space. The shape of a molecule on the coating of a tumor cell floated next to it. I could use the feedback arm to try to fit the molecules together like pieces in a puzzle—and feel the molecular forces as actual physical resistance.

If you could find a way to link human cognitive and perceptual abilities to the robot's strength and ability to operate in hostile environments, you could train human technicians to supervise the operations of flocks of robots in automated factories or undersea mines. In Japan, I had the eerie experience of locking my head and arm into a VR control apparatus to tele-operate a robot on the other side of the room; the eerie part came in when I looked over at myself through the robot's eyes and realized that my sense of presence had been transferred effectively to the robot. In Hawaii, at a high-security U.S. Marine base, I saw the prototype for a tele-operated machine-gun vehicle. And in Manchester, England, I saw the first components of a tele-operated firefighter tested.

THE ETHICAL QUESTIONS

From what we know about the potential for tele-operation today, ethical implications already begin to emerge—implications we would do well to ponder and debate before the technology becomes an industry with a momentum of its own. The three most important ethical questions posed by possible VR applications are:

- What is the morality of virtualizing warfare, which blurs the difference between video games and bombing runs?

- Who will own virtual reality? Who will control it? Who will have access to it?

- What are the ethical problems inherent in using VR technology to change people's beliefs and opinions?

VIRTUAL WAR

The most immediate downside to VR is the advent of the age of virtual war. During the Gulf War, the restriction of news photography to those now-famous shots of "smart-bombs" blowing up bunkers presented a kind of virtual war to the world. At the same time, pilots of aircraft and tanks saw similar views of landscapes they had seen before in simulations; one of the things I witnessed when I was researching my book on VR was SIMNET, the U.S. military simulation network that trains tank crews, helicopter pilots, and jet pilots in mock battles on simulated battlefields based on Defense Intelligence Agency digital maps of expected combat zones. The Gulf War was the first war that was rehearsed in virtual space before it took place—and was presented to the world *while* it was taking place—in images that closely resemble those of simulations. As culture theorist Jean Baudrillard warned, the map now precedes the territory.[2]

When we blur the line between playing a video game and blowing up real people, aren't we doing serious damage to the social fabric, the web of agreements about meaning that knits societies together? The role of semi-autonomous weaponry is worth serious public discussion. Whether or not war is a good idea is a separate issue. The question here is whether we are sure that we want to turn over human judgment to computer systems when it comes to combat.

Questions of power and control are always important when technology creates a new entertainment or communication medium: will there be a market for realities, or will we all have to buy regulation reality from Fujitsu or Disney? Will a large number of people be able to use the technology to discover new knowledge, create new wealth, and share it with others, or will it be controlled by a few who will reap enormous revenues from everyone else?

THE REALITIES WE WANT

The question of whether VR will be an open system or a proprietary one might be one of the most important questions the human race has faced. A certain amount of responsibility for managing this new technology lies in the citizenry beyond the small circles of technical experts. We are faced with decisions about fundamental human values, not just decisions about technology. The important questions that as citizens we must confront have to do with the kinds of realities we want to encourage—proprietary or free-of-charge, centrally controlled or libertarian, funded for science and education applications or funded for military or economic dominance. These questions can be answered only by an informed citizenry—which is why it is important that people learn to talk more intelligently about a future in which it might be possible to manufacture any conceivable experience.

Howard Rheingold has written numerous articles on virtual reality, as well as *The Virtual Community* (Addison-Wesley, 1993), *Virtual Reality* (Summit, 1991), *The Cognitive Connection: Thought and Language in Man and Machine* (Prentice Hall, 1987), and *Tools for Thought: the People and Ideas Behind the Next Computer Revolution* (Simon & Schuster, 1985). Internet: <hlr@well.sf.ca.us>.

REFERENCES

1. "Being and Believing: Ethics of Virtual Reality," *Lancet*, August 3, 1991: 283.

2. Jean Baudrillard, Simulations. New York: Semiotext(e), Columbia University Press, 1983.

CYBERCULTURE: THE PATTERN THAT CONNECTS

Gareth Branwyn

It is as though progress were making the real world invisible.

O.B. Hardison, *Disappearing Through the Skylight*

FROM DADA TO DATA

Art, technology, and science in the twentieth century have followed trajectories that have brought them increasingly closer together. Avant-garde art, for instance, has consistently shown a concern for the effects that technology and science are having on culture, even as science and technology have looked to art for new ways to design and package their discoveries. Conversations between art and technoscience have taken many forms. The Italian futurists in the 1910s celebrated the machine, almost to the point of worship, while the dadaists in the twenties poked fun at mechanization and alienation, as evidenced in such works as the machine portraits of Raoul Hausmann, Francis Picabia, and others.[1] The French situationists of the 1950s and 1960s wrote extensively about the somnambulistic effects of media driven by commodity fetishism. In such statements as "everything that was directly lived has moved away into a representation" (Debord), they foresaw the displacement of the real by the simulated that now characterizes our postmodern condition.

In the past decade, artists, scientists, and technologists have found themselves in unique collaborations over such projects as visualizing 3D computer worlds and modeling theoretical mathematical constructs such as hyperspace and fractals. In his book *Disappearing through the Skylight*, O. B. Hardison examines the co-evolution of art and technoscience from Dada to virtual reality: "Computers complete the democratization of art begun by Dada, and as they do, they announce a change so fundamental in the idea of art that it can legitimately be called a disappearance."

This emergence of computers and other "personal" technologies (modems, copiers, video cameras, fax machines, and other "desktop" devices) has had a tremendous impact on technological societies. Inexpensive miniaturized technology has revolutionized the ability of one person or a small group of people to greatly expand the bandwidth (spectrum) of their communications. Lots of people have brought this technology into their lives (or had it foisted on them), even as they seem confused or ignorant as to the impact the technology is having on them. As Larry McCaffery states in the introduction to *Storming the Reality Studio*, "this unprecedented expansion ... has profoundly altered not only the daily textures of the world(s) we inhabit but the way we think about the world and ourselves in it."

As our world becomes saturated by more powerful and sophisticated end-user technologies, economists, philosophers, political scientists, and artists (to name a few) struggle to keep up with the significance of these rapid developments. Personal cybernetic technologies, along with other technoscientific developments (such as bioengineering, high-tech medicine, artificial intelligence, and virtual reality) are once again calling into question such classic opposites as real and artificial, human and machine, organic and inorganic, life and death, original and copy, and even male and female. As would be expected, interpretations regarding what all this portends cover a broad spectrum, from technophobic doomsaying to the longstanding techno-utopian tradition of throwing more technology at the technology that has already failed us.

Onto this fragmented postmodern landscape there has recently emerged a new subculture that is deeply committed to keeping pace with all the leading-edge technology and the cultural artifacts and debates that surround it. This subculture, largely connected through telecommunication networks and "samizdat" publishing,[2] has glimpsed not only the ways these technologies are reshaping our world, but also their vast potential for building new forms of community and fostering creative autonomy. While this subculture is too young and too anarchistic to have an agreed upon name or a handy definition, it is increasingly being referred to as the cyberculture.[3] Computer hackers, the denizens of the world's computer networks and bulletin boards, visionary researchers into artificial intelligence, virtual reality, robotics, and artificial life, and a diverse range of artists and musicians might all be considered active participants in this new subculture.

While a full map of this cyberculture has yet to be plotted, certain historical trends offer some clues as to the aesthetics from which it is drawn. Here we will look at four areas of influence—art, literature, technology, and politics—and at some of the important texts that will help the interested reader explore further this new cultural trend.

JUST SAY NO (to the Dominant Culture)

As the Hardison quote above points out, it is not hard to see various ideas behind cyberculture as continuing a conversation that began at the turn of the century with the futurists and the dadaists. The futurists were obsessed with technology and its awesome potential to transform the natural world into the image of humanity. Futurist art also showed a contempt for dominant culture and the limitations of "the common people." While these two aesthetic concerns later fell into the hands of the fascists, dadaism picked up these threads in the 1920s, expressing similar ideas with a more leftist spin. Dadaists were far more suspicious of technology, art, and anything else that "high" culture held sacred. In his book *Lipstick Traces*, Greil Marcus follows a thinly veiled path through these twentieth-century "negationist movements." He maps his trail through dada (and what it absorbed from futurism), surrealism, the lettrists, and the situationists, ending up in the punk movement of the late 1970s. *The Assault on Culture*, a similar survey by Stewart Home, follows the same path all the way up to the samizdat publishing scene of the 1980s.

It is here that the cyberculture could trace a link to this lineage. The 1980s desktop publishing "revolution" created an explosion of small publications covering a staggering variety of subjects. Many of these 'zines were influenced by the dadaists, the situationists, the punk movement, and various other fringe cultures. In the late 1980s, these 'zines started to enter into the crude cyberspace of telecom services such as Usenet, The WELL, and CompuServe.[4] Other subgroups orbiting this scene such as mail artists and concrete poets also started to maintain a presence in these new "virtual communities."[5] Numerous arts organizations started their own online conferences such as the pathbreaking Art Com on the WELL and Usenet, and the more recent ArtsWire service. Out of this interface between avant-garde/underground art, samizdat publishing, the burgeoning virtual communities, and pop culture grew such cyberculture publications as *Mondo 2000*, *bOING-bOING*, and *Intertek*.

Two cultural strategies also run straight through these historical movements toward the cyberculture. "Detournement," a term coined by the situationists, refers to the turning of existing images back onto themselves to make sociopolitical statements. This idea of recycling and recontextualizing the output of the commodity culture has been a key confrontation strategy from Dada collage and ready-mades to the audio sampling of 1980s industrial music and the war machine mutations of Survival Research Labs (SRL). Obviously, the issues of intellectual property, sampling, and copying go to the heart of all postmodern discourse, but they are perhaps made most explicit and argued most vigorously throughout the cyberculture.

The second strategy that is employed often in confrontational avant-garde art is what the anarchist Hakim Bey has labeled poetic terrorism. This involves the use of various shock tactics and semantical shifts in an effort to get people to wake up to what is really going on behind the facade of our slick, commercialized, and cosmetized cultures. Examples of poetic terrorism would include everything from Duchamp's famous "Fountain" (a urinal) to the situationist Guy Debord's blank films, to the AIDS activism group, Act Up. Within the cyberculture, one could point to numerous acts of benign hacker mischief, the work of a number of techno-performance and installation artists (SRL, Alan Rath, Comfort/Control, Julia Scher, Stelarc), and others who use technology as "a powerful and appropriate vehicle of cultural confrontation and discursive commentary upon the technological religion of our times."[6] A new organization called the Immediasts was recently formed to help organize and support "media activists" in using the media arts as a way to create an all-out poetic assault on the commercial media. In their first communiqué, "Seizing the Media," they call on hackers, artists, and activists to use all available do-it-yourself (DIY) media technologies to detourne the "ecology of coercion" that they believe the mainstream media has perpetrated.

TECHNO-SURREAL FICTION

The single most influential artistic contribution to the coalescence of the cyberculture was the emergence of cyberpunk science fiction in the mid-1980s. The term "cyberpunk" was coined to refer to the literary dispatches of a small group of science fiction writers including William Gibson (*Neuromancer*, 1984), Bruce Sterling (*Schismatrix*, 1985), John Shirley (*Eclipse*, 1985), and Rudy Rucker (*Software*, 1982). These writers created a collective body of work that tore open the naive utopian veneer of golden-age sci-fi. Bruce Sterling, in his preface to *Mirrorshades: The Cyberpunk Anthology* (1986), points out that "certain central themes spring up repeatedly in cyberpunk. The theme of body invasion; prosthetic limbs, implanted circuitry, cosmetic surgery, genetic alteration. The even more powerful theme of mind invasion: brain-computer interfaces, artificial intelligence, neurochemistry techniques radically redefining the nature of humanity, the nature of the self." The cyberpunk aesthetic, fully realized in these literary works, was prefigured in other art of the period, such as the films *Blade Runner* and *Videodrome*, and in such industrial art as Survival Research Labs' mechanized performances and Throbbing Gristle's experiments in art noise. But, while these various explorations were developing separately, books like *Neuromancer* provided a full landscape view of all these aesthetic threads coming together in the very near future. Unlike a lot of science fiction before it, cyberpunk simply projected our current conditions twenty minutes into the future. Things in Gibson's near-future world have not radically changed as much as they have grown progressively better in one direction and worse in another. Classes are more stratified, megacorporations are more powerful, entertainment technologies are more addictive, and technology has become so small and sophisticated that it has trickled down to the street level and disappeared inside of us. Everyone is a cyborg, everyone and everything is wired and transmitting.

While cyberpunk literature has been repeatedly pronounced dead and most of its preeminent architects have tried to divorce themselves from the label, cyberpunk itself continues to have a tremendous influence on those interested in real-world cyberculture. Larry McCaffery sums up the contribution of the cyberpunks: "Their work represents the most concerted effort yet by artists to find a suitable means for displaying the powerful and troubling technological logic that underlies our postmodern condition. Mixing equal measures of anger and bitter humor, technological know-how and formal inventiveness, [cyberpunk] science-fiction should be seen as the breakthrough 'realism' of our time. It is an art form that vividly represents the most salient features of our lives, as these lives are being transformed and redefined by technology. It also seeks to empower us by providing a cognitive mapping that can help situate us in a brave new postmodern world that systematically distorts our sense of who or where we are, of what is 'real' at all, of what is most valuable about human life."

DO-IT-YOURSELF: The Hacker Ethic

In *War in the Age of Intelligent Machines*, Manuel De Landa explores how the early years of the personal computer industry were shaped by "young obsessed programmers" (hackers) who "developed an unwritten ethical code which would become one of the driving forces behind the interactive movement, and the force that would eventually bring the personal computer to the marketplace. This ethical code was never encoded in a manifesto, but was embodied instead in the hacker's practices. It involved the idea that information should flow freely without bureaucratic controls and that computers should be used to build better, more interactive computers. Without hackers and hackerlike scientists, I believe, the amount of interactivity that would have found its way into computers would not have reached by itself the minimum threshold needed for the bootstrapping process to acquire its own momentum." This mentality of experimentation, exploration, and free access was a hallmark of early personal computer development. Even within today's highly commercial and litigious computer industry, this ethic lives on among hardcore computer enthusiasts, virtual community "residents," and other members of the cyberculture. It is interesting to note that the DIY philosophy of the early hacker community (largely within academic and research sectors) developed right alongside the late seventies and eighties punk DIY culture. Punk culture in Europe and the United States readily embraced the use of inexpensive technology and its ability to help spread punk rock music and ideas. Copying music, reappropriating images, and making cultural products available as inexpensively as possible were all part of the punk ethos. In the current cyberculture, both the hacker and the punk expressions of DIY live on in such things as 'zine publishing and the so-called "cassette culture" (punk DIY) and in the desire to create an "electronic frontier" of free (or inexpensive) access to the world's databases and virtual communities (hacker DIY).

In the spring of 1990, U.S. law enforcement officers of the FBI, the Secret Service, and numerous local police departments set in motion a series of coordinated arrests aimed at ferreting out alleged computer criminals using computers and telecom networks to organize crimes, exchange stolen documents, break into systems, and steal money electronically. The media had a field day with these arrests, presenting the suspects as "notorious hackers," "computer terrorists," and "high-tech burglars." Within the media and law enforcement, the word "hacker" was being redefined as a term of derision and criminality. The actual hacking community, most of which was not involved in any criminal activity, was shocked by these arrests and the media circus that ensued. "Hacking" had gone from the noble realm of the scientific and technological quest to low-life thievery and electronic intrusion. While there was some criminality involved, most of the arrests and equipment confiscations turned out to be of questionable merit. Many innocent users were left out in the cold as their systems or the systems they networked on were confiscated.

Out of all this chaos emerged a new organization called the Electronic Frontier Foundation (EFF). Co-founder Mitch Kapor's desire was to form an organization that would "protect Constitutional guarantees of free speech and freedom from unreasonable search and seizure. We believe that these fundamental civil liberties must apply to all users of computer networks." The EFF also chose to concern itself with educating the media, policymakers, and the general public on the opportunities and challenges posed by rapidly evolving telecommunications and online networking. The creation of the EFF and the publication of such books such Hafner and Markoff's *Cyberpunk: Outlaws and Hackers on the Computer Frontier* and Bruce Sterling's The *Hacker Crackdown* have gone a long way toward sensibly and nonhysterically addressing issues of freedom, security, and law enforcement in regard to "cyberspace." The computer terrorism scare is not without substance, however. As computer networks connect more and more of the world's databases, financial institutions, corporate and government information sources, and so on, the threat of computer break-in (called "cracking" by the hacker community), theft, and sabotage could pose a big problem. As De Landa concludes: "What used to be a healthy expression of the maxim that information should flow freely is now in danger of becoming a new form of terrorism and organized crime which could create a new era of unprecedented repression."

TEMPORARY AUTONOMOUS ZONES

> Lay down a map of the land; over that, set a map of political change; over that, a map of the Net, especial the [web] with its emphasis on clandestine information—flow and logistics—and finally, over all, the 1:1 map of the creative imagination, aesthetics, and values. The resultant grid comes to life, animated by unexpected eddies and surges of energy, coagulations of light, secret tunnels, surprises.
>
> Hakim Bey, *T.A.Z.*

> Cybernetic identity is never used up—it can be recreated, reassigned, and reconstructed with any number of different names and under different user accounts.
>
> Andrew Ross, *Technoculture*

The politics that influence cybercultural sensibilities are diverse and difficult to pin down. Many of those active within the cyberculture might describe themselves as anarchists, Marxists, socialists, anarcho-libertarians, right wing libertarians, individualists, greens, bohemians, or more likely, none of the above. A large segment of cyberculture participants are generally leery of labels and "group thinks" of all kinds. Running through all these fringe political traditions, however, are a few key similarities. The autonomy of the individual, the value of nonconsensus thinking, the hunger for a better world, an interest in decentralized systems and distributive networks, and a suspicion of the dominant society—all these notions inform cybercultural political discourse. There is also a very strong belief that all the old ways of looking at politics and governance are not adequate for addressing a globalized world that moves at the velocity of electrons.

A glimpse of a new politic that might emerge from computer-mediated communication can be gleaned from Hakim Bey's poetic rant/essay "The Temporary Autonomous Zone." The concept of a temporary autonomous zone, a fluid and free-arising "island" of activity in the world's technosphere, is perhaps fully realizable in the invisibility, temporality, and omnipresence afforded by cyberspace. A networked group of people can come together for a moment, a week, a year, or for a specific project, and once their task has been completed, they can disappear back into the 'net, ready to pop up someplace else. This kind of dynamically fluid polity might be the shape of things to come, at least for certain types of organizing, educating, protesting, and insurgency. Bey sees a kind of "psychic nomadism" as being a possible future lifestyle. He draws a distinction between the "'nets," which are the world's "official" information transfer and communication systems, and the "web," which is the open-structured communication exchange and conviviality connections that each user weaves together for himself or herself using the official channels of the 'net. The more local, national, and special interest groups link into cyberspace, the greater the possibilities become for constructing more complex webs of communication and influence within the 'net.

I, CYBORG

What we need is a new integrative metaphor—like religion or science—that is not based on the idea of ultimate truth.

Mary Catherine Bateson

While not the master metaphor suggested above, Donna Haraway's "Cyborg Manifesto" is one of the first attempts at high tech myth-making to emerge from cybercultural discourse. Initially published in the *Socialist Review* and later in her book *Simians, Cyborgs, and Women,* the manifesto seeks to use the popular sci-fi concept of the cyborg as a tool for personal, social, and political change. Haraway writes: "A cyborg is a cybernetic organism, a hybrid of machine and organism, a creature of social reality as well as a creature of fiction....I am making an argument for the cyborg as a fiction mapping our social and bodily reality and as an imaginative resource suggesting some fruitful couplings." Haraway believes that a lot of leftist political discourse, especially feminism, is antitechnology and based on the idea of a return to a natural state that does not and cannot ever exist again. She suggests a pragmatic and empowered approach toward technology, working with the notion that you can build yourself, your social relations, and your politics using all available resources. Here are a few excerpts from the manifesto:

> The relation between organism and machine has been a border war. The stakes in this war have been the territories of production, reproduction, and imagination. The cyborg manifesto is an argument for pleasure in the confusion of boundaries and for responsibility in their construction.

> Cyborgs are not relevant; they do not remember the cosmos. They are wary of holism, but needy for connections. Cyborgs are the illegitimate offspring of militarism and patriarchal capitalism, not to mention state socialism. But illegitimate offspring are exceedingly unfaithful to their origins. Their fathers, after all, are inessential.

> A cyborg world might be about lived social and bodily realities in which people are not afraid of their joint kinship with animals and machines, not afraid of permanently partial identities and contradictory standpoints. The political struggle is to see from both perspectives at once because each reveals both dominations and possibilities unimaginable from the other vantage point. Single vision produces worse illusions than double vision or many-headed monsters.

> The cyborg is a kind of disassembled and reassembled, postmodern collective and personal self. Communications technologies and biotechnologies are the crucial tools recrafting our bodies. These tools embody and enforce new social relations.

In cybernetics, options (multifold feedback loops) are usually the best way to build flexibility into a system. Flexibility is almost always good. The cyborg manifesto reinforces the idea that we in technological societies have a huge number of options available in constructing the shape our lives. We can have access to an expanding universe of knowledge, myriad lifestyle options, and lots of choices for technological augmentation and amplification. Haraway's manifesto cuts to the heart of what cyberculture is all about. Cyberculture simply represents the vanguard of those who are "imagineering" the new realities that are emerging from our increasingly intimate relationship with machines. Whether we like it or not, we are becoming cyborgs.

Many attuned to cyberculture feel that we now have a golden opportunity to forge the evolutionary path between humans and machines. If we, as informed individuals, do not contribute to directing the course of this partnership, it may fall into the hands of forces that could direct it away from humane ends. In his conclusion to *War in the Age of Intelligent Machines*, Manuel De Landa emphasizes "the need to use computer networks as a means for creating new forms of collective intelligence, of getting humans to interact with one another in novel ways. At every step we will find a similar mixture of new roads to explore and new dangers to avoid. And at all times we will have to play it by ear, since there is no way to predict in advance where these roads will lead, or what kinds of dangers they will present us with." This challenge is what those involved in the cyberculture have chosen to accept.

FURTHER READING

This essay only touches on the history, issues, and cultural productions with which cyberculture is concerned. The texts and organizations cited below can provide further information.

Books

Benedikt, Michael, editor. *Cyberspace: First Steps*. Cambridge, Mass.: MIT Press, 1991. An excellent series of papers exploring the social, artistic, architectural, and philosophical implications of cyberspace.

Bey, Hakim. *T.A.Z.* New York: Autonomedia, 1991. A collection of rants from the anarchist Hakim Bey. While there is a lot of hysteria and delirium in his writing, there are also some useful insights into the possibilities of a new form of computer-mediated nomadism.

Branwyn, Gareth, and Peter Sugarman, eds. *Beyond Cyberpunk*. Rt. 4, Box 54C, Louisa, VA, 23093: The Computer Lab, 1992. Hypercard-based computerized catalog of cyberpunk and cyberculture.

Debord, Guy. *Society of the Spectacle*. Detroit, Mich.: Black & Red, 1983. The principal manifesto of the situationists.

Hafner, Katie, and John Markoff. *Cyberpunk*. New York: Simon and Schuster, 1991. Detailed accounts of three mischievous hackers and how they were caught.

Haraway, Donna Jeanne. *Simians, Cyborgs, and Women: The Reinvention of Nature*. New York: Routledge, 1991. A feminist historian of science looks at how issues of gender have effected scientific perception.

Hardison, O. B. *Disappearing through the Skylight: Culture and Technology in the Twentieth Century*. New York: Viking, 1989. An interpretive history of the co-evolution of science, technology, and avant-garde art.

Home, Stewart. *The Assault on Culture*. London: Aporia Books, 1988. A brief analysis of twentieth-century negationist art movements.

Kroker, Arthur, and Marilouise Kroker. *Panic Encyclopedia*. New York: St. Martin's, 1989. A panicked A-Z journey through a postmodern alphabet. Looks at various aspects of our contemporary condition with the notion that our age is about the simultaneous experience of ecstasy and dread. "Architecture," "Panic Fashion," "Panic Sex," and so forth. Interesting attempt at creating a "Panic Academia."

De Landa, Manuel. *War in the Age of Intelligent Machines*. New York: Zone Books, 1991. A fascinating study of the evolution of warfare and the increasing reliance on "smart" technology over human decision-making.

Marcus, Greil. *Lipstick Traces*. Boston, Mass.: Harvard, 1989. A whimsical history of the twentieth century from the point of view of negationist art movements from Dada to punk rock.

Motherwell, Robert, ed. *The Dada Painters and Poets*. Cambridge, Mass.: Belknap/Harvard, 1989. A comprehensive collection of essays, manifestoes, and illustrations covering all the major Dada figures and cities of origin (New York, Zurich, Paris, Berlin).

McCaffery, Larry. *Storming the Reality Studio*. Chapel Hill, N. C.: Duke University Press, 1992. A casebook of cyberpunk sci-fi and other related forms of postmodern fiction.

Penley, Constance, and Andrew Ross, eds. *Technoculture*. Minneapolis, Minn.: University of Minnesota Press, 1991. An anthology of academic essays exploring various ways in which technology is impacting popular culture.

Quarterman, John. *The Matrix*. Digital Press, 1989. The first attempt to articulate and map the length and breadth of the world's telecom networks.

Raymond, Eric S., ed. *The New Hacker's Dictionary*. Cambridge, Mass. : MIT Press, 1991. A dictionary and cultural artifact of the hacker movement.

Rheingold, Howard. *Virtual Reality*. New York: Summit Books, 1991. A readable account of the early development of VR at NASA, VPL, University of North Carolina, and elsewhere.

Rucker, Rudy, and R. U. Sirius, eds. *Mondo's Guide to the New Edge*. New York: Harper and Collins, 1992. An anthology of *Mondo 2000* magazine.

Sterling, Bruce. *Hacker Crackdown*. New York: Bantam, 1992. Reports on the events leading up to and the aftermath of the 1990 "hacker raids."

Vale, V., and Andrea Juno, eds. *Industrial Culture Handbook*. San Francisco: RE/Search Publications, 1981. A series of interviews with industrial artists and musicians including Survival Research Labs, Throbbing Gristle, SPK, and others.

Fiction

Gibson, William. *Count Zero*. New York: Arbor House, 1986.

Gibson, William. *Mona Lisa Overdrive*. New York: Bantam Books, 1988.

Gibson, William. *Neuromancer*. New York: Ace, 1984.

Rucker, Rudy. *Software*. New York: Avon Books, 1982.

Rucker, Rudy. *Wetware*. New York: Avon Books, 1988.

Shirley, John. *Eclipse*. New York: Bluejay, 1985.

Sterling, Bruce. *Artificial Kid*, New York: Harper and Row, 1980.

Sterling, Bruce. *Schismatrix*. New York: Arbor House, 1985.

Booklets

Hughes, Carolyn, ed. *Black Hole*. Baltimore: Institute for Publications Design, University of Baltimore, 1992. A reader assembled for a cyberculture panel at the 1992 Word and Image conference held in Baltimore.

Ruggiero, Greg. *Seizing the Media*. PO Box 2726, Westfield, NJ 07091: The Immedaists, 1992. The first in a series of booklets centered around the theme of media insurgency and DIY media production.

'Zines

bOING-bOING, 11288 Ventura Blvd. #818, Studio City, CA 91604.

Gareth Branwyn writes frequently on issues on culture and technology and is a contributor to *Mondo 2000* and *Wired*. He can be reached at 4905 Old Dominion Drive, Arlington, VA 22207; Internet: <gareth@well.sf.ca.us>.

REFERENCES

1. See especially Hausmann's *Spirit of Our Times* assemblage and Picabia's machine-based portraits done for the various dada magazines such as Alfred Stieglitz's *291*. I do not want to create the impression that the dadaists rejected technology. They shared much of the futurists' passion for technology, but it was mixed with the cynicism and dark humor of the post-WWI era. Hugo Ball: "An epoch disintegrates—A thousand-year-old culture disintegrates. There are no columns and supports, no foundations anymore—they have all been blown up."

2. *Samizdat* is the Russian word for self-publishing. In its original context, it usually referred to underground or subversive publications. The word, and its underground implications, was picked up by desktop 'zine publishers in the United States and Europe in the 1980s.

3. Keep in mind while reading this essay that there is certainly not a fixed thing called cyberculture with an attendant politics, lifestyle, and belief system. Cyberculture is only a vague pattern of ideas, conversations, and behaviors that can be seen by taking a core sample of the art, literature, and cultural discourse that centers over the area where technology, science, and avant-garde art overlap. It should also be pointed out that I, given my own participation in this "movement," cannot be objective about what is important about it. I am not really describing the cyberculture here as much as I am constructing for you the filter through which I view it. Other names that have been floated over this same territory are "technoculture," "the new edge," "the computer (or silicon) underground," and the "cyberpunk movement" (the latter more often associated with the radical fringe of cyberculture and the science fiction literary movement of the 1980s).

4. The word *cyberspace* was coined by sci-fi writer William Gibson for his "Sprawl" series of novels (*Neuromancer, Count Zero, Mona Lisa Overdrive*). In Neuromancer, he describes it as "A consensual hallucination experienced daily by billions of legitimate operators, in every nation....A graphic representation of data abstracted from the banks of every computer in the human system. Unthinkable complexity. Lines of light ranged in the nonspace of the mind, clusters and constellations of data ..." Cyberspace may have started out as sci-fi, but it has quickly caught on as a useful label for the real-world global telecommunication grid. As more and more links and bridges are installed in the major national and international computer nets (such as Internet, Usenet, Bitnet), anyone with a modem and a PC has almost instant access to thousands of people, information data bases, services, and virtual communities that are being "built" by their users. Increasing numbers of people work, play, socialize, and wander around in a crude version of Gibson's cyberspace. While today's cyber-residents have to use their imaginations to see beyond the text-based communication, developments in virtual reality will soon provide them with interactive visual representations of data.

5. In his recent essay "A Slice of Life in My Virtual Community" (*EFFector Online* 2.11, June 22, 1992), Howard Rheingold defines a virtual community as "a group of people who may or may not meet one another face to face, and who exchange words and ideas through the mediation of computer bulletin boards and networks. In cyberspace, we chat and argue, engage in intellectual intercourse, perform acts of commerce, exchange knowledge, share emotional support, make plans, brainstorm, gossip, feud, fall in love, find friends and lose them, play games and metagames, flirt, create a little high art and a lot of idle talk. We do everything people do when they get together, but we do it with words on computer screens, leaving our bodies behind. Millions of us have already built communities where our identities commingle and interact electronically, independent of local time or location. The way a few of us live now might be the way a larger population will live, decades hence."

6. Jim Pomeroy, "Black Box S-thetics: Labor, Research and Survival in the He[art] of the Beast," *Technoculture.*

YOU DON'T WIN AT PINBALL WITH THE FIRST QUARTER: TURF WARS AND AGENTS

Tom Hargadon

Most folks get to experience virtual reality by putting on a head-mounted display for five or ten minutes. This is barely enough time to get used to the navigation scheme and make a move or two. But these VR surfers become instant experts on virtual reality. They usually say that the graphics were crude or the moves too obvious.

PHOTOREALISM OR INTERACTIVITY?

Turf wars between those who believe high-quality photorealism is needed for good interactive presentation and those who feel that changeability, movement, and multiple users generate adequate interest have been going on for years in the worlds of computer graphics and animation. Virtual reality is just another arena. I, for one, am not sure that this dichotomy is a useful one.

Of course, it would be helpful if more people had the opportunity to experience virtual reality for a longer period. It would be even better if the experience had some inherent interest, and was not just another pretty demonstration of technology or photography.

It is certainly true that the world presented is not photorealistic. The inherent capacity of most personal computers or low-end workstations to develop world scenes in real time places substantial limits on resolution. The HMDs themselves are often unable to reproduce even that limited resolution.

The first, and quite effective, way to get around the resolution problem is to allow users to move instantly around the virtual world. That is just what game designers have used for years! Nintendo is not high resolution!

A second important characteristic is a feeling of immediacy, of interactivity—you shoot something; it dies fast. This has not been well implemented on most virtual reality demonstrations. The rebuilding of the scene as one moves has meant perceived delays and jerkiness.

The advocates of photorealism have an important point—without enough detail in virtual worlds, they quickly become boring. But these worlds are being developed in real time at thirty frames per second. Detail, like immediacy, requires substantial computing power. The question is, How much is detail a function of how long one stays in a virtual world? That is, if you stay in a virtual world for a substantial length of time, does low-resolution begin to seem more realistic.

One can make the entire world more challenging. In some arcade games the number of worlds or levels can be daunting: nine or ten commercially, and up to fifty or more on noncommercial, student-developed games. The amount of work required to create exciting, interactive, detailed visual virtual experiences in multiple worlds is beyond the capacity of most media developers today.

In the Networked Virtual Art Museum project at Carnegie Mellon University (described elsewhere in this anthology) and Seigo Matsuoka's Opera project at the Editorial Engineering Laboratory in Tokyo, similar moves are used as mechanisms to continue interest and links.

The CMU project uses the abilities of Sense8, one of the few PC-based authoring systems, to change textures on the fly to give the user a taste of the capability to change a world! The project connected Pittsburgh and Munich in September 1992 using a fun house to try out interactive science-related trips. The researchers found that the half-second delay between Pittsburgh and Munich was not a problem when something still seemed to be going on in your world, and you couldn't see what was going on in the other world.

PROTOCOLS FOR INTERACTIVITY

Most Americans seem to want to move more quickly, experience a your move–my move interaction with each move taking perhaps ten seconds to complete. With faster interaction, it is probable that this method will work well only when all parties have had substantial experience with this world.

To push the envelope of these developments in interaction means looking at how people communicate interactively, conversationally, in real time with others who share the same virtual world on their machines. If two people are in the same world together, how do they relate to each other? The protocols are not obvious. When Sense8 demonstrated a multiple-user world-building exercise in Boston in April 1992 (see Pimentel's "The Workroom" in this anthology) the common way users got organized was for both parties to go to an obvious spot and slowly work their way to another position from there.

Even simpler is to allow one person to tell a story, perform a task, and announce he or she is done, then have the next person take over. Researchers can do this with a simple protocol of giving each person a certain amount that gives to do what he or she wants to do. A more sophisticated version has a token passing between parties.

AGENTS

The addition of multiple characters generates substantial interest in itself. With multiple characters, there is little talk of how low the resolution is or, surprisingly, how fast the moves are. Brenda Laurel defines an agent as "a character, enacted by the computer, who acts on behalf of the user in a virtual (computer-based) environment. Their usefulness can range from managing mundane tasks like scheduling, to handling customized information searches that combine both filtering and the production (retrieval) of alternative representations, to providing companionship, advice, and help throughout the spectrum of known and yet-to-be-invented interactive contexts."[1]

Users consider these characters, which are usually anthropomorphic, considered their trusted assistants for certain tasks. On the simplistic side is a wake-up call agent, Phil, the bow-tied professor of Apple's *Knowledge Navigator*; at the other end of the spectrum is HAL of the movie *2001*, an incredibly complex, responsive, almost human agent. We are still far away from a HAL agent.

The most advanced agents are those that help users to handle large databases, obtaining relevant material in personalized, systematic ways. Behind the agent interface is complex software that does the categorizing, inferring and deciding. The first such software consisted of the Boolean logic strings developed by information brokers to systematize complex searches.

More recently, personalized news services using similar techniques have become commercially available. One example is a news-gathering system developed by Phillips at Los Alamos for NeXT computers. More complex searches use approaches such as "information refineries" to obtain, manipulate, and slice information into relevant structures. One example is the *Christian Science Monitor* publishing project from Coopers and Lybrand Advanced Technology in Boston.

Ever-more complex database retrieval systems will be needed as we get serious about accessing and manipulating different data types (text, numeric, visual, graphic, and voice). The text-based notational structure of present databases may not work in this new environment. But that is another, longer story. Back to agents.

You can create your own agent by developing search routines, by using a macro, a template, developed by others, or by modifying an already-defined agent. You might choose a character with a predisposition that you know, trust, or want to experience. How would Abraham Lincoln function as an agent?

One of the more advanced such agent-types occurs in is the Guides Project in Advanced Technology at Apple Computer, which presents guides (frontiersmen and -women or Indians) as they react to historical topics based on their own values.[2] These guides display such characteristics as yawning or sleeping when they are not interested, or beckoning one to come closer when they are very interested and want to tell a story. Version 3 of Guides can perform complex positioning from multiple dimensions to get closer and closer to the material desired. Other mechanisms, such as artificial intelligence and expert systems, have been used to develop more sophisticated agents.

The most recent experiments have added some narrative or theatrical (time-oriented) quality to the present agents, which are fundamentally space-oriented (one thing at a time, or frame-oriented). Amy Bruckman at the MIT Media Lab is attempting to see whether she can obtain connections without programming specific linking in advance.[3] Patti Maes at the Media Lab is investigating contextual narrative.[4] Joe Bates at Carnegie Mellon has been designing characters who develop as the story continues.[5] Abbe Don believes she has developed methods to embed narrative structure and obtain much richer materials from visual bases, audio bases, data bases. Her project, *We Make Memories,* allows one to follow the lives of three generations of Don's family by following the linear story line of a single individual, the issues that come up across individuals and generations, or a combination of the two.[6]

The boundaries around agents and other smart mechanisms are still undefined. Those developing Boolean logic searches often just call the file that invokes an agent. This is also often the case with the use of macros and templates. Objects that have embedded within them run timed versions of software that often exhibit "agentlike" qualities. Tom Malone, with his Information Lens program at MIT, tries to filter information as an assistant would, but does not speak of "agents."[7] Those developing theatrical methodologies probably use "character" in a more substantive sense than the scheduling agent who pops up on the screen.

In their attempts to have someone appear as present even though they are actually miles away, researchers in tele-existence or telepresence do not find agents to be a useful metaphor. (The most progressive work in tele-existence seems to be at the Advanced Telecommunications Research Labs in Osaka, Japan.)[8] Those doing virtual reality can use agents as assistants or selectors, but the primary thrust of researchers has been on development of worlds, passage through and modification of worlds and, most recently, networking of such worlds—especially the higher bandwidth interactions available over the Internet now and soon on your local home cable television system.

Those who take the time to build or modify worlds become totally engrossed in the details and interrelations of these worlds. Perhaps it is only by linking that many of VR toys will actually be used, not as a completed product sold as a commodity to an individual. Ten minutes just is not enough.

Tom Hargadon is managing director of Distributed Simulations. He is an authority on broadband interactive communication. He can be reached at 1320 18th St., San Francisco, CA 94107; telephone: (415) 431-9368; Internet: <foxhedge@well.sf.ca.us>.

REFERENCES

1. Brenda Laurel, "Interface Agents: Metaphors with Character" in *Art of Human-Computer Interface Design*, Brenda Laurel, ed., Reading, Mass.: Addison-Wesley, 1990.

2. See Tim Oren et al., "Guides: Characterizing the Interface" in Laurel's *Art of Human-Computer Interface Design*.

3. Amy Bruckman, in CHI *Proceedings* (1992).

4. Patti Maes, ed., *Designing Autonomous Agents*, special issue of *Robotics and Autonomous Systems* , Cambridge, Mass.: MIT Press, 1990.

5. See his essay in this collection, and also W. Scott Reilly and Joseph Bates, *Building Emotional Agents*, Pittsburgh, Pa.: School of Computer Science, Carnegie Mellon University, May 1992, Technical Report CMU-CS-92-143; Joseph Bates, A. Bryan Loyall, and W. Scott Reilly, "Broad Agents," *SIGART Bulletin* 2(4), August 1991: 38-40; Joseph Bates, A. Bryan Loyall, and W. Scott Reilly, "Integrating Reactivity, Goals, and Emotion in a Broad Agent" in *Proceedings of the Fourteenth Annual Conference of the Cognitive Science Society*, July 1992, Bloomington, Ind.; and A. Bryan Loyall and Joseph Bates, *Hap: a Reactive, Adaptive Architecture for Agents*, Pittsburgh, Pa.: School of Computer Science, Carnegie Mellon University, June 17,1991, Technical Report CMU-CS-91-147.

6. Abbe Don, "Narrative and Interface" in Laurel's *Art of Human-Computer Interface Design*.

7. Kum-Yew Lai and Thomas W. Malone, "Object Lens: Letting End-Users Create Cooperative Work Applications," *Human Factors in Computing Systems. Reaching Through Technology: CHI '91*, S.P. Robertson, G. M. Olson, and J. S. Olson, eds., proceedings of a conference held in New Orleans, La., April 27 - May 2, 1991. New York: ACM, 1991: 425-6.

8. See, for example, Nobuyoshi Terashima, "Cooperative Works in Teleconference System with Realistic Sensations" in *HyperNetwork '92 Beppu Bay Conference*, proceedings of the conference held February 28-29, 1992 at Oita, Japan. Oita: Conference '92 Steering Committee, 1992: 115-119.

IT'S NOT THE TECHNOLOGY:
IT'S THE CONTENT

David Fox

AUGUST 1959

"David! Your Auntie Lee just got a new color TV! Want to go over and see it?"

I was eight years old, and already a dedicated technophile (though the word wouldn't be invented for several decades). My face lit up, "Wow! A *color TV?* You bet!!"

We drove to her house and found my younger cousins sitting around the large television console, two feet from its screen. Danny was rapidly switching channels while black-and-white scenes flashed by, one after another. "Wait, there's one!" They had stopped at a scene in full color! There was Bucky Beaver singing the Ipana toothpaste jingle, "Brusha brusha brusha, here's the new Ipana ..."

"Wow!" we all exclaimed in unison. We were transfixed. No matter that the picture was blurry and the colors oversaturated and inaccurate, as if it had been painted by a drunken preschooler. It was in COLOR!

The commercial ended. The regular program started up again, but was in boring black and white. Danny jumped to the knob and began switching again until he found the next color commercial. "Oooh!" we all crooned.

And so it went for an hour or so. We watched one awful commercial after another until the moms made us turn off the TV.

"That was neat!" I said. "Can we get a color TV?"

SEPTEMBER 1989

It was finally my turn. All eyes turned to me as I donned the helmet and glove. The helmet banged me in the eye, and then caught (and pulled out) several of my hairs as it slid down over my head. It was uncomfortably heavy. The images on the tiny screens before my eyes looked like an animated wall of mosaic tiles—much coarser than the large display monitor I had been watching moments before. I had to balance the helmet with one hand to keep the jerky image of a kitchen in focus.

"Wow!" I turned my head to look around, and soon after, the image changed as well. Okay, so I had to move in slow motion to keep the time lag to a minimum. No problem. I moved (stumbled) to the sink, and thrust my computer hand toward the faucet. A steady stream of water appeared (actually, it was a featureless vertical blue polygon). It was wonderful! I had made something happen in virtual reality! I broke into a wide grin.

I had just experienced the 1989 version of an early color-TV commercial. I was delighted to spend half an hour exploring several crude worlds, even though the interaction was almost nonexistent—there was absolutely no story, plot, or goal to be achieved. I even endured a slight case of motion sickness from the image lag and slow frame rate. But I still had a great time.

PROGRESS IS MADE?

Every subsequent visit to virtual reality showed me incremental improvements in the technology—the eyephones got a bit clearer, the helmet a bit lighter, the frame rate a bit faster, and the head-tracking lag a bit shorter. There is no doubt that the VR hardware will continue to improve dramatically. In fact, it will get so good that we'll be laughing at what we had to put up with in the early nineties, just as we now laugh at those early color commercials.

So, if we don't have to worry about the hardware getting better, what should we be concerned with?

THE SOFTWARE: THE ACTUAL VR EXPERIENCE

Even though the hardware is getting better, the virtual worlds I have entered are still as crude as that of my first visit. I'm not talking about the quality of the image, but the level of interaction or involvement that the worlds provide. It is clear that VR is still largely in the hands of the technologists. Story tellers, screen writers, game designers, and artists have not yet made an impact on this new realm. This is understandable, since most of the "world building" to date is done primarily to show off the technology, to get additional funding. Build the hardware, get the system up, create a short demo to prove it works, and then immediately move on to the next incremental technological improvement. There's no time or budget allocated to implement a truly innovative world. And this is no small undertaking. It takes anywhere from nine months to two years for a team of professional computer game designers, programmers, artists, and musicians to create a commercial computer or arcade game. This equates to budgets ranging from $300,000 to several million dollars, depending on the scale of the project. It will take no less time or money to implement a high-quality gaming experience on a VR platform.

True, there *are* a few companies doing full blown VR games (for instance, Battletech and Virtuality), but their first attempts are still basic arcade games with the added gimmick of taking place in a VR universe (see figures 34-1 to 34-3). The mere inclusion of VR automatically adds to the gaming

Figure 34-1. The pod for *Mirage*, a networked VR game developed by Lucasarts and Hughes training.
• Credit: Hughes Training Inc.

Figure 34-2. Multiple players participate simultaneously in *Mirage*.
• Credit: Hughes Training, Inc.

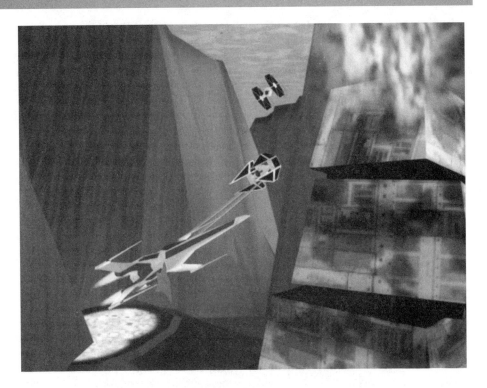

Figure 34-3. Networking allows players to interact with real people in a shared universe. • Credit: Hughes Training, Inc.

experience in the same way that color added to the experience of watching those early TV commercials, by increasing the "gee whiz" factor. But this does not necessarily improve game play, nor does it disguise the fact that the games are still primarily shoot-'em-ups that appeal to a young male audience.

But this too is understandable. VR is a brand new medium with new, not yet understood, potential. We game designers only have our previous experience to draw upon, so naturally our first VR games resemble our previous, nonimmersive games.

One important feature that most VR games have borrowed from some earlier forms of computer games is that they take place in a shared, multiplayer universe. No matter how good game designers get at creating computer-controlled characters, interacting with real people in the virtual world is much more rewarding. It's extremely important to game players that they play against (or with) other people and not just a machine. It's that much more fun if the players *know* the people they are interacting with. If the game is properly designed to allow the players the creative freedom to invent their own strategies, the game will remain fresh, innovative, and forever changing as the players experiment with new moves.

How do we really take advantage of the impact of immersion and of having other humans in the computer-generated universe? The answer will emerge as we gain experience implementing these games.

Here is an analogy: filmmakers at the turn of the century had only one related field from which to draw inspiration, the theater. So they plopped the camera at the edge of the stage and filmed the actors playing their roles. The scripts were not changed and the camera never moved. There were no close ups, two-shots, or cutaways. But no one noticed this lack of innovation because suddenly, people who never went to see plays could watch them at the movie theater. It took almost two decades before D. W. Griffith used all he had learned about the potential of film as a new story-telling medium in his ground breaking film, *The Birth of a Nation* (1915). He discovered that film did not have to be used as a linear recording medium. The film industry was forever changed.

We are just a few years into the experiment of VR as public entertainment. Let's hope it doesn't take us twenty years to take advantage of its possibilities!

LUCID DREAMING

For inspiration, maybe we should look beyond current forms of entertainment. There is an experience many people have from time to time called lucid dreaming, in which you become aware that you are dreaming. You can then often take control of your dream, choose to fly, rendezvous with someone special, perform feats of magic (much to the astonishment of all the other dream characters), vanquish monsters, or talk back to domineering relatives (often the same thing as vanquishing monsters). Upon awakening, the dreamer often experiences an overwhelming sense of well-being, a feeling of empowerment that may last for days. In fact, the experience may alter the way the person views and deals with life ever after!

This is pretty heady stuff! Is it possible to give someone the opportunity to have a similar experience in a virtual world? What if we could confront our personal demons and subdue them while fully awake? Wouldn't that be even more empowering?

Science-fiction writer Orson Scott Card seems to have thought of this in his book *Ender's Game* (1985). The main character, a young boy named Ender is being trained on a large space station. Installed on Ender's laptop computer is a remarkable adventure game that has been customized for his benefit by the computer itself. The computer knows everything about Ender's history, his blind spots, his weaknesses, his mindset. The obstacles the computer puts in Ender's game path are precisely those obstacles that he most needs to overcome as a person. When Ender gets stuck in the game, he spends hours mulling over the problem as he goes about his day-to-day life. When the solution finally hits him, it is often accompanied by a realization about the way he views the world. By changing his attitude, his point of view, or his approach to life in general, he also comes up with the solution to the adventure's puzzle. The game forces him to put his full powers of concentration into solving puzzles that change his life for the better. Ender becomes a capable leader, more flexible in dealing with the problems that his tumultuous life presents to him. What a wonderful concept!

FILM POWER

Despite the myriad forms of media entertainment that exist today, film is still the most powerful. The film image fills a significant portion of our vision; we are bathed in high-quality sound, and surrounded by people who reinforce and amplify the emotions we are feeling. But this alone is not enough. In its ongoing pursuit to move increasingly jaded audiences, Hollywood has learned how to manipulate us through strikingly intense visuals, hyper-real sound effects, and overpowering musical scores. Film, when done effectively, elicits emotions and feelings we rarely experience in everyday life. As a result, film has the potential to change our lives by transporting us to other places and times and allowing us to view the world from new perspectives.

There are two broad categories of film. The first makes up the vast majority of those produced in this country. This kind of film is the media equivalent of cotton candy—fun to eat, but with no lasting impression. We forget the characters and story are as soon as we reach the theater lobby.

The second category are films with the power to haunt our consciousness for days or even years. These feed us the concentrated substance of life experience. Upon leaving the theater, we feel we have just lived the adventure along with the characters. We may feel transformed by their insights, elevated by their triumphs, and inspired to strive for more in our own lives.

Or the film may be a very disturbing experience. The images might be nightmarish, the themes brutal, the characters distasteful, leaving us with feelings of fear, paranoia, distrust. The images may spring into our minds uncalled for, like a flashback from a bad acid trip. Either way, the impact is undeniably real.

WHICH WAY TO GO?

Currently, our computer games and VR experiences are cartoonlike. It is harder to suspend disbelief and become emotionally involved when interacting with jerky cartoon characters than with realistic images. As the experiential "resolution" of VR advances, and as VR world builders begin using Hollywood production values, this new media will rival and then surpass the emotional impact of films. Because we are fully immersed while in VR, it will be easier to allow ourselves to believe and act as if the experience is real. We can't glance to the side and be reminded we're just sitting in a theater. Because VR is an interactive experience, much more of our mental and emotional selves will become engaged.

The same broad categories that we see in film will appear in VR, but the experiential "volume" will be greatly amplified. The cotton candy experiences will taste sweeter, but will still leave us feeling empty. The powerful, life-altering experiences will have even more potential to affect us, either positively or negatively. Will they balance each other out, or will one become the predominant form of VR entertainment? As an optimist, I'd like to believe that people will choose positive, life-transforming experiences rather than nightmares.

David Fox cofounded the world's first public-access microcomputer center in 1977. After ten years with LucasGames in the Bay Area, he is now consulting with various entertainment companies on virtual reality projects. He can be reached at Electric Eggplant, 11 Indian Rock Road, San Anselmo, Calif.; telephone: (415) 485-0882; fax: (415) 485-5232; Internet: <fox@eeggplnt.nbn.com>.

DESIGNING IN VIRTUAL SPACE

Robert Jacobson

W e stand on the brink of a great advance in human communication. We are the inheritors of a century of progress in electronics. In our time, human beings using highly evolved computer technology will gain the ability to share with one another their most intimate impressions of places, things, people, and relationships. The experiences they will share we call *virtual worlds*.

In the future, computer-generated virtual worlds will help us to bridge the gap between the "outside" material world and the conceptual worlds we carry around on the "inside," in our heads and bodies. This transcendental process, this unification of inside and outside, will alter the way we live—perhaps as profoundly as did the inventions of philosophy, science, and printing in the common language.

But before we skip ahead to receive this penultimate wisdom—the only thing greater being the meaning of life itself!—we must first refine the virtual world technology with which we will mingle our interior and exterior worlds. We especially must pay attention to learning how to work with this technology and put it to use for the sharing of information and understanding. I call this information design.

Too often in the past, information technology of all types—most recently, television, computers, and CD-ROM multimedia—have been foisted on the public by engineers and marketers whose only purpose has been to push technology and to "move product." We have been confronted with the likelihood not only of overt misuse, which is obvious to everyone (exploitative children's advertising on television is an egregious example), but also the careless or ineffectual use of these powerful technologies. To illustrate the latter point, we need only look to American industry, where investments in information technology have increased by more than fifty percent over the past two decades, while white-collar productivity has risen by one percent. Obviously, to the question of how to increase the productivity of America's workforce, merely adding more technology has not been the right answer.

INFORMATION DESIGN

We need not continue to implement technology in this directionless fashion. When we are ready to begin applying virtual world technology, perhaps the most powerful medium of communication ever, we can look beyond the technology itself to what it is we are trying to do. We are trying to convey experience. This is the essence of information design.

Let us consider the nature of experience more closely. Experience is an encounter with the world. We translate this "meeting" with the objective conditions of a situation into subjective mental meanings. That is, we see, hear, touch, taste, and smell things; then we turn these haptic, whole-body impressions into memories and understandings in our minds. Experience is not a one-way path, however: our prior memories and understandings often determine what it is we are capable of sensing in the world. If I know that something exists, I am far more likely to sense it in my environment (if it is there) than if I have no prior knowledge about it. In fact, I may sense it in the environment, based on my prior knowledge, even if it is not there at all! These vagaries of human perception are what makes information design so exciting—these uncertain rules that we must discover and by which we must play if we are to craft virtual worlds that will help us to better understand the worlds in and around us.

If an experience is pallid, uninspiring, or misinformative, what is the point of passing it on? There is none. On the other hand, if an experience is colorful and exciting, and leads to greater understanding, then it is worth turning into a virtual world. How we determine the quality of an experience and the virtual world that represents it is one of the challenges facing information designers. Two of the methods by which we can make these judgments are way-finding—which architects use to let people know where they are and how to get to where they are going—and sense-making, a way to help people to understand how things work. These are sometimes considered to be parts of the new field of cognitive science, but I prefer to think of them as devices in the information designer's tool chest. At least for now, evaluating the quality of experiences is more an art than a science.

Once an experience has been identified as worth sharing, turning it into a virtual world is the fun work. At Worldesign, Inc., the information design studio I helped to found, we call people who understand the meaning of the experience "counselors," indicating their role as helpers to the client. Counselors get together with designers who know about conveying meaning, and worldsmiths who can create computer-driven tools, to build a virtual world. This is where we invoke virtual reality, putting to use the tools created by the worldsmiths according to directions given by the designers, who craft virtual worlds that fit the client's needs as described by the counselors. It is a more complicated process than simply strapping on goggles and a DataGlove and dancing in beautiful, digital abstractions. To make the distinction between sensory hacking and the crafting of useful worlds, at Worldesign, we don't talk about "virtual reality" except as a buzzword; our profession is information design.

VIRTUAL WORLD TECHNOLOGY

Let us now consider the technology behind virtual world technology itself—virtual reality. So much has been written about virtual reality that you may be wondering why it is not here already, why you cannot turn on your home VR system and float away into a virtual world.

The technology itself is conceptually elegant. The idea is to program computers so that their outputs, transmitted through the right input/output devices, mimic other types of sensory communication between the person and the external environment. If we link many computers, we should be able to generate the type of power that is necessary to produce high resolution images—sights, sounds, and eventually physical sensations—that look a lot like the real world. In fact, progress is being made to do just that, but it will be a few more years before the technology lives up to our expectations.

Take our ability to see things. Our eyes—which are really extensions of our brains—are remarkably acute. In the past, when our ancestors were chasing down small animals and running away from big ones, visual acuity was essential to survival. Until eyeglasses were invented, human beings with poor eyesight were prone to attacks and accidents that often resulted in death. As a result, those who survived developed excellent stereoscopic eyesight. We see exceptionally well and require visual imagery of an equally high standard.

Of course, there are exceptions. When we laugh at a simply drawn cartoon, we are willing to give the artist some leeway to get the point across. Similarly, the most powerful modern art often comprises only a few elements; again, the emotional quality of this expression has a lot to do with the understanding we bring to it. Remember my comments about the two-way street of perception? But the word "reality" in virtual reality has been taken to mean "exactly like the material world" (even though reality is seldom so clearly perceived) and people expect virtual reality to feature high-resolution graphics equal to or better than those of television.

A simple picture on a computer screen will not do. In order to experience immersion or inclusion in a virtual world, we need to stimulate the entire visual field, including our peripheral vision. The magic number for a convincing field of vision, according to technological pioneer Thomas Furness, is 120 degrees. That means that the virtual world image has to subtend, or cover, fully one third of the circle of things around us. As we move our heads, this super-widescreen imagery has to keep up with where we are looking, so the virtual world has to continually reproduce and update the "window" that appears to surround us. Doing this requires not only special projectors or head-mounted displays capable of presenting extremely clear pictures, but also a lot of computer power to constantly alter and maintain the changing imagery.

The problems with tracking our hearing—where we focus our attention—the parts of our bodies, with which we interact with the virtual world, are a little easier, but not much. When you add up all these inputs and outputs, you are talking about a mighty computer processor. If we link many computers to overcome this problem, then we have a new problem: coordinating all the models being generated within the various computers. This requires very fast, very capable communications networks and software that is still in its earliest stages of development.

And this is the situation for only one person. Add one, two, a dozen, or a thousand people to the virtual world, so that they are all perceiving and interacting with one another, and the difficulties are magnified almost infinitely.

THE INDUSTRY TODAY

Perhaps these problems could be overcome if large corporations with adequate resources were more interested in investing to solve them. Unfortunately, the companies working exclusively in the field of virtual world technology are for the most part tiny; the largest has fewer than thirty employees! Every so often we hear rumblings of interest on the part of larger firms, but inevitably we discover that only a few people within these companies are actually working on virtual world technology, or that they are working on something they call virtual reality but that really is something else.

The big companies are sitting back, waiting for their smaller counterparts to spend all their energy on the new technology, which the large companies hope to then pick up for a song.

It cannot happen that way. The technology is crawling forward far slower than our hopes for what it can accomplish. People's expectations have been raised to a high level; disappointment and disillusion could set in at any time.

That is the main reason I founded Worldesign: to accelerate the use of existing virtual world technology and thereby stimulate investment in the development of new technology. I am confident that if we focus on how we use the technology rather than on perfect performance, there's a lot we can do...and then we can look forward to the wonders I will discuss later.

WORLDESIGN, INC.

At Worldesign, we emphasize the flexibility and appropriateness of the virtual world itself—however it is presented, whether with projectors or headsets, joysticks or DataGloves—and concentrate on putting this concept to use solving our clients' information problems. We search out companies that make heavy use of information, including firms in almost every line of business. Then we closely examine how these companies use information and how they craft information environments that make it easier to use information. We do not need the best possible graphics or total wraparound imagery. In our work so far, we have found that people bring a lot to a virtual world presentation. Moreover, the really exciting challenges in representing information have to do with processes and relationships that are invisible to us under normal circumstances. We can do a lot to make these processes and relationships visible and understandable. We surmise that simple illustrations and three-dimensional sound displayed in a theaterlike setting are more conducive to the sharing of common experiences and shared understanding than goggles, which isolate people in their own crude virtual worlds. This is not yet Star Trek's Holodeck, but you have to start somewhere.

The worlds on which we at Worldesign are working, for all their simplicity, are valuable to the people who pay us to build these environments. For example, for a major European auto manufacturer, we are proposing to create information environments useful for designing, manufacturing, and marketing automobiles; training workers; and running the corporation. A large Japanese utility has asked us to build a multidimensional map of the region served by the utility, including subterranean infrastructure, surface phenomena like traffic flows, and invisible processes like the influx of economic investments expected as the utility improves the infrastructure. To do this, we will employ not only virtual world technology but also other important technologies that are now reaching maturity, like management support systems that describe an organization's performance and geographic information systems that show where things are taking place. Other applications we have considered include a "cockpit" for operators of telecommunications networks, so that they can navigate around the networks to make adjustments and repairs, and various forms of educational and entertainment systems, like nonviolent games that encourage collaborative activity and that can be used by schools and museums as well as by amusement arcades and theme parks.

NEW APPLICATIONS

As firms demonstrate the competitive advantage they gain by using information design to build practical information environments, other companies will want to have environments crafted for them, too. Once this process has begun, our industry will be on its way. With each new application, there will be greater incentives to develop new technology. Eventually, information designers at firms throughout the United States and around the world will be creating environments like these:

- A surgeon learns a new technique by wielding a simulated scalpel on a three-dimensional electronic body before trying the innovation on a living human. Work has already begun under the direction of U. S. Army Colonel Rick Satava at California's Monterey Medical Hospital, in cooperation with the consulting firm SRI International. "Medicine Meets VR" is now one of the best attended and most serious conferences in our field, attracting hundreds of doctors and researchers each year.

- Two people meet in a telecommunication-supported virtual world. Together they explore an Aztec pyramid—complete with Aztec priests and nobles. Three large telephone companies, BT and Cable & Wireless in Britain and Saskatchewan Telecommunications in Canada, are looking at providing a service like this. Michael Naimark, the San Francisco video artist, has developed an excellent hypermedia tour of the pyramids of Tlaquepaque; its translation into a three-dimensional virtual world that can be transmitted over the telephone wires is only a matter of time.

- An executive using a "corporate visualizer" can decompose and recompose the manufacturing process with the help of managers and workers. Work similar to that for the European auto company is underway in Japan, supported by a consortium organized by the prominent consulting firm, the Nomura Research Institute.

- Scientists in San Diego have linked up a powerful electron microscope to a computer and are composing three-dimensional portraits of cells. They can blow up these pictures and then walk around inside them, getting a good feeling for how the cells are structured and how they work.

- School children share three-dimensional pictures of their homes with other children, building understanding across cultural barriers. This is the great dream of our profession, the idea that virtual world technology, skillfully designed and deployed, can contribute to cross-cultural understanding (since experience can transcend language) and international peace. Sensational movies like *Lawnmower Man*, which gained some notoriety, argue that people are essentially evil and will misuse this technology. It does not have to end this way, especially if the students of today, who have so much to gain from this technology, become adept at its use and are given a chance to guide its development.

Those working in the virtual world domain bring diverse skills to this integrative science, as information designers, world builders, and technologists. Many are scientists and engineers—our traditional technological heroes—but an even larger number come, unexpectedly, from the social sciences and the humanities. Worldesign's small staff, for example, is already more diverse than you might imagine, including individuals with backgrounds in music, psychology, organizational management, museum exhibition design, software programming, educational technology, finance, aerospace engineering, critical social theory, human factors engineering, philosophy, and urban planning. One third of our professional employees made anthropology—the study of human community—their undergraduate college careers and another third are deeply involved in architecture. How we live is obviously important to people working in this field.

Our employees and others successfully involved in information design and virtual world technology share some characteristics that set them apart from more traditional technologists. First, they have a strong sense of spatiality and how human beings react to spaces and places. Second, they are enormously enthusiastic and energetic about our mission, which is important when the industry is still small and vulnerable to economic and political shocks. Third, and perhaps most important, these successful professionals have the ability to submerge their egos to the collective purpose of advancing our field and its technological tools. Our field is superheated by press attention, premature competition among a few firms, and the adventure inherent to the pursuit of new knowledge and skills; these are stressful conditions under which to work.

CONCLUSION

I began this paper by saying that we are on the brink of a precipice, about to take a big step into the future. The metaphor of the cliff is correct. This is a perilous moment. We can don wings of wisdom and, like a hang-glider, sail off into a remarkable future where communication among human beings is both natural and conducive to greater understanding of the world in which we live. Or we can make the terrible mistake of allowing this virtual world technology to slip away from us and into the hands of those who would debase its promise, turning it into something cheap or silly.

Information design is the best way that I can help to ensure that virtual world technology serves humane ends. While we await the new technology, patience is called for, but not inaction. Those who choose to work in the field must bring to it the personal qualities of enthusiasm and community that will be conducive to our collective success.

Robert Jacobson, Ph.D., is President and Chief Executive Officer of Worldesign, Inc., in Seattle. He can be reached at 128 NW 56th St., Seattle, WA 98107; Internet: <cyberoid@u.washington.edu>.

Note

This paper was adapted from the Hammerle Memorial Lecture delivered at Oakland University, Rochester, Michigan, on November 5, 1992. My thanks to Oakland University and Howard Witt and his staff.

APPENDICES
AND
ANNOTATED
BIBLIOGRAPHY

APPENDIX A

A GUIDE TO THE LITERATURE

Tim Anderson

The literature of virtual reality, artificial reality, tele-existence, remote presence, cyberspace, et al., is especially challenging to track. The very proliferation of terms suggests one part of the problem; the newness of the field is another. The nature of VR research and development is yet another, since it comprises elements of computer science, telecommunications engineering, robotics, psychophysiology, epistemology, dramatics, fiction, aesthetics, and more. This mixture of disciplines is, however, one of the field's greatest attractions. The literature ranges from highly academic to journalistic to promotional, with a high proportion of hype.

This bibliography is meant to be an initial guide for the nontechnical artist, designer, educator, or cultural worker interested in virtual reality. It is necessarily incomplete and arbitrary, and will be outdated to some degree by the time it is published. Print materials, videorecordings, computer files, and online sources are all included.

Many of the articles, books, and videos in the field combine application descriptions with reports of technical research, development with theoretical speculation, and so forth, creating a literature that is especially messy to categorize. I will use the following headings to try to provide some nominal guidance to the literature:

- Overviews
- Theory and Design
- Applications
- Keeping Current
- Background
- Political and Cultural Issues
- Policy
- Fiction and Cyberculture
- Technical
- Bibliographies
- Indexes
- Directories
- FTP Sites and BBSs

Some works are simply listed in the bibliography, and are not discussed under any of these categories.

OVERVIEWS

The best overview for a nontechnical reader is Rheingold's journalistic account, *Virtual Reality*. Kalawsky and Pimentel and Texeira provide an excellent introductory look across the field as of the end of 1992. Aukstakalnis and Blatner provide a similar description of the hardware but less of a sense of how the field is developing. A briefer introduction is Stewart's article in *Smithsonian*. A short survey from a corporate viewpoint is by Hamilton in *Business Week*, October 5, 1992. The anthology edited by Helsel and Roth is another useful starting point, with sections on theory, practice, and promise. A similar survey with completely unrestrained enthusiasm is in the cyberculture magazine *Mondo 2000*'s first theme issue on virtual reality. Hattori's book is an authoritative survey of the field from Japan (in Japanese). Kahaner surveys aspects of Japanese work more briefly in English.

Although not edited as overviews, various conference proceedings present cross sections of current research and development. Some of these are also available as videorecordings. For poetic, philosophical, and theoretical treatments, the papers from the 1990 Austin, Texas, conference collected in Benedikt's *Cyberspace: First Steps* are provocative, while the collected abstracts of that conference (some sixty of them, also edited by Benedikt) report on a wide range of experimentation and speculation. The conference papers in Earnshaw, Gigante, and Jones; the ICAT proceedings; and the Conference on Virtual Reality (SRI) are more technical. The annual CyberArts conferences present a variety of papers addressed to arts and entertainment applications of new technologies, including virtual reality (see Linda Jacobson and *CyberArts*). The various conference proceedings (and related videorecordings) tend to offer mixed bags of technical papers, reports on applications, and observations on design (see Helsel, Virtual Reality, Virtual Reality '92, VR Conference, VRAIS 93, and others).

Tachi and Robinett each provide useful taxonomies of virtual reality, tele-existence, and related terms, as do Goldman-Pach, Hart, and Gigante (in Earnshaw, Gigante, and Jones). In the article "Virtual Environments," Zeltzer constructs a classification scheme to dissect the dimensions of interaction, autonomy, and presence. Barlow's articles capture the subjective experience of entering a virtual world; he also provides the memorable definition of virtual reality as "a Disneyland for epistemologists." Stampe, Roehl, and Eagan's book/disk package provides demonstration programs and code for those interested in exploring the possibilities for building virtual worlds on IBM PC-compatibles. The papers by Binkley and Brown offer general considerations on artistic uses of virtual realities. The papers by Bricken ("Languages for Virtual Reality" and "A Formal Foundation for Cyberspace"), Conn et al., Farmer, Fisher, Furness, and Gullichsen and Walser serve as starting points for more technical approaches to virtual world development.

THEORY AND DESIGN

While the contradictory qualities of virtuality versus reality and remoteness versus presence have spawned a great deal of speculation, there has been little in the way of theory written on these topics. In many publications, theoretical comments are interwoven with proposals for design of virtual environments, so it may be helpful to consider these writings together rather than to force onto them a more academic distinction.

Woolley, in *Virtual Worlds*, provides the most systematic introduction to theorizing about virtual reality; he writes as a perceptive science journalist and grounds the new field in contemporary philosophy, physics, and mathematics. VR pioneer and impresario Jaron Lanier has spoken frequently on his view of the nature of virtual reality, often with insight. William Bricken has contributed mathematical rigor in specifying general properties of virtual worlds (in "Formal Foundations for Cyberspace" and other papers). For considerations of the concept of presence in ordinary reality, virtual reality, and telepresence, see Ludvigsen, Naiman, Sheridan's "Musings on Telepresence and Virtual Presence," Steuer, and Zeltzer's "Autonomy, Interaction, and Presence."

Laurel has written most widely on principles of design applied to virtual world building. For a Brechtian viewpoint that contrasts with her use of Aristotelian drama as a design model, see Gigliotti. Benedikt, Ludvigsen, and Novak have each developed approaches to understanding the spatial structure of virtual worlds. Webb and Barna situate such design in the trajectory of twentieth century-architecture.

Other articles with a substantial focus on design include Bates's "Virtual Reality, Art, and Entertainment," Benedikt, Furness's "Designing in Virtual Space," Kay, Krueger's "An Architecture for Artificial Realities," Novak, McFadden, McLellan, Spring, Stoppi, Thomas, Tice and Jacobson, Tollander, Walker, and Walser. Also relevant are many of the pieces in the overview collections mentioned above, in Ascott and Loeffler, and in *Cyberspace, Power and Culture*.

APPLICATIONS

Because the construction of virtual worlds is so recent and because so much emphasis has been placed on technical issues, it is difficult to find substantial descriptions of individual projects. Consequently, the listing below is less complete than other sections of this bibliography, and the works range in nature from serious academic papers to brief journalistic stories to video documentation. The 1991 SIGGRAPH catalog, edited by Tice and Beirne, is an especially helpful roundup of some twenty leading-edge projects. Numerous descriptions of particular projects can be found in Rheingold's *Virtual Reality*, Benedikt's *Cyberspace* and *Collected Abstracts*, and the proceedings of the various virtual reality conferences, including *ICAT* and Linda Jacobson's *Cyberarts*. General considerations can be found in "Applications of Virtual Reality: Reports from the Field," Breen's "Near Term Applications" and "The Reality of Fantasy," Emmett, and Romkey.

Several references expand on projects described in chapters in this anthology: Bates et al., *Virtual Seminar on the Bioapparatus*, Brill, Fukuda, Haggerty, Hughes et al., Krueger, Loeffler, Morningstar and Farmer, Moshell et al., Peterson, Pimentel and Texeira, Robinett and Naimark, Shaw, Stelarc, Stenger, Truck, and Vamplew.

The Arts

Artists' use of virtual worlds technology is surveyed in the Art Futura catalog, Dery, "Gallery," *Informatique '92*, Linda Jacobson's *Cyberarts*, Laurel's "Art and Activism," Hagen, Princenthal, Robinett and Naimark, Rotzer and Weibel, and TISEA. The connections between theater and virtual reality are explored in Bates, Kelso et al., Krueger, Laurel's *Computers as Theatre*, "Dramatic Action and Virtual Reality" and "The Role of Drama in the Evolution of Virtual Reality," Smith and Bates, and Truck's "The Prompt and Virtual Reality." A telepresence art installation is described in Kac. Applications in music are described in Cadoz et al., and Lanier's "Music from Inside Virtual Reality." For general considerations, see Binkley, Cornwell, Garber, and Mallary. Some of the art works described in this anthology are further documented in Bates et al., Brill, Dery, Loeffler's "Networked Virtual Reality," Peterson, Papper and Gigante, Shaw, Stelarc, Stenger, TISEA, and Truck.

Scientific Visualization

Scientific visualization has been one of the most important driving motives in the development of virtual worlds technology. Work at NASA's Ames Research Center in space exploration, including the virtual representation of Mars, has propelled much of the recent development in immersion technology; see Anzovin, Bolas and Fisher, Bryson, Fisher, Fisher et al., McDowall et al., McGreevy and Stoker, Rheingold's *Virtual Reality*, and the *Virtual Reality* videorecording. The modeling of complex molecules that can be manipulated by hand is perhaps the best known of the important series of scientific projects at the University of North Carolina; see Bajura et al., Brooks et al., Fuchs et al., Rheingold's *Virtual Reality*, Robinett, and the videorecordings *Virtual Reality* and *Virtual Reality: Head Mounted Display Research*. A virtual wind tunnel is described in Bryson and Levitt and in Bancroft et al.

Current work at UNC is reported in the technical reports from their Computer Science Department; see University of North Carolina. Ongoing work from the Human Interface Technology Laboratory at the University of Washington, Seattle, is reported in their *HIT Lab Review*.

Medicine

Closely related to scientific visualization are some of the experiments in virtual medicine. These include virtual modeling of patients' organs for planning radiation treatment; for prenatal diagnosis, and for training doctors and surgeons. For general considerations, see Dutton, Fuchs, Levoy and Pizer,

Hamit, "Innovative Medical VR Research," *Lancet, Medicine Meets Virtual Reality*, Molendi and Patriarca, Pace, Rheingold's Virtual Reality, Robinett, Stix's "See-Through View," *Virtual Reality in Medicine* (videorecording), Weghorst, and Whalley. On cancer treatment, see Rosenman, et al., Sherouse and Chaney, and Sherouse, et al. For speculation about the use of VR in psychiatry, see the exchange between Tart and Begelman. For other projects, see Bains, Bajura, et al., and the several items by Joseph Henderson. A very helpful bibliography is *VR/Telepresence and Medicine Sources*, compiled by Prothero, Emerson, and Weghorst.

Education and training

Training pilots was the first major application of virtual environments; see Furness, Moshell, Rheingold's *Virtual Reality*, and Vince. For extensions of this kind of training, see Dowding, Moshell et al.'s "Networked Virtual Environments for Simulation and Training," and Sterling's "War is Virtual Hell."

For general considerations on the use of virtual environments in education see Alluisi, M. Bricken's "Virtual Reality Learning Environments," W. Bricken's *Learning in Virtual Reality*, Durlach et al., Helsel's "Virtual Reality and Education", Hiltz and Turoff, Lanier's "Virtual Reality: The Promise of the Future", McCluskey, McLellan's "Virtual Environments and Situated Learning," Osberg, Regian, Shebilske, and Monk, Resnick, "Surreal Science ...," the various articles by Traub, and *Virtual Reality and Learning* For particular projects, see M. Bricken's *A Description of the Virtual Reality Learning Environment*, Bricken and Byrne, W. Bricken's "Languages for Virtual Reality," Christel, Davidson, and Winn and Bricken. For networked education, see Alluisi, and Hughes et al., "Cooperative Problem Solving in a Networked Simulation Environment." See also the bibliography by Pantelidis.

Entertainment

For general considerations on virtual worlds as a new entertainment technology, see Cook, Fukuda et al., Glenn, Haverstock, Morningstar and Farmer, Ramanathan, Rangan, and Vin, Sims, and Stratton. For examples of VR arcade games, see Heeter, Kinnaman, Latta, Laurel, Rowley's "'Virtuality' Entertainment Systems", Whittington, and Woolley's "Lifting the Veil." On virtual movies, see Laurel, Brill, Solman, and Stenger. Snapshots of the current status of the industry can be found in Brill's Home VR," Gradecki's "Virtual Reality Arcade Systems," "Money Games," and Sprout.

Communication

Shared virtual workspaces and expanded teleconferencing are receiving considerable attention as possible applications of virtual reality, especially in Japan and Scandinavia. See Biocca, "Communication within Virtual Reality," Burg et al., Forchheimer, Hirose, Hughes et al., "Cooperative Problem Solving in a Networked Simulation Environment," Kvarnström, Ishii and

Miyake, Ohkubo and Ishii, Pruitt and Barrett, Ståhl, Stanger, and Suzuki and Kouno. The Networked Virtual Art Museum and Virtual Polis are also host to experiments with virtual communication of various sorts; see Loeffler's chapters in this anthology.

Information Management

In various articles, Robert Jacobson has argued the importance of seeing virtual environments as a means for information management; see his chapter in this anthology and the interview with him in *Virtual Reality Report*. For some general considerations, see Coull and Rothman, Fairchild et al., Larue, Miller's "Virtual Reality and Online Databases," Newby's "An Investigation of the Role of Navigation for Information Retrieval," Nilan, Nugent, Poulter, Quarendon, and Zeltzer's "Virtual Environment Technology." For examples in financial analysis, see Bradford Smith, Stuart, and Surprenant.

Disabilities Adaptation

The proceedings of the conference, *Virtual Reality and Persons with Disabilities*, edited by Murphy, are the prime source. In addition to the articles by Trimble and Morris and Vamplew in this anthology, see Dockery and Littman, Fels and Hinton, Pausch, Vogtle and Conway, Pausch and Williams, Vamplew, and Vamplew and Adams.

Architecture and Design

In addition to the article by Pimentel in this anthology, see M. Bricken's *Building the VSX Demonstration*, Machlis, Neugebauer, Nomura, Richmond, Rolf, Schraft, Strommer, and Neugebauer, and Yu.

Military

Like many advanced technologies, virtual reality began in the military, which still funds much research. Bruce Sterling has written the best description of the current military application of VR in "War is Virtual Hell." He also situates the technology in political and military contexts.

For general background, see Arnett. For the background to VR development in the super cockpit project, see "Virtual Cockpit." Recent extensions of the virtual cockpit are reported in Kaye et al. and Long et al. Moshell provides a brief sketch of VR's origins in simulator training.

Other military applications are surveyed in Rheingold's *Virtual Reality*. For reports on SIMNET, the networked virtual combat simulator used for training tank crews and others, see Alluisi, "The Development of Technology for Collective Training," Garvey, Harvey, Schaffer and McGarry, Kanarick, Moshell et al.'s "Nap-of-earth Flight," Rabines and Mohler, Schneider, and Weatherly, Seidel, and Weissman. NPSNET is the Navy's proposed successor to SIMNET; see Zyda et al. For other applications, see Adams, and Arbogast and Coviello. For telepresence in battle, see Blais and Lyons.

KEEPING CURRENT

In a field as diverse and rapidly developing as virtual reality, keeping current is a major challenge. The sources below include print journals, electronic journals, a hypermedia journal, online computer conferences, and newsgroups. Printed journals and newsletters that cover both industry and technical developments include *CyberEdge Journal* (Sausalito, California), *PIX-Elation, Virtual Reality News* (Farmington Hills, Michigan), *Virtual Reality Report* (Westport, Connecticut), *Virtual Reality World* (Westport, Connecticut), and *VR Monitor* (Lathrup Village, Michigan). In Europe, VR News (London, England) plays a similar role, as do *Realtá Virtuale* (Milan, Italy) and *Matrixx* (Helsinki, Finland).

For current comment on topics ranging across technology, science, philosophy, applications, who's who (and where's who), and new publications, the Usenet newsgroup <sci.virtual-worlds> is outstanding. In 1993, a closely related Usenet newsgroup, <sci.virtual-worlds.apps>, was created to focus on VR applications.

For tracking applications of virtual reality in the arts, *Art Com* and *Leonardo Electronic News* (both electronic journals) are helpful. For new writing in science fiction, *bOING-bOING, Intertek*, and *Science Fiction Eye* tend to publish stories of particular interest, although many of the science fiction magazines occasionally publish cyber stories; *Omni* published a good deal of the early cyberpunk fiction. For more general coverage of cyberculture, *AZIMUTH, bOING-bOING, Intertek, MONDO 2000*, and *Wired* are helpful. Some of these also cover virtual reality specifically—for example, Issue 7 of *MONDO 2000* includes interviews with Brenda Laurel and Myron Krueger, an article on do-it-yourself VR, and an item on BattleTech games. Editors and contributors include Gareth Branwyn, John Barlow, and Jas. Morgan.

Policy issues concerning access, freedom of expression and association, privacy, and control by U.S. government agencies are covered extensively in the electronic journal of the Electronic Frontier Foundation, *EFFector Online.*

There are active conferences devoted to virtual reality on several private computer networks, including the WELL (Whole Earth 'Lectronic Link), BIX, and Compuserve. Access requires an account on the particular network. The conference on the WELL, founded by Howard Rheingold and now moderated by Peter Rothman, is especially active and wide-ranging. There are also network discussion lists on particular topics; see Netgame and Glove-list.

PCVR is devoted to technical issues of programming virtual environments with low-tech equipment on IBM-compatible PCs. It is a noncommercial, nonacademic publication from the do-it-yourself (or "garage") school of VR developers. Many issues come with a diskette containing source code.

The only academic journal devoted to virtual reality and telepresence is MIT's new quarterly, *Presence*. Articles from *Presence* include Bates, Hester, Meyer et al., Naiman, Piantanida, Robinett, Robinett and Naimark,

Sheridan, and Zeltzer. Business concerns receive special attention in *The Green Sheet*, edited by Tom Hargadon, which emphasizes strategic discussions of the convergence of visual computing with high bandwidth telecommunications.

BACKGROUND

As research and development extend the advancing edge of virtual reality, they also extend its background. As more directions for research are opened up – in computer science, physiology of perception, psychology, narrative theory, graphic design, gaming, and other areas—more antecedents are recognized. The references listed are just a sample of the many intellectual threads leading into cyberspace. In making these selections, I have emphasized works cited as influences by current VR researchers and developers.

The work of Ivan Sutherland is most often cited as the beginning of the field of virtual reality as a distinct field; see Sutherland, and Burton and Sutherland. Other computer scientists who pioneered work that led to VR interfaces are Vannevar Bush, Douglas Engelbart, J. C. R. Licklider, Joseph Weizenbaum, and Alan Kay. For the history of VR see Goldberg, Goodman, Levine and Rheingold, Rheingold's *Tools for Thought* and his *Virtual Reality*. More immediate background is provided in Brand, and in Gelernter. Although not concerned with immersion environments, Theodor Nelson's longstanding concern with hypertext has contributed much to concepts of virtuality and interactivity.

A decade before Sutherland's first work, Morton Heilig was developing models of virtual environments based in cinema rather than in computing; see his writings, Lipton, and Rheingold's Virtual Reality. A number of the artists working with virtual environments come from interactive networked computer art projects, which are well documented in Ascott and Loeffler; see also Couey, Loeffler's "Interactive Computer-based Art," and Truck's *Art Engine*. Some recent work in the physiology of perception has helped to propel virtual interfaces, and is described in Gregory and in Johnson.

Finally, lest we think that the fiction of cyberspace started with Gibson's *Neuromancer*, we should look again at Joyce's *Finnegan's Wake* (1939), well explicated in this context by Theall.

POLITICAL AND CULTURAL ISSUES

As an expensive and powerful new extension of computing with the most intimate connections to human perception, virtual reality technology raises many political issues, but few have been addressed, and those only superficially. The greatest development of virtual environments has been sponsored by the military; a history is traced briefly in Rheingold's overview, *Virtual Reality*. De Landa, Druckrey, and Ronell suggest some of the problems in making war appear to be "virtual" while the actual military use of VR technology makes it all the more deadly.

Beardon, the *Lancet* editorial, Shapiro and MacDonald, and Whalley raise more general cautions, especially concerning the medical application of virtual environments; some of these are discussed in Rheingold's contribution to this volume.

The place of virtual environments in Western culture is given critical attention in this volume and other papers by Penny, who sees it as an extension of Cartesian rationality rather than the escape from it claimed by Lanier and other enthusiasts. The nature of the virtualized body and related gender issues are examined by Richards and Tenhaaf in this volume and in the Bioapparatus seminar proceedings, and also raised by M. Bricken in *Gender Issues in Virtual Reality Technology*, by Heim, Lanza, Little, Piercy, Stone, and Weghorst, as well as by various participants in the videotaped discussion of *Cyberspace, Power & Culture*. Heim also considers a wide range of philosophical questions about cyberspace.

Hall and Moser use the conventions of advertising to deflate the hyperbolic claims for virtual technology better than any number of more sober columnists. Joans explores the dichotomy between the technical culture of the VR engineers and the imagination of the VR promoters. Bleecker, Gigliotti, and Manovich all situate virtual worlds in the historical development of visual technologies and the economics of the computer industry.

POLICY

Two issues concerning virtual reality have surfaced as important public policy questions in the United States. One is whether this is a leading technology that should receive government support. The United States Senate Subcommittee on Science, Technology and Space hearing is a key document in this debate. The report by Fuchs et al. is the product of an invitational workshop that was held in March 1992 at the request of the National Science Foundation "to identify and recommend future research directions in the area of 'virtual environments'"—directions that might be considered strategic for government funding. For a summary, see Bishop et al.

A more important question is how to extend civil liberties, especially freedom of expression, freedom of association, and privacy, to cyberspace in the face of Federal laws and regulations that do not recognize digital communications as constitutionally protected. The Electronic Frontier Foundation in its many publications—some cited below—has developed major proposals in this area. John Perry Barlow and Mitch Kapor, co-founders of the foundation, have written extensively on these concerns; see also Branscomb, Gans, Russo and Risch, and Sirius and Gleason.

FICTION AND CYBERCULTURE

Fiction has played an unusually influential role in the development of thinking about virtual reality—William Gibson is commonly credited with creating the word "cyberspace" in his novel, *Neuromancer*. The scientific and public-policy literature is filled with references to this seminal work, as well as to the other titles in his trilogy, *Count Zero* and *Mona Lisa Overdrive*. Works on the architecture, design, philosophy, and politics of virtual worlds make even greater reference to these and related works of fiction.

Other science-fiction writers whose works have directly influenced thinking on virtual reality include Orson Scott Card, Rudy Rucker, John Shirley, Bruce Sterling, and Vernor Vinge. Marge Piercy's novel *He, She and It* explores deep cultural issues of virtual reality, robotics, and artificial intelligence. Only the most often cited works are listed below, plus a small sampling of statements by and interviews with the most prominent "cyberpunk" authors—a label some accept more readily than others. For a sampling of criticism, see McCaffery, Tomas, and Slusser and Shippey.

The relation of cyberculture and of cyberpunk fiction to virtual world building is best laid out in Gareth Branwyn's essay in this volume, "Cyberculture: The Pattern That Connects." Since that essay was completed, a new magazine has appeared: *Wired*. It covers much the same technological front as *Mondo 2000* with more social consciousness and less infatuation with drugs and fashion. Anthologies that provide overviews include Branwyn and Sugarman, Hughes, Penley and Ross, Rucker and Sirius, Vale and Juno, and *Cyberpunk* (videorecording). On virtual communities, see *Intertek* (Winter 1992), Rheingold's "A Slice of My Life," and Stone. On hackers, see Hafner and Markoff, Hughes, Saffo, Sobchack, and Sterling's "GURPS' Labors Lost" and *Hacker Crackdown*.

TECHNICAL

Although this guide is for nontechnical readers, understanding a field like virtual reality requires some acquaintance with the technologies involved. The references mentioned here are selected to emphasize key articles in the development—both historic and current—of virtual environment technologies.

Introductions

Three recent books provide introductions to the technology. Pimentel and Teixeira's *Virtual Reality* devotes one part to a technical overview while other parts trace the development of the field and survey current applications. Aukstakalnis and Blatner's *Silicon Mirage* focuses entirely on the technology, organized around types of sensory input and output. The most thorough technical treatment is Kalawsky's *Science of Virtual Reality*. Gigante's "Virtual Reality: Enabling Technologies" provides a shorter introduction. Biocca's "Virtual Reality Technology," McLellan's "Virtual Reality Design Notes," and Walser's "Doing It Directly" are directed toward nonscientist audiences and are more accessible than some of the others. The Virtual Interface Technology course notes (1991) may be helpful for serious beginning students of the technology.

Types of virtual environments

Taxonomies of ideal types of virtual environments are given in Tachi and in Robinett. Pimentel and Teixeira provide overviews of systems available today. Sutherland's early papers first described the immersive environments with visual displays that are the most common today, typified by the VPL and VIEW systems. The VPL system is described by Blanchard et al. and is demonstrated in the videos *Applications Development Toolkits* and *Jaron Lanier: Report from the Field*. The VIEW system is described by Fisher et al.

Cruz-Neira et al. report on the Cave, a virtual environment that the participant enters physically, rather than by projection; see also Robertson, Card and Mackinlay.

Krueger's *Artificial Reality II* and various presentations on VIDEO-PLACE describe his nonimmersive (unencumbered) environment into which the participant is projected. A variation on this is the Mandala system described by Vincent and Jacobson.

For a sampling of approaches to combining virtual environments with real ones, see the papers collected in Wellner, Mackay and Gold.

For low-tech, do-it-yourself systems, see Isdale, Linda Jacobson's *Garage Virtual Reality*, Lavroff, and *PCVR* as well as Stampe and Roehl's contribution to this anthology. Stampe, Roehl, and Eagan's *Virtual Reality Creations* contains the code of the REND386 system for IBM-compatible PCs as well as extensive documentation.

Display

Sutherland's 1965 paper on "The Ultimate Display" may be said to have started the field of virtual reality. Ever since, display technology has been a central concern. Many aspects of it are covered by Bajura et al., Blanchard et al., Bogdanski, Bolas et al., Bryson and Fisher, Coull, Fairchild et al., Feiner and Beshers, Fisher et al., Hirose et al., Iwata and Matsuda, R. Jacobson's "The Ultimate User Interface," Kijima and Hirose, *Jaron Lanier: Report from the Field* (videorecording), Lee, et al., Long, McDowall et al., Pausch, Piantanida et al., "Retina Projection, Tactile Fields and Other Toys", Robinett and Rolland, Smith, Snowdon et al., Starks, Stix's "Reach Out," Sutherland, Tachi et al., Vincent and Jacobson, and West et al. See also the various *Proceedings* of the Symposiums on Interactive 3D Graphics.

Tracking

Tracking a participant's position and motion is a central aspect of virtual world technologies and has generated a large technical literature. Major articles include Applewhite, Eglowstein, Ferrin, Meyer, Applewhite, and Biocca, Sturman, Tachi, Arai, and Maeda, Väänänen and Böhm, and Zimmerman et al.

Sound

Sound could simply be considered another aspect of display. However, it has received much separate attention in the literature. Major articles include Begault, Chan, Foster, Linda Jacobson's "Sound Enters the Third Dimension," Pope and Fahlén, Takala and Hahn, Wenzel, and Wenzel et al.

Architectures and operating systems

Many standard operating systems have been used for virtual environments, and some that have been developed specifically for this purpose are proprietary. However, at least two research centers have developed VR operating systems that are documented and offered for use (or at least consideration) by other researchers. The Human Interface Technology Lab in Seattle has developed VEOS, described in Emmett, "An Operating System for Virtual Reality", Bricken and Jacobson, and Jacobson, "What Is VEOS?" Sony has developed Muse and Apertos, described in Tenma, Yokote, and Tokoro, Teraoka, Yokote, and Tokoro (1988), Tokoro, and Yokote. Off-the-shelf VR development programs are surveyed in Brill, "Kicking the Tires of VR Software."

Networking and teleconferencing

Much of the general networking literature applies to networking virtual environments. Articles that address the specifics of shared virtual worlds include Burg et al., Hughes et al.'s "Cooperative Problem Solving in a Networked Simulation Environment," Moshell et al., *System Architectures and Networks* (videorecording). Work at the Sony Computer Science Laboratory is reported in Takeuchi and Nagao, Teraoka, Teraoka, Claffyl, and Tokoro, and Teraoka, Yokote, and Tokoro (1990). Work from the MultiG group in Sweden is reported in Carlsson and Hagsand, Fahlén, Fahlén and Brown, Fahlén and Hagsand, Forchheimer, Hagsand, Marmolin, Sundblad, and Pehrson, and Pehrson, Gunningberg and Pink, See also the proceedings of the various MultiG Workshops, edited by Fahlén and Jää-Aro, Pehrson, and Sundblad.

Teleconferencing in virtual conference worlds is discussed in M. Bricken's *The Virtual Conference Room*, W. Bricken's "Coordination of Multiple Pariticipants ...," Ishii, Ishii and Miyake, and Ohkubo and Ishii. Other networked virtual applications are reported in Fukuda, Tahara and Miyoshi, and in Loeffler's "Networked Virtual Reality."

BIBLIOGRAPHIES

The recent emergence of virtual reality as a distinct field and the dispersion of the literature across many academic disciplines have limited the compilation of bibliographies. An excellent introductory bibliography that includes online sources, conferences, and other resources is Emerson. For additional technical literature, see her *Selected Bibliography on Virtual Interface Technology*. McLellan's is the most general bibliography to have been published as of this writing. Newby's survey in ARIST is a well-researched bibliographic essay. Carande's *Information Sources* is an essential guide to research sources. Ellis's bibliographic essay traces the development of virtual reality as a field.

The bibliography in Earnshaw et al. is substantial; it draws heavily on the bibliography from the <sci.virtual-worlds> newsgroup built over time by multiple contributors; see "Citations." For sources on medicine and virtual reality, see Prothero, Emerson and Weghorst. Much of the work done at the Department of Computer Science at the University of North Carolina at Chapel Hill can be found in the "Bibliography of Virtual Worlds Research " available from the department. Campbell's slim bibliography is a now outdated list of articles from the popular business press.

INDEXES

Only the *Multi-Index to Cyberspace, Virtual and Artificial Reality,* first published in 1992, attempts to systematically cover the field. Although its coverage does not yet match its ambitions, it is substantial. Many indexes cover aspects of the field, from such specialist tools as the bibliography of the Modern Language Association (for criticism of cyberpunk fiction) to newspaper indexes. In preparing the bibliography in this volume, however, *INSPEC* was especially useful in finding computer science literature, and *Computer Contents* and *Periodical Abstracts* were good sources of popular articles and product announcements. These indexes all provide searchable abstracts fields, a feature that is particularly helpful in a field with no established subject headings and few standard keywords.

DIRECTORIES

Suppliers of virtual environment technologies can be found listed in McNaughton and Rowley (both in Earnshaw, Gigante, and Jones), and in the annual "Virtual Reality Resource Guide" in *AI Expert.* Directories of businesses and academic organizations in the field are provided by *Virtual Reality Market Place,* Panos, and Thompson.

FTP SITES, WWW SITES, AND COMPUTER BULLETIN BOARDS

The rapid pace of virtual reality research and development, combined with its concentration in computer-intensive campuses and laboratories, has generated a valuable literature of notes and documents that are not published in traditional print media. Rather, they are distributed as computer files and printed, if at all, by individual readers from their own computers. While many of these are circulated privately, a substantial body of these files have been made publicly available on the Internet. Generally these can be retrieved by any computer on the Internet using the net's File Transfer Protocol (FTP). For information about using FTP, see any guide to computer networking; Kehoe and Krol are among the best introductions. World Wide Web sites allow computers on the Internet to access multimedia documents including graphics, formatted text, sound, animation, and other formats. Krol provides an introduction to WWW also. Bulletin Board Systems, better known as BBSs or b-boards, do not require an Internet connection. They can be dialed up across telephone lines with a modem.

The accessibility of FTP and WWW sites as well as their organization and contents change rapidly. Those listed in the bibliography under FTP and World Wide Web are among the main sites available as of June 1994. Bulletin Board Systems are equally changeable; only a few are listed (under BBS).

APPENDIX B

SUPPLIERS OF HARDWARE AND SOFTWARE FOR VIRTUAL REALITY APPLICATIONS

3-D ImageTec Corp.
25251 Paseo De Alicia, Suite 100 A, Laguna Hills, CA 92653
Telephone: (714) 455-1806; fax: (714) 455-1990
LCD 3D display system and wireless LCD glasses.

The 3DO Company
1820 Gateway Drive, Suite 109, San Mateo, CA 94404
Telephone: (415) 574-6789; fax: (415) 573-5772
Digital interactive multiplayer, hardware, and software.

3DTV Corp.
P.O. Box Q, San Rafael, CA 94913-4316
Telephone: (415) 479-3516; fax: (415) 479-3316
Virtual reality hardware and software.

4th Wave, Inc.
Box 6547, Alexandria, VA 22306
Telephone: (703) 360-4800; fax: (703) 360-2311
Virtual reality products, applications, and markets.

Advanced Gravis Computer Technology, Ltd.
7400 MacPherson Avenue #111, Burnaby, British Columbia V5J 5B6,
CanadaTelephone: (604) 431-5020; fax: (504) 431-5155
Input devices and sound cards.

Advanced Technology Systems, Inc.
800 Follin Lane, Suite 270, Vienna, VA 22180
Telephone: (703) 242-0030; fax: (703) 242-5220
Head-mounted display.

Alternate Worlds Technology
P.O. Box 43003, Louisvillle, KY 40253
Telephone: (502) 426-0903
Head-mounted display.

Art Com
P.O. Box 193123, Rincon Annex, San Francisco, CA 94119-3123
Telephone: (415) 431-7524; fax: (415) 431-7841
Distributor for virtual reality applications.

Art + Com
Hardenbergplatz 2, 1000 Berlin 12, Germany
Telephone: (49) 30 2629301; fax: (49) 30 2619036
Virtual reality applications.

Artificial Reality Corp.
P.O. Box 786, Vernon, CT 06066
Telephone: (203) 871-1375; fax: (203) 871-7738
Applications design.

Artlab
2590 Walnut Street, Suite 7, Boulder, CO 80302-5706
Telephone: (303) 447-3817; fax: (303) 449-7732
Virtual reality projects and applications.

Ascension Technology Corporation
P.O. Box 527, Burlington, VT 05402
Telephone: (802) 860-6440; fax: (802) 860-6439
6D tracker and tracking system.

Autodesk
2320 Marinship Way, Sausalito, CA 94965
Telephone: (415) 332-2344; fax: (415) 332-8893
Virtual reality development system and environments.

Banff Centre for the Arts
Office of the Registrar, Banff Centre for the Arts, Box 1020, Station 28, 107
Tunnel Mountain Drive, Banff, Alberta TOL OCO, Canada
Telephone: (403) 762-6180; fax: (403) 762-6345
Education projects in virtual reality.

BBN Systems and Technologies
10 Moulton Street, Cambridge, MA 02138
Telephone: (617) 873-2000; fax: (617) 873-6244
Virtual reality hardware and software.

BioControl Systems, Inc.
430 Cowper Street, Palo Alto, CA 94301
Telephone: (415) 329-8494; fax: (415) 329-8498
Nerve impulse sensor.

Boeing Computer Services
499 Boeing Boulevard, MS JY-58, Huntsville, AL 35758
Telephone: (205) 464-4965; fax: (205) 464-4964
Virtual reality simulators.

Cadonmac
665 Finchley Road, London NW2 2HN, England
Telephone: (44) 81 208122
Stand-alone system for prerecorded walk-throughs.

California Medical Research Corporation
3658 Mt. Diablo Boulevard, Lafayette, CA 94549
Telephone: (510) 284-6944; fax: (510) 283-3948
Biomedical devices, instrumentation for surgery.

Center for Electronic Art
950 Battery #3D, San Francisco, CA 94111
Telephone: (415) 956-6500; fax: (415) 362-1989
Consulting and applications design.

CiS 285
1 Stiles Road, Salem, NH 03074
Telephone: (603) 894-5999; fax: (603) 894-5995
6D joystick.

Clarity
Nelson Lane, Garrison, NY 10524
Telephone: (914) 424-4071; fax: (914) 424-3467
Audio development system.

Convex Computer
701 North Plano Road, Richardson, TX 75081
Telephone: (214) 934-2500; fax: (214) 808-0934
Real-time supercomputers.

Covox, Inc.
675 Conger Street, Eugene, OR 97402
Telephone: (503) 342-1271; fax: (503) 342-1283
Voice recognition system.

Crystal River Engineering
12350 Wards Ferry Road, Groveland, CA 95321
Telephone: (209) 962-6382; fax: (209) 962-4873
Systems for 3D audio digital signal processing.

CyberEvent Group Inc.
355 Degraw Street, Brooklyn, NY 11231
Telephone: (718) 802-9415; fax: same
Virtual reality systems for arcades and advertising.

Cybernet Systems Corporation

1919 Green Road, Suite B101, Ann Arbor, MI 48105-2554
Telephone: (313) 668-2567; fax: (313) 668-8780
People-centered systems applying human computer interfaces, computer-aided instruction and training, robotics and automation, and artificial intelligence.

CyberStudio

2490 Mariner Square Loop, Alameda, CA 94501
Telephone (510) 522-3584; fax: (510) 522-3587
Entertainment software for the virtuality systems of W Industries.

David Sarnoff Research Center

201 Washington Road, Princeton, NJ 08540
Telephone: (609) 734-2861; fax: (609) 734-2443
Virtual reality hardware and software.

DEC, Artificial Life and Virtual Reality Applications Group

Technology Centre, 111 Lacke Drive, Marlborough, MA 01752
Telephone: (508) 480-6628; fax: (508) 408-5822
Virtual reality applications research.

Digital Image Design, Inc.

170 Claremont Avenue, Suite 6, New York, NY 10027
Telephone: (212) 222-5236; fax: (212) 864-1189
Hardware/software system, stereoscopic glasses, 3D input device.

Dimension International

Zephyr One, Calleva Park, Aldermaston, Berkshire RG7 4QZ, England
Telephone: (44) 734 810077; fax: (44) 734 816940
Hardware/software system.

Dimension Technologies, Inc.

315 Mt. Read Boulevard, Rochester, NY 14611
Telephone: (716) 436-3530; fax: (716) 436-3280
Autostereoscopic 3D displays.

Distributed Simulations

1320 18th Street, San Francisco, CA 94107
Telephone: (415) 861-1317; fax: (415) 431-8368
Development of distributed virtual reality applications.

Division, Ltd.

19 Apex Court, Woodlands, Almondsbury, Bristol, BS12 4JT, England
Telephone: (44) 454 615554; fax: (44) 454 615532
Integrated virtual reality system with body tracking, gesture interface, stereoscopic display, and stereo audio.

Domark Software, Inc.
1900 S. Norfolk Street, #202, San Mateo, CA 94403
Telephone: (415) 513-8929; fax: (415) 571-0437
Virtual reality software.

Evans & Sutherland
600 Komas Drive, P.O. Box 59700, Salt Lake City, UT 9415
Telephone: (801) 582-5847; fax: (801) 582-5848
Computer image generator for virtual reality applications.

EXOS, Inc.
8 Blanchard Road, Burlington, MA 01803
Telephone: (617) 229-2075; fax: (617) 270-5901
Tactile feedback system and exoskeleton for measuring hand positions /motions.

Fakespace, Inc.
935 Hamilton Avenue, Menlo Park, CA 94025
Telephone: (415) 688-1940; fax: (415) 688-1949
Counterbalanced stereoscopic CRT-based viewer and teleoperated camera.

Focal Point 3D Audio
1402 Pine Avenue, Suite 127, Niagara Falls, NY 14301
Telephone: (716) 285-3930
Convolved binaural sound system.

Fraunhofer Institute for Manufacturing Engineering and Automation (IPA)
Nobelstrasse 12, Postfach 800469, 7000 Stuttgart, Valhing 800469, Germany
Telephone: (49) 711 97000; fax: (49) 711 971-1399
Virtual reality workstation.

G. E. Aerospace
1800 Volusia Avenue, Daytona Beach, FL 32114
Telephone: (904) 239-2906; fax: (904) 239-2176
Computer image generators.

George Mason University
Visual Information Technologies Program
Fairfax, VA 22030-4444
Telephone: (703) 993-1020; fax: (703) 993-8714
Virtual reality applications.

Global Devices
6630 Arabian Circle, Granite Bay, CA 95661
Telephone: (916) 791-3533; fax: (916) 791-4358
Motion controller.

Greenleaf Medical
2248 Park Boulevard, Palo Alto, CA 94306
Telephone: (415) 321-6135; fax: (415) 321-0419
Computer-based evaluation workstations for the medical market.

Gyration, Inc.
12930 Saratoga Avenue, Bldg. C, Saratoga, CA 95070
Telephone: (408) 255-3016; fax: (408) 2255-3016
Optically sensed gyroscopic device.

Horizon Entertainment, Inc.
501 North Broadway, St. Louis, MO 63102
Telephone: (314) 331-6049; fax: (314) 331-6002
Interactive entertainment systems.

Human Interface Technology Laboratory (HIT Lab)
University of Washington, FJ-15, Seattle, WA 98195
Telephone: (206) 543-5075; fax: (206) 543-5380
Virtual reality research.

Imagetects
P. O. Box 4, Saratoga, CA 95071
Telephone: (408) 252-5487; fax: (408) 252-7409
Libraries of texture maps for virtual worlds.

Intel Digital Education and Arts Department (IDEA)
2200 Mission College Boulevard, MS RN5-25, Santa Clara, CA 95052
Telephone (408) 765-8080
Virtual reality applications research.

ISCAN, Inc.
125 Cambridge Park Drive, Cambridge, MA 02140
Telephone: (617) 868-5353; fax: (617) 868-9231
Eye and head tracking systems.

Iterated Systems, Inc.
5550A Peachtree Parkway, Suite 545, Norcross, GA 30092
Telephone: (404) 840-0633; fax: (404) 840-0806
Image-compression tools.

Ixion, Inc.
1335 N. North Lake Way, Seattle, WA 98103
Telephone: (206) 282-6809; fax: (206) 547-8802
Virtual reality game for the home.

LC Technologies, Inc.
9455 Silver King Court, Fairfax, VA 22031
Telephone: (703) 385-7133; fax: (703) 385-7137
Eye tracking system.

Latent Image Development Corp.
2 Lincoln Square, New York, NY 10023
Telephone: (212) 873-5487
Process for converting 2D media into 3D format.

LEEP Systems, Inc.
241 Crescent Street, Waltham, MA 02154
Telephone: (617) 647-1395; fax: (617) 647-1109
Head-mounted display and wide-angle stereoscopic optical assembly.

Liquid Image
582 King Edward Street, Winnipeg, Manitoba R3H OPI, Canada
Telephone: (204) 772-0137; fax: (204) 772-0239
Head-mounted display.

Logitech, Inc.
6505 Kaiser Drive, Freemont, CA 94555
Telephone: (510) 795-8500; fax: (510) 792-8901
Mice, head trackers, and ultrasonic devices for data input.

Marconi Simulation
Fulmar Way, Donibristle Industrial Park, Fife, Dunfermline KY 11 5JX,
    Scotland
Telephone: (44) 383 821921; fax: (44) 383 824227
Flight simulators and training systems.

Metaware, Inc.
2161 Delaware Avenue, Santa Cruz, CA 95060-5706
Telephone: (408) 429-6382
High-C 386 compiler.

Micron Green, Inc.
1240 N.W. 21st Avenue, Gainesville, FL 32609
Telephone: (904) 376-1529; fax: (904) 376-0466
Real-time software package for virtual reality simulations.

Mondo-tronics, Inc.
24 San Anselmo Avenue #107, San Anselmo, CA 94960
Telephone: (415) 455-9330; fax: (415) 455-9333
Tactile feedback devices.

n-Vision, Inc.
800 Follin Lane, Suite 270, Vienna, VA 22180
Telephone: (703) 242-0030; fax: (703) 242-5220
Head-mounted display system.

NASA Ames Research Center/Advanced Display of Spatial Perception
Aerospace Human Factors Division, MS 262-2, Moffett Field, CA 94035-1000
Telephone: (415) 604-6147; fax: (415) 604-3729
Virtual reality applications research.

Nintendo of America
4820 150th Avenue N.E., Redmond, WA 98052
Telephone: (206) 882-2040

Norwegian Telecom Research
Postboks 83, N-2007 Kjeller, Norway
Telephone: (47) 63 809100; fax: (47) 6 810076
Distributed multimedia.

NYNEX Science and Technology, Inc.
500 Westchester Avenue, White Plains, NY 10604
Telephone: (914) 644-2362; fax: (914) 644-2211
3D audio and network visualization tools.

Phar Lap Software, Inc.
60 Aberdeen Ave., Cambridge, MA 02138
Telephone: (617) 661-1510
386 DOS-extender.

Polhemus, Incorporated
1 Hercules Drive, P.O. Box 560, Colchester, VT 05446
Telephone: (802) 655-3159; fax: (802) 655-1439
3D position/orientation tracking systems.

Primary Image, Ltd.
Lever House, St. James's Road, Kingston, Surrey KT12BA, England
Telephone: (44) 81 5464908; fax: (44) 81 5498035
Computer graphics and image-processing tools.

RPI Advanced Technology Group
P.O. Box 14607, San Francisco, CA 94114
Telephone: (415) 777-3226; fax: (415) 495-5124
Personal simulation systems, virtual reality hardware and software.

Real World Graphics, Ltd.
5 Bluecoats Avenue, Hertford SG141PB, England
Telephone: (44) 992 554442; fax: (44) 992 554827
Computer image generators.

Research Triangle Institute
P.O. Box 12194, Research Triangle Park, NC 27709-2194
Telephone: (919) 541-7123; fax: (919) 541-8746
Biomedical engineering.

Royal Melbourne Institute of Technology, Advanced Computer Graphics Centre
CITRI Building, 723 Swanston Street, Carlton, Victoria 3053, Australia
Telephone: (61) 3-282-2463; fax: (61) 3-282-2444
Research in virtual reality applications.

Sacred Heart University, Conceptual Visualization Institute
5151 Park Avenue, Fairfield, CT 06432-1000
Telephone: (203) 371-7794; fax: (203) 365-7520
Virtual reality applications.

Sarcos Research Corporation
261 East 300 South, Suite 150, Salt Lake City, UT 84111
Telephone: (801) 581-1098; fax: (801) 581-1151
Virtual world input and robotic control device, force and positon feedback system.

Sega of America
6573 Forbes Boulevard, San Francisco, CA 94080
Telephone: (415) 742-9300
Games and consumer virtual reality.

Sense8 Corp.
4000 Bridgeway, Suite 101, Sausalito CA 94965
Telephone: (415) 331-6318; fax: (415) 331-9148
Virtual world development software.

Shooting Star Technology
1921 Holdom Avenue, Burnaby, British Columbia V5B 3W4, Canada
Telephone: (604) 298-8574; fax: (604) 298-8580
Mechanical tracking system for head position and orientation.

Swedish Institute of Computer Science, MultiG
Distributed Systems Laboratory
Box 1263, S-164 28 KISTA, Sweden
Telephone: (46) 8 7521570; fax: (46) 8 7517230
Distributed multimedia.

Silicon Graphics, Inc.
2011 North Shoreline Boulevard, Mountain View, CA 94039
Telephone: (415) 960-1980; fax: (415) 961-0595
Visual computing systems.

SimGraphics Engineering Corp.
1137 Huntington Drive, South Pasadena, CA 910301
Telephone: (213) 255-0900; fax: (213) 255-0987
Virtual reality software and input devices.

Sintef SI
Forskningsveien 1, N-0314 Oslo, Norway
Telephone: (47) 22 067300; fax: (47) 22 067350
Machine vision and telemanipulation.

Softis hf
Tæknigardur, Dunhaga 5, IS-107 Reykjavik, Iceland
Telephone: (354) 1 694732; fax: (354) 1 23363
Interface software.

Sony Corporation of America
Sony Drive, Park Ridge, NJ 07656
Telephone: (201) 930-1000

Sowerby Research Centre, British Aerospace
FPC267 P.O. Box 5, Filton, Bristol BS127QW, England
Telephone: (44) 272 366259; fax: (44) 272 363733
Virtual reality simulators.

Spaceball Technologies, Inc.
2063 Landings, Sunnyvale, CA 94043
Telephone: (508) 970-0330
Six-degrees-of-freedom 3D input device.

Specom Technologies
2322 Walsh Avenue, Santa Clara, CA 95051
Telephone: (408) 982-1880; fax: (408) 982-1883
Teleconferencing hardware.

Spectrum Dynamics
2 Greenway Plaza, Suite 640, Houston, TX 77046-0203
Telephone: (713) 520-5020; fax: (713) 520-7395
Virtual reality development system.

Spectrum Holobyte
2490 Mariner Square Loop, Alameda, CA 94501
Telephone: (510) 522-3584; fax: (510) 522-3587
Design and development of entertainment applications.

StereoGraphics Corp.
2171 E. Francisco Boulevard, San Rafael, CA 94901
Telephone: (415) 459-4500; fax: (415) 459-3020
Data eyephones viewing stereoscopic images.

StrayLight Corp.
150 Mt. Bethel Road, Warren, NJ 07059
Telephone: (908) 580-0086; fax: (908) 580-0092
Desktop virtual reality system for photorealistic imaging.

Studio for Creative Inquiry
College of Fine Arts, Carnegie Mellon University, Pittsburgh, PA 15213-3890
Telephone: (412) 268-3452; fax: (412) 268-2829
Development of distributed virtual reality applications.

Telepresence Research
320 Gabarda Way, Portola Valley, CA 94028
Telephone: (415) 854-4420; fax: (415) 854-3141
Boom-mounted stereoscopic viewer incorporating camera system and sensors.

TeleRobotics, Inc.
7325 Oak Ridge Highway, Suite 104, Knoxville, TN 37931
Telephone: (615) 690-5600; fax: (615) 690-2913
Camera system for omnidirectional image viewing applications.

Tellurian, Inc.
1 Pearl Court, Allendale, NJ 07401
Telephone: (201) 818-4885; fax: (201) 808-4876
High-resolution head-mounted display systems.

UNIK (UNIVERSITETSSTUDIENE PÅ KJELLER)
Granav. 33, Boks 70, 2007 Kjeller, Norway
Telephone (44) 63 814570; fax: (44) 63 818146
Virtual reality applications research.

University of Central Florida, Institute for Simulation and Training
12424 Research Parkway, Suite 300, Orlando FL 32826
Telephone: (508) 658-5000; fax: (407) 658-5059
Research in the field of virtual reality.

University of Illinois at Chicago
Department of Electrical Engineering and Computer Science (M/C 154), Box 4348, Chicago, IL 60680-4348
Telephone: (312) 996-3002
Virtual reality applications, research.

University of North Carolina at Chapel Hill, Department of Computer Science
CB#3175, Sitterson Hall, Chapel Hill, NC 27599-3175
Telephone: (919) 962-1900; fax: (919) 962-1799
Research in the field of virtual reality.

Virtual Images, Inc.
4356 Langport Road, Columbus, OH 43220
Telephone: (614) 459-1232; fax: (614) 764-7852
Virtual reality entertainment systems, custom virtual reality systems.

Virtual Reality, Inc.
485 Washington Avenue, Pleasantville, NY 10570
Telephone: (914) 769-0900; fax: (914) 769-7106
Low-end and high-end head-mounted displays.

Virtual Reality Laboratories, Inc.
2341 Ganadour Court, San Luis Obispo, CA 93401
Telephone: (805) 545-8515; fax: (805) 781-2259
World-building software for landscapes.

Virtual Research
3193 Belick Street, Suite #2, Santa Clara, CA 95054
Telephone: (408) 748-8712; fax: (408) 748-8714
Head-mounted display.

Virtual 'S' Limited
123 Mortlake High St., London SW14 8SN, England
Telephone: (44) 813922424
Virtual reality applications.

Virtual Scene Systems
18 Waterhouse Rd., Bourne, MA 02532
Telephone: (508) 759-2459; fax: (508) 759-2257
Image compression tools.

Virtual Technologies
P.O. Box 5984, Stanford, CA 94309
Telephone: (415) 599-2331; fax: (415) 723-0010
Virtual reality hardware, software, and force feedback system.

Virtual Vision, Inc.
7659 178th Place NE, Redmond, WA 98052
Telephone: (206) 882-7878; fax: (206) 882-7373
Monocular head-mounted display.

Virtual World Entertainment
4444 Lakeside Drive, Suite 320, Burbank, CA 91505
Telephone: (818) 973-4200; fax: (818) 557-8372
Virtual reality games, entertainment centers.

Virtus Corporation
112 Edinburgh South, Suite 204, Cary, NC 27511
Telephone: (919) 467-9700; fax: (919) 460-4530
3D drawing tool and stereoscopic display system.

The Vivid Group
317 Adelaide Street West, Suite 302, Toronto, Ontario M5V 1P9, Canada
Telephone: (416) 340-9290; fax: (416) 348-9809
Virtual worlds authoring system.

Volumetric Imaging
2200 Kendall Square Bldg., Cambridge, MA 02139
Telephone: (617) 621-7007; fax: (617) 577-1209
3D volumetric imaging device.

VPL, Inc. (Virtual Programming Language Research)
3977 E. Bayshore Road, Palo Alto, CA 94303
Telephone: (415) 988-2550; fax: (415) 998-2557
*Complete virtual reality systems, tracking system, software for importing 3D
models into virtual reality environments, 3D sound spatialization system.*

VREAM, Inc.
2568 North Clark Street, Suite 250, Chicago, IL 60614
Telephone: (312) 477-0425 ; fax: (312) 477-9702
Virtual reality development software.

VRontier Worlds of Stoughton, Inc.
809 E. South Street, Stoughton, WI 53589
Telephone: (608) 873-8523; fax: (608) 877-0575
Head-mounted display.

W Industries, Ltd.
Virtuality House, 3 Oswin Road, Brailsford Industrial Park,
Leicester LE3 1HR, England
Telephone: (44) 533 542127; fax: (44) 533 471855
Virtual reality hardware, software, and arcade games.

Worldesign, Inc.
128 NW 56th Street, Seattle, WA 98107
Telephone: (206) 782-8630; fax: (206) 782-8630
Information design and virtual environments.

Xing Technology Corporation
Box 950, 1540 W. Branch, Arroyo Grande, CA 93420-1818
Telephone: (805) 473-0145; fax: (805) 473-0147
Compression software.

Xtensory, Inc.
140 Sunridge Drive, Scotts Valley, CA 95066
Telephone: (408) 439-0600; fax: (408) 439-8845
Virtual worlds development software and tactile feedback system.

ANNOTATED BIBLIOGRAPHY

Adams, C. "If Looks Could Kill: The Eyes Have It." *Military and Aerospace Electronics*, March 1990: 35-37.

AI Expert. San Francisco: Miller Freeman. Monthly, since 1986.

AI Expert. Virtual Reality Special Report 1993. San Francisco: Miller Freeman, 1993. Includes "Virtual Reality, Phase Two" by Howard Rheingold, "Authoring Virtual Worlds on the Desktop" by Andy Tait, "Where Virtual Rubber Meets the Road" by Ben Delaney, "Designing Virtual Worlds" by Tony Asch, "The Lessons of Lucasfilms's Habitat" by Chip Morningstar and F. Randall Farmer, "The VR Technology Agenda in Medicine" by Michael S. Nilan, Joanne L. Silverstein,and R. David Lankes, "Reading, 'Riting, 'Rithmetic, and Reality" by Linda Jacobson, "Virtual Reality Resource Guide" by Julie Shaw, "Virtual Phone Sex: Is It in Your Future?" by Harvey P. Newquist III, "Developing a Market for Virtual Reality" by Kathleen Maher, "Naval Applications of Virtual Reality" by Mark Gembicki and David Rousseau,and other articles.

AI Expert. Virtual Reality '93. Fall Special Report. Larry O'Brien, ed. San Francisco: Miller Freeman, 1993. Includes "After the Shoot-'Em-Up: Entertainment's Future" by R. V. Kelly, "The Fruits of War for Fun and Profit" by H. P. Newquist, "Virtual Reality in Education" by P. Richert-Boe, "A Survey of Head Mounted Displays" by B. Delaney, "Low-Cost VR for the Virtual Hacker" by R. Suding, "Virtual Reality for Decision Support Systems" by T. Coull and P. Rothman, "Telerobotic Vehicle Control: NASA Preps for Mars" by B. Eisenberg, B. Hine, and D. Rasmussen, "On the Cutting Edge: VR and Surgery" by R. M. Satava, "Biocontrollers for Virtual Environments" by H. S. Lusted, R. B. Knapp, and A. M. Lloyd, "In the Eye of the Beholder" by J. Fenn, "I'm Rubber and You're Glue" by D. Persons, and "Virtual Reality Resource Guide" by J. Shaw.

Alluisi, E. A. "Network and Virtual-World Technologies for Training." *34th Annual Proceedings of the Human Factors Society*. Santa Monica, Calif., 1990: 1405-1406.

Alluisi, E. A. "The Development of Technology for Collective Training: SIM-NET, A Case History." *Human Factors*. June 1991, 33(3): 343-362.

America Online (computer network). VR Folder, in Virtus Folder. Sponsored by Virtus Corporation.

"Amusement Trade Show Features Simulation: VR and Simulation Well-Represented at IAAPA." *Real Time Graphics.* January 1994, 1 ff.

Anderson, R. L. "A Real Experiment in Virtual Environments: A Virtual Batting Cage." *Presence,* Winter 1993, 2(1): 16-33.

Andersson, Jerker, and Lasse Hellquist. "Telepresence: Some Aspects of the Interface." *Telepresence — A New Concept for Teleconferencing: Proceedings of the First COST #229 WG.5 Workshop,* Forchheimer, Robert, ed. Conference held October 1991 at Stockholm.

Andersson, Johan. "Prototype Remote Inclusive Interface." *Telepresence — A New Concept for Teleconferencing: Proceedings of the First COST #229 WG.5 Workshop,* Forchheimer, Robert, ed. Conference held October 1991 at Stockholm.

Andersson, Magnus, Lennart E. Fahlén, and Torleif Söderlund. "A Virtual Environment User Interface for a Robotic Assistive Device." *Proceedings of the Second European Conference on the Advancement of Rehabilitation Technology.* Stockholm, Sweden, 1993: 33-57. Conference held May 1993 at Stockholm, Sweden.

Anzovin, Steven. "Pathways: Your Ticket to Mars." *Compute!* May 1991, 13(5): 96.

Applewhite, "Position Tracking in Virtual Reality" See Helsel, *Beyond the Vision.*

Applications Development Toolkits. (videorecording). Distributed by Art Com, San Francisco. 120 minutes. Chuck Blanchard, then Director of Software Engineering at VPL, Inc., speaks about the design and workings of Body Electric, VPL's software environment.

"Applications of Virtual Reality: Reports from the Field." *Computer Graphics.* July 1, 1991, 25(4): 365.

Arbogast, G. W., and G. J. Coviello. "Impact of New Technologies Assessed by Defense Agency: Workstation Three-Dimensional Artificial Reality Emerges." *Signal.* August 1990, 44(12): 59 ff.

Arnett, Eric H. "Welcome to Hyperwar." *Bulletin of the Atomic Scientists.* September 1992, 48(7): 14-21.

Art and Artistry in Virtual Reality: Brenda Laurel and Scott Fisher (videorecording). Distributed by Art Com, San Francisco. 60 minutes.

Art Com (electronic journal). San Francisco: Art Com. Internet: artcomtv@well.sf.ca.us. Monthly electronic journal distributed by e-mail. Also on the WELL (computer network) in the Art Com Electronic Network conference, and on the <alt.artcom> newsgroup of Usenet.

Art Futura: Virtual Reality/1990. Barcelona, Spain: Ajuntament Barcelona, 1990. Catalog of the exhibition Art Futura, held in Barcelona, Spain in 1990. Includes essays by Rebecca Allen, Scott Fisher, William Gibson, Eric Gullichsen, Timothy Leary, and Luis Racionero, and works by Rebecca Allen, Max Almy, Susan Amkraut/Michael Girard, Geoff Campbell, Degraf /Wahrman/Montxo Algora, David Em, Masaki Fujihata, Yoichiro Kawaguchi, Kleiser/Walczak, William Latham, Shelly Lake, Links Corporation, Nappi/Winkler, Alan Norton, Pixar, Zbig Rybczynski, Karl Sims, and Zush.

Ascott, Roy, and Carl Eugene Loeffler, eds. *Connectivity: Art and Interactive Telecommunications.* Special issue of *Leonardo* 24(2). Elmsford, N.Y.: Pergamon Press, 1991. Includes "Modem Dialing Out" by Carl Eugene Loeffler, "Connectivity: Art and Interactive Telecommunications" by Roy Ascott, "Art Works As Organic Communications Systems" by Anna Couey, "Communication Arts for A New Spatial Sensibility" by Derrick De Kerckhove, "Aesthetics and Telecommunications Systems" by Fred Forest, "The Many Worlds of Art, Science and the New Technologies" by Don Foresta, "Cultural Implications of Integrated Media" by Beverly Jones, "Oracular Art and the Global Telecommunication Net" by Timothy O'Neill, "Primary Devices: Artists' Strategic Use of Video, Computers and Telecommunications Networks" by Tom Sherman, "Electronic Space in Contemporary Australian Art: Practice and Theory" by Urszula Szulakowska, "The Prompt and Virtual Reality" by Fred Truck, "Noise on the Line: Emerging Issues in Telecommunications-Based Art" by Stephen Wilson, "Telecommunications Art and Play: Intercities Sao Paulo-Pittsburgh" by Artur Matuck, "Notes on Telecommunications Art: Shifting Paradigms" by Dana Moser, "Ornitorrinco: Exploring Telepresence and Remote Sensing" by Eduardo Kac, "Chronology and Working Survey of Select Telecommunications Activity" by Carl Eugene Loeffler and Roy Ascott, and other papers.

Astheimer, Peter. "Sonification Tools to Supplement Dataflow Visualization." *Third Eurographics Workshop on Visualization in Scientific Computing.* Conference held April 1992 at Vlareggio, Italy.

Astheimer, Peter. "Sonification in Scientific Visualization and Virtual Reality Applications." *GI-Workshop "Visuallsierung — Rolle von Interaktivität und Echtzeit".* St. Augustin, Germany: GMD, 1992. Conference held June 1992.

Astheimer, Peter. "Realtime Sonification to Enhance the Human-Computer-Interaction in Virtual Worlds." *Fourth Eurographics Workshop on Visualization in Scientific Computing.* Conference held April 1993 at Abingdon, England.

Astheimer, Peter, and Wolfgang Felger. "Virtuelle Realität in der Architektur." *Bau-Informatik,* Heft 2. Düsseldorf: Werner-Verlag, 1993.

Astheimer, Peter, and Martin Goebel. "Integration Akustischer Effekte und Simulationen in VR-Entwicklungsumgebungen." *Virtual Reality '93*. H. J. Bullinger and H. J. Warnecke, eds. Conference held February 1993. Berlin: Springer-Verlag, 1993: 187-208.

Aukstakalnis, Steve. "Too Hot to Handle: Using CAD, Virtual Reality and Telepresence to Manage Nuclear Waste." *CADalyst*, August 1993, 10(8): 46-50.

Aukstakalnis, Steve, and David Blatner. *Silicon Mirage: The Art and Science of Virtual Reality*. Berkeley, Calif.: Peachpit Press, 1992.

Avis, N. J. "Medical Applications of Virtual Environments" (online text file). *Proceedings of the 1st UK VR-SIG Conference*. Nottingham, England: United Kingdom Virtual Reality Special Interest Group, 1994. Proceedings available through World Wide Web URL=<http://pipkin.lut.ac.uk/ WWW docs/LUTCHI/people/sean/vr-sig/Proceedings.html>.

AZIMUTH. Distributed by Media Magic, Nicasio, Calif. Macintosh-based hypermedia journal.

Badler, Norman I., Cary B. Phillips, and Bonnie Lynn Webber. *Virtual Humans and Simulated Agents*. New York: Oxford University Press, 1993.

Bains, S. "Scientists Slice Virtual Leg." *New Scientist*. July 6, 1991, 131(1776): 28.

Bajura, Michael, Henry Fuchs, and Ryutarou Ohbuchi. *Merging Virtual Reality with the Real World: Seeing Ultrasound Imagery within the Patient*. Chapel Hill, NC: Computer Science Department, University of North Carolina, 1992. Technical Report TR92-005.

Balaguer, Francis, and Angelo Mangili. "Virtual Environments." *New Trends In Animation and Visualization*, Daniel Thalmann and Nadia Magnenat-Thalmann, eds. Lausanne, Switzerland: John Wiley, 1991: 91-105.

Bancroft, G., et al. "Tools for 3D Scientific Visualization in Computational Aerodynamics at NASA Ames Research Center." *Three Dimensional Visualization and Display Technologies, Proceedings of the SPIE - The International Society for Optical Engineering*, W. E. Robbins and S. S. Fisher, eds. Bellingham, Wash.: SPIE, 1989, 1083: 161-172.

Barlow, John Perry. "Being and Nothingness: Virtual Reality and the Pioneers of Cyberspace" and "Life in the DataCloud: Scratching Your Eyes Back In." *Mondo 2000*, June 1990 (2).

Barlow, John Perry. "Electronic Frontier: Coming into the Country." *Communications of the ACM* (Association for Computing Machinery), March 1991, 34(3): 19-21.

Barlow, John Perry. "Private Life in Cyberspace." *Communications of the ACM* (Association for Computing Machinery), August 1991, 34(8): 23-25.

Barlow, John Perry. "Decrypting the Puzzle Palace." *Communications of the ACM* (Association for Computing Machinery), July 1992, 35(7): 25-31.

Barlow, John Perry. "The Great Work." *Communications of the ACM* (Association for Computing Machinery), July 1992, 35(1): 25-28.

Barlow, John Perry. "Will Japan Jack In?" *Communications of the ACM* (Association for Computing Machinery), October 1992, 35(3): 27 ff.

Barlow, John Perry. Interview. *See* Gans and Sirius, Gosney.

Bates, Joseph. "Virtual Reality, Art, and Entertainment." *Presence*, December 1992, 1(1): 133-138.

Bates, Joseph. "The Role of Emotion in Believable Agents." *Communications of the ACM* (Association for Computing Machinery), July 1994.

Bates, Joseph, A. BryanLoyall, and W. Scott Reilly. "Broad Agents." *Proceedings of AAAI Spring Symposium on Integrated Intelligent Architectures.* Conference held March 1991 at Stanford, Calif. Also in *SIGART Bulletin*, August 1991, 2(4): 38-40.

Bates, Joseph, A. BryanLoyall, and W. Scott Reilly. "An Architecture for Action, Emotion, and Social Behavior." *Proceedings of the Fourth European Workshop on Modeling Autonomous Agents in a Multi-Agent* World. Conference held July 1992 at San Martino al Cimino, Italy.

Bates, Joseph, A. BryanLoyall, and W. Scott Reilly. "Integrating Reactivity, Goals, and Emotion in a Broad Agent." *Proceedings of the Fourteenth Annual Conference of the Cognitive Science Society.* Conference held July 1992 at Bloomington, IN.

Bates, Joseph. *See also* Kantrowitz and Bates; Kelso, Weyhrouch, and Bates; Loyall and Bates; Reilly and Bates; and Smith and Bates.

Bauer, W. "VODIS - Virtual Office Design, ein Konzept für die Ganzheltllche Bürogestaltung." *Forschung und Praxis*, H. J. Warnecke, and H. J. Bullinger, eds. 1993, T 35: 281-297.

Bauer, W., H. J. Bullinger, and O. Riedel. "Virtual Reality as a Tool for Office Design Applications - Visions and Realities." *International Conference on Human Computer Interaction (HCI-5)*. Tarrytown, N.Y.: Elsevier Science, 1993. Conference held August 8-13, 1993 at Orlando, Fla.

Bauer, W., and O. Riedel. "Virtuelle Realität als Werkzeug für die Bürogestaltung." *Office Design*. 1992: 36-41.

Bauer, W., and O. Riedel. *Der Blick in eine Faszinierende Künstliche Welt.* Stuttgart, Germany: Fraunhofer-Institut für Arbeitswirtschaft und Organisation IAO, 1993. Technical Report 15/93.

Bauer, W., and O. Riedel. "New Techniques for Interaction in Virtual Worlds-Contents of Development and Examples." *HCI International "93.* Conference held 1993.

Bauer, W., and O. Riedel. "VILAGE - Virtueller Layoutgestalter." *Forschung und Praxis*, H. J. Warnecke, and H. J. Bullinger, eds. 1993, T 35: 47-59.

Bauer, W., and O. Riedel. "Virtual Reality Design in Office Workplaces." *ICPR '93.* Conference held 1993 at Lappeenranta, Finland.

BBS, Hacker-Art. Italy. 39-55-485997.

BBS, Toronto Virtual Reality Special Interest Group Bulletin Board Service (TOR-VR-SIG). Shawn Knight, sysop. Toronto, Ontario, Canada: Canada Remote Systems. (416) 631-6625; 24 hours/7 days; 16.8K baud. Offers "information, code and objects: VR FAQs; suppliers, addresses, specs; REND386 PLGs, WLDs, converters, source [code]; home brew VR — Power Glove code, Sega 3D glasses code; objects — TDDDs, converters, 3D-Studio PLG's; rendering — ray tracing, scenes, converters; graphics gems and more."

BBS, VRontier Worlds BBS. Laramie, Wyo. (608) 873-8523; 6p.m. to 7 a.m. CST weekdays, 24 hours on weekends. The electronic home of *PCVR magazine.*

Beardon, C. "The Ethics of Virtual Reality." *Intelligent Tutoring Media*, February 1992, 3(1): 23-8.

Beck, Stephen. "Virtual Light." *See Mondo 2000.*

Begault, Durand K. "The Virtual Reality of 3-D Sound." *See* Jacobson, *Cyberarts.*

Begelman, D. A. "Virtual Realities and Virtual Mistakes: A Comment on Tart." Dissociation: Progress in the Dissociative Disorders, December 1991, 4(4): 214-215.

Benedikt, Michael, ed. *Collected Abstracts from the First Conference on Cyberspace.* Austin, Tex.: University of Texas at Austin, 1990. Conference held May 4, 1990 at Flawn Academic Center, The University of Texas at Austin.

Benedikt, Michael, ed. *Cyberspace: First Steps.* Cambridge, Mass.: MIT Press, 1991. Includes "Academy Leader" by William Gibson, "Old Rituals for New Space: Rites de Passage and William Gibson's Cultural Model of Cyberspace" by David Tomas, "Mind is a Leaking Rainbow" by Nicole Stenger, "The Erotic Ontology of Cyberspace" by Michael Heim, "Will the Real Body Please Stand Up?: Boundary Stories about Virtual Cultures" by Allucquere

Rosanne Stone, "Cyberspace: Some Proposals" by Michael Benedikt, "Liquid Architectures in Cyberspace" by Marcos Novak, "Giving Meaning to Place: Semantic Spaces" by Alan Wexelblat, "The Lessons of Lucasfilm's Habitat" by Chip Morningstar and F. Randall Farmer, "Collaborative Engines for Multiparticipant Cyberspaces" by Carl Tollander, "Notes on the Structure of Cyberspace and the Ballistic Actors Model" by Tim McFadden, "Virtual Worlds: No Interface to Design" by Meredith Bricken, "Corporate Virtual Workspace" by Steve Pruitt and Tom Barrett.

Benford, Steve, and Lennart E. Fahlén. "Awareness, Focus and Aura: A Spatial Model of Interaction in Virtual Space." *Proceedings of HCI International '93.* Conference held August 1993 at Orlando, Fla.

Benford, Steve, and Lennart E. Fahlén. "A Spatial Model of Interaction in Large Virtual Environments." ECSCW '93: *Proceedings of the Third European Conference on Computer- Supported Cooperative Work.* Giorgio De Michelis, Carla Simone, and Kjeld Schmidt, eds. Boston: Kluwer Academic Publishers, 1993. Conference held September 13-17, 1993 at Milan, Italy.

Best of TED2 [Technology Entertainment Design 2] (videorecording). Distributed by Art Com, San Francisco. 6 hours 33 minutes. Includes "NASA Virtual Environment Workstation Demonstration" by Scott Fisher, "VPL Virtual Reality Demonstration" by Jaron Lanier and presentations by Alan Kay, Ted Nelson and others.

Bey, Hakim. *T.A.Z.: The Temporary Autonomous Zone, Ontological Anarchy, Poetic Terrorism.* Brooklyn, N.Y.: Autonomedia, 1991.

"Bibliography of Virtual-Worlds Research at Department of Computer Science, University of North Carolina at Chapel Hill." Chapel Hill: University of North Carolina, Department of Computer Science, 1992.

Binkley, Timothy. "Camera Fantasia: Computed Visions of Virtual Realities." *Millennium Film Journal.* 1989, (20/21).

Binkley, Timothy. "The Quickening of Galatea: Virtual Creation Without Tools or Media." *Art Journal*, September 1990, 49: 233-240.

Bioapparatus seminar. See Virtual Seminar on the Bioapparatus.

Biocca, Frank. "Communication Within Virtual Reality: Creating a Space for Research." *Journal of Communication*, 1992, 42(4): 5-22.

Biocca, Frank. "Virtual Reality Technology: A Tutorial." *Journal of Communication*, 1992, 42(4): 23-72.

Bishop, G., et. al. "Research Directions in Virtual Environments: Report of an NSF Invitational Workshop." *Computer Graphics*, 1926: 153-177.

BIX (computer network). Virtual-Reality Conference, <virtual.world>. Moderated by Dan Duncan, e-mail: dunc.

Blackburn, Dave. "Virtual Tennis, Anyone?" *Virtual Reality World*, July /August 1994: 35-40.

Blais, C., and R. D. Lyons. "Telepresence: Enough is Enough (Remote Combat Vehicles Control)." *Teleoperation and Control 1988*, C. A. Mason, ed. Bedford, England: IFS Publications, 1988: 217-26. Conference held July 12, 1988 at Bristol, England.

Blanchard, C., et al. "Reality Built for Two: a Virtual Reality Tool." *Computer Graphics*. March 1990, 24(2): 35-6.

Blanchard, Chuck. *See* Applications Development Toolkits (videorecording).

Bleecker, Julian. "Vision Culture: Information Management and the Cultural Assimilation of VR." *Afterimage*, October 1992, 20(3): 11-13.

Bleecker, Julian C. *Coherent Light: Virtual Reality, Culture Politics and the New Humanism in Science*. University of Washington, 1992. Unpublished thesis.

Bogdanski, Jan. "Color Helmet-Mounted Display." *Proceedings from the 4th MultiG Workshop*, Björn Pehrson, ed. Conference held May 1992 at Stockholm. Stockholm, 1992.

Bogdanski, Jan. "Helmet Mounted Display Based on Tektronics LC NuColor Shutter." *Proceedings of the Society for Display Technology Conference*. Conference held May 1993 at Seattle, Washington.

Böhm, K., W. Hubner, and K. Väänänen. "GIVEN: Gesture Driven Interactions in Virtual Environments. A Toolkit Approach to 3D Interactions." *Informatique '92: International Conference Interface to Real and Virtual Worlds*. Nanterre, France: EC2, 1992: 243-254. Conference held March 23, 1992 at Montpellier, France.

bOING-bOING. Quarterly, since 1988. Studio City, Calif.

Boire, Christopher P. *The Epistemology of Natural and Virtual Realities*. Clark University, 1992. Unpublished thesis.

Bolas, Michael T., and Scott S. Fisher. "Head-Coupled Remote Stereoscopic Camera System for Telepresence Applications." *Stereoscopic Displays and Applications: Proceedings of the SPIE - The International Society for Optical Engineering*. Santa Clara, Calif.: SPIE, 1990, 1256: 113-23. Conference held February 12, 1990.

Bolt, R. "Put-that-there: Voice and Gesture at the Graphics Interface." Computer Graphics, 14(3):262-270. Also in *Proceedings of ACM SIGGRAPH 1980*. New York: ACM (Association for Computing Machinery), 1980.

Bonacic, Vladimir. "A Transcendental Concept for Cybernetic Art in the 21st Century." *Leonardo*, 1989, 22(1): 109-11.

Brand, Stewart. *The Media Lab: Inventing the Future at MIT*. New York: Viking Press, 1987.

Branscomb, A. W. "Common Law for the Electronic Frontier." *Scientific American*, September 1991, 265(3): 112-16.

Branwyn, Gareth, and Peter Sugarman, eds. *Beyond Cyberpunk: A Do-It-Yourself Guide to the Future* (Hypercard stack for Macintosh computers). Louisa, Va.: The Computer Lab, 1992. A compilation of cyberpunk and cyberculture; among the contributors are Hakim Bey, Stephen Brown, Mike Gunderloy, Richard Kadrey, Rudy Rucker, Bruce Sterling, and Robert Anton Wilson.

Branwyn, Gareth. "Jamming the Media" *See* Hughes, Carolyn.

Bray, Faustin. "Mutations in the 4th Dimension: A Conversation with Rudy Rucker." *Mondo 2000*, September 1989, (1): 74-79.

Breen, P. T. , Jr. "Near-term Applications for Virtual Environment Technology." *1992 Summer Computer Simulation Conference*, P. Luker, ed. San Diego, Calif.: SCS, 1992: 1258-62. Conference held July 27, 1992 at Reno, Nev.

Breen, P. T. , Jr. "The Reality of Fantasy: Real Applications for Virtual Environments." *Information Display*, November 1992, 8(11): 15-18.

Brennan, J. P., and J. A. Brennan. "Virtual Reality in the Delivery Room." *Virtual Reality Systems*, 1994, 1(3): 24-27.

Bricken, Meredith. *Inventing Reality*. Seattle, Wash.: HITL (Human Interface Technology Laboratory), 1989. Technical Memo M-89-2.

Bricken, Meredith. *A Description of the Virtual Reality Learning Environment*. Seattle, Wash.: HITL (Human Interface Technology Laboratory), 1990. Technical Memo M-90-4.

Bricken, Meredith. *The Virtual Conference Room: A Shared Environment for Remote Collaboration*. Seattle, Wash.: HITL (Human Interface Technology Laboratory), 1990. Technical Memo M-90-8.

Bricken, Meredith. *Building the VSX Demonstration: Operations with Virtual Aircraft in Virtual Space*. Seattle, Wash.: HITL (Human Interface Technology Laboratory), 1990. Technical Memo M-90-9.

Bricken, Meredith. *Gender Issues in Virtual Reality Technology*. Seattle, Wash.: HITL (Human Interface Technology Laboratory), 1991. Technical Presentation P-91-6.

Bricken, Meredith. "Virtual Reality Learning Environments: Potential and Challenges." *Computer Graphics*, 1991, 25: 178-84.

Bricken, Meredith. "Virtual Worlds: No Interface to Design." See Benedikt, *Cyberspace*.

Bricken, Meredith, and Chris Byrne. *Summer Students in Virtual Reality: A Pilot Study on Educational Applications of VR Technology*. Seattle, Wash.: HITL (Human Interface Technology Laboratory), 1992. Technical Report R-92-1.

Bricken, William, "Cyberspace 1999: The Shell, the Image, and Now, the Meat." *Mondo 2000*, June 1990 (2).

Bricken, William. *Coordination of Multiple Participants in Virtual Space*. Seattle,Wash.: HITL (Human Interface Technology Laboratory), 1990. Technical Presentation P-90-4.

Bricken, William. *Learning in Virtual Reality*. Seattle, Wash.: HITL (Human Interface Technology Laboratory), 1990. Technical Memo M-90-5.

Bricken, William. "Virtual Reality, As Unreal As It Gets." DIAC-90: *Directions and Implications of Advanced Computing*. Palo Alto, Calif.: Computer Professionals for Social Responsibility, 1990: 265-7. Conference held July 28, 1990, at Boston.

Bricken, William. "Languages for Virtual Reality: Spatial Representation of Elementary Algebra." *1992 IEEE Workshop on Visual Languages*. Los Alamitos, Calif.: IEEE Computer Society Press, 1992: 56-62.

Bricken, William, "A Formal Foundation for Cyberspace." *See* Helsel, *Beyond the Vision*.

Bricken, William. *See* Virtual Reality Conference (videorecording).

Bricken, William, and Linda Jacobson. "Virtual Environment Operating System." *AI Expert: Virtual Reality Special Report*. San Francisco: Miller Freeman, July 1992: 55-8.

Brill, Louis. "Virtual Reality Research Grows: Cinema Butterfly in the Making." *Film Journal*, June 1991, 94(5). Continued as "Virtual Reality Environments Prepare for Interactive Cinema" in July 1991, 94(6).

Brill, Louis M. "Facing Interface Issues." *Computer Graphics World*, April 1992, 15(4): 48-55.

Brill, Louis. "An Interactive Trip into a Virtual Paradise." *Computer Graphics World*, September 1992.

Brill, Louis. "Art Meets Cyberspace in a VR Museum." *Computer Graphics World*, December 1992.

Brill, Louis. "Where Art Meets Cyberspace – Application: The Networked Virtual Art Museum." *CyberEdge Journal*, November/December 1992: 6.

Brill, Louis. "Metaphors for the Traveling Cybernauts." *Virtual Reality World*, Spring 1993, 1(1): q-s. Insert in *Multimedia Review*, Summer 1993.

Brill, Louis. "Kicking the Tires of VR Software." *Computer Graphics World*, June 1993: 40-53.

Brill, Louis. "Designing, Authoring, and Toolkit Cyber Software." *Virtual Reality World*, Part One, May/June 1994; Part Two, July/August 1994.

Brooks, F. P. , Jr., et al "Project GROPE: Haptic Displays for Scientific Visualization." *Computer Graphics*, August 1990, 24(4): 177-85. Special issue containing proceedings of SIGGRAPH 1990, 17th Annual ACM Conference on Computer Graphics and Interactive Techniques, held August 6-10, 1990, at Dallas, Tex.

Brooks, Fred. *See* United States Congress, New Developments in Computer Technology.

Brown, Paul. "Metamedia and Cyberspace: Advanced Computers and the Future of Art." *Culture, Technology & Creativity in the Late Twentieth Century*, Philip Hayward, ed. London, England: John Libbey & Company, 1990: 227-241.

Bryson, Steve. "Virtual Spacetime: An Environment for the Visualization of Curved Spacetimes via Geodesic Flows." *Proceedings: Visualization '92*. Los Alamitos, Calif.: IEEE Computer Society Press, 1992: 291-8. Conference held October 19-23, 1992, at Boston, Mass.

Bryson, Steve, and Scott S. Fisher. "Defining, Modeling, and Measuring System Lag in Virtual Environments." *Stereoscopic Displays and Applications: Proceedings of the SPIE - The International Society for Optical Engineering*. Santa Clara, Calif.: The International Society for Optical Engineering, 1990, 1256: 98-109. Conference held February 12, 1990.

Bryson, Steve, and Creon Levit. "The Virtual Wind Tunnel." *IEEE Computer Graphics and Applications*, July 1992, 12: 25-34.

Bryson, Steve. *See* ICAT '92.

Burdea, Grigore, and Philippe Coiffet. *La Réalité Virtuelle*. Paris: Hermes Publishing, 1993.

Burg, Jennifer, et al. "Behavioral Representation in Virtual Reality." *Behavioral Representation Symposium, April 1991*. Orlando, Fla.: Institute for Simulation and Training, 1991.

Burgin, Victor. "Realising the Reverie." *Ten.8*, 1991, 2(2): 5-15.

Burnett, Christopher. "Hieroglyphs of the Hyperreal." *Ten.8*, 1991, 2(2): 44-45.

Burton, R. P., and I. E. Sutherland. "Twinkle Box: A Three-Dimensional Computer Input Device." *National Computer Conference and Exhibition.* APIPS, 1974, 43.

Bush, Vannevar, James M. Nyce, and Paul Kahn. *From Memex to Hypertext: Vannevar Bush and the Mind's Machine.* Boston, Mass.: Academic Press, 1991. Includes: "As We May Think" and "Selections from Of Inventions and Inventors" by Vannevar Bush, "Letter to Vannevar Bush" and "Program on Human Effectiveness" by Douglas C. Engelbart, "As We Will Think" by Theodor H. Nelson, and other papers.

Buss, Martin and Hideki Hashimoto. "Intelligent Cooperative Manipulation." *See* ICAT '93.

Cadoz, Claude, Jean-Loup Florens, and Annie Luciani. "Responsive Input Devices and Sound Synthesis by Simulation of Instrumental Mechanisms: the CORDIS System." *Computer Music Journal*, 1984, 8(3): 60-73.

Cadoz, Claude, Leszek Lisowski, and Jean-Loup Florens. "Modular Feedback Keyboard." *Computer Music Journal*, 1990, 14(2): 47-51.

Cadoz, Claude, and Christophe Ramstein. "Capture, Representation, and Composition of the Instrumental Gesture." *Proceedings of ICMC '90.* Conference held 1990 at Glasgow.

Calvin, J., et al. "The SIMNET Virtual World Architecture." *Proceedings of IEEE 1993 Virtual Reality Annual International Symposium, VRAIS '93.* Piscataway, N.J.: IEEE Service Center, 1993: 450-455. Conference held September 1993, at Seattle, Washington.

Campbell, Colin. *Virtual Reality.* Albany, N.Y.: University of the State of New York, State Education Department, 1992.

Carande, Robert. *Information Sources for Virtual Reality: A Research Guide.* Westport, Conn.: Greenwood Press, 1993.

Card, Orson Scott. *Unaccompanied Sonata & Other Stories.* New York: Dial Press, 1980. Includes "Ender's Game," "Kingsmeat," "Deep Breathing Exercises," "Closing the Timelid," "I Put My Blue Genes On," "Eumenides in the Fourth Floor Lavatory," "Mortals Gods," "Quietus," "The Monkeys Thought 'Twas All in Fun," "The Porcelain Salamander," "Unaccompanied Sonata," and "Afterword: On Origins".

Card, Orson Scott. *Ender's Game.* New York: T. Doherty Associates, 1985.

Carlsson, Christer, and Lennart E. Fahlén. "Integrated CSCW Tools Within a Shared 3D Virtual Environment." *INTERCHI '93 Conference Proceedings: Bridges between Words.* Stacey Ashlund, et al., eds. Conference on Human

Factors in Computing Systems, INTERACT '93 and CHI '93, held April 1993 at Amsterdam, the Netherlands.

Carlsson, Christer, and Olof Hagsand. "DIVE — A Platform for Multi-User Virtual Environments." *Computers & Graphics*, 1993, 17(6): 663-669.

Carlsson,Christer, and Olof Hagsand. "DIVE — A Multi-User Virtual Reality System." *VRAIS: IEEE Virtual Reality Annual Symposium, Symp. 1.* Piscataway, N.J.: IEEE Service Center, 1993: 394-400. Conference held September 1993 at Seattle, Washington.

Carlsson, Christer, and Olof Hagsand. "The Distributed Interactive Virtual Environment — Architecture and Applications." *IEE Colloquium on 'Distributed Virtual Reality'* (Digest No. 121). London: IEE, 1993: 3/1-3. Conference held May 21, 1993 at London, England.

Chan, Curtis. "Sound Localization and Spatial Enhancement with the Roland Sound Space System." *See* Jacobson, *Cyberarts*.

Christel, Michael. "Virtual Reality Today on a PC." *Instruction Delivery Systems*, July-August 1992, 6(4): 6-9.

Citations (a bibliography) (online text file). Multiple contributors. FTP: <ftp.u.washington.edu>. Directory ~ftp/public/virtual-worlds File: citations. In LateX format, but readable as plain text. Selections are not systematic; most are technical, but some are popular. Revised and reprinted as the bibliography in Earnshaw, Gigante, and Jones.

CompuServe (computer network). Virtual Reality section in the Cyberforum. Sysops: Neil Shapiro and John Eagan. E-mail: 71333.2650@compuserve.com.

Computer Database (online database). Foster City, Calif.: Information Access Corporation, since 1983. Online bibliographic database covering some 90 journals in computers, telecommunications and electronics.

Conn, C., et al. "Virtual Environments and Interactivity: Windows to the Future." *Proceedings of ACM SIGGRAPH '89. Computer Graphics* 23(5): 7-18. Conference held August 1989, at Boston, Mass.

Cook, R. "Serious Entertainment." *Computer Graphics World*, May 1992, 15(5): 40-48.

Cornwell, R. "Where is the Window? Virtual Reality Technologies Now." *Artscribe International*, January 1991, 85: 52-55.

Couey, Anna. "Shapes of Virtual Reality: Interactive Experimentation in the Arts Online." *NCGA '90.* Fairfax, Va.: National Computer Graphics Association, 1990, 3: 354-8. Conference held March 19, 1990, at Anaheim, Calif.

Coull, Tom. "Texture-based Virtual Reality on a Desktop Computer Using WorldToolKit." See Helsel, *Beyond the Vision.*

Coull, Tom, and Peter Rothman. "Virtual Reality for Decision Support Systems." *AI Expert.*, August 1993, 8(8): 22-25.

Cruz-Neira, Carolina, et al. "The Cave: Audio Visual Experience Automatic Virtual Environment." *Communications of the ACM* (Association for Computing Machinery), June 1992, 35(6): 64-72.

CyberArts 1991 (videorecording). Distributed by Art Com, San Francisco, 1991. Tape 1: 60 minutes; tape 2: 120 minutes. Second Annual Cyber Arts International Conference & Expo held November, 1991, at Pasadena, Calif.

CyberEdge Journal. Ben Delaney, ed. Sausalito, Calif.: The Delaney Companies. E-mail: MCI Mail, BENDEL1; CompuServe, 76217,3074; Internet: bdel@well.sf.ca.us. Bimonthly since 1991.

Cyberpunk. (videorecording). Distributed by Art Com, San Francisco. 60 minutes. Includes William Gibson, Jaron Lanier, and Timothy Leary.

Cyberspace, Power & Culture (videorecording). Distributed by Art Com, San Francisco. Palo Alto, Calif.: Pure Grain Film & Video, 1991. 106 minutes. Second Annual Conference on Cyberspace, held 1991, at University of California, Santa Cruz. Panelists include John Perry Barlow, Michael Benedikt, Kathleen Biddick, Scott Bukarman, Scott Fisher, Jean-Claude Guedon, Eric Gullichsen, Barbara Joans, Brenda Laurel, Nicole Stenger, and Allucquère Roseanne Stone.

D'Amato, Brian. "The Last Medium: the Virtues of Virtual Reality." *Flash Art* (International Edition). January 1992, 162: 96-98.

Davidson, Clive. "Pupils Put Virtual Reality to the Test: Dimension International's Desktop VR system." *Computer Weekly*, April 30, 1992: 42.

Degenhart, E., J. Neugebauer, and M. Wapler. "VR4RobotS: Virtual Reality for Robot Systems." *IPA/IAO Forum Virtual Reality '93*. Conference held 1993 at Stuttgart, Germany.

De Landa, Manuel. *War in the Age of Intelligent Machines*. New York: Zone Books, 1991.

Delaney, Ben. "Meeting the Angels." *CyberEdge Journal*, May 1992.

Dery, Mark. "Fast Forward: Art Goes High Tech." *Art News*, February 1993, 92(2): 74-83.

Dockery, J., and D. Littman. "Intelligent Virtual Reality as a Universal Interface for the Handicapped." *Informatique '92 International Conference: Interface to Real and Virtual Worlds. Proceedings and Exhibition Catalog.*

Nanterre, France: EC2, 1992: 515-522. Conference held March 23, 1992, at Montpellier, France.

Dowding, Tim J. "A Self-Contained Interactive Motorskill Trainer." *See* Helsel, *Beyond the Vision.*

Dowding, Tim. *See* VR Conference — Applications (videorecording).

Druckrey, Timothy. "Deadly Representations." *Ten.8*, 1991, 2(2): 16-27.

Druckrey, Timothy. "Revenge of the Nerds (interview with Jaron Lanier)." *Afterimage.* May 1991, 18:5-9.

Druckrey, Timothy. "Lost in Cyberspace: Writing the History of Virtual Reality." *Afterimage*, December 1991, 19:8-9.

Durlach, N. I., et al., eds. *Virtual Environment Technology for Training (VETT).* Cambridge, Mass.: Bolt Beranek and Newman, Inc., March 1992. BBN Report No. 7661.

Dutton, Gail. "Medicine Gets Closer to Virtual Reality." *IEEE Software*, September 1992, 9: 108.

Earnshaw, R. A., M. A. Gigante, and H. Jones, eds. *Virtual Reality Systems.* London: Academic Press, 1993. Contains papers presented at the British Computer Society conference, Virtual Reality Systems, held May 1992, at London and additional contributions. Includes foreword by Henry Fuchs, "Virtual Reality: Definitions, History, Applications" by M. A. Gigante, "Virtual Reality: Enabling Technologies" by M. A. Gigante, "SuperVision - A Parallel Architecture for Virtual Reality" by C. Grimsdale, "Virtual Reality Products" by T. W. Rowley, "A Computational Model for the Stereoscopic Optics of a Head-Mounted Display" by W. Robinett and J. P. Rolland, "A Comprehensive Virtual Environment Laboratory Facility" by R. S. Kalawsky, "Gesture Driven Interaction as a Human Factor in Virtual Environments: An Approach with Neural Networks" by K. Väänänen and K. Böhm, "Using Physical Constraints in a Virtual Environment" by M. J. Papper and M. A. Gigante, "Device Synchronization Using an Optimal Linear Filter" by M. Friedmann, T. Starner and A. Pentland, "Virtual Reality Techniques in Flight Simulation" by J. A. Vince, "Using Virtual Reality Techniques in the Animation Process" by D. Thalmann, "Dynamic FishEye Information Visualizations" by K. M. Fairchild, L. Serra, N. Hern, L. B. Hai and A. T. Leong, "Virtual Reality: A Tool for Telepresence and Human Factors Research" by R. J. Stone, "Critical Aspects of Visually Coupled Systems" by R. S. Kalawsky, "AVIARY: A Generic Virtual Reality Interface for Real Applications" by A. J. West, T. L. J. Howard, R. J. Hubbold, A. D. Murta, D. N. Snowdon and D. A. Butler, "Using Gestures to Control a Virtual Arm" by M. J. Papper and M. A. Gigante, "Toward Three-Dimensional Graphical Models of Reality" by P. Quarendon, "Back to the Cave - Cultural Issues on Virtual Reality" by G. L. Mallen, "Ethical Issues in the Application of Virtual Reality to the Treatment of Mental Disorders" by L. J. Whalley, and "Overview of Virtual Reality Software Suppliers" by C. McNaughton.

Edwards, Thomas M. *Virtual Worlds Technology as an Interface to Geographic Information.* Seattle, Wash.: Department of Geography, University of Washington, 1991. Unpublished thesis.

EFFector Online (electronic journal). Cambridge, Mass.: Electronic Frontier Foundation, Inc. E-mail: eff-request@eff.org. Also on the <comp.org.eff.news> newsgroup of Usenet.

Eglowstein, Howard. "Reach Out and Touch Your Data: Hand-tracking Devices." *BYTE,* July 1990, 15(7): 283-290.

Electronic Frontier Foundation. "The Electronic Frontier Foundation's Open Platform Proposal" (online text file). FTP: <ftp.eff.org> Directory pub/EFF/papers File: open-platform-proposal.

Ellis, Steven R. "Nature and Origins of Virtual Environments: a Bibliographical Essay." *Computing Systems in Engineering,* 1991, 2(4): 321-47.

Ellis, Steven R. "The Design of Virtual Spaces and Virtual Environments." *Human Vision, Visual Processing and Digital Display III: Proceedings of the SPIE - The International Society for Optical Engineering.* San Jose, Calif.: SPIE, 1992, 1666: 536-40. Conference held February 10, 1992.

Ellis, Steven R. "What Are Virtual Environments?" *See* ICAT '93.

Emerson, Toni. *Information Resources in Virtual Reality.* Seattle, Wash.: HITL (Human Interface Technology Laboratory), April 1993. Bibliography B-93-1. Updated versions available online. FTP: <ftp.u.washington.edu> Directory: /public/VirtualReality/HITL/papers/tech-reports File: irvr.txt.

Emerson, Toni. *Selected Bibliography on Virtual Interface Technology: Selected Citations from the Literature.* Seattle, Wash.: HITL (Human Interface Technology Laboratory), 1993. Bibliography B-93-2. Updated versions available online. FTP: <ftp.u.washington.edu> Directory: /public/VirtualReality /HITL/papers/tech-reports File: emerson-B-93-2.txt.

Emerson, Toni. *Virtual Audio Bibliography* (online text file). Seattle, Wash.: HITL (Human Interface Technology Laboratory), 1994. FTP: 140.142.56.2 Directory: ./public/HITL/Bibliographies File: Virtual-Audio-Bibliography.txt.

Emmett, Arielle. "Down to Earth: Commercial Applications of Virtual Reality." *Computer Graphics World,* March 1992, 15(3): 43-48.

Emmett, Arielle. "An Operating System for Virtual Reality: Development of the Virtual Environment Operating System at the University of Washington's Human Interface Technology Laboratory." *Computer Graphics World,* January 1993, 16: 14.

Engelbart, Douglas. "A Conceptual Framework for Augmenting Man's Intellect." *Vistas in Information-Handling*, Paul W. Howerton and David C. Weeks, eds. Washington, DC: Spartan Books, 1963.

Fahlén, Lennart E.. "Issues in Telepresence." *Proceedings from the 2nd MultiG workshop*, Björn Pehrson and Yngve Sundblad, eds. Conference held June 1991 at Stockholm.

Fahlén, Lennart E. "The MultiG TelePresence System." *Proceedings from the 3rd MultiG Workshop*, Yngve Sundblad, ed. Conference held December 1991 at Stockholm.

Fahlén, Lennart E. "Virtual Reality and the MultiG Project." *VR93:Virtual Reality International 93. Proceedings of the Third Annual Conference on Virtual Reality.* London, England: Meckler, 1993: 78-86. Conference held April 1993 at London, England.

Fahlén, Lennart E., and Charles Brown. "Use of a 3D Aura Metaphor for Computer Based Conferencing and Teleworking." *Proceedings from the 4th MultiG workshop*, Björn Pehrson, ed. Conference held May 1992 at Stockholm.

Fahlén, Lennart E., and Olof Hagsand. "The SICS TelePresence System." *Telepresence — A New Concept for Teleconferencing: Proceedings of the First COST #229 WG.5 Workshop*, Forchheimer, Robert, ed. Conference held October 1991 at Stockholm.

Fahlén, Lennart E., et al. "A Space Based Model for User Interaction in Shared Synthetic Environments." *INTERCHI '93 Conference Proceedings: Bridges between Words.* Stacey Ashlund, et al., eds. Conference on Human Factors in Computing Systems, INTERACT '93 and CHI '93, held April 1993 at Amsterdam, the Netherlands.

Fahlén, Lennart E., and Kai-Mikael Jää-Aro, eds. *Proceedings of the 5th MultiG Workshop.* Stockholm: Royal Institute of Technology, 1993. Conference held December 18, 1992 at Stockholm. Includes "Networked Virtual Reality" by Carl Loeffler, "Aura, Focus and Awareness" by Steve Benford and Lennart E. Fahlén, "The MultiG Distributed Interactive Virtual Environment" by Christer Carlsson and Olof Hagsand", "A Virtual Reality: Possibilities for the Handicapped?" by Torleif Söderlund, "Telepresens in Conference Applications" by Jonas Yngvesson and Bengt Kvarnström, "Achieving Object Persistence for DIVE" by Olivier Démoulin and Kai-Mikael Jää-Aro, "Building Sound into a Virtual Environment" by Stephen Travis Pope and Lennart E. Fahlén, "Advanced Visualization as an Aid to Effective Design and Marketing" by Mats Werke, and other papers.

Fairchild, K. M., et al. "Dynamic FishEye Information Visualizations." *See* Earnshaw, Gigante and Jones.

Farmer, F. Randall. "Cyberspace: Getting There from Here." *Journal of Computer Game Design*, October 1988.

Feiner, S., and C. Beshers. "Worlds within Worlds: Metaphors for Exploring n-Dimensional Virtual Worlds " *UIST: Third Annual Symposium on User Interface Software and Technology*. New York: ACM (Association for Computing Machinery), 1990: 76-83. Proceedings of the ACM SIGGRAPH Symposium held October 3-5, 1990, at Snowbird, Utah.

Feldman, Tony, ed. *Virtual Reality International 92: Impacts and Applications*. Proceedings of the 2nd annual Conference on Virtual Reality International: Impacts & Applications. London: Meckler, 1992. Conference held April 1992 at London.

Felger, Wolfgang. "How Interactive Visualization can Benefit from Multi-dimensional Input Devices." *GI-Workshop "Visuallsierung: Rolle von Interaktivität und Echtzeit"*. Conference held June 1992 at St. Augustin, Germany.

Felger, Wolfgang. "Konzept und Realisierung eines Labors fuer Anwendungen der Virtuellen Realitaet angenommen fuer." *Proceedings. GI-Workshop "Sichtsysteme: Visualisierung in der Simulationstechnik."* Berlin: Springer-Verlag, 1993. Conference held November 1993.

Felger, Wolfgang, Torsten Froehlich, and Martin Goebel. "Techniken sur Navigation durch Virtuelle Welten."*Virtual Reality '93*. H. J. Bullinger, and H. J. Warnecke, eds. Springer-Verlag, 1993: 209-222. Conference held February 1993.

Fels, S. Sydney, and Geoffrey E. Hinton. "Glove-Talk: A Neural Network Interface Between a Data-glove and a Speech Synthesizer." *IEEE Transactions on Neural Networks*, January 1993, 4: 2-8.

Ferrin, Frank J. "Survey of Helmet Tracking Technologies." *Proceedings of the SPIE - The International Society for Optical Engineering*. Santa Clara, Calif.: SPIE, 1991, 1456. Conference held 1991.

Fineart Forum (electronic journal). Berkeley, Calif.: International Society for Art, Science and Technology. Monthly. E-mail: fast@garnet.berkeley.edu or CONSERVA@IFIIDG.FI.CNR.IT or OKUNO@NTT-20.JP.

Fisher, Scott S. "NASA Virtual Environment Workstation Demonstration." *See* Best of TED2 (videorecording).

Fisher, Scott S. "Virtual Interface Environments." *See* Laurel, ed.

Fisher, Scott S. "Virtual Environments: Personal Simulations and Telepresence." *See* Helsel and Roth.

Fisher, Scott S. *See* Art and Artistry in Virtual Reality.

Fisher, Scott, and Jane Tazelaar. "Living in a Virtual World." *BYTE*, July 1990: 215-221.

Fisher, Scott S., et al. "Virtual Environment Display System." *1986 Workshop on Interactive 3D Graphics*, F. Crow and S. M. Pizer, eds. New York: ACM (Association for Computing Machinery), 1987: 77-87.

Fisher, Scott S., et al. "Virtual Interface Environment for Telepresence Applications." *ANS International Topical Meeting on Remote Systems and Robotics in Hostile Environments*, J. D. Berger, ed. 1987: x-y.

Flaig, T. "Einsatz von Transputersystemen zur Simulation und Steuerung von Industrierobotern." *IPA/IAO Forum Virtual Reality 93*. Conference held 1993 at Stuttgart, Germany.

Fleischmann, Monika. "A Virtual Walk Through Berlin: Visiting a Virtual Museum." *Virtual Reality World*, Spring 1993, 1(1): n-p. Insert in *Multimedia Review*, Summer 1993.

Fontaine, Gary. "The Experience of a Sense of Presence in Intercultural and International Encounters." *Presence*, Fall 1992, 1(4): 482-490.

Foley, J. D. "Interfaces for Advanced Computing." *Scientific American*, October 1987, 257(4): 83-90.

Forchheimer, Robert, ed. *Telepresence - A New Concept for Teleconferencing: Proceedings of the First COST #229 WG.5 Workshop*. Conference held October 1991 at Stockholm.

Foster, Scott. "The Convolvotron Concept." *See* Linda Jacobson, *Cyberarts*.

Friedmann, M., T. Starner and A. Pentland. "Device Synchronization Using an Optimal Linear Filter." *See* Earnshaw, Gigante and Jones.

FRIEND 21: '91 International Symposium on Next Generation Human Interface. Tokyo: Institute for Personalized Information Environment. Conference held November 25, 1991 at Tokyo.

FTP site at Apple, Inc. FTP: <ftp.apple.com> (machine address: 130.43.2.3). Maintained by Bill Cockayne, e-mail: billc@apple.com. Directory: /pub/vr. Files include information on Macintosh virtual reality applications and CAD projects. The file vr_sites lists other FTP sites.

FTP site at Electronic Frontier Foundation. FTP: <ftp.eff.org>. Cambridge, Mass. Directories include pub/EFF. The EFF Gopher service is available on gopher.eff.org, port 70. WAIS access is available on wais.eff.org, port 210. Mail service is handled through archive-server@eff.org; use "index eff" for a list of documents and document sections. E-mail: eff@eff.org.

FTP site at HITL (Human Interface Technology Laboratory). Seattle, Wash. FTP: <ftp.u.washington.edu> Directory: ./public/VirtualReality/HITL. HITL notes that, "This site is still under construction. However, there are technical reports (./public/VirtualReality/HITL/papers/tech-reports) and masters theses (./public/VirtualReality/HITL/papers/Thesis) available. The HIT Lab is also collecting documents in the ./public/VirtualReality area. There are a couple UNC technical reports, the Virtual Education Bibliography, and more."

FTP site at National Center for Supercomputing Applications (NCSA). FTP: <ftp.ncsa.uiuc.edu> Directory: ./VR.

FTP site at <src.doc.ic.ac.uk> (machine address: 146.169.2.1). The directories /usenet/comp.archives/auto/comp.sys.isis and /usenet/comp.archives/auto/sci.virtual-worlds contain archives of the newsgroups <sci.virtual-worlds> and <comp.sys.isis>.

FTP site at University of North Carolina. FTP: FTP: <sunsite.unc.edu> (machine address: 152.2.22.81). University of North Carolina at Chapel Hill. The directory /pub/academic/computer-science/virtual-reality contains numerous subdirectories with VR demos, papers, 3-D objects, viewing software, DOS and Silicon Graphics VR programs, proposed standards and files mirrored from the <sci.virtual-worlds> archive and the glove-list.

FTP site at University of Waterloo. Waterloo, Ontario, Canada. FTP: <sunee.uwaterloo.ca> (machine address: 129.97.50.50). REND386 freeware is archived in the directory /pub. Directories also include /pub/vr and various directories on powerglove, raytracing, graphics, demos, and other topics. As described by the sysop, the directory /pub/vr "contains a hodgepodge of text files relating to the idea of shared VR's or networked games." Some proposals include Michael Snoswell's Open Systems Cyberterminal, KLUGE by Brennan Underwood, Multi-User Network Generic Gaming System by Darryl Palmer, and a model of a shared VR by Bernie Roehl.

FTP site at VR-SIG (U. K.). FTP: <eta.lut.ac.uk> (machine address: 158.125.96.29).

FTP site at Washington University. St. Louis, Mo. FTP: <wuarchive.wustl.edu> (machine address: 128.252.135.4). Contains a mirror of the usenet newsgroup <sci.virtual-worlds> and a graphics archive.

FTP site at Xerox PARC. FTP: <parcftp.xerox.com>. The directory /pub/MOO/papers archives papers on Multi-User Dimension (MUD) text-based virtual worlds. Titles include: "Mudding: Social Phenomena in Text-Based Virtual Realities," "MUDs Grow Up: Social Virtual Reality in the Real World," "Better Living Through Language: The Communicative Implications of a Text-Only Virtual Environment, or, Welcome to LambdaMOO!," "Conversational Structure and Personality Correlates of Electronic Communication," "Electropolis: Communication and Community on Internet

Relay Chat," "Virtual Reality: Reflections of Life, Dreams, and Technology: An Ethnography of a Computer Society," and "Identity Workshop: Emergent Social and Psychological Phenomena in Text-Based Virtual Reality."

Fuchs, Henry, et al. "Interactive Visualization of 3D Medical Data." *IEEE Computer*, August 1989, 22(8): 46-51.

Fuchs, Henry, et al. *Research Directions in Virtual Environments: An Invitational Workshop on the Future of Virtual Environments Research Sponsored by the National Science Foundation*. Chapel Hill, N.C.: Department of Computer Science, University of North Carolina, 1992. Technical Report TR92-027. Electronic text available from the University of North Carolina, Department of Computer Science. To obtain, send e-mail to netlib@cs.unc.edu and in either the subject line or message body, send the request *get 92-027.ps from techreports* The file will be returned via e-mail.

Fukuda, K., T. Tahara, and T. Miyoshi. "Hypermedia Personal Computer Communication System: Fujitsu Habitat." *Fujitsu Scientific and Technical Journal*, 1990, 26(3).

Furness, Thomas A., III. "Designing in Virtual Space." *System Design*. William B. Rouse and Kenneth R. Boff, eds. Amsterdam: North Holland.

Furness, Thomas A., III. *Putting Humans into Virtual Space*. Seattle, Wash.: HITL (Human Interface Technology Laboratory), 1986. Report No. R-86-1.

Furness, Thomas A., III. "Creating Better Virtual Worlds." *Society for Information Display Digest*, May 1988.

Furness, Thomas A., III. "Harnessing Virtual Space." *1988 SID International Symposium*. Playa del Rey, Calif.: SID, 1988: 4-7. Conference held May 24, 1988 at Anaheim, Calif.

Furness, Thomas A., III. "Creating Better Virtual Worlds. " *Proceedings: Human-Machine Interfaces for Teleoperators and Virtual Environments*. March 1990: 48-51.

Furness, Thomas A., III. "Exploring Virtual Worlds with Tom Furness" (interview). *Communications of the ACM* (Association for Computing Machinery), July 1991, 34: S1(2).

Furness, Thomas A., III. *See* United States Congress.

Furness, Thomas A., III. *See* also Miller.

Fusco, Mike. *See* Virtual Reality Conference (videorecording).

"Gallery: Virtual Reality and Interactive Multimedia." *Verbum*, 1991, 5(2): 26-35.

Gans, Davidand R. U. Sirius. "Civilizing the Electronic Frontier: An Interview with Mitch Kapor and John Barlow of the Electronic Frontier Foundation." *Mondo 2000*, December 1991, (3): 45-49.

Garber, S. "A Vision of VR as Art." *Verbum*, 1992, 5(2): 13.

Garvey, R. E. "SIMNET-D: Extending Simulation Boundaries." *National Defense*, November 1989: 40-43.

Gelernter, David. *Mirror Worlds, or, The Day Software Puts the Universe in a Shoebox: How It Will Happen and What It Will Mean.* New York: Oxford University Press, 1991.

Geshwind, David M. "Adapting Traditional Media for Virtual Reality Environments." *See* Helsel, *Beyond the Vision.*

Gibson, William. *Neuromancer*. West Bloomfield, Mich.: Phantasia Press, 1986.

Gibson, William. *Count Zero*. New York: Arbor House, 1986.

Gibson, William. *Burning Chrome*. New York: Ace Books, 1987.

Gibson, William. *Mona Lisa Overdrive*. New York: Bantam Books, 1988.

Gibson, William. "Sci-fi Writer William Gibson Explores the Final Frontier: Information." *Computerworld*, October 15, 1990, 24: 107.

Gibson, William. *Virtual Light*. New York: Bantam Books, 1993.

Gibson, William. "Academy Leader" See Benedikt, *Cyberspace.*

Gibson, William. "The King of Cyberpunk" (interview). *See* Hamburg.

Gibson, William. *See* Cyberpunk (videorecording).

Gigante, M. A. "Virtual Reality: Enabling Technologies." *See* Earnshaw, Gigante and Jones.

Gigliotti, Carol. "VR, or the Modern Frankenstein." *Interface*, November 1992, 4(2): 5-8.

Glenn, "Real Fun, Virtual Experience Amusements and Products in Public Space Entertainment." *See* Helsel, *Beyond the Vision.*

Glove-list (online mailing list). Since 1991. J. Eric Townsend, administrator. E-mail: jet@nas.nasa.gov. For information on adapting the Power Glove for VR systems. To subscribe, send e-mail to listserv@boxer.nas.nasa.gov, with only the following text in the body of the message: subscribe glove-list Yourname. For more information, consult the Glove-list FAQ (electronic text). FTP: <ftp.u.washington.edu> Directory: /public/virtual-worlds/faq/other File: FAQ-glovelist.

Goebel, Martin. "Virtuelle, Realität - Technologie und Anwendungen." *Multimedia und Imageprozessing.* L. Nastansky, ed. AIT Verlag, 1992.

Goldberg, Adele ed. *A History of Personal Workstations.* Reading, Mass.: Addison-Wesley Pub. Co., 1988. ACM Conference on the History of Personal Workstations, held 1986 at Palo Alto, Calif. Includes papers by Douglas Engelbart, J. C. R. Licklider, Allen Newell, and others.

Goldman-Pach, Janine. *Virtual Reality and Virtual Boundaries.* Tucson, Ariz.: University of Arizona, 1993. Unpublished Ph.D. dissertation.

Goldsby, M., et al. "A Virtual Reality Browser for Space Station Models." *Proceedings of the 1993 Conference on Intelligent Computer-Aided Training and Virtual Environment Technology.* Houston, Tex.: NASA, 1993: 2-9.

Goodman, Nelson. *Ways of Worldmaking.* Indianapolis, Ind.: Hackett Publishing, 1978.

Gosney, Michael. "The Verbum Interviews: John Barlow, Timothy Leary, Myron Krueger." *Verbum,* 1992, 5(2): 18-20.

Gradecki, Joe. "Virtual Reality Arcade Systems." *PCVR,* May/June 1994, 15:5-9.

Gradecki, Joe. *Virtual Reality Construction Kit.* New York: Wiley, 1994.

Grantham, Charles E. "Visual Thinking in Organizational Analysis." *See* Helsel, *Beyond the Vision.*

Green Sheet. Thomas J. Hargadon, ed. San Francisco: Conference Communications. Monthly.

Gregory, R. L. *Eye and Brain,* 4th edition. Princeton, N.J.: Princeton University Press, 1990.

Grimsdale, C. "SuperVision: A Parallel Architecture for Virtual Reality." *See* Earnshaw, Gigante and Jones.

Gullichsen, Eric. "Morton L. Heilig and the Genesis of Synthetic Realities." *See* *Mondo 2000.*

Gullichsen, Erich. *See* Virtual Reality Conference (videorecording).

Gullichsen, Eric, and Randall Walser. "Cyberspace: Experiential Computing." *Nexus '89 Science Fiction and Science Fact.* 1989.

Hafner, Katie, and John Markoff. *Cyberpunk: Outlaws and Hackers on the Computer Frontier.* New York: Simon & Schuster, 1991.

Hagen, Charles. "Virtual Reality: Is It Art Yet?" *New York Times,* July 5, 1992: Section 2:1 ff. Review of the exhibition "Through the Looking Glass: Artists' First Encounters with Virtual Reality" at the Jack Tilton Gallery, New York

City, July 1992; the exhibit included works by Brian D'Amato, Lynn Hershman and Sara Roberts, Myron Krueger, Jaron Lanier, Matt Mullican, Nicole Stenger, and Dennis Wilson.

Haggerty, Michael. "The Art of Artificial Reality." *IEEE Computer Graphics and Applications*, 1991, 11: 8.

Haggerty, Michael. "Serious Lunacy: Art in Virtual Worlds." *IEEE Computer Graphics and Applications*, March 1992, 12: 5-7.

Hagsand, Olof. "Consistency and Concurrency Control in Distributed Virtual Worlds." *Proceedings from the 2nd MultiG workshop*, Björn Pehrson and Yngve Sundblad, eds. Stockholm: Royal Institute of Technology, 1991. Conference held June 1991 at Stockholm.

Hall, Jennifer, and Dana Moser. *Virtual Reality: A 30-Second Self-Administered Training Course.* Boston, Mass.: Pro-Reality Concern — Do While Studio, 1992.

Hamburg, Victoria. "The King of Cyberpunk" (interview with writer William Gibson). *Interview*, January 1989, 19(1): 84 ff.

Hamilton, Joan O'C. "Virtual Reality: How a Computer-Generated World Could Change the Real World." *Business Week*, October 5, 1992: 96-105.

Hamilton, Joan O'C. "Trials of a Cyber-Celebrity: Fallen Virtual Technology Pioneer Jaron Lanier" (interview). *Business Week*, February 22, 1993: 95.

Hamit, Francis. "Innovative Medical VR Research." *CyberEdge Journal*, March 1991, 2: 4-5.

Hamit, Francis. *Virtual Reality: An Exploration of Cyberspace.* Carmel, Indiana: Howard W. Sams/Prentice-Hall Publishers, 1993.

Handelman, Eliot. "Permeable Space." *See* ICAT '93.

Harashima, Hiroshi. "Face, Expression and Communication." *See* ICAT '93.

Haraway, Donna. "A Manifesto for Cyborgs: Science, Technology, and Socialist Feminism in the 1980's." *Socialist Review.* 1985, 80: 65-107. Reprinted in Donna Jeanne Haraway. *Simians, Cyborgs, and Women: The Reinvention of Nature*, New York: Routledge, 1991.

Haraway, Donna. "Cyborgs at Large" and "The Actors Are Cyborg." *See* Penley and Ross.

Hardison, O. B. *Disappearing through the Skylight: Culture and Technology in the Twentieth Century.* New York: Viking, 1989.

Hargadon, Thomas J. "Network Virtual Reality and Other Visions." *Office*, May 1992, 115(5): 24.

Hart, John J. *In Search of a Definition of Virtual Reality*. Wellington, N.Z.: Victoria University. Unpublished thesis.

Harvey, E. P., R. L. Schaffer, and S. M. McGarry. "High Performance Fixed-wing Aircraft Simulation Using SIMNET Protocols." *1991 Summer Computer Simulation Conference.:Twenty-Third Annual Summer Computer Simulation Conference*, D. Pace, ed. San Diego, Calif.: CSC, 1991: 965-70. Conference held July 22, 1991, at Baltimore, Md.

Hashimoto, H., et al. "Visual Servo Control of Robotic Manipulators Based on Artificial Neural Network." *IECON '89: 15th Annual Conference of IEEE Industrial Electronics Society*. New York: IEEE, 1989, 4: 770-774. Conference held November 6-10, 1989, at Philadelphia.

Hattori, Katsura. *Jinko Genjitsukan No Sekai* [What Is Virtual Reality?]. Tokyo: Kogyo Chosakai, 1991. In Japanese.

Haverstock, Mark. "Virtual Gaming." *PCM: Personal Computer Magazine*, July 1993, XI(1):16-23.

HDTV and the Quest for Virtual Reality (videorecording). Itasca, Ill.: ACM (Association for Computing Machinery), 1990. 120 minutes. *ACM SIG-GRAPH Video Review*, special issue 60. Part 1 covers HDTV (High Definition Television). Part 2 provides a history of virtual reality and a look at current workstations.

Head-mounted Display Research at UNC-Chapel Hill, July 1991 (videorecording). Chapel Hill, N.C.: University of North Carolina, Department of Computer Science, 1992. 52 minutes. Distributed by Media Magic, Nicasio, Calif., and Art Com, San Francisco. Documents head-mounted display research at the University of North Carolina, Chapel Hill, including architecture walk-throughs, molecular modeling, medical imaging, general 3-D modeling, and flight simulation.

Hedberg, S. "VR Art Show at the Guggenheim." *Virtual Reality Special Report*, 1994, (1): 73-76.

Heeter, Carrie. "BattleTech Masters: Emergence of the First U.S. Virtual Reality Subculture." *Multimedia Review*, December 1992, 3(4): 65-70.

Heilig, Morton. "El Ciné del Futuro: The Cinema of the Future." *Espacios* , January 1955, 23-24. In English and Spanish. Reprinted in English in *Presence*, Summer 1992, 1(3): 279-294.

Heilig, Morton. "Enter the Experiential Revolution." *See* Jacobson, *Cyberarts*.

Heilig, Morton. *See* Virtual Reality Conference (videorecording).

Heim, Michael. *The Metaphysics of Virtual Reality*. New York: Oxford University Press, 1993.

Heim, Michael. "The Erotic Ontology of Cyberspace." *See* Benedikt, *Cyberspace.*

Heim, Michael. "The Metaphysics of Virtual Reality." *See* Helsel and Roth. For a videorecording of the presentation, see *Virtual Reality: Theory, Practice, Promise.*

Helsel, Sandra K. "Virtual Reality and Education." *Educational Technology,* May 1992, 32(5): 38-42.

Helsel, Sandra K., ed. *Beyond the Vision:The Technology, Research, and Business of Virtual Reality: Proceedings of Virtual Reality '91, the Second Annual Conference on Virtual Reality, Artificial Reality, and Cyberspace.* London, England and Westport, Conn.: Meckler, 1992. Conference held September 23-25, 1991 at San Francisco, Calif. Includes "Position Tracking in Virtual Reality" by Hugh L. Applewhite, "Extended Abstract: A Formal Foundation for Cyberspace" by William Bricken, "Cyberspace Representation of Vietnam War Trauma" by Joseph V. Henderson, "How Many Ds in Reality?" by Theodor Holm Nelson, "Texture-based Virtual Reality on a Desktop Computer Using WorldToolKit" by T. B. Coull, "The Sense of Touch in Virtual Reality" by Paul Cutt, "A Self-Contained Interactive Motorskill Trainer" by Tim J. Dowding, "Adapting Traditional Media for Virtual Reality Environments" by David M. Geshwind, "Real Fun, Virtual Experience Amusements & Products in Public Space Entertainment" by Steve Glenn, "Visual Thinking in Organizational Analysis" by Charles E. Grantham, "An Evolution of Synthetic Reality and Tactile Interfaces" by David Hon, "When Will Reality Meet the Marketplace?" by John N. Latta, "Realities of Building Virtual Realities" by Bryan J. Lewis, "Educational Applications of Virtual Reality: Medium or Myth?" by Jim McCluskey, "Virtual Perception Program at SRI International" by Tom Piantanida, "Virtual Reality in Japan" by Jack Plimpton, "The Use of Animation to Analyze and Present Information About Complex Systems" by Bradford Smith, "Stereoscopic Video and the Quest for Virtual Reality" by Michael Starks, and "Virtual Reality at NYNEX" by Rory Stuart.

Helsel, Sandra K., and Jeffrey Jacobson, eds. *Virtual Reality Market Place 1994.* Westport, Conn.: Meckler, 1994.

Helsel, Sandra K., and Judith Paris Roth, eds. *Virtual Reality: Theory, Practice, and Promise.* Westport, Conn.: Meckler, 1991. Includes "Informating with Virtual Reality" by Michael B. Spring, "Artificial Reality: Past and Future" by Myron W. Krueger, "The Metaphysics of Virtual Reality" by Michael Heim, "The Emerging Technology of Cyberspace" by Randall Walser, "The Virtual World of HDTV" by Bret C. McKinney, "Elements of a Cyberspace Playhouse" by Randall Walser, "Designing Realities: Interactive Media, Virtual Realities, and Cyberspace" by Joseph Henderson, "Fluxbase: a Virtual Exhibit" by Joan S. Huntley and Michael Partridge, "Virtual Reality Design: a Personal View" by Brenda Laurel,

"Virtual Environments: Personal Simulations and Telepresence" by Scott S. Fisher, and "Simulated World as Classroom: the Potential for Designed Learning within Virtual Environments" by David C. Traub. *See also* video-recording of the same title.

Henderson, Joseph. "Cyberspace Representation of Vietnam War Trauma." *See* Helsel, *Beyond the Vision.*

Henderson, Joseph. "Designing Realities: Interactive Media, Virtual Realities, and Cyberspace." *See* Helsel and Roth.

Henderson, Joseph. *See* VR Conference – Overview of VR (videorecording).

Henry, Tyson R., et al. "A Nose Gesture Interface Device: Extending Virtual Realities." *Presence*, Spring 1992, 1(2): 258-261. Responses by Elizabeth M. Wenzel, Gary L. Payne and Connor T. Payne; Nat Durlach; Warren Robinett; and John P. Cater in Fall 1992, 1(4): 491-494.

Herrmann, G., and O. Riedel. "VIRUSI: Virtual User Interface: Iconorientierte Benutzerschnittstelle für VR-Applikationen." *Forschung und Praxis*, H. J. Warnecke, and H. J. Bullinger, eds. 1993, T 35: 227-243.

Hester, C. "Being There." *Presence*, 1992, 1(2).

Hiltz, Starr Roxanne, and Murray Turoff. "Teaching Computers and Society in a Virtual Classroom." *Computers and Society*, October 1990, 20(3).

Hirose, M. "Virtual Reality and Collaboration." *Journal of the Society of Instrument and Control Engineers*, 1991, 30(6): 457-464.

Hirose, M., K. Hirota, and R. Kijima. "Human Behaviour in Virtual Environments." *Human Vision, Visual Processing and Digital Display III: Proceedings of the SPIE — The International Society for Optical Engineering.* Santa Clara, Calif.: SPIE, 1992, 1666: 548-59. Conference held February 10-13, 1992, at San Jose, Calif.

Hirose, M., et al. "A Study on Synthetic Visual Sensation through Artificial Reality." *7th Symposium on Human Interface.* 1991: 675-682.

HIT Lab Review: a Periodic Review of Research at the Human Interface Technology Laboratory at the Washington Technology Center. Seattle, Wash.: HITL. Occasional since 1992.

Hollands, Robin. "The 'Garage' VR Solution." *Virtual Reality World*, July /August 1994: 21-27.

Hon, David. "Ixion's Realistic Medical Simulations." *Virtual Reality World*, July/August 1994: 58-62.

Horgan, John. "Technology: Robots Rampant." *Scientific American*, August 1988, 259(2).

Hughes, Carolyn, ed. *Black Hole: A Virtual Vacuum of Cyberpunk Musings, Street Tech, Bits and Bytes.* Baltimore, Md.: Institute for Publications Design, University of Baltimore, 1992. Includes "Jamming the Media" by Gareth Branwyn, "Confessions of a Hacker: An Interview with Asides" by Carolyn Hughes, "GURPS' Labor Lost: The Cyberpunk Bust" by Bruce Sterling, "The Electronic Frontier Foundation and Computer Cracking" by Mitch Kapor, "Cutting Up: Cyberpunk, Punk Music and Urban Decontextualization" by Larry McCaffery, and "All I Really Need to Know I Learned from my Computer" by Ann Gordon.

Hughes, Charles E., J. Michael Moshell, Sean G. Hughes, and Marc Smith. "Cooperative Problem Solving among K-12 Students: The ExploreNet Project." *Proceedings of Frontiers in Education '92*, November 1992.

Hughes, Charles E., et al. "Cooperative Problem Solving in a Networked Simulation Environment." *Space Education Conference.* Conference held October 23, 1991, at Cocoa Beach, Fla.

HyperNetwork '92 Beppu Bay Conference: Groupmedia Creation: Proceedings. Oita, Japan: the conference, 1992. Conference held February 28, 1992, at Oita, Japan. In Japanese and English.

ICAT '91: The First International Conference on Artificial Reality and Tele-Existence. Tokyo: ICAT at Japan Technology Transfer Association (JTTAS), 1991. Conference held July 9, 1991, at Tokyo, Japan. Includes "Telepresence and Artificial Reality: Some Hard Questions" by Thomas B. Sheridan, "A Virtual Environment for the Exploration of Three Dimensional Steady Flows" by Steve Bryson, "Virtual Thinking in Organizational Analysis" by Charles Grantham, "Virtual Reality for Home Game Machines" by Allen Becker, "What Should You Wear to an Artificial Reality?" by Myron W. Krueger, "Bringing Virtual Worlds to the Real World: Toward A Global Initiative" by Robert Jacobson , "Virtuality™, The Worlds First Production Virtual Reality Workstation" by Jonathan D. Waldern, "Toward Virtual Existence in Real and/or Virtual Worlds" by Susumu Tachi, "Visualization Tool Applications of Artificial Reality" by Michitaka Ilirose, "Virtual Work Space for 3-dimensional Modeling" by Makoto Sato, "Force Display for Virtual Worlds" by Hiroo Iwata, "Psychophysical Analysis of the 'Sensation of Reality' Induced by a Visual Wide-Field Display" by Toyohiko Hatada, and "Undulation Detection of Virtual Shape by Fingertip Using Force-feedback Input Device" by Yukio Fukui.

ICAT '92: The Second International Conference on Artificial Reality and Tele-Existence. Tokyo: ICAT at Japan Technology Transfer Association (JTTAS), 1992. Conference held July 1, 1992, at Tokyo, Japan. Includes "Artificial Reality and Tele-Existence – Present Status and Future Prospect" by Susumu Tachi, "Virtual Environments in Scientific Visualization" by Steve Bryson, "Haptic Walkthrough Simulator: Its Design and Application to Studies on Cognitive Map" by Hiroo Iwata and Keigo Matsuda, "Virtual

Baseball" by John Latta and Dave Oberg, "Networked Virtual Reality" by Carl Eugene Loeffler, "Virtual Worlds Research at the University of North Carolina" by Warren Robinett and "Virtual Collaborative Workspace" by Gen Suzuki and Takashi Kouno.

ICAT '93: The Third International Conference on Artificial Reality and Tele-Existence. Tokyo: ICAT at Japan Technology Transfer Association (JTTAS), 1993. Conference held July 6, 1993, at Tokyo, Japan. Includes "Distributed Virtual Reality: Applications for Education, Entertainment, and Industry" by Carl Loeffler, "Evaluation Experiments of Tele-Existence Manipulation System" by Susumu Tachi and Kenichi Yasuda, "Distributed Processing Architecture for Virtual Space Teleconferencing System" by Haruo Takemura, Yasuichi Kitamura, Fumio Kishino and Jun Ohya, "Hypermedia and Networking in the Development of Large-Scale Virtual Environments" by Michael Zyda, Chuck Lombardo and David R. Pratt, "Virtual Sand Box: A Development of an Application of Virtual Environment for Clinical Medicine" by Ryugo Kijima and Michitaka Hirose, "Visual Communication Environment Using Virtual Space Technology" by Gen Suzuki, Shouhei Sugawara and Machio Moriuchi, "PC Based VR System" by Kazuo Itoh, "Face, Expression and Communication" by Hiroshi Harashima, "What are Virtual Environments?" by Steve Ellis, "Artificial Life in Haptic Virtual Environment" by Hiroo Iwata and Hiroaki Yano, "A Direct Deformation Method of Free Forms for CAD Interface" by Juli Yamashita and Yukio Fukui, "A 3D Interface Device with Force Feedback for Pick-and-Place Tasks" by Masahiro Ishii and Makota Sato, "Intelligent Cooperative Manipulation Using Dynamic Force Simulator" by Martin Buss and Hideki Hashimoto, "An Architecture for Orientation Mapping Post Rendering" by Matthew Regan and Ronald Pose, and "Permeable Space: A Language of Virtual Perception" by Eliot Handelman.

IEE Colloquium on 'Distributed Virtual Reality." London: IEE, 1993. Digest No.121. Conference held May 21, 1993, at London.

IEEE Computer Graphics and Applications. Special issue on virtual reality. January 1994.

Implementation of Immersive Virtual Environments (videorecording). New York: ACM (Association for Computing Machinery), 1992. Course 9 at ACM SIGGRAPH '92.

Informatique '92. Interface to Real and Virtual Worlds: Proceedings and Exhibition Catalog. Paris: EC2, 1992. March 23, 1992, at Montpellier, France. In English and French.

INSPEC. London: Institution of Electrical Engineers. Since 1969. An online bibliographic database, including abstracts, covering more than 5600 scholarly publications in communications, computer science and engineering, physics and information technology.

Intertek. San Carlos, Calif. Steven G. Steinberg, ed. One or two issues per year, since 1991. E-mail: tek@well.com.

Intertek. Special issue on Virtual Communities. Goleta, Calif.: Intertek. Winter 1992. Includes "Electropolis: Communication and Community on Internet Relay Chat" by Elizabeth Reed, "Social Organization of the Computer Underground" by Gordon Meyer, "Mudding: Social Phenomena in Text-Based Virtual Realities" by Pavel Curtis, and "Bury Usenet" by Steve Steinberg with responses by Peter Denning, Mitch Kapor, John Quarterman, and Bruce Sterling.

Isdale, Jerry. "What Is VR? A Homebrew Introduction" (online text file). FTP: <sunee.uwaterloo.ca> Directory: pub/vr/documents File: whatisvr.zip.

Ishii, H. "Translucent Multiuser Interface for Realtime Collaboration." *IEICE Transactions on Fundamentals of Electronics, Communications and Computer Science,* February 1992, E75-A(2): 122-31.

Ishii, H., and N. Miyake. "Toward an Open Shared Workspace: Computer and Video Fusion Approach of TeamWorkStation." *Communications of the ACM (Association for Computing Machinery),* December 1991, 34(12): 37-50.

Ishii, M., et al. "Teaching Robot Operations and Environments by Using a 3-D Visual Sensor System." *Intelligent Autonomous Systems: An International Conference,* L. O. Hertzbergerand F. C. A. Groen, eds. Conference held December 8-11, 1986, at Amsterdam, Netherlands. Amsterdam: North-Holland, 1987: 283-9.

Ishii, Masahiro, and Makota Sato. "3D Interface Device with Force Feedback." *See* ICAT '93.

Itoh, Kazuo. "PC Based VR System." *See* ICAT '93.

Iwata, Hiroo. "Artificial Reality with Force-feedback: Development of Desktop Virtual Space with Compact Master Manipulator." *Computer Graphics,* August 1990, 24(4): 165-70. SIGGRAPH 1990: 17th Annual ACM Conference on Computer Graphics and Interactive Techniques held August 6-10, 1990, at Dallas, Tex.

Iwata, Hiroo, and Keigo Matsuda. "Artificial Reality for Walking About Uneven Surface of Virtual Space." *6th Symposium on Human Interface.* 1990: 21-25.

Iwata, Hiroo, and Keigo Matsuda. "Haptic Walkthrough Simulator: Its Design and Application to Studies on Cognitive Map." *See* ICAT '92.

Iwata, Hiroo, and Hiroaki Yano. "Artificial Life in Haptic Virtual Environment." *See* ICAT '93.

Jää-Aro, Kai-Mikael. "The X-ray Factory: Some Experiments with Three-dimensional, Iconic Control Displays." *Proceedings from the 3rd MultiG*

Workshop, Yngve Sundblad, ed. Stockholm: Royal Institute of Technology, 1991. Conference held December 1991 at Stockholm.

Jacobson, Karie, ed. *Simulations: 15 Tales of Virtual Reality*. New York: Citadel Twilight, 1993. Includes "The Veldt" (1950) by Ray Bradbury, "Overdrawn at the Memory Bank" (1976) by John Varley, "Walking the Moons" (1990) by Jonathan Letham, "Virtual Reality" (1993) by Michael Kandel, "Dogfight" (1985) by Michael Swanwick and Willian Gibson, "The Shining Dream Road Out" (1993) by M. Shayne Bell, "The Total Perspective Vortex" (1980) by Douglas Adams, "Plug-in Yosemite" (1985) by Marc Laidlaw, "This Life and Later Ones" (1987) by George Zebrowski, "Steelcollar Worker" (1992) by Vonda McIntyre, "I Hope I shall Arrive Soon" (1980) by Philip K. Dick, "From Here to Eternitape" (1992) by Daniel Pearlman, "Pretty Boy Crossover" (1986) by Pat Cadigan, "A Guide to Virtual Death" (1992) by J.G. Ballard, "The Happy Man" (1963) by Gerald Page, and a bibliography of VR fiction.

Jacobson, Linda. "Homebrew VR." *Wired*, 1993, 1(1): 84-5.

Jacobson, Linda. *Garage Virtual Reality: The Affordable Way to Explore Virtual Worlds*. Indianapolis, IN: Sams/Prentice Hall Computer Books, 1994.

Jacobson, Linda, ed. *Cyberarts: Exploring Art and Technology*. San Francisco, Calif.: Miller Freeman, Inc., 1992. Selected papers from the first and second Cyberarts International conferences of 1990 and 1991. Includes "Sound Enters the Third Dimension" by Linda Jacobson, "The Virtual Reality of 3-D Sound" by Durand R. Begault, "Launching Sounds into Space" by Elizabeth M. Wenzel, "The Convolvotron Concept" by Scott Foster, "Sound Localization and Spatial Enhancement with the Roland Sound Space System" by Curtis Chan, "Virtual Audio: New Uses for 3-D Sound" by Christopher Currell, "Virtual World Without End: The Story of Xanadu™" by Ted Nelson, "The 'Art' in Artificial Reality: Videoplace and Other New Forms of Human Experience" by Myron Krueger, "The Mandala System: An Alternative Approach to Virtual Reality" by Vincent John Vincent and Linda Jacobson, "Virtual Reality: A Status Report" by Jaron Lanier, "The Art of Building Virtual Realities" by Steve Tice and Linda Jacobson, and "Enter the Experiential Revolution: A VR Pioneer Looks Back to the Future" by Morton L. Heilig.

Jacobson, Robert. *Virtual Places: Strolling the Electronic Neighborhood*. Seattle,Wash.: HITL (Human Interface Technology Laboratory), 1989. HITL Memo M-89-4.

Jacobson, Robert. *Televirtuality: "Being There" in the 21st Century*. Seattle,Wash.: HITL (Human Interface Technology Laboratory), 1990. Memo M-90-1.

Jacobson, Robert. *Virtual Worlds, Inside and Out*. Seattle, Wash.: Human Interface Technology Laboratory, 1990. Technical Memo M-90-12.

Jacobson, Robert. *Bringing Virtual Worlds to the Real World.* Seattle,Wash.: Human Interface Technology Laboratory, 1991. Technical Memo M-91-2.

Jacobson, Robert. "What is VEOS?" *CyberEdge Journal*, March 1991, 2: 9.

Jacobson, Robert. "The Ultimate User Interface." *BYTE*, April 1992: 175-181.

Jacobson, Robert. "Interview with Robert Jacobson." *Virtual Reality Report*, June 1992: 2(5).

Jacobson, Robert. "Virtual Worlds: A New Type of Design Environment." *Virtual Reality World*, May 1994, 2(3): 46-52.

Jacobson, Robert. *See* "Retina Projection."

Joans, Barbara. *Cyberspace: A Wedding.* Mill Valley, Calif.: CyberEdge Journal, 1991.

Johnson, Mark. *The Body in the Mind: The Bodily Basis of Meaning, Imagination, and Reason.* Chicago: University of Chicago Press, 1987.

Joyce, James. *Finnegans Wake.* London: Faber and Faber, 1939.

Kac, Eduardo. "Towards Telepresence Art." *Interface*, November, 1992, 4(2): 2-4.

Kahaner, David. "Virtual Reality in Japan." *IEEE Micro*, April 1993, 13(2): 66-73.

Kahaner, David. *vr.791* (online text file). September 5, 1991. "Brief summary of Artificial Reality/Tele-Existence Symposium, July 1991, Tokyo Japan." FTP: <cs.arizona.edu> machine address (192.12.69.5) Directory: japan/kahaner.reports.

Kahaner, David. *vr.991* (online text file). October 9, 1991. "Comments on Virtual/Artificial Reality research in Japan." FTP: <cs.arizona.edu> machine address (192.12.69.5) Directory: japan/kahaner.reports.

Kahaner, David. *vr-10.92* (online text file). October 26, 1992. "A summary of recent Japanese activities in Virtual Reality (VR)." FTP: <cs.arizona.edu> machine address (192.12.69.5) Directory: japan/kahaner.reports.

Kalawsky, Roy S. *The Science of Virtual Reality and Virtual Environments: A Technical, Scientific and Engineering Reference on Virtual Environments.* Reading, Mass.: Addison-Wesley, 1993.

Kalawsky, Roy S. "A Comprehensive Virtual Environment Laboratory Facility", and "Critical Aspects of Visually Coupled Systems." *See* Earnshaw, Gigante and Jones.

Kallman, Ernest A. "Ethical Evaluation: A Necessary Element in Virtual Environment Research." *Presence*, Spring 1993, 2(2): 143-146.

Kanarick, C. M. "A Technical Overview and History of the SIMNET Project." V. Madisetti, D. Nicol, and R. Fujimoto, eds. *Advances in Parallel and Distributed Simulation: Proceedings of the SCS Multiconference.* San Diego, Calif.: SCS, 1990: 104-111. Conference held January 23, 1991, at Anaheim, Calif.

Kantrowitz, Mark, and Joseph Bates, Joseph. "Integrated Natural Language Generation Systems." *Aspects of Automated Natural Language Generation,* R. Dale, et al., eds. LNAI Volume 587. Berlin: Springer-Verlag, 1992.

Kapor, Mitchell. "Civil Liberties in Cyberspace." *Scientific American,* September 1991, 265(3): 116-20.

Kapor, Mitchell. "The Electronic Frontier Foundation and Computer Cracking." *See* Hughes, Carolyn.

Kapor, Mitchell. "Interview." *See* Gans and Sirius.

Kay, Alan. "Microelectronics and the Personal Computer." *Scientific American,* 1977, 237(3): 230.

Kay, Alan. "Computer Software." *Scientific American,* September 1984, 251(3): 52-59.

Kaye, M. G., et al. "Evaluation of Virtual Cockpit Concepts During Simulated Missions." *Proceedings of the SPIE - The International Society for Optical Engineering.* Santa Clara, Calif.:SPIE, 1990, 1290: 236-45.

Kehoe, Brendan P. *Zen and the Art of the Internet: A Beginner's Guide to the Internet* (online text file). Rev. 1.0. Chester, Penn., February 2, 1992. FTP: <ftp.cs.widener.edu> Directory: pub/zen.

Kelly, Kevin. "Virtual Reality: An Interview with Jaron Lanier." *Whole Earth Review,* 1989, (64): 108-109.

Kelso, Margaret Thomas, Peter Weyhrauch, and Joseph Bates. "Dramatic Presence." *Presence,* Winter 1993, 2(1): 1-15.

Kijima, R., and M. Hirose. "'Virtual Science' of Accuracy in Generated Environments: Focusing on the Effect of Time Delay in Virtual Space." *Human Interface News and Report,* 1991, 6(2): 140-145.

Kijima, R., and Hirose, M. "Virtual Sand Box." *See* ICAT '93.

Kinnaman, Daniel E. "Batter Up!" *Technology & Learning,* April 1992, 12(7): 78.

Kroker, Arthur. *SPASM: Virtual Reality, Android Music, and Electric Flesh.* New York: St. Martin's Press, 1993.

Kroker, Arthur, and Marilouise Kroker. *Panic Encyclopedia.* New York: St. Martin's Press, 1989.

Krol, Ed. *The Hitchhiker's Guide to the Internet.* Urbana, Ill.: University of Illinois, 1989.

Krueger, Myron W. *Artificial Reality.* Reading, Mass.: Addison-Wesley, 1983.

Krueger, Myron W. *Artificial Reality II.* Reading, Mass.: Addison-Wesley, 1991.

Krueger, Myron W. "An Architecture for Artificial Realities." *COMPCON Spring 1992: Thirty-Seventh IEEE Computer Society International Conference.* Los Alamitos, Calif.: IEEE Computer Society Press, 1992: 462-465. Conference held February 24, 1992, at San Francisco, Calif.

Krueger, Myron W. "The Experience Society." *Presence*, Spring 1993, 2(2): 162-168.

Krueger, Myron W. "Environmental Technology: Making the Real World Virtual." *Communications of the ACM* (Association for Computing Machinery). July 1993, 36(7): 36-37.

Krueger, Myron W. "The 'Art' in Artificial Reality." *See* Jacobson, *Cyberarts.*

Krueger, Myron W. "Artificial Reality: Past and Future." *See* Helsel and Roth.

Krueger, Myron W. "Shaping Cultural Consciousness with Artificial Reality." *See* Virtual Reality: Theory, Practice, Promise (videorecording).

Krueger, Myron W. *See* VR Conference – Overview of VR (videorecording) and Virtual Reality Conference (videorecording).

Krueger, Myron W. *See also* Gosney and Haggerty.

Kum-Yew Lai, and Thomas W. Malone. "Object Lens: Letting End-users Create Cooperative Work Applications." *Human Factors in Computing Systems. Reaching Through Technology: CHI '91*, Robertson, S. P., et al., eds. New York: ACM (Association for Computing Machinery), 1991: 425-426. Conference held April 2, 1991 at New Orleans, La.

Kvarnström, Bengt. "Telepresence, a Proposal to Facilitate Communication between Humans." *Telepresence — A New Concept for Teleconferencing: Proceedings of the First COST #229 WG.5 Workshop*, Forchheimer, Robert, ed. Conference held October 1991 at Stockholm.

Lancet. "Being and Believing: Ethics of Virtual Reality." August 3, 1991: 283.

Lanier, Jaron. *Jaron Lanier: Report from the Field and Group World Design* (videorecording). Distributed by Art Com, San Francisco. 105 minutes. An overview of the technology developed by VPL, Inc.

Lanier, Jaron. "Virtual Reality: the Promise of the Future." *Third National College Teaching and Learning Conference.* Conference held April 9, 1992 at Jacksonville, Fla.

Lanier, Jaron. "Music from Inside Virtual Reality: The Sound of One Hand." *Whole Earth Review,* June 1993: 30-34.

Lanier, Jaron. "Virtual Reality: A Status Report." *See* Jacobson, *Cyberarts.*

Lanier, Jaron. "VPL Virtual Reality Demonstration" *See* Best of TED2 (video-recording).

Lanier, Jaron. *See also* Blanchard et al., Conn et al., Cyberpunk (videorecording), Druckrey, Hamilton, Kelly, Porter, Snider, United States Congress, Virtual Reality Conference (videorecording), and Zimmerman et al.

Lanier, Jaron, and Frank Biocca. "An Insider's View of the Future of Virtual Reality." *Journal of Communication,* 1992, 42(4) : 136-149.

Lanza, Joseph. "Female Rollercoasters (And Other Virtual Vortices)." *Performing Arts Journal,* May 1992, 41: 51-63.

Larue, James. "Microcomputing: The Virtual Library." *Wilson Library Bulletin,* March 1991, 65(7): 100-102.

Latta, John and Dave Oberg. *See* ICAT '92.

Laurel, Brenda. *Interface as Mimesis. User-Centered System Design: New Perspectives on Human-Computer Interaction.* D. A. Norman and S. Draper, eds. Hillsdale, N.J.: Lawrence Erlbaum Associates, 1986.

Laurel, Brenda. "Reassessing Interactivity." *Journal of Computer Game Design,* 1987, 1(3).

Laurel, Brenda. "Culture Hacking." *Journal of Computer Game Design,* 1988, 1(8).

Laurel, Brenda. "Dramatic Action and Virtual Reality." *NCGA '89: Interactive Arts.* Fairfax, Va.: National Computer Graphics Association, 1989. Conference held 1989, at Los Angeles.

Laurel, Brenda. "New Interfaces for Entertainment." *Journal of Computer Game Design,* 1989, 2(5).

Laurel, Brenda. "On Dramatic Interaction." *Verbum,* 1989, 3(3).

Laurel, Brenda. "A Taxonomy of Interactive Movies." *New Media News* (The Boston Computer Society), 1989, 3(1).

Laurel, Brenda. "Art and Activism in VR." *Verbum,* 1991, 3.3.

Laurel, Brenda. *Computers as Theatre.* Reading, Mass.: Addison-Wesley, 1991.

Laurel, Brenda. "Virtual Reality Design: a Personal View." *See* Helsel and Roth.

Laurel, Brenda. "The Role of Drama in the Evolution of Virtual Reality." *See* Virtual Reality: Theory, Practice, Promise (videorecording).

Laurel, Brenda. *See* Art and Artistry in Virtual Reality (videorecording) and Virtual Reality Conference (videorecording).

Laurel, Brenda, ed. *The Art of Human-Computer Interface Design.* Reading, Mass.: Addison-Wesley Publishing Co., 1990. Includes "Conversation as Direct Manipulation" by Susan Brennan, "Through the Looking Glass" by John Walker, "User Interface: A Personal View" by Alan Kay, "Interface Agents: Metaphors with Character" by Brenda Laurel, "Guides: Characterizing the Interface" by Tim Oren, Gitta Salomon, Kristee Kreitman and Abbe Don, "Narrative and the Interface" by Abbe Don, "VIDEOPLACE and the Interface of the Future" by Myron Krueger, "What's the Big Deal about Cyberspace?" by Howard Rheingold, "Realness and Interactivity" by Mark Naimark, "Designing a New Medium" by Tim Oren, "Virtual Interface Environments" by Scott Fisher, and more.

Laurel, Brenda, Abbe Don, and Tim Oren. "Issues in Multimedia Interface Design: Media Integration and Interface Agents." *Proceedings of CHI '90.* New York: ACM (Association for Computing Machinery), 1990.

Lavroff, Nicholas. *Virtual Reality Playhouse.* Corte Madera, Calif.: Waite Group Press, 1992.

Leary. Timothy. *See* Cyberpunk (videorecording) and Gosney.

Lee, Haibo, Pertti Roivainen, and Robert Forchheimer. "Analysis/Synthesis of Human Facial Movements." *Telepresence — A New Concept for Teleconferencing: Proceedings of the First COST #229 WG.5 Workshop*, Forchheimer, Robert, ed. Conference held October 1991 at Stockholm.

Leonardo Electronic Almanac (electronic journal). Cambridge, Mass.: MIT Press. Craig Harris, ed. Monthly, since 1993. E-mail: craig@well.com. Successor to *Leonardo Electronic News.*

Leonardo Electronic News (electronic journal). Berkeley, Calif.: International Society for Art, Science and Technology. Monthly 1990 - 1993. E-mail: fast@garnet.berkeley.edu. FTP: <ftp.msstate.edu> Directory: pub/archives/fineart_online. Succeeded in Fall 1993 by *Leonardo Electronic Almanac.*

Levine, Howard, and Howard Rheingold. *The Cognitive Connection: Thought and Language in Man and Machine.* New York: Prentice Hall Press, 1987.

Lewis, J. B., L. Koved, and D. T. Ling. "Dialogue Structures for Virtual Worlds." *Human Factors in Computing Systems: Reaching Through Technology: CHI '91*, S. P. Robertson, G. M. Olson, and S. J. Olson, eds. Reading, Mass.: Addison-Wesley, 1991: 131-136. Conference held April 2, 1991, at New Orleans, La.

Licklider, J. C. R. "Man-Computer Symbiosis." *IRE Transactions on Human Factors in Electronics*, March 1960, HFE-1.

Licklider, J. C. R., and Robert William Taylor. *In memoriam, J.C.R. Licklider, 1915-1990.* Palo Alto, Calif.: Digital Equipment Corp., Systems Research Center, August 7,1990. Technical report 61. Includes reprints of "Man-Computer Symbiosis" by J. C. R. Licklider, "The Computer as a Communication Device" by J. C. R. Licklider and Robert W. Taylor, and more.

Lipton, L. "New Step into a Movie: Sensorama." *Popular Photography*, July 1964, 55(1): 114, 116.

Little, Gregory. "Gallery (Identity Selection Sequence)." *Interface.* November 1992, 4(2): 9-13.

Loeffler, Carl Eugene. "The Art Com Electronic Network." *Leonardo*, 1988, 21(3): 320-321.

Loeffler, Carl Eugene. "Telecomputing und die digitale Kultur [Telecomputing and Digital Culture]." *Kunstforum International* (proceedings of the Ars Electronica conference held 1989 at Linz, Austria). September-October 1989, 103 : 128-133.

Loeffler, Carl Eugene. "Telecomputing and the Arts." *NCGA '89.* Fairfax, Va.: National Computer Graphics Association, 1989. Conference held 1989, at Los Angeles.

Loeffler, Carl Eugene. "Interactive Computer-based Art." *NCGA '90.* Fairfax, Va.: National Computer Graphics Association, 1990, 3: 405-408. Conference held March 19, 1990, at Anaheim, Calif.

Loeffler, Carl Eugene. "How to Do It: Tools for Tele-Computing" and "Serving the Business Needs of Art Organizations." *Electronic Citizenship.* San Francisco: Pacific Bell Telephone, 1990: 4.3 - 4.6 and 11.3 - 11.6.

Loeffler, Carl Eugene. "Virtual Communities." *Interface '91.* Conference held November 1991 at Hamburg, Germany.

Loeffler, Carl Eugene. "Virtual Communities." *Asia-Pacific Computer Networking Forum.* Conference held December 1991 at Seoul, Korea.

Loeffler, Carl Eugene. "Networked VR Museum." *HyperNetwork '92 Beppu Bay Conference: Groupmedia Creation: Proceedings.* Oita, Japan: the conference, 1992. Conference held February 28, 1992, at Oita, Japan.

Loeffler, Carl Eugene. "Networked Virtual Reality." *See* ICAT '92 and Fahlén and Jää-Aro.

Loeffler, Carl Eugene. "Networked Virtual Reality." *Artificial Intelligence in Media.* Conference held November 1992 at Nagoya, Japan.

Loeffler, Carl Eugene. "Distributed Virtual Reality: Applications for Education, Entertainment, andIndustry." *Telektronikk*, 1993, (4): 83-88.

Loeffler, Carl Eugene. "Interview with Carl Eugene Loeffler, Studio for Creative Inquiry, Carnegie Mellon University." *Nikkei Computer Graphics*. 1993, 76-79. In Japanese.

Loeffler, Carl Eugene. "Networked Virtual Reality: Applications for Industry, Education and Entertainment." *Virtual Reality World*. Summer 1993; 1(2):g-i. Insert in *Multimedia Review*, Summer 1993.

Loeffler, Carl Eugene. "Networked Virtual Reality." *The Simulated Presence: Critical Response to Electronic Imaging*. Tempe: University of Arizona Press, forthcoming. Conference held February 1993 at Tempe, Arizona.

Loeffler, Carl Eugene. "Una città nella rete." *Virtual*, Febbraio 1994, (6): 18-22.

Loeffler, Carl Eugene. "Virtual Polis: A Networked Virtual Reality Application." *See* Networked Reality '94.

Loeffler, Carl Eugene. "Rencontres dans le virtuel." *La Recherche*, Mai 1994, (265): 514-517.

Loeffler, Carl Eugene, ed. *Virtual Realities: Anthology of Industry and Culture*. Tokyo: Gitjusu Hyoron Sha, 1993. In Japanese.

Loeffler, Carl Eugene. *See also* Ascott and Loeffler, Brill, "Where Art Meets Cyberspace," and *Multimedia Frontier '93*.

Long, M., et al. "Virtual Environment Debriefing Room for Naval Fighter Pilots: Phase I." *Visual Data Interpretation*, J. R. Alexander, ed. 1992, 1668: 49-60.

Long, Mark, ed. *Next Generation Head Mounted Displays Workshop*. Princeton, N.J. Princeton, N.J.: The David Sarnoff Research Center, 1992. Conference held June 30, 1992 at Princeton.

Loyall, A. Bryan, and Joseph Bates. *Hap: a Reactive, Adaptive Architecture for Agents*. Pittsburgh: School of Computer Science, Carnegie Mellon University, June 17 1991. Technical report CMU-CS-91-147.

Loyall, A. Bryan, and Joseph Bates. "Realtime Control of Animated Broad Agents." *Proceedings of the 15th Annual Conference of the Cognitive Science Society*. Hillsdale, N.J.: L. Erlbaum, 1993. Conference held June 1993 at Boulder, Colorado.

Ludvigsen, Børre. "Content and Context in the Architecture of Cyberspace." Norwegian Informatics Conference held November 1992 in Norway.

Ludvigsen, Børre. "Med Cyberspace inn i en virtuell virkelighet." *C-World*, 1992, (3): 10-11. (In Norwegian).

Ludvigsen, Børre. "Presence and Form in the Architecture of Cyberspace." Halden, Norway: Department of Computer Science, Østfold Distriktshøgskole, March 1992.

Lurins, S. L., ed. "Virtual Reality in the Real World." *CADalyst*. August 1993, 10(8):37-58.

Machlis, Sharon. "Computers Create a New Reality." *Design News*, October 26, 1992, 48: 60 ff.

MacLeod, Douglas. "A Lot of Hype about Hyper: CyberArts International, Los Angeles." *The Canadian Architect*. November 1990, 35: 35 ff.

Mallary, R. "Synthesthetic Art Through 3D-Projection: The Requirements of a Computer-Based Supermedium." *NASA, Ames Research Center: Spatial Displays and Spatial Instruments*, S. R. Ellis, M. K. Kaiser, and A. J. Grunwald, eds. Moffett Field, Calif.: Ames Research Labs, 1989. Technical Report N90-22962. An expanded version of this paper can be found in the journal *Leonardo*, 23:1:3-16.

Mallen, G. L. "Back to the Cave: Cultural Issues in Virtual Reality." *See* Earnshaw, Gigante and Jones.

Manovich, Lev. "Virtual Cave Dwellers: SIGGRAPH '92." *Afterimage*, October 1992, 20(3): 3-4.

Marmolin, Hans. *Multimedia From the Perspectives of Psychology*. Stockholm, Sweden: Royal Institute of Technology, Interaction and Presentation Laboratory, 1991. Technical report TRITA-NA-P9115; IPLab-43; MultiG report no. 3.

Marmolin, Hans, Yngve Sundblad, and Björn Pehrson. *Models of Distributed Design and Collaboration*. Stockholm, Sweden: Royal Institute of Technology, Interaction and Presentation Laboratory, 1991. Technical report TRITA-NA-P9103; IPLab-36; MultiG report no. 1.

Matrixx. Kari Hintikka, ed. Occasional since 1992. Helsinki, Finland: Matrixx. E-mail: klammer@mits.mdata.fi or klammer@clinet.fi. In Finnish.

McCaffery, Larry, ed. *Storming the Reality Studio*. Chapel Hill, N.C.: Duke University, 1992.

McCluskey, Jim. "A Primer on Virtual Reality." *T.H.E. Journal: Technological Horizons in Education*. December 1992, 20(5): 56-59.

McDowall, I. E., M. Bolas, S. Pieper, S. S. Fisher, and J. Humphries. "Implementation and Integration of a Counterbalanced CRT-based Stereoscopic Display for Interactive Viewpoint Control in Virtual Environment Applications." *Stereoscopic Displays and Applications: Proceedings of the SPIE - The International Society for Optical Engineering*. Santa Clara, Calif.: SPIE, 1990, 1256: 136-146. Conference held February 12, 1990.

McFadden, Tim. "Notes on the Structure of Cyberspace and the Ballistic Actors Model." See Benedikt, *Cyberspace*.

McGreevy, Michael W. "The Presence of Field Geologists in Mars-Like Terrain." *Presence*, Fall 1992, 1(4): 375-403.

McGreevy, M. W., and C. R. Stoker. "Telepresence for Planetary Exploration." *Cooperative Intelligent Robotics in Space*. Santa Clara, Calif.: SPIE, 1991, 1387: 110-23. Conference held November 6, 1990 at Boston, Mass.

McKenna, Michael, Steve Pieper, and David Zeltzer. "Control of a Virtual Actor: The Roach." *Computer Graphics*, March 1990, 24(2).

McLellan, Hilary. "Virtual Environments and Situated Learning." *Multimedia Review*, September 1991, 2(3): 30-7.

McLellan, Hilary. *Virtual Reality: A Selected Bibliography*. Englewood Cliffs, N.J.: Educational Technology Publications, 1992.

McLellan, Hilary. "Virtual Reality Design Notes." *Virtual Reality Report*, June 1992, 2(5).

McNaughton, C. "Overview of Virtual Reality Software Suppliers." *See* Earnshaw, Gigante and Jones.

Medicine Meets Virtual Reality: Discovering Applications for 3-D Multi-media Interactive Technology in the Health Sciences (A symposium sponsored by The Plastic Surgery Research Foundation and Office of Continuing Medical Education, University of California, San Diego). San Diego, Calif.: Aligned Management Associates, 1992. Conference held June 4, 1992 at San Diego, Calif. Includes "Dexterity Enhancement in Microsurgery Using Telemicrorobotics" by Steve Charles, Roy E. Williams and Ian W. Hunter, "Diagnostic/Rehabilitation Systems Using Force Measuring and Force Feedback Destrous Masters" by Grigore Burdea, Noshir Langrana, Deborah Silver, Robert Stone, and Deneca M. DiPaolo, "Surgical Simulation Models: From Body Parts to Artificial Person" by David T. Chen, Joseph Rosen, and David Zeltzer, "Experimental Analysis of Problems in Perception and Manipulation in Endoscopic Surgery" by Frank Tendick, Russell Jennings, Gregory Tharp and Lawrence Stark, "Biocontrollers: A Direct Link form the Nervous System to Computer" by Hugh S. Lusted and R. Benjamin Knapp, and more.

Meissner, Gerd. "Engel zum Anfassen." *Der Spiegel*, August 10, 1992.

Meyer, Kenneth, Hugh L. Applewhite, and Frank A. Biocca. "A Survey of Position Trackers." *Presence*, 1992, 1(2).

Milhon, Jude. "Call it Revolutionary Parasitism: A Conversation with John Shirley." *Mondo 2000*, September 1989 (1): 88-92.

Milhon, Jude. "Coming in under the Radar: A Conversation with Bruce Sterling." *Mondo 2000*, September 1989 (1): 98-101.

Miller, C. "Dr. Thomas A. Furness III, Virtual Reality Pioneer," *Online*, November 1992, 16(6): 14-27.

Miller, C. "Virtual Reality and Online Databases: Will 'Look and Feel' Literally Mean 'Look' and 'Feel'?" *Online*, November 1992, 16(6): 12-13.

Miller, R. Bruce, and Milton T. Wolf, eds. *Thinking Robots, An Aware Internet, and Cyberpunk Librarians: The 1992 LITA President's Program.* Chicago: Library and Information Technology Association, 1992. Includes "Free as Air, Free as Water, Free as Knowledge" by Bruce Sterling, "After the Deluge: Cyberpunk in the '80s and '90s" by Tom Maddox, "Transcendence at the Interface: The Architecture of Cyborg Utopia, or Cyberspace Utopoids as Postmodern Cargo Cult" by David Porush, "Virtual Reality in Medicine and Medical Education" by Cheryl S. Pace, and other essays.

Milman, E. "Fluxus: A Conceptual Country." *Visible Language*, Winter-Spring 1992, 26(1-2): 11-16.

Molendi, Gloria, and Matteo Patriarca. *Virtual Reality: Medical Researches.* Milano, Italy: Universita' degli Studi di Milano, 1992. Technical Report Number 1/92. Available as online text. FTP: <ghost.dsi.unimi.it> Directory: pub2/papers/patriarca File: med_VR.txt.Z.

MONDO 2000. Queen Mu, Domineditrix; R. U. Sirius, Editor in Chief. Berkeley Calif.: Fun City MegaMedia E-mail: mondo2k@well.sf.ca.us. Quarterly since 1990.

Mondo 2000. No. 2, June 1990. Special issue on virtual reality including "Being in Nothingness: Virtual Reality and The Pioneers of Cyberspace" by John Perry Barlow, "Life in the DataCloud: Scratching Your Eyes Back In" by John Perry Barlow, "Virtual Light: Visual Sensology for the 1990's and Beyond" by Stephen Beck, "Cyberspace 1999: The Shell, The Image And Now The Meat" by William Bricken, "Morton L. Heilig and the Genesis of Synthetic Realities" by Eric Gullichsen, "ImagineNation: 'Virtual Reality' For Entertainment" by Bob Stratton, "Hyperwebs" by Wes Thomas, and "Spacemakers and The Art Of The Cyberspace Playhouse" by Randall Walser.

"Money Games." *PC Week*, July 26, 1993.

Moravec, Hans P. *Mind Children: The Future of Robot and Human Intelligence.* Cambridge, Mass.: Harvard University Press, 1988.

Morgan, Anne. "Interactive Art." *Sculpture*, May 1991.

Morgan, Anne. "Interactivity: From Sound to Motion to Narrative." *Art Papers*, October 1991.

Morningstar and Farmer, "The Lessons of Lucasfilm's Habitat." *See* Benedikt, *Cyberspace.*

Morris, Ted, and Max Donath. "Using a Maximum Error Statistic to Evaluate Measurement Errors in 3D Position and Orientation Tracking Systems." *Presence,* Fall 1993, 2(4): 1-28.

Moshell, J. Michael. "Three Views of Virtual Reality: Virtual Environments in the U. S. Military." *IEEEComputer,* February 1993, 26(2): 81-2.

Moshell, J. Michael, and Richard Dunn-Roberts. "A Survey of Virtual Environments: Research in North America" Part One. *Virtual Reality World,* November/December 1993. Part Two. January/February 1994.

Moshell, J. Michael, and Charles E. Hughes. "Shared Virtual Worlds for Education." *Virtual Reality World,* January/February 1994: 63-74.

Moshell, M., B. Blau, and R. Dunn-Roberts. "Virtual Environments for Military Training: SIMNET, Ender's Game, and Beyond." *Virtual Reality World,* Summer 1993, 1(2):v-ad. Insert in *Multimedia Review,* Summer 1993.

Moshell, J. Michael, Charles E. Hughes, Brian Blau, Richard Dunn-Roberts, Curtis R. Lisle, and Xin Li. "Networked Virtual Environments: Issues and Approaches." *SRI Virtual Worlds Symposium.* Conference held June 17, 1991, at Menlo Park, Calif.

Moshell, J. Michael, Charles E. Hughes, Brian Blau, Xin Li, and Richard Dunn-Roberts. "Networked Virtual Environments for Simulation and Training." *SIMTEC '91.* Orlando, Fla.: Simulation Computer Society, 1991. Conference held October 21, 1991, at Orlando.

Moshell, J. M., Xin Li, C. E. Hughes, B. Blau, and B. Goldiez. "Nap-of-earth Flight and Realtime Simulation of Dynamic Terrain." *Cockpit Displays and Visual Simulation.* Santa Clara, Calif.: SPIE, 1990, 1289: 118-129. Conference held April 17, 1990, at Orlando, Fla.

Mueller, Stefan, Matthias Unbescheiden, and Martin Goebel. "GENESIS - Eine Interaktive Forschungsumgebung zur Entwicklung Effizienter und Parallelislerter Algorithmen fuer VR-Anwendungen." *Virtual Reality '93.* H. J. Bullinger and H. J. Warnecke, eds. Berlin: Springer-Verlag, 1993: 321-341. Conference held February 1993.

Mullican, Matt. *See* Tarantino.

Multi-Index to Cyberspace, Virtual and Artificial Reality. Robert Carande, ed. Pine Valley, Calif.: Carande Press. Quarterly since 1992.

Multimedia Frontier '93. Special issue of Multimedia Creators' Magazine. Tokyo: Pioneer, 1993. Interviews with John Perry Barlow, Scott Fisher, Tom Hargadon, Jaron Lanier, Brenda Laurel, Carl Eugene Loeffler, Howard Rheingold, David Traub, and others. In Japanese with English introductions.

Murphy, Harry J., ed. *Virtual Reality and Persons with Disabilities: Proceedings.* Northridge, Calif.: Office of Disabled Student Services, California State University, 1992. Conference held March 18, 1992 at Northridge, Calif. Includes: "DataGlove, DataSuit and Virtual Reality: Advanced Technology for People with Disabilites" by Walter J. Greenleaf, "Updating the Eyegaze Language Board with Software Design" by Fran Lexcen, "Orientation Enhancement through Virtual Reality and Geographic Information Systems" by Erik G. Urdang and Rory Stuart, "The SLARTI System: Applying Artificial Neural Networks to Sign Language Recognition" by Peter Vamplew and Anthony Adams, and others.

Murphy, Harry J., ed. *Virtual Reality and Persons with Disabilities: Proceedings.* Northridge, Calif.: Office of Disabled Student Services, California State University, 1993. Conference held June 17-18, 1993, at San Francisco, Calif.

Nagashima, Y., H. Agawa, and F. Kishino. "3D Face Model Reproduction Method Using Multi View Images." *Proceedings of the SPIE, Visual Communications and Image Processing '91.* Santa Clara, Calif.: SPIE, 1991, 1606 (1): 566-73. Conference held November 11-13, 1991, at Boston, Mass.

Naiman, Alaric. "Presence, and Other Gifts: or, What is Reality? Why? Who Cares Anyway?" *Presence,* December 1992, 1(1).

Nelson, Ted. "Interactive Systems and the Design of Virtuality: The Design of Interactive Systems, Tomorrow's Crucial Art Form, Rests on New Philosophical Principles." *Creative Computing.* November 1980, 6(11-12).

Nelson, Theodor H. *Literary Machines: the Report on, and of, Project Xanadu Concerning Word Processing, Electronic Publishing, Hypertext, Thinkertoys, Tomorrow's Intellectual Revolution, and Certain Other Topics Including Knowledge, Education and Freedom.* Swarthmore, Penn.: Ted Nelson, 1981.

Nelson, Theodor H. *Computer Lib/Dream Machines.* Redmond, Wash.: Tempus Books of Microsoft Press, 1987.

Nelson, Theodor H. "How Many Ds in Reality?" *See* Helsel, *Beyond the Vision.*

Nelson, Theodor H. "Virtual World Without End: The Story of Xanadu™." See Jacobson, *Cyberarts.*

Netgame (online mailing list). Bernie Roehl, moderator. Focuses on multi-user virtual environments. E-mail: netgame-request@sunee.uwaterloo.ca.

Networked Reality '94: First International Workshop on Networked Reality in Telecommunication. Tokyo: NTT Media Lab, 1994. Conference held May 13-14, 1994, at Tokyo. Includes "Networked Virtual Environment System SPIDAR" by Masahiro Ishii, Masanori Nakata, and Makoto Sato, "Putting Spatial Sound into Voicemail" by Michael Cohen and Nobuo Koizumi, "VideoPeek: An Intuitive Video Representation in Cyberspace" by Akihito

Akutsu et al., "Mt. Fuji Project" by Masaki Fujihata, "The CyberCube Project" by Derek Dowden, "Virtual Playground and Communication Environments for Children" by Michitaka Hirose et al., "NPSNET: Ensuring World Consistency in a Shared Networked Virtual Environment" by David R. Pratt et al., "Virtual Polis: A Networked Virtual Reality Application" by Carl Eugene Loeffler, "InterSpace: Networked Virtual World for Visual Communication" by Shohei Sugawara, et al., "TwisterGame on Network" by Masaki Fujihata and Nobuya Suzuki, "Is Virtual Reality a Gentle Technology for Humans?" by H. Igarashi, et al., "Networked Teleexistence" by Susumu Tachi, "Merging Real and Virtual Worlds" by Paul Milgram, Haruo Takemura, and Fumio Kishino, "Distributed Virtual Environment System for Cooperative Work" by Nobutatsu Nakamura, Keiji Nemoto, and Katsuya Shinohara, "The Hyper Hospital: A Networked Reality Based Medical Care System" by J. Noritake, et al., "How the Human Being Survives in an Online Virtual World" by Atsuya Yoshida, and other papers.

Neugebauer, J. G. "Virtual Reality: More Than Just Simulation." *The Industrial Robot.* 1992, 19(3): 30-4.

Neugebauer, J. G. "Virtual Reality Applied to Industry." *Imagina 93.* Conference held 1993 at Monte Carlo.

Neugebauer, J. G. "Virtual Reality: The Demonstration Centre." *VR93 Virtual Reality International '93.* London: Meckler, 1993: 72-77. Proceedings of the Third Annual Conference on Virtual Reality held April 6-7, 1993 at London.

Neugebauer, J. G., and W. M. Strommer. "Virtual Reality Applied to Industrial Robot Control and Simulation." *Automation 92.* Conference held 1992 at Genoa, Italy.

Newby, Gregory B. "An Investigation of the Role of Navigation for Information Retrieval." *Annual Meeting of the American Society for Information Science.*, Deborah Shaw, ed. Medford, N.J.: Learned Information, Inc., 1992: 20-25.

Newby, Gregory B. "Virtual Reality." *Annual Review of Information Science and Technology* (28). Medford, N.J.: Learned Information, 1993.

Nilan, Michael S. "Cognitive Space: Using Virtual Reality for Large Information Resource Management Problems." *Journal of Communication,* 1992, 42(4) : 115-135.

Nomura, J. "Virtual Reality and its Application to Consumer Showrooms." *Joint Conference for Automatic Control.* Amsterdam: North Holland Publishing Company, 1990, 33: 11-14.

Novak, Marcos. "Liquid Architectures in Cyberspace." *See* Benedikt, *Cyberspace.*

"Now's the Time to Make Rules for Cyberspace." *PC Week,* October 5, 1992: 70.

Nugent, William R. "Virtual Reality: Advanced Imaging Special Effects Let You Roam in Cyberspace." *Journal of the American Society for Information Science.* September 1991, 42(8): 609-617.

Ødegård, Ola. *Hvordan skapes elektronisk kultur ? - Endrede vilkr med data-kommunikasjon* . Kjeller, Norway: Norwegian Telecom Research, 1992. Technical Report TF-F 22/92. In Norwegian.

Ødegård, Ola. "Telecommunications and Social Interaction: The Social Construction of Virtual Space." *Telektronikk,* 1993, (4): 76-82.

Ødegård, Ola, ed. *Virtuell Virkelighet og det sosiale liv* [Virtual Reality and Social Life]. Kjeller, Norway: Norwegian Telecom Research, 1992. Technical Report TF-R 32/93. Report from the Telematics Seminar '93, held December 16, 1992, in Oslo. Includes "Ider er billige: syntetiske virkeligheter p norsk" by Hakon W. Lie, "Networked Virtual Reality" by Carl Eugene Loeffler, and other papers. In Norwegian and English.

O'Brien, Timothy. "The Art of Multimedia." *Electronic Entertainment,* May 1994: 64-70.

Ohkubo, M., and H. Ishii. "Design and Implementation of a Shared Workspace by Integrating Individual Workspaces." *1990 Conference on Office Information Systems.* Special issue of *SIGOIS Bulletin,* 1990, 11(2-3): 142-146. Conference held April 25, 1990 at Cambridge, Mass.

Omni. New York: Omni Publications International. Monthly since 1978.

Orr, James. *See* Virtual Reality Conference (videorecording).

Osberg, K. *Virtual Reality and Education: A Look at Both Sides of the Sword* (online text file). 1993. FTP: <ftp.u.washington.edu> Directory: ./public/VirtualReality/HITL/papers/tech-reports File: osberg-r-93-7.ps.

L'ouevre d'art à l'époque de la réalité numérique (Art work in the Age of Digital Reality). Conference held May 28, 1993 at l'Ecole Nationale Supérieure des Beaux Arts, Paris.

Panos, Gregory, ed. *Virtual Reality Sourcebook.* Lakewood, Calif.: SophisTech Research, 1992.

Pantelidis, Veronica. *VR in Education Bibliography* (online text file). 1994. FTP: <ftp.u.washington.edu> Directory: ./public/VirtualReality/misc/papers File: Pantelidis-VR-Education-Bibl.txt.

Papper, M. J. and M. A. Gigante. "Using Gestures to Control a Virtual Arm." *See* Earnshaw, Gigante and Jones.

Papper, M. J. and M. A. Gigante. "Using Physical Constraints in a Virtual Environment." *See* Earnshaw, Gigante and Jones.

Pausch, Randy. "Virtual Reality on $5 a Day."*Human Factors in Computing Systems: Reaching Through Technology*, Scott P. Robertson, Gary M. Olson, and Judith S. Olson, eds. Proceedings of CHI '91 conference held April 27 - May 2, 1991, at New Orleans, La. New York: ACM (Association for Computing Machinery), 1991: 265-270.

Pausch, Randy, and Ronald D. Williams. "Giving CANDY to Children: User Tailored Gesture Input Driving an Articulator-Based Speech Synthesizer." *Communications of the ACM* (Association for Computing Machinery), January 1993.

Pausch, Randy, Laura Vogtle, and Matthew Conway. "One Dimensional Motion Tailoring for the Disabled: A User Study." Penny Baversfeld, John Bennett, and Gene Lynch, eds. CHI '92. New York: ACM (Association for Computing Machinery), 1992: 405-412.

PCVR Magazine. Joseph D. Gradecki, ed. Stoughton, Wis.: PCVR Magazine. E-mail: PCVR@fullfeed.com. Six issues per year, since 1991.

Pehrson, Björn, ed. *Proceedings from the 1st MultiG workshop.* Stockholm: Royal Institute of Technology, 1990. Conference held November 1990 at Stockholm.

Pehrson, Björn, ed. *Proceedings from the 4th MultiG Workshop.* Stockholm: Royal Institute of Technology, 1992. Conference held May 1992 at Stockholm.

Pehrson, Björn, and Yngve Sundblad, eds. *Proceedings from the 2nd MultiG Workshop.* Stockholm: Royal Institute of Technology, 1991. Conference held June 1991 at Stockholm.

Pehrson, Björn, Per Gunningberg, and Stephen Pink. MultiG – *A Research Program on Distributed Multimedia Applications and Gigabit Networks.* Stockholm: Royal Institute of Technology, 1991.

Penley, Constance, and Andrew Ross, eds. *Technoculture.* Cultural Politics, vol. 3. Minneapolis, Minn.: University of Minnesota Press, 1991. Includes "Cyborgs at Large: Interview with Donna Haraway" by Constance Penley and Andrew Ross, "The Actors Are Cyborg, Nature Is Coyote, and the Geography Is Elsewhere: Postscript to 'Cyborgs at Large'" by Donna Haraway, "The Lessons of Cyberpunk" by Peter Fitting, and other essays.

Penny, Simon. "Kinetics, Cybernetics, Art Practice in the Age of the Thinking Machine." *Irrelevant Ethics: Notes on Art Practice in a Technological Context*, Simon Penny, ed. [Melbourne?], Australia, 1988: 5-11.

Penny, Simon. "2000 Years of Virtual Reality." *Through the Looking Glass, Artists' First Encounters with Virtual Reality* , Janine Cirincione and Brian D'Amato, eds. New York: Jack Tilton Gallery, 1992. Catalog of an exhibition held at Jack Tilton Gallery, 1992.

Penny, Simon. "Virtual Bodybuilding." *Media Information Australia*, August 1993.

Periodical Abstracts. Louisville, Ken.: UMI, since 1986. Online bibliographic database, with abstracts, indexing more than a thousand academic and general journals in the social sciences, humanities, general science and current affairs.

Peterson, Ivars. "Wizard of Oz." *Science News*, December 19, 1992, 142(25-26): 440-441.

Piantanida, T. P. "Virtual Perception Program at SRI International." *See* Helsel, *Beyond the Vision*.

Piantanida, T. P., D. K. Boman, and J. Gille. "Perceptual Issues in Virtual Reality." *Presence*, 1993.

Piantanida, T. P., et al. "Studies of the Field-of-View/Resolution Tradeoff in Virtual-Reality Systems." *Human Vision, Visual Processing and Digital Display III: Proceedings of the SPIE — The International Society for Optical Engineering*. Bellingham, Wash.: SPIE, 1666,1992. Conference held February 10-13, 1992 at San Jose, Calif.

Piantanida, Tom. "Cyberhead: Am I Really Existing?" *Virtual Reality World*, July/August 1994: 67-68.

Pickover, Clifford, ed. *Visions of the Future: Art, Technology and Computing in the Twenty-First Century*. New York: St. Martin's Press, 1993.

Piercy, Marge. *He, She, and It: A Novel*. New York: Knopf, 1991.

Pimentel, Kenneth. "Texturing Reality." *Multimedia Review*, June 1991, 2(2): 28-33.

Pimentel, Kenneth, and Kevin Teixeira. *Virtual Reality, Through the New Looking Glass*. Windcrest/McGraw-Hill, 1992.

PIX-Elation. Official newsletter of VRASP: the Virtual Reality Alliance of Students and Professionals. Writers' queries and submissions to Tod Foley : asif@well.sf.ca.us. Advertising and VRASP membership to Karin August: kaugust@caip.rutgers.edu. Occasional since 1992.

Pope, Stephen Travis, and Lennart E Fahlén. *Building Sound into A Virtual Environment: An Aural Perspective Engine for a Distributed Interactive Virtual Environment: A Progress Report*. Sweden, 1992.

Pope, Stephen, and Lennart E. Fahlén. "The Use of 3-D Audio in a Synthetic Environment: An Aural Renderer for a Distributed Virtual Reality System." *VRAIS: IEEE Virtual Reality Annual Symposium, Symp. 1*. Piscataway, N.J.: IEEE Service Center, 1993: 176-182. Conference held September 1993 at Seattle, Washington.

Porter, S. "Interview: Jaron Lanier." *Computer Graphics World*, April 1992, 15(4): 61-63.

Poulter, Alan. "Towards a Virtual Reality Library." *ASLIB Proceedings*, Alan Poulter, ed. London: ASLIB, January 1993, 45(1): 11-17.

Presence: The Journal of Teleoperators and Virtual Environments. Cambridge, Mass.: MIT Press Journals. Quarterly since 1992.

Princenthal, Nancy. "Review of Exhibitions: 'Virtual Reality' at Jack Tilton." *Art in America*, October 1992, 80(10): 146-147.

Proceedings: 1990 Symposium on Interactive 3D Graphics. Conference held March 25-28, 1990 at Snowbird, Utah. Special issue of *Computer Graphics*. March 1990, 24(2).

Proceedings: 1992 Symposium on Interactive 3D Graphics. Computer Graphics, 1992. Conference held March 29 to April 1, 1992, at Cambridge, Mass.

Proceedings of IEE Colloquium on 'Using Virtual Worlds'. London: IEE, 1992, (Digest No.093).

Prothero, J., T. Emerson, and S. Weghorst. *VR/Telepresence and Medicine Sources*. Seattle, Wash.: HITL (Human Interface Technology Laboratory), 1993. Technical report BMed-93-1.

Pruitt, Steven, and Tom Barrett, "Corporate Virtual Workspace." *See* Benedikt, *Cyberspace.*

Quarendon, P. "Toward Three-Dimensional Graphical Models of Reality." *See* Earnshaw, Gigante and Jones.

Quarterman, John S. *The Matrix: Computer Networks and Conferencing Systems Worldwide*. Bedford, Mass.: Digital Press, 1990.

Queau, P. "The Virtues and the Vertigo of the Virtual." *Journal of Visualization and Computer Animation*, July 1991, 2(3): 114-115.

Rabines, R., and J. Mohler. "Battlefield Realism Flows via Distributed Simulation." *Signal*, November 1990, 45(3): 47-9.

Ramanathan, Srinivas, P. Venkat Rangan, and Harrick M. Vin. "Integrating Virtual Reality, Tele-conferencing, and Entertainment into Multimedia Home Computers." *IEEE Transactions on Consumer Electronics*, May 1992, 38: 70-6.

Rassmussen, T., and M. Søby. *Kulturens digitale felt*. Oslo: Aventura Forlag, 1993.

Raymond, Eric S., ed. *The New Hacker's Dictionary*. Cambridge, Mass.: MIT Press, 1991.

Real Time Graphics (newsletter). Roy Latham, ed. Mountain View, Calif.

Realtá Virtuale. Milan, Italy: A.R.S. (Artificial Realities Systems). E-mail: montefus@dsi.unimi.it. Monthly since 1992. In Italian.

Regan, Matthew, and Ronald Pose, "Architecture for Orientation Mapping." *See* ICAT '93.

Regian, J. Wesley, Wayne L. Shebilske, and John M. Monk. "Virtual Reality: An Instructional Medium for Visual-Spatial Tasks." *Journal of Communication*, 1992, 42(4): 136-149.

Reilly, W. Scott, and Joseph Bates. *Building Emotional Agents*. Pittsburgh: School of Computer Science, Carnegie Mellon University, May 1992. Technical Report CMU-CS-92-143.

Resnick, M. "Collaboration in Simulated Worlds: Learning Through and About Collaboration." *SIGCUE Outlook*, March 1992, 21(3): 36-8.

"Retina Projection, Tactile Fields and Other Toys." *Broadcasting* (supplement), December 9, 1991: 66-67.

Rheingold, Howard. *Tools for Thought: The People and Ideas Behind the Next Computer Revolution*. New York: Simon & Schuster, 1985.

Rheingold, Howard. *Virtual Reality*. New York: Summit Books, 1991.

Rheingold, Howard. "A Slice of Life in My Virtual Community." *EFFector ONline* (electronic journal), 1992, 2(11)-3(0) in three parts. FTP: <ftp.eff.org> Directory: pub/EFF/newsletters.

Rheingold, Howard. *The Virtual Community*. Reading, Mass.: Addison-Wesley, 1993.

Rheingold, Howard. *See* VR Conference – Overview of VR (videorecording).

Rheingold, Howard. *See also* Levine and Rheingold.

Riedel, O. *Faktor 10: Cyberspace auf dem Mac*. Stuttgart, Germany: Fraunhofer-Institut für Arbeitswirtschaft und Organisation IAO, August 1992. Technical Report. In German.

Riedel, O. "Fraunhofer-Institut Develops Office Design Tools." *VR News*, 1992: 8.

Riedel, O., and A. Ebeling. *Begrenzte Welten: Fraunhofer Institut (IAO) Präsentiert Virtuelle Realität auf dem Grafikrechner "SkyWriter."* Stuttgart, Germany: Fraunhofer-Institut für Arbeitswirtschaft und Organisation IAO, May 1992. Technical Report. In German.

Robertson, George G., Stuart K. Card, and Jock D. Mackinlay. "Nonimmersive Virtual Reality." *Computer*, February 1993, 26: 81.

Robinett, Warren. "Synthetic Experience: A Proposed Taxonomy." *Presence*, 1992, 1(2): 229-247.

Robinett, Warren. "Electronic Expansion of Human Perception." *Whole Earth Review*, 72: 16-22. Reprinted as "Virtual Worlds Research at the University of North Carolina" in ICAT '92.

Robinett, Warren. *Synthetic Experience: A Taxonomy, Survey of Earlier Thought, and Speculations on the Future.* Chapel Hill, N.C.: University of North Carolina, 1992. Technical Report TR92-022.

Robinett, Warren. "Synthetic Experience: A Proposed Taxonomy". *Presence*, Spring 1992, 1(2): 229-247.

Robinett, Warren. "Artificial Reality at the UNC at Chapel Hill." *See* Virtual Reality (videorecording).

Robinett, Warren, and Michael Naimark. "Artists Explore Virtual Reality: The Bioapparatus Residency at Banff Centre for the Arts." *Presence*, Spring 1992, 1(2): 248-250.

Robinett, Warren, and J. P. Rolland. "A Computational Model for the Stereoscopic Optics of a Head-Mounted Display." *See* Earnshaw, Gigante and Jones.

Rolf, John. "Virtual Lobby." *See* Virtual Reality (videorecording).

Romkey, J. "Whither Cyberspace?" *Journal of the American Society for Information Science*, September 1991, 42(8): 618-620.

Ronell, Avital. "Support Our Tropes II: Or, Why in Cyburbia There Are a Lot of Cowboys." *Yale Journal of Criticism*, March 1992, 5(2): 73-80. Reprinted in collage form in *Semiotext[e]/Architecture*, Hraztan Zeitlian, ed. New York: Semiotext[e], 1992: 144-145.

Rosenberg, L. B. (1994). "Medical Applications of Virtual Reality." *Virtual Reality Systems*, 1994, 1(3): 48-50.

Rosenman, J., et al. "Virtual Simulation: Initial Clinical Results." *International Journal of Radiation: Oncology-Biology-Physics*, April 1991, 20(4): 843-851.

Rotzer, Florian, and Peter Weibel, eds. *Strategien des Scheins: Kunst, Computer, Medien.* Munchen: Boer, 1991. In German.

Rowley, "Virtual Reality Products" *See* Earnshaw, Gigante and Jones, eds.

Rubine, Dean. "Specifying Gestures by Example." Presented at *SIGGRAPH 91*, 1991. This and other gesture recognition papers and software are available via anonymous FTP from <emsworth.andrew.cmu.edu> machine address: (128.2.30.62) in the directory /gestures. The entire directory, including the paper, the gesture recognizer, and recognition software is in the compressed file gestures/gesture.tar.Z.

Rucker, Rudy. *Software*. New York: Avon Books, 1982.

Rucker, Rudy. *Wetware*. New York: Avon Books, 1988.

Rucker, Rudy. "Mutations in the 4th Dimension." *See* Bray.

Rucker, Rudy, Quenn Mu, and R. U. Sirius, eds. *Mondo 2000: A User's Guide to the New Edge*. New York: HarperCollins, 1992.

Russo, Jack, and Michael Risch. "New Frontiers." *National Law Journal*, October 12, 1992, 15(6): S1 ff.

Saffo, Paul. "Consensual Realities in Cyberspace." *Computers Under Attack: Intruders, Worms, and Viruses*, Peter J. Denning, ed. New York: Addison-Wesley, 1990.

Schneider, W. "SIMNET: A Breakthrough in Combat Simulator Technology?" *International Defense Review*, April 1989, 22(4): 489-91.

Shneiderman, Ben. *Designing the User Interface: Strategies for Effective Human Interaction*. Reading, Mass.: Addison-Wesley, 1992.

Schraft, R. D., W. M. Strommer, and J. G. Neugebauer. "Virtual Reality Applied to Industrial Robots." *Informatique '92: International Conference Interface to Real and Virtual Worlds*. Nanterre, France: EC2, 1992: 297-307. Conference held March 23, 1992 at Montpellier, France.

Schraft, R. D., W. M. Strommer, and J. G. Neugebauer. "A Virtual Reality Testbed for Robot Applications." *International Symposium for Industrial Robots* (ISIR 92). Conference held 1992 at Barcelona, Spain.

sci.virtual-worlds (online). Seattle, Wash.: HITL (Human Interface Technology Laboratory). A Usenet newsgroup "aimed at the discussion of aspects of virtual reality and its related technologies." Founded by Bob Jacobson and moderated by Toni Emerson and a team from HITL. E-mail: scivw@u.washington.edu. For readers with access to e-mail but not to Usenet, see virtu-l.

sci.virtual-worlds.apps (online). Cambridge, Massachusetts: Massachusetts Institute of Technology. This Usenet newsgroup, spun off from <sci.virtual-worlds> in 1993, focuses on applications of virtual worlds technology. Moderated by Bob Jacobson and Mark De Loura. E-mail: cyberoid@u.washington.edu. For readers with access to e-mail but not to Usenet, see vrapp-l.

Science Fiction Eye. Stephen P. Brown, ed. Three issues per year, since 1987. Asheville, N.C.

Seizing the Media. Westfield, N.J.: The Immedaists, 1992.

Shapiro, Michael A., and Daniel G. McDonald. "I'm not a Doctor, but I Play One in Virtual Reality: Implications of Virtual Reality for Judgments About Reality." *Journal of Communication*, 1992, 42(4): 94-114.

Shaw, Jeffrey. "The Legible City." *Ten.8*, 1991, 2(2): 46-48.

Shaw, Jeffrey. "EVE: Extended Virtual Environment." *Virtual Reality World*, May/June 1994: 59-61.

Shaw, Jeffrey. "Revolution/Revolutions" (interactive video sculpture). *Leonardo*, 1991, 24(4): 489.

Sheridan, Thomas B. "Musings on Telepresence and Virtual Presence." *Presence*, Winter 1992, 1(1): 120-126.

Sheridan, Thomas B. "Defining Our Terms." *Presence*, Spring 1992, 1(2): 272-274.

Sheridan, Thomas B. "My Anxieties about Virtual Environments." *Presence*, Spring 1993, 2(2): 141-142.

Sheridan, Thomas B. *Telerobotics*, Automation, and Human Supervisory Control. Cambridge, Mass.: The MIT Press, 1992.

Sherman, Barrie, and Phil Judkins. *Glimpses of Heaven, Visions of Hell: Virtual Reality and Its Implications*. London: Hodder & Stoughton, 1992.

Sherouse, George W., and Edward L. Chaney. "The Portable Virtual Simulator." *International Journal of Radiation, Oncology, Biology, Physics*, 1991, 21(2): 475-482.

Sherouse, George W., et al. "Virtual Simulation in the Clinical Setting: Some Practical Considerations." *International Journal of Radiation, Oncology, Biology, Physics*. October 1990, 19(4): 1059-1065.

Shirley, John. *Heatseeker*. Los Angeles: Scream/Press, 1989.

Shirley, John. "Call It Revolutionary Parasitism." *See* Milhon.

Sims, Dave. "Virtual Violence Takes Center Stage at Cyber Arts." *IEEE Computer Graphics and Applications*, January 1993, 13: 104.

Sirius, R. U., and George Gleason. "Do G-Men Dream of Electric Sheep?" *Mondo 2000*, December 1991, (3): 40-43.

Sjöland, Thomas. *Using SICStus Objects in the Design of Graphical User Interfaces*. Stockholm: SICS (Swedish Institute for Computer Science), August 1992. SICS Research Report R92:10.

Slater, M., and M. Usoh. "Presence in Immersive Virtual Environments." *Proceedings of IEEE 1993 Virtual Reality Annual International Symposium, VRAIS '93*. Piscataway, N.J.: IEEE Service Center, 1993: 90-96. Conference held September 1993 at Seattle, Washington.

Slusser, George Edgar, and T. A. Shippey, eds. *Fiction2000: Cyberpunk and the Future of Narrative*. Athens: University of Georgia Press, 1992. Includes

"Inside the Movement: Past, Present, and Future" by Lewis Shiner, "The Frankenstein Barrier" by George Slusser, "Deus Ex Machina in William Gibson's Cyberpunk Trilogy" by Paul Alkon, "'The Gernsback Continuum': William Gibson in the Context of Science Fiction" by Gary Westfahl, "Of AIs and Others: William Gibson's Transit" by John Christie, and other papers.

Smith, Bradford. "The Use of Animation to Analyze and Present Information About Complex Systems." *See* Helsel, *Beyond the Vision.*

Smith, Sean, and Joseph Bates. *Towards a Theory of Narrative for Interactive Fiction.* Pittsburgh: School of Computer Science, Carnegie Mellon University, 1989. Technical Report CMU-CS-89-121.

Snider, Burr. "Jaron." *Wired,* May/June 1993, 1(2): 76-81.

Snowdon, David N., Adrian J. West and Toby L. J. Howard. "Towards the Next Generation of Human-Computer Interface." *Informatique '92: International Conference Interface to Real and Virtual Worlds.* Nanterre, France: EC2, 1992. Conference held March 23, 1992 at Montpellier, France.

Sobchack, Vivian Carol. "What in the World: Vivian Sobchack on New Age Mutant Ninja Hackers." *Artforum,* April 1991, 29: 24-26.

Søby, Morten, and Ola Ødegård. *To Be is to Connect.* Kjeller, Norway: Norwegian Telecom Research, 1993. Technical Report TF-F 15/93.

Solman, Gregory. "Through the Looking Glass (Stepping Beyond 3-D to Flirt with a Wonderland Called Cyberspace)." *American Film,* September 15, 1990, 15: 50.

Spring, Michael, and Michael Jennings. "VR and Abstract Data: Virtualizing Information." *Virtual Reality World,* Spring 1993, 1(1): c-m. Insert in *Multimedia Review,* Summer 1993.

Spring, Michael. "'Being There,' or Models for Virtual Reality." *See* Virtual Reality: Theory, Practice, Promise (videorecording).

Spring, Michael. "Informating with Virtual Reality." *See* Helsel and Roth, eds.

Sprout, Randy. "Virtual Reality Entertainment Developers: An Industry Overview." *Pix-Elation.* 2(2), April/May 1993.

Ståhl, Olov. "Tools for Cooperative Work in the MultiG TelePresence Environment." *Proceedings from the 4th MultiG workshop,* Björn Pehrson, ed. Stockholm: Royal Institute of Technology, 1992. Conference held May 1992 at Stockholm.

Stampe, Dave, Bernard Roehl, and John Eagan. *Virtual Reality Creations.* Corte Madera, Calif.: Waite Group Press, 1993.

Stanger, V. J. "Telecommunications Applications of Virtual Reality." *IEE Colloquium on 'Using Virtual Worlds'*. London, England: IEE, 1992, 7 (Digest No. 093): 1-3,40.

Stanger, V. J. "Networked Virtual Reality Applications." *IEE Colloquium on 'Distributed Virtual Reality'*. London: IEE, 1993, (Digest No.121): 1/1-4. Conference held May 21, 1993 at London.

Stark, L. W., et al. "Visual Search in Virtual Environments." *Human Vision, Visual Processing and Digital Display III: Proceedings of the SPIE - The International Society for Optical Engineering*. Bellingham, Wash.: SPIE, 1666, 1992: 577-89. Conference held February 10-13, 1992 at San Jose, Calif.

Starks, Michael. "Stereoscopic Video and the Quest for Virtual Reality: An Annotated Bibliography of Selected Topics." *Stereoscopic Displays and Applications III: Proceedings of the SPIE—The International Society for Optical Engineering*. John O. Merritt and Scott S. Fisher, eds. Bellingham, Wash.: SPIE, 1992, 1669: 216-227. Conference held February 12-13, 1992 at San Jose, Calif.

Starks, Michael. "Stereoscopic Video and the Quest for Virtual Reality." *See* Helsel, *Beyond the Vision*.

Stelarc. "Event for Amplified Body, Laser Eyes and Third Hand." *Irrelevant Ethics: Notes on Art Practice in a Technological Context*, Simon Penny, ed. [Melbourne], Australia, 1988: 28-31.

Stelarc and James D. Paffrath. *Obsolete Body: Suspensions: Stelarc*. Davis, Calif.: J. P. Publications, 1984.

Stenger, Nicole. "Kitsch, Kommerz und Kunst." *Vraiment Faux*. Versailles, France: Fondation Cartier, 1988. Catalog of an exhibition held 1988 at Fondation Cartier pour l'Art Contemporain, Versailles, France.

Stenger, Nicole. "Brave New Virtual World." *SCAN Proceedings*. Philadelphia: Small Computers in the Arts Network (SCAN), 1989. Conference held 1989 at Philadelphia.

Stenger, Nicole. "Real-time Movies: A New Industry." *Informatique '92: International Conference Interface to Real and Virtual Worlds*. Nanterre, France: EC2, 1992: 37-38. Conference held March 23, 1992 at Montpellier, France.

Stenger, Nicole. "Mind is a Leaking Rainbow." *See* Benedikt, *Cyberspace*.

Stenger, Nicole. *See* VR Conference – Applications (videorecording) and Cyberspace, Power and Culture (videorecording).

Stenger, Nicole. *See also* Meissner, Delaney, "Meeting the Angels," Morgan, "Interactive Art," and "Interactivity."

Sterling, Bruce. *The Artificial Kid*. New York: Harper & Row, 1980.

Sterling, Bruce. *Schismatrix*. New York: Arbor House, 1985.

Sterling, Bruce. "Cyberspace (™)." *Interzone*. November 1990.

Sterling, Bruce. *Hacker Crackdown*. New York: Bantam, 1992.

Sterling, Bruce. "War is Virtual Hell." *Wired*. 1993, 1(1): 46 ff.

Sterling, Bruce. "Coming in under the Radar." *See* Milhon.

Sterling, Bruce. "GURPS' Labor Lost: The Cyberpunk Bust." *See* Hughes, Carolyn.

Sterling, Bruce, ed. *Mirrorshades: The Cyberpunk Anthology*. New York: Arbor House, 1986. Includes "The Gernsback Continuum" by William Gibson, "Snake-Eyes" by Tom Maddox, "Rock On" by Pat Cadigan, "Tales of Houdini" by Rudy Rucker, "400 Boys" by Marc Laidlaw, "Solstice" by James Patrick Kelly, "Petra" by Greg Bear, "Till Human Voices Wake Us" by Lewis Shiner, "Freezone" by John Shirley, "Stone Lives" by Paul Di Filippo, "Red Star, Winter Orbit" by Bruce Sterling and William Gibson, and "Mozart in Mirrorshades" by Bruce Sterling and Lewis Shiner.

Sterling, Bruce. *Bruce Sterling: Speaking the Unspeakable* (videorecording). Distributed by Art Com, San Francisco. 50 minutes.

Steuer, Jonathan. "Defining Virtual Reality: Dimensions Determining Telepresence." *Journal of Communication*, 1992, 42(4): 73-93.

Stewart, Doug. "Artificial Reality: Don't Stay Home Without It." *Smithsonian*, January 1991, 21(10).

Stix, G. "Reach Out: Touch is added to Virtual Reality Simulations." *Scientific American*, February 1991, 264(2): 134.

Stix, G. "See-Through View: Virtual Reality May Guide Physicians' Hands." *Scientific American*, September 1992, 267(3): 166.

Stone, Allucquère Roseanne. "The Architecture of Elsewhere: Gender, Structure & Schizophrenia." *Semiotext[e]/Architecture*. Hraztan Zeitlian, ed. New York: Semiotext[e], 1992: 136-143.

Stone, Allucquère Roseanne. "Virtual Systems." *Zone*, 1993, 6 (Incorporations): 608-621.

Stone, Allucquère Roseanne. "Will the Real Body Please Stand Up?: Boundary Stories about Virtual Cultures." *See* Benedikt, *Cyberspace*.

Stone, Allucquère Roseanne. "The Drunken Terminal: Desire, Virtual Worlds, and the Problem of the Diffracted Subject." *Lost Boundaries: A History of Media Induced Experience*. Norman Klein, ed. Forthcoming.

Stone, Allucquère Roseanne. "How Robots Grew Gonads: A Cautionary Tale." Funaro and Joans, eds. *Collected Proceedings of the Contact Conferences.* Forthcoming.

Stone, R. J. "The UK Virtual Reality & Telepresence Project: One Year On." Computer Graphics. *Computer Animation, Virtual Reality, Visualisation.* Pinner, England: Blenheim Online, 1991: 131-40. Conference held November 5-7, 1991 at London.

Stone, R. J. "Virtual Reality: A Tool for Telepresence and Human Factors Research." *See* Earnshaw, Gigante and Jones.

Stone, Valerie E. "Social Interaction and Social Development in Virtual Environments." *Presence,* Spring 1993, 2(2): 153-161.

Stoppi, J.U.L. "'VR-chitecture': A New Discipline." *IEE Colloquium on 'Distributed Virtual Reality'* (Digest No. 121). London: IEE, 1993: 6/1-3. Conference held May 21, 1993 at London, England.

Stratton, Bob. "ImagineNation: 'Virtual Reality' For Entertainment." *See* Mondo 2000.

Strommer, W. M., and J. G. Neugebauer. "Robot Simulation with Virtual Reality." ESA *Workshop on Simulators for the European Space Programmes.* Conference held 1992 at ESTEC, Noordwijk, Netherlands.

Strommer, W. M., J. G. Neugebauer, and T. Flaig. "Transputerbased Virtual Reality Workstation." *Informatique '92: International Conference Interface to Real and Virtual Worlds.* Nanterre, France: EC2, 1992. Conference held March 23, 1992 at Montpellier, France.

Stuart, Rory. "Virtual Reality at NYNEX." *See* Helsel, *Beyond the Vision.*

Sturman, David. *Whole-Hand Input.* Cambridge, Mass.: MIT. Unpublished thesis. Text available online as a .dvi file by anonymous ftp to <medialab.media.mit.edu> in directory /tmp/djs File: WholeHandInput.

Sundblad, Yngve. *A Distributed Multimedia Interface Builder.* Stockholm, Sweden: Royal Institute of Technology, Interaction and Presentation Laboratory, 1991. Technical Report TRITA-NA-P9113; IPLab-41; MultiG report no.2.

Sundblad, Yngve, ed. *Proceedings from the 3rd MultiG workshop.* Stockholm: Royal Institute of Technology, 1991. Conference held December 1991 in Stockholm. Stockholm, 1991.

Surprenant, Thomas. "Information Dreams." *Wilson Library Bulletin,* October 1991, 66(2): 95 ff.

"Surreal Science: Virtual Reality Finds a Place in the Classroom." *Scientific American,* February 1993, 268(2): 103.

Survival Research Laboratories. *Mark Pauline, Menacing Machine Mayhem* (videorecording). San Francisco: Re/Search, 1982. 30 minutes.

Survival Research Laboratories. *Virtues of Negative Fascination: Videorecording: Five Mechanized Performances by Survival Research Laboratories* (videorecording). San Francisco: S.R.L., 1986. 103 minutes.

Survival Research Laboratories. *See also* Horgan.

Sutherland, Ivan. *Sketchpad, a Man-Machine Graphical Communication System.* New York: Garland Publishers, 1980; reprint of his 1963 Ph.D. dissertation at MIT. Summarized in "Sketchpad, a Man-Machine Graphical Communication System." AFIPS Spring Joint *Computer Conference.* Arlington, Va.: American Federation of Information Processing Societies, 1963, 23: 329-346.

Sutherland, Ivan. "The Ultimate Display." *Proceedings of the IFIP Congress 65, Vol. 2*, Wayne A. Kalenich, ed. Washington, DC: Spartan Books, 1965: 506-509.

Sutherland, Ivan. "A Head-Mounted Three-Dimensional Display." *Proceedings of the Fall Joint Computer Conference, AFIPS Conference Proceedings, Vol. 33.* New York: American Federation of Information Processing Societies, 1968: 757-764.

Sutherland, Ivan. "Computer Displays." *Scientific American,* June 1970, 222(6): 56-81.

Suzuki, Gen, and Takashi Kouno. *See* ICAT '92.

Suzuki, G., et al. "Virtual Collaborative Workspace." *NTT Review,* March 1993, 5(2): 74-81.

Suzuki, Gen, Shouhei Sugawara, and Machio Moriuchi. "Visual Communication Environment." *See* ICAT '93.

Synergy, Michael. "Hurtling Towards the Singularity: a Conversation with Vernor Vinge." *Mondo 2000,* September 1989 (1): 114-117.

System Architectures and Networks for Virtual Environments (videorecording). 120 minutes. Includes presentations by Larry Koved, Michael Moshell, Warren Robinett and Herbert Taylor.

Tachi, Susumu. "Artificial Reality and Tele-Existence: Present Status and Future Prospect." *See* ICAT '92.

Tachi, Susumu, and Kenichi Yasuda. "Evaluation Experiments." *See* ICAT '93.

Tachi, S., H. Arai, and T. Maeda. "Tele-existence Master-Slave System for Remote Manipulation." *IROS '90: IEEE International Workshop on Intelligent Robots and Systems '90. Towards a New Frontier of Applications.* New York: IEEE, 1990, 1: 343-8. Conference held July 3, 1990 at Ibaraki, Japan.

Tachi, S., et al. "Tele-existence (I): Design and Evaluation of a Visual Display with Sensation of Presence." *RoManSy '84: The Fifth CISM-IFToMM Symposium.* London: Hermes Publishing: 245 ff. Conference held June 1984 at Udine, Italy.

Tachi, Susumu, et al. "Tele-existence in Real World and Virtual World." *ICAR '91* (Fifth International Conference on Advanced Robotics). Conference held June19-22, 1991, at Pisa, Italy.

Tachi, S., and M. Hirose, eds. *Virtual Technology Laboratory.* Japan: Kogyo-Cyosa-Kai, 1992.

Takahashi, T., and F. Kishino, F. "A Hand Gesture Recognition Method and Its Application." *Systems and Computers in Japan,* 1992, 23(3): 38-48.

Takahashi, T., and T. Sakai. "Teaching Robot's Movement in Virtual Reality." *Proceedings IROS '91: IEEE/RSJ International Workshop on Intelligent Robots and Systems.* New York: IEEE,1991 (3): 1583-8. Conference held November 3-5, 1991, at Osaka, Japan.

Takala, Tapio, and James Hahn. "Sound rendering." *Computer Graphics,* July 1992, 26(2): 211-219.

Takemura, H., A. Tomono, and F. Kishino. "A Usability Study of the Virtual Environment." *Human Interface,* 1990, 6: 577-582.

Takemura, Haruo, et al. "Distributed Processing Architecture." *See* ICAT '93.

Takeuchi, Akikazu, and Katashi Nagao. *Communicative Facial Displays as a New Conversational Modality.* Tokyo, Japan: Sony Computer Science Laboratory, September 1992. Technical Report SCSL-TR-92-019. Also published in the *Proceedings of ACM/IFIP INTERCHI.* New York: ACM (Association for Computing Machinery), 1993. Conference held April 24 - 29, 1993 at Amsterdam, The Netherlands.

Tarantino, Michael. "Die Darstellung der Wirklichkeit mittels fiktiver Architektur [The City Project: Interview with Matt Mullican]." *Werk, Bauen + Wohnen,* January/February 1992, 79/46: 68-71.

Tart, Charles T. "Multiple Personality, Altered States and Virtual Reality: The World Simulation Process Approach." *Dissociation: Progress in the Dissociative Disorders,* December 1990, 3(4): 222-233.

Tart, Charles T. "On the Uses of Computer-Generated Realities: A Response to Begelman." *Dissociation: Progress in the Dissociative Disorders,* December 1991, 4(4): 216-217.

Telepresence Research: Be There Here (videorecording). Menlo Park, Calif.: Penrose Productions, 1991. Distributed by Telepresence Research. 15 minutes.

Tenma, Takao, Yasuhiko Yokote, and Mario Tokoro. *Implementing Persistent Objects in the Apertos Operating System.* Tokyo, Japan: Sony Computer Science Laboratory, September 1992. Technical Report SCSL-TR-92-015.

Teraoka, Fumio. *Host Migration in Virtual Internet Protocol.* Tokyo: Sony Computer Science Laboratory, June 1992. Technical Report SCSL-TR-92-006.

Teraoka, Fumio, Kim Claffy, and Mario Tokoro. *Design, Implementation, and Evaluation of Virtual Internet Protocol.* Tokyo: Sony Computer Science Laboratory, June 1992. Technical Report SCSL-TR-92-003.

Teraoka, Fumio, Yasuhiko Yokote, and Mario Tokoro. *Inter-Object Communication in the Muse Operating System.* Tokyo: Sony Computer Science Laboratory, September 1988. Technical Report SCSL-TR-88-002.

Teraoka, Fumio, Yasuhiko Yokote, and Mario Tokoro. *Virtual Network: Towards Location Transparent Communication in Large Distributed Systems.* Tokyo: Sony Computer Science Laboratory, June 1990. Technical Report SCSL-TR-90-005.

Teixeira, Kevin. "Behind the Scenes at the Guggenheim." *Virtual Reality World*, May/June 1994: 66-70.

Thalmann, D. "Using Virtual Reality Techniques in the Animation Process." *See* Earnshaw, Gigante and Jones.

Thalmann, Nadia Magnenat, and Daniel Thalmann, eds. *Animation of Synthetic Actors and 3D Interaction.* Lausanne, Switzerland: Computer Graphics Lab, Swiss Federal Institute of Technology and MIRALab Group, University of Geneva, November 1991.

Theall, Donald F. "Beyond the Orality/Literacy Dichotomy: James Joyce and the Pre-History of Cyberspace". *PostModern Culture: An Electronic Journal of Interdisciplinary Criticism* (electronic journal), May 1992, 2(3). FTP: <ncsuvm.cc.ncsu.edu> Directory: PMC Filename THEALL 592.

Theasby, P. J. "The Virtues of Virtual Reality." *GEC Review*, 1992, 7(3): 131-145.

Thomas, John. "Cyberspace, VR and the Principle of Commonality: Cyberspace Design." *See* Virtual Reality: Theory, Practice, Promise (videorecording).

Thomas, John C., and Rory Stuart. "Virtual Reality and Human Factors." *Proceedings of the 36th Annual Meeting of the Human Factors Society*, Part 1. Santa Monica, Calif.: Human Factors Society, 1992: 207-210. Conference held October 12-16 at Atlanta, Ga.

Thomas, Wes. "Hyperwebs." *See* Mondo 2000.

Thomas, Wes. *See* Virtual Reality Conference (videorecording).

Thompson, Jeremy B., ed. *Virtual Reality: An International Directory of Research Projects*, Westport, Conn.: Meckler, 1993.

Tice, Steve, and Linda Jacobson. "The Art of Building Virtual Realities." *See* Jacobson, *Cyberarts.*

Tice, Steve E., and Gary Beirne. *Tomorrow's Realities: Virtual Reality, Hypermedia.* New York: ACM (Association for Computing Machinery), 1991. SIGGRAPH 91 conference held July 2, 1991 at Las Vegas, Nevada. Includes descriptions of the following projects: Michael Naimark and Company, EAT: A Virtual Dining Environment; Michael Naimark, VBK: A Moviemap of Karlsruhe; SimGraphics Engineering Corp., Assembly Modeller; Mark Bolas, Be Here Now; Suresh Balu et al, Radiation Therapy Treatment Planning with a Head-Mounted Display; Richard Holloway and Warren Robinett, Flying Through Protein Molecules; Jeff Butterworth et al., 3dm: A 3-Dimensional Modeling System; John Alspaugh et al., An Interactive Building Walkthrough System; Erik Erikson et al., A Mountain Bike with Force Feedback for Indoor Exercise; SimGraphics Engineering Corp., Performance Cartoons; The Vivid Group, The Mandala VR System; Boeing, The Boeing VSX; Silicon Graphics, Plasm: Above the Drome; Incredible Technologies, Throwing Real Objects into Virtual Space; DIVISION, Ltd., PROvision; Luc Courchesne, Portrait One; Michael J. Zyda and David R. Pratt, PNSNET: A 3D Visual Simulator for Virtual World Exploration and Experience; Myron Krueger and Katrin Hinrichsen, VIDEODESK Teletutoring; Scott H. Foster and Elizabeth M. Wenzel, Virtual Acoustic Environments: The Convolvotron.

TISEA. Cultural Diversity in the Global Village: The Third International Symposium on Electronic Art. Sydney: Australian Network for Art and Technology, 1992. Exhibition catalog of the conference and exhibition held November 9, 1992 at Sydney, Australia. Includes "Response is the Medium" by Myron W. Krueger, "Global Media, Common Ground and Cultural Diversity" by Brenda Laurel, "Commentaries on Metacommentaries on Interactivity" by Erkki Huhtamo, "Autonomy and Antipodality in Global Village" by McKenzie Wark, "Virtual Environments as Intuition Synthesisers" by Manuel de Landa, "Real Time Synthesis of Complex Acoustic Environments" by Scott Foster, Elizabeth Wenzel and R. Michael Taylor, plus abstracts of other papers and documentation of art by Tim Gruchy, Stelarc, and other artists.

Tokoro, Mario. *Toward Operating Systems for the 2000's.* Tokyo: Sony Computer Science Laboratory, May 1991. Technical Report SCSL-TR-91-005.

Tollander, Carl. "Collaborative Engines for Multiparticipant Cyberspaces." *See* Benedikt, *Cyberspace.*

Tomas, David. "Old Rituals for New Space: Rites de Passage and William Gibson's Cultural Model of Cyberspace." *See* Benedikt, *Cyberspace.*

Train, John. "Jacking In, Jerking Off: Review of the Conference Towards the Aesthetics of the Future, Institute of Contemporary Arts, London." *Creative Camera,* June 1991, (310): 12-14.

Traub, David. "Neomedia: To Live and Learn in 3D." *Verbum,* 1991, 5(2): 22-24.

Traub, David. "Simulated World as Classroom: the Potential for Designed Learning within Virtual Environments." *See* Helsel and Roth.

Traub, David. "Educational Implications for Virtual Reality." *See* Virtual Reality: Theory, Practice, Promise (videorecording).

Truck, Fred. "Musings on an Interactive Postmodern Metaphor: Robert Edgar's Interactive Computer Art." *High Performance,* 1987, 10(1): 50-1.

Truck, Fred."Interactivity: Conversation with the Machine." *NCGA '90.* Fairfax, Va.: National Computer Graphics Association, 1990, 3:469-477. Conference held March 19, 1990, at Anaheim, Calif.

Truck, Fred. *Art Engine* (computer program). Des Moines, Ia.: Fred Truck, 1991. Distributed by Art Com, San Francisco. Program for Macintosh computer.

Truck, Fred. *Illustrated Art Engine.* Des Moines, Ia.: Fred Truck, 1991.

Truck, Fred. "My Experience in the Bioapparatus Residency." *Art Com* (electronic journal). December 1991, 55. E-mail: artcomtv @well.com.

Truck, Fred. "The Prompt and Virtual Reality." *Leonardo,* 1991, 24(2): 171-173.

Truck, Fred. *Archaeopteryx.* Des Moines, Ia: Fred Truck, 1992.

Truckenbrod, J. and B. Mones-Hattal. "Interactive Computer Graphics via Telecommunications." *Proceedings of Interactive Learning through Visualization. The Impact of Computer Graphics in Education.* S. Cunningham and R. Hubbold, eds. Berlin: Springer-Verlag, 1992: 173-188.

United States Congress. Senate Committee on Commerce, Science and Transportation. Subcommittee on Science, Technology, and Space. *New Developments in Computer Technology: Virtual Reality.* Hearing before the Subcommittee on Science,Technology, and Space of the Committee on Commerce, Science, and Transportation, United States Senate, One Hundred Second Congress, first session, May 8, 1991. Washington: U.S. G.P.O., 1992. Videorecording available from Virtual Reality Film Documentary, Palo Alto, Calif. Robert Miller, producer. Includes Jaron Lanier, Fred Brooks, Thomas A. Furness III, Senator Al Gore and others.

University of North Carolina. Chapel Hill, N.C.. Technical Reports. To receive hard copies, contact Research Access, Inc. at (800) 685-6510 or (412) 682-6510. To receive the reports electronically, send e-mail to netlib@cs.unc.edu and in either the subject line or message body, send the request, "get <report> from techreports". For questions, e-mail softlab@cs.unc.edu. For an index, send the request "get index from techreports".

Väänänen, K., and K. Böhm. "Gesture Driven Interaction as a Human Factor in Virtual Environments: An Approach with Neural Networks." *See* Earnshaw, Gigante and Jones.

Vale, V., and Andrea Juno, eds. *Industrial Culture Handbook*. Special issue of *Re/Search*, No. 6/7. San Francisco, Calif.: Re/Search, 1983.

Vamplew, Peter. "Computer Recognition of Sign Language." *Paper Clips to Silicon Chips: Proceedings of the 2nd National Conference on Disability Issues and Technology*, John Thorne, ed. Conference held 1991 at Hobart, Tasmania, Australia.

Vamplew, Peter, and A. Adams. "The Slarti System: Applying Artificial Neural Networks to Sign Language Recognition." *Virtual Reality and Persons with Disabilities: Proceedings*, Harry J. Murphy, ed. Northridge, Calif.: Office of Disabled Student Services, California State University, 1992. Conference held March 18, 1992 at Northridge, Calif.

Verlinden, Jouke C. *Virtual Books: Integrating Virtual Reality and Hypertext* (online text file). Delft University of Technology, August 1993. FTP: <ftp.twi.tudelft.nl> Directory: pub/publications/masters-thesis File: J.C.Verlinden.ps.gz.

Verlinden, Jouke C., Jay David Bolter, and Charles van der Mast. *Virtual Annotation: Verbal Communication and Virtual Reality*. Delft University of Technology, 1993. Technical Report DUT-TWI-93-67. Electronic version available FTP: <ftp.twi.tudelft.nl> Directory: pub/publications/Reports File: DUT-TWI-93-67.ps.gz.

Verlinden, Jouke C., Jay David Bolter, and Charles van der Mast. *The World Processor: Effective Manipulation of Textual Information in Virtual Environments*. Technical Report DUT-TWI-93-55. Electronic version available FTP: <ftp.twi.tudelft.nl> Directory: pub/publications/Reports File: DUT-TWI-93.55.ps.gz.

VIGIS-L (online discussion list). Moderated by Thomas Edwards. Newsgroup for discussion of uses of VR interfaces for Geographic Information Systems (GIS) and spatial information support systems. E-mail: listserv@uwavm.bitnet with message Subscribe VIGIS-L Yourname.

Viire, Erik. "A Survey of Medical Issues and Virtual Reality Technology." *Virtual Reality World*, July/August 1994: 16-20.

Vince, J. A. "Virtual Reality Techniques in Flight Simulation." *See* Earnshaw, Gigante and Jones.

Vincent, Vincent John, and Linda Jacobson. "The Mandala System." *See* Jacobson, *Cyberarts*.

Vinge, Vernor. *True Names.* New York: Bluejay Books, 1984. Reprinted in Vinge's *True Names – And Other Dangers.* New York: Baen, 1987.

Vinge, Vernor. "Hurtling Towards the Singularity." *See* Synergy.

virtu-l (online mailing list). List owner: Greg Newby, e-mail: gbnewby@alexia.lis.uiuc.edu. This mailing list is an e-mail redistribution of the Usenet newsgroup <sci.virtual-worlds>, for readers who do not have access to Usenet. Internet e-mail: listserv@vmd.cso.uiuc.edu with the message: subscribe virtu-l Yourname. BITNET e-mail: listserv@uiucvmd with the same message.

Virtual: Mensile di Realtà Virtuale e Immagini di Sintesi. Milan, Italy. Monthly since 1993. E-mail: virtual@relay1.iunet.it. In Italian.

"Virtual Cockpit's Panoramic Displays Afford Advanced Mission Capabilities." *Aviation Week & Space Technology*, January 14, 1985, 122(2): 143-152.

Virtual Interface Technology. New York: Association for Computing Machinery, 1991. Course C3 at SIGGRAPH 1991, 18th International Conference on Computer Graphics and Interactive Techniques, held July 28 - August 2, 1991 at Las Vegas. With contributions by Meredith Bricken, William Bricken, Thomas A. Furness, and Robert Jacobson.

Virtual Reality (videorecording). Compiled by Media Magic. Distributed by Art Com, San Francisco. Nicasio, Calif.: Media Magic; 1990. 60 minutes. Includes "VIEW , The Ames Virtual Environment Workstation" and "Virtual Workstation for Telepresence and Supervisory Control" by NASA, "Artificial Reality at the UNC at Chapel Hill" by Warren Robinett, "Head-Mounted Display" by University of North Carolina at Chapel Hill, "Virtual Lobby" by John Rolf, "I 'm a Little Tea Pot" by VPL Research, and "The Bolio Virtual Environment System" by MIT Media Lab.

Virtual Reality '90: Theory, Practice, Promise (videorecording). Three volumes. Westport, Conn.: Meckler; 1991. 360 mins. Distributed by Art Com, San Francisco. Virtual Reality Conference and Exhibition sponsored by Multimedia Review and Virtual Reality Report held December 10-11, 1990, at San Francisco, Calif. Includes "Shaping Cultural Consciousness with Artificial Reality" by Myron Krueger, "The Role of Drama in the Evolution of Virtual Reality" by Brenda Laurel, "'Being There,' or Models for Virtual Reality" by Michael Spring, "The Metaphysics of Virtual Reality" by Michael Heim, "The Emerging Technology of Cyberspace" by Randy Walser, "Bringing Affordable Virtual Reality Systems to Market" by Eric Gullichsen,

"The Virtual Body" by Suzanne Weghorst, "Educational Implications for Virtual Reality" by David Traub, "Cyberspace, VR and the Principle of Commonality: Cyberspace Design" by John Thomas, "Cooperative Work Environment: The Virtual Heartland" by Tom Barrett, plus reports on projects at the Human Interface Technology Lab, University of Washington.

Virtual Reality '91. See Helsel, *Beyond the Vision.*

Virtual Reality and Learning (videorecording). Distributed by Art Com, San Francisco, 1991. 120 minutes. A panel discussion on the possibilities of virtual reality applications in education, moderated by Barbara Means at the 1991 SRI International/VPL Conference on Virtual Worlds.

Virtual Reality Conference: Anaheim Convention Center, March 22, 1990. 11th National Computer Graphics Association Conference (videorecording). Monterey Park, Calif.: Cutting Edge Video, 1990. 300 min. Includes presentations by William Bricken, Mike Fusco, Eric Gullichsen, Morton Heilig, Myron Krueger, Jaron Lanier, Brenda Laurel, James Orr, Wes Thomas, and Randall Walser.

Virtual Reality Handbook. Bari, Italy: Minus Habens Records, 1992. In English and Italian.

Virtual Reality: Impacts and Applications: Proceedings of the First Annual Conference on Virtual Reality. Westport, Conn.: Meckler, 1991. Conference held June 1991 at London. Includes "Virtual Reality: Directions of Growth" by William Bricken, "Effective Human Interface Desigh in Virtual Reality" by Brian Karr, "A Parallel Vision for Virtual Reality" by Charles Grimsdale, "How Virtual is Reality?" by Florian Brody, "Virtual Reality, The Serious Side: Where Next, and How?" by Robert J. Stone, "Virtuality: The World's First Production Virtual Reality Workstation" by Jonathan Waldern, "Cyberzone: Virtual Reality Comes to the TV Screen" by Ian Andrew, "Virtual Reality and Telepresence: A UK Initiative" by Robert J. Stone, and "Training in Virtual Reality" by William Bricken.

Virtual Reality in Medicine (videorecording). Princeton, N. J., 1992. 30 minutes. From the series The Doctor Is In. Includes Joseph Henderson and Joseph Rosen.

Virtual Reality News. Farmington Hills, Mich.: Magellan Marketing, Inc. Bimonthly.

Virtual Reality Products Catalogue and Resource Guide. Houston, Tex.: Spectrum Dynamics, Inc., 1993.

Virtual Reality Report. Westport, Conn.: Meckler Publishing. E-mail: meckler@jvnc.net. Ten issues per year.

"Virtual Reality Resource Guide." *AI Expert*, August 1993: 34-42.

Virtual Reality: The Next Revolution in Computer/Human Interface. Lathrup Village, Mich.: Matrix Information Services, 1990.

Virtual Reality Update (VRU) (electronic journal). Toni Emerson, ed. Seattle, Wash.: HITL (Human Interface Technology Laboratory). Bimonthly since 1993. Available online on <sci.virtual-worlds> newsgroup and FTP: <ftp.u.washington.edu> machine address (140.142.56.2) Directory: ./public/VirtualReality/HITL/Bibliographies Filename: vru-v#n#.txt where # is the volume and issue number. Current updates on bibliographic sources.

Virtual Reality World. Sandra K. Helsel, ed. Westport, Conn.: Meckler Publishing. Bimonthly since 1993. First issue (Spring 1993) an insert in *Multimedia Review* 4(1).

Virtual Reality World. Los Angeles: VR World. One issue only, 1991.

Virtual Seminar on the Bioapparatus. Banff: Banff Centre for the Arts, 1991. Proceedings of a seminar held October 28 and 29, 1991 at Banff, Alberta, Canada.

Virtual Worlds: Real Challenges: Papers from SRI's 1991 Conference on Virtual Reality. Westport, Conn.: Meckler, 1992. Conference held 1991, at Menlo Park, Calif.

Virtuoso. London: Cydata Ltd. Six issues per year, 1993. Succeeded by *VR News* in 1994.

VR Becomes a Business: Proceedings of Virtual Reality '92. Westport, Conn.: Meckler, 1993. Conference held September 1993 at San Jose, Calif. Includes "Photorealistic VR on the desktop" by Tony Asch, "An Introduction to 3-D Sound for Virtual Reality " by Durand R. Begault, "Communication Design in Virtual Reality " by Frank Biocca, "A Virtual Environment System Architecture for Large-Scale Simulations" by Rudy Darken and Daria Bergen, Supercomputing and Virtual Reality " by Wotjek Furmanski, "Where in the (Virtual) World Are We?: Building a Virtual Worlds Industry" by Robert Jacobson, "Sonification and Virtual Reality I: An Introduction" by Gregory Kramer, "Accuracy, Resolution, Latency and Speed: Key Factors in Virtual Reality Tracking Environments" by James C. Krieg, "Biosignal Processing in Virtual Reality " by Hugh S. Lusted, R. Benjamin Knapp, and Anthony Lloyd, "Doorways to the Virtual Battlefield" by James McDonough, "Virtual Reality Research at the National Center for Supercomputing Applications" by Michael McNeill, "Immersive Visualization System Architectures" by Joshua S. Mogal, "System Architecture Issues Related to Multiple-User VR Systems: Teaching Your System to Share" by Ken Pimentel and Brian Blau, "Experiential advertising" by David B. Polinchock, "Telepresence surgery: medical Implications for Virtual Reality" by Richard M. Satava, "Virtual Auditory Worlds: An Overview" by Rory Stuart, "The Mandala Virtual Reality System: The Vivid Group" by Vincent John Vincent, "A De Facto Anti-Standard for Cyberspace" by Randal

Walser, "A Video Pan/Tilt/Magnify/Rotate System with No Moving Parts for Motion Simulation and Telepresence" by Steve Zimmermann and Daniel P. Kuban, "Educational and Technological Foundations for the Construction of a 3-D Virtual World" by John S. Falby et al., "Virtual Reality Market Place 1993: Insights from the Meckler Database" by Sandra Kay Helsel and Susan DeNoble Doherty, "The Emperor's New Realities" by Myron W. Krueger, "VREAM: Virtual Reality Development System" by Edward R. LaHood, "Implications of Learning Theory and Strategies for the Design of Synthetic Environments" by Joseph S. Mattoon and Lyn Mowafy, and "The Potential Integration of Virtual Reality into Theme Parks: An Introduction" by Leigh Shipley.*VR Conference: Overview of VR* (videorecording). Distributed by Art Com, San Francisco. 120 minutes. Includes presentations by Joseph Henderson, Myron Krueger, and Howard Rheingold.

VR Conference: Applications (videorecording). Distributed by Art Com, San Francisco. 120 minutes. Includes presentations by Tim Dowding, Roland Hjerppe, Erland Jungert , Ted Nelson, Nicole Stenger, and others.

VR Monitor: A Technical Newsletter on Virtual Reality. Lathrup Village, Mich.: Matrix Information Services. Bimonthly, since 1991. E-mail: matrix@well.sf.ca.us.

VR News. London: Cydata Ltd. Ten issues per year, since 1991. An industry newsletter.

VR93:Virtual Reality International 93. Proceedings of the Third Annual Conference on Virtual Reality. London, England: Meckler, 1993. Conference held April 1993 at London, England.

VRAIS: IEEE Virtual Reality Annual Symposium, Symp. 1. Piscataway, N.J.: IEEE Service Center, 1993. Conference held September 1993 at Seattle, Washington.

vrapp-l (online mailing list). List owner: Greg Newby, e-mail: gbnewby @alexia.lis.uiuc.edu. This mailing list is an e-mail redistribution of the Usenet newsgroup <sci.virtual-worlds.apps>, for readers who do not have access to Usenet. Internet e-mail: listserv@vmd.cso.uiuc.edu with the message: subscribe vrapp-l Yourname. BITNET e-mail: listserv@uiucvmd with the same message.

Walker, John. "Through the Looking Glass." *See* Laurel, *The Art of Human-Computer Interface Design.*

Walser, Randall. "Elements of a Cyberspace Playhouse." *NCGA '90.* Fairfax, Va.: National Computer Graphics Association, 1990, 1:403-411. Conference held March 19, 1990, at Anaheim, Calif.

Walser, Randy. "Doing It Directly: The Experiential Development of Cyberspaces." *Proceedings of the 1990 SPIE/SPSE Symposium on Electronic Imaging Science and Technology.* Santa Clara, Calif.: SPIE, 1990.

Walser, Randy. "Spacemakers and the Art of the Cyberspace Playhouse." *See* Mondo 2000.

Walser, Randy. "The Emerging Technology of Cyberspace" and "Elements of a Cyberspace Playhouse." *See* Helsel and Roth.

Walser, Randy. "The Emerging Technology of Cyberspace." *See* Virtual Reality: Theory, Practice, Promise (videorecording).

Walser, Randy. *See* Virtual Reality Conference (videorecording).

Warwick, Kevin, John Gray, and David Roberts, eds. *Virtual Reality in Engineering.* Londin: Institute of Electrical Engineers, 1993.

Weatherly, R., D. Seidel, and J. Weissman. "Aggregate Level Simulation Protocol." 1991 *Summer Computer Simulation Conference.:Twenty-Third Annual Summer Computer Simulation Conference*, D. Pace, ed. San Diego, Calif.: CSC, 1991: 953-958. Conference held July 22, 1991, at Baltimore, Md.

Webb, Bruce C., and Joel Warren Barna. "After Deconstruction: Beyond the Meat World." *Texas Architect*, July 1992, 42(4): 36-41.

Weghorst, Suzanne. *Inclusive Biomedical Visualization.* Seattle, Wash.: HITL (Human Interface Technology Laboratory), 1991. Technical Report R-91-2.

Weghorst, Suzanne. "The Virtual Body" *See* Virtual Reality: Theory, Practice, Promise (videorecording).

Weghorst, Suzanne. *See* Prothero, Emerson and Weghorst.

Weizenbaum, Joseph. "Eliza." *Communications of the ACM* (Association for Compting Machinery), 1966, 9: 36-45.

WELL (Whole Earth 'Lectronic Link) (computer network). Virtual reality conference, <vr>. Moderated by Peter Rothman.

Wellner, Pierre, Wendy Mackay, and Rich Gold, eds. "Computer-Augmented Environments: Back to the Real World." Special issue of *Communications of the ACM* (Association for Compting Machinery), July 1993, 36(7):24-97.

Wenzel, Elizabeth M., P. K. Stone, Scott S. Fisher, and S. H. Foster. "A System for Three-Dimensional Acoustic 'Visualization' in a Virtual Environment Workstation." *Proceedings of the First IEEE Conference on Visualization. Visualization '90*; A. Kaufman, ed. Los Alamitos, Calif.: IEEE Computer Society Press, 1990: 329-37. Conference held October 23, 1990, at San Francisco, Calif.

Wenzel, Elizabeth M. "Launching Sounds into Space." *See* Jacobson, *Cyberarts.*

West, A. J., et al. "AVIARY: A Generic Virtual Reality Interface for Real Applications." *See* Earnshaw, Gigante and Jones.

Wexelblat, Alan, ed. *Virtual Reality: Applications and Explorations*. Boston: Academic Press Professional, 1993. Includes "Artificial Realities as Data Visualization Environments" by Thomas Erickson, "The Reality of Cooperation: Virtual Reality and CSCW" by Alan Wexelblat, "Information Management Using Virtual Reality-Based Visualizations" by Kim Michael Fairchild, "Writing Cyberspace: Literacy in the Age of Simulacra" by Stuart Moulthrop, "The Creator's Toolbox" by Brian R. Gardner, "Full-Body Unencumbered Immersion in Virtual Worlds" by Susan Wyshynski and Vincent John Vincent, "An Easy Entry Artificial Reality" by Myron Krueger, "Virtual Reality and Planetary Exploration" by Michael W. McGreevy, "Summer Students in Virtual Reality: A Pilot Study on Educational Applications of Virtual Reaality Technology" by Meredith Bricken and Chris M. Byrne, and "Visualization of Information Flows: Virtual Reality as an Organizational Modeling Technique" by Charles Grantham.

Wexelblat, Alan. "Giving Meaning to Place: Semantic Spaces." *See* Benedikt, *Cyberspace*.

Whalley, L. J. "Ethical Issues in the Application of Virtual Reality to the Treatment of Mental Disorders." *See* Earnshaw, Gigante and Jones.

Whitbeck, Carolyn. "Virtual Environments: Ethical Issues and Significant Confusions." *Presence*, Spring 1993, 2(2): 14147-152.

Whittington, Amanda. "Fun with Eric the Spider." *New Statesman & Society*, May 29, 1992, 5(204): 33.

Winn, W., and W. Bricken. "Designing Virtual Worlds for Use in Mathematics Education: the Example of Experimental Algebra." *Educational Technology*, December 1992, 32(12): 12-19.

Wired. Louis Rossetto, ed. San Francisco: Wired USA. Bimonthly since 1993.

Woolley, Benjamin. "Lifting the Veil: The Virtuality System." *Sight & Sound*, July 1991, 1: 64.

Woolley, Benjamin. *Virtual Worlds: A Journey in Hype and Hyperreality*. Cambridge, Mass.: Blackwell, 1992.

World Wide Web site at Electronic Visualization Lab, University of Illinois, Urbana-Champaign. The Uniform Resource Locator (URL) for this page is: <http://www.ncsa.uiuc.edu/EVL/docs/supercomp/EVL.CAVE.html>.

World Wide Web site at GVU. The Uniform Resource Locator (URL) for this page is: <http://www.gatech.edu/gvu/people/Masters/Rob.Kooper/Meta.VR.html>. For informtion contact Rob Kooper at kooper@cc.gatech.edu.

World Wide Web site at National Center for Supercomputing Applications (NCSA). The Uniform Resource Locator (URL) for this page is: <http://www.ncsa.uiuc.edu/VR/vr_homepage.html>.

World Wide Web site at Naval Postgraduate School. Monterey, Calif. The Uniform Resource Locator (URL) for this page is: <http://taurus.cs.nps.navy.mil/pub/mosaic/nps_mosaic.html>. Files include NPSNET papers.

World Wide Web site at VR-SIG (UK). The Uniform Resource Locator (URL) for this page is: <http://pipkin.lut.ac.uk/WWWdocs/LUTCHI/people/sean/vr-sig/vr-sig.html>.

Yamashita, Juli, and Yukio Fukui. "Direct Deformation Method of Free Forms." *See* ICAT '93.

Yokote, Yasuhiko. *The Apertos Reflective Operating System: The Concept and Its Implementation.* Tokyo: Sony Computer Science Laboratory, October 1992. Technical Report SCSL-TR-92-014. Also published in Proceedings of the Conference on Object-Oriented Programming, Systems, Languages, and Applications, 1992.

Yu, Larry. "3D Design: Cyberspace and Beyond." *Progressive Architecture.* October 1991, 72: 126-127.

Zeltzer, David. "Virtual Environments: Where Are We Going?" *IDATE. 12th International Conference: Key Technologies, Experiments, New Concepts. Proceedings.* Montpellier, France: IDATE, 1990: 507-13. Conference held November 14, 1990, at Montpellier.

Zeltzer, David L. "Virtual Environment Technology in Extracting Meaning from Complex Data: Processing, Display, Interaction II." *Proceedings of the SPIE—The International Society for Optical Engineering.* Santa Clara, Calif.: SPIE, 1991, 1459: 86. Conference held 1991.

Zeltzer, David. "Autonomy, Interaction, and Presence." *Presence,* December 1992, 1(1).

Zimmerman, Thomas G., Jaron Lanier, Chuck Blanchard, Steve Bryson, and Young Harvill. "A Hand Gesture Interface Device." *CHI + GI 1987 Conference: Human Factors in Computing Systems and Graphics Interface - IV,* John M. Carroll and Peter P. Tanner, eds. New York: ACM (Association for Compting Machinery), 1987. SIGCHI Bulletin. Special issue, 1987: 189-92. Conference held April 5, 1987 at Toronto.

Zyda, M. J., et al. "NPSNET, Constructing a 3D Virtual World." *Proceedings of 1992 Symposium on Interactive 3D Graphics.* D. Zelter, E. Catmull, and M. Levoy, eds. New York: ACM (Association for Computing Machinery), 1992: 147-156.

Zyda, M. J., et al. "The Software Required for the Computer Generation of Virtual Environments." *Presence*, Spring 1993, 2(2): 130-140.

Zyda, Michael, et al. "Hypermedia and Networking." *See* ICAT '93.

Acknowledgments

Acknowledgment is gratefully made to the University Libraries and the STUDIO for Creative Inquiry of Carnegie Mellon University for their support. Thanks to Joe Bates, Gareth Branwyn, Toni Emerson, Randy Farmer, Carl Loeffler, Geoff Thomas, Peter Vamplew, and the others whose suggestions have improved this bibliography, and to Henry Pisciotta for his encouragement. Special thanks to Nick Madjerick for all his help.

– Tim Anderson

INDEX